A·N·N·U·A·L E·D·I·T·I·O·N·S

Psychology

Thirty-Fourth Edition

04/05

EDITOR

Karen G. Duffy

SUNY at Geneseo (Emerita)

Karen G. Duffy holds a doctorate in psychology from Michigan State University, and she is an emerita Distinguished Service Professor of State University of New York at Geneseo. Dr. Duffy continues to work on her books and research, and she is also involved in several community service projects both in the United States and Russia.

McGraw-Hill/Dushkin

530 Old Whitfield Street, Guilford, Connecticut 06437

Visit us on the Internet
http://www.dushkin.com

Credits

1. **The Science of Psychology**
   Unit photo—Photo by Harvard University Press.
2. **Biological Bases of Behavior**
   Unit photo—WHO photo.
3. **Perceptual Processes**
   Unit photo—© 2004 by Cleo Freelance Photography.
4. **Learning and Remembering**
   Unit photo—© 2004 by PhotoDisc, Inc.
5. **Cognitive Processes**
   Unit photo—© 2004 by Cleo Freelance Photography.
6. **Emotion and Motivation**
   Unit photo—United Nations photo.
7. **Development**
   Unit photo—Courtesy of McGraw-Hill/Dushkin.
8. **Personality Processes**
   Unit photo—WHO photo.
9. **Social Processes**
   Unit photo—© 2004 by Sweet By & By/Cindy Brown.
10. **Psychological Disorders**
    Unit photo—Courtesy of Cheryl Greenleaf.
11. **Psychological Treatments**
    Unit photo—© 2004 by PhotoDisc, Inc.

Copyright

Cataloging in Publication Data
Main entry under title: Annual Editions: Psychology. 2004/2005.
1. Psychology—Periodicals. I. Duffy, Karen G., *comp.* II. Title: Psychology.
ISBN 0–07–286149–5   658'.05   ISSN 0272–3794

Thirty-Fourth Edition

Cover image © 2004 PhotoDisc, Inc.
Printed in the United States of America   1234567890BAHBAH54   Printed on Recycled Paper

Editors/Advisory Board

Members of the Advisory Board are instrumental in the final selection of articles for each edition of ANNUAL EDITIONS. Their review of articles for content, level, currentness, and appropriateness provides critical direction to the editor and staff. We think that you will find their careful consideration well reflected in this volume.

EDITOR

Karen G. Duffy
SUNY at Geneseo (Emerita)

ADVISORY BOARD

Jeffery L. Arbuckle
Harford Community College

Michael Atkinson
University of Western Ontario

Timothy Barth
Texas Christian University

John Cross
St. Louis University

Joan F. DiGiovanni
University of Arizona

Mark J. Friedman
Montclair State University

Rebecca Ganes
Modesto Junior College

Florine A. Greenberg
Northern Virginia Community College

Robert L. Hale
Shippensburg University

C. Harry Hui
University of Hong Kong

Angela J.C. LaSala
Community College of Southern Nevada

Nancy G. McCarley
Mississippi State University

Carroll Mitchell
Cecil Community College

Quentin Newhouse
Tennessee State University

Paul Nochelski
Canisius College

Terry F. Pettijohn
Ohio State University

Janice Rafalowski
County College of Morris

Edward Raymaker
Eastern Maine Technical College

Mitchell W. Robins
New York City Technical College

Virginia F. Saunders
San Francisco State University

Stephen P. Stelzner
College of Saint Benedict

Harry Strub
University of Winnipeg

David W. Wolfe
Ocean County College

Staff

Jeffrey L. Hahn, Vice President/Publisher

To the Reader

In publishing ANNUAL EDITIONS we recognize the enormous role played by the magazines, newspapers, and journals of the public press in providing current, first-rate educational information in a broad spectrum of interest areas. Many of these articles are appropriate for students, researchers, and professionals seeking accurate, current material to help bridge the gap between principles and theories and the real world. These articles, however, become more useful for study when those of lasting value are carefully collected, organized, indexed, and reproduced in a low-cost format, which provides easy and permanent access when the material is needed. That is the role played by ANNUAL EDITIONS.

Ronnie's parents couldn't understand why he didn't want to be picked up and cuddled as did his older sister when she was a baby. As an infant, Ronnie did not respond to his parents' smiles, words, or attempts to amuse him. By the age of two, Ronnie's parents knew that he was not like other children. He spoke no English, was very temperamental, and often rocked himself for hours. Ronnie is autistic. His parents feel that some of Ronnie's behavior may be their fault. As young professionals, they both work long hours and leave both of their children with an older woman during the workweek. Ronnie's pediatrician assures his parents that their reasoning, while logical, does not have merit, because the causes of autism are little understood and are likely to be biological rather than parental. What can we do about children like Ronnie? From where does autism come? Can autism be treated or reversed? Can autism be prevented?

Psychologists attempt to answer these and other complex questions with scientific methods. Researchers, using carefully planned research designs, try to discover the causes of complex human behavior—normal or not. The scientific results of psychological research typically are published in professional journals and therefore may be difficult for the lay person to understand.

Annual Editions: Psychology 04/05 is designed to meet the needs of lay people and introductory level students who are curious about psychology. This Annual Edition provides a vast selection of readable and informative articles primarily from popular magazines and newspapers. These articles are typically written by journalists, but a few are written by psychologists with writing styles that are clear yet retain the excitement of the discovery of scientific knowledge.

The particular articles selected for this volume were chosen to be representative of the most current work in psychology. They were selected because they are accurate in their reporting and provide examples of the types of psychological research discussed in most introductory psychology classes. As in any science, some of the findings discussed in this collection are startling, while others confirm what we already know. Some articles invite speculation about social and personal issues; others encourage careful thought about potential misuse of research findings. You are expected to make the investment of effort and critical reasoning necessary to answer such questions and concerns.

I believe that you will find this collection of articles readable and useful. I suggest that you look at the organization of this book and compare it to the organization of your textbook and course syllabus. By examining the topic guide provided after the table of contents, you can identify those articles most appropriate for any particular unit of study in your course. Your instructor may provide some help in this effort or assign articles to supplement the text. As you read the articles, try to connect their contents with the principles you are learning from your text and classroom lectures. Some of the articles will help you better understand a specific area of research, while others are designed to help you connect and integrate information from diverse research areas. Both of these strategies are important in learning about psychology or any other science; it is only through intensive investigation and subsequent integration of the findings from many studies that we are able to discover and apply new knowledge.

Please take time to provide me with some feedback to guide the annual revision of this anthology by completing and returning the article rating form in the back of the book. With your help, this collection will be even better next year. Thank you.

Karen Grover Duffy

Karen Grover Duffy
Editor

Contents

UNIT 1
The Science of Psychology

In this unit, three articles examine psychology as the science of behavior.

Unit Overview   xviii

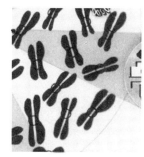

UNIT 2
Biological Bases of Behavior

Three unit selections discuss the biological bases of behavior. Topics include the nature-nurture controversy and the brain's control over the body.

Unit Overview   12

The concepts in bold italics are developed in the article. For further expansion, please refer to the Topic Guide and the Index.

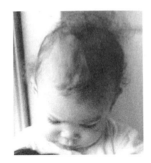

UNIT 3
Perceptual Processes

The impact of the senses on human perceptual processes is addressed in five unit articles.

UNIT 4
Learning and Remembering

Four selections in this section examine scientific principles of learning and remembering, explaining how forgetting occurs, and exploring the basis of implicit learning.

The concepts in bold italics are developed in the article. For further expansion, please refer to the Topic Guide and the Index.

UNIT 5
Cognitive Processes

Three unit articles examine how social skills, common sense, and intelligence affect human cognitive processes.

UNIT 6
Emotion and Motivation

In this unit, four articles discuss the influence of mental states, motivation, and emotion on the mental and physical health of the individual.

The concepts in bold italics are developed in the article. For further expansion, please refer to the Topic Guide and the Index.

UNIT 7
Development

Six articles in this section consider the importance of experience, discipline, familial support, and biological and psychological aging during the normal human development process.

The concepts in bold italics are developed in the article. For further expansion, please refer to the Topic Guide and the Index.

UNIT 8
Personality Processes

A few of the processes by which personalities are developed are discussed in this section's three selections. Topics include psychoanalysis, the influence of media violence, and the secrets of happiness.

UNIT 9
Social Processes

Four unit selections discuss how interpersonal interactions, irrational fears, and sexuality issues can affect an individual's social development.

The concepts in bold italics are developed in the article. For further expansion, please refer to the Topic Guide and the Index.

UNIT 10
Psychological Disorders

In this unit, five articles examine several psychological disorders. Topics include severe anxiety, the impact of depression on a person's well-being, post-traumatic stress disorder, and schizophrenia.

UNIT 11
Psychological Treatments

Six selections in this unit discuss a few psychological treatments, including empirically supported psychotherapy, Internet-based interventions, and self-care.

The concepts in bold italics are developed in the article. For further expansion, please refer to the Topic Guide and the Index.

The concepts in bold italics are developed in the article. For further expansion, please refer to the Topic Guide and the Index.

Topic Guide

This topic guide suggests how the selections in this book relate to the subjects covered in your course. You may want to use the topics listed on these pages to search the Web more easily.

On the following pages a number of Web sites have been gathered specifically for this book. They are arranged to reflect the units of this *Annual Edition*. You can link to these sites by going to the DUSHKIN ONLINE support site at *http://www.dushkin.com/online/*.

ALL THE ARTICLES THAT RELATE TO EACH TOPIC ARE LISTED BELOW THE BOLD-FACED TERM.

Adolescents
26. The Future of Adolescence: Lengthening Ladders to Adulthood

Aggression
31. The Verdict on Media Violence: It's Ugly…and Getting Uglier

Aging
23. The Biology of Aging
28. Start the Conversation

Alzheimer's disease
14. The Seven Sins of Memory: How the Mind Forgets and Remembers
15. Memory's Mind Games

Anxiety disorder
38. The Science of Anxiety

Assessment
17. Intelligent Intelligence Testing

Autism
18. The Inner Savant

Biological issues
4. What Makes You Who You Are
5. The Blank Slate
6. Neuroscience: Breaking Down Scientific Barriers to the Study of Brain and Mind
19. Fundamental Feelings
23. The Biology of Aging
27. Midlife Changes: Utilizing a Social Work Perspective

Brain
6. Neuroscience: Breaking Down Scientific Barriers to the Study of Brain and Mind
11. Brains in Dreamland
16. Mind in a Mirror
19. Fundamental Feelings
20. Medical Detection of False Witness
22. How to Multitask
38. The Science of Anxiety

Children
13. New Evidence for the Benefits of Never Spanking
25. Parenting: The Lost Art
31. The Verdict on Media Violence: It's Ugly…and Getting Uglier

Cognition
16. Mind in a Mirror
18. The Inner Savant

Computers
43. Computer- and Internet-Based Psychotherapy Interventions

Criticisms of psychology
1. Mind Games: Psychological Warfare Between Therapists and Scientists
2. Teaching Skepticism via the CRITIC Acronym and the Skeptical Inquirer

Deafness
9. It's a Noisy, Noisy World Out There!

Death
28. Start the Conversation

Depression
37. The Lowdown on Depression

Development
13. New Evidence for the Benefits of Never Spanking
23. The Biology of Aging
24. Inside the Womb
25. Parenting: The Lost Art
27. Midlife Changes: Utilizing a Social Work Perspective

Dreams
11. Brains in Dreamland

Drug treatment
10. Pain and Its Mysteries
37. The Lowdown on Depression
40. The Schizophrenic Mind

Emotions
19. Fundamental Feelings
28. Start the Conversation
38. The Science of Anxiety

Environment
4. What Makes You Who You Are
5. The Blank Slate
24. Inside the Womb

Fear
34. Rational and Irrational Fears Combine in Terrorism's Wake
39. Post-Traumatic Stress Disorder

Fetus
24. Inside the Womb

Forgetting
14. The Seven Sins of Memory: How the Mind Forgets and Remembers
15. Memory's Mind Games

Freud, Sigmund
11. Brains in Dreamland
29. Psychoanalyst: Sigmund Freud

World Wide Web Sites

The following World Wide Web sites have been carefully researched and selected to support the articles found in this reader. The easiest way to access these selected sites is to go to our DUSHKIN ONLINE support site at *http://www.dushkin.com/online/*.

AE: Psychology 04/05

The following sites were available at the time of publication. Visit our Web site—we update DUSHKIN ONLINE regularly to reflect any changes.

General Sources

APA Resources for the Public
http://www.apa.org/psychnet/

Use the site map or search engine to access *APA Monitor,* the American Psychological Association newspaper, APA books on a wide range of topics, PsychINFO, an electronic database of abstracts on scholarly journals, and the HelpCenter.

Health Information Resources
http://www.health.gov/nhic/Pubs/tollfree.htm

Here is a long list of toll-free numbers that provide health-related information. None offer diagnosis and treatment, but some do offer recorded information; others provide personalized counseling, referrals, and/or written materials.

Mental Help Net
http://mentalhelp.net

This comprehensive guide to mental health online features more than 6,300 individual resources. Information on mental disorders and professional resources in psychology, psychiatry, and social work is presented.

Psychology: Online Resource Central
http://www.psych-central.com

Thousands of psychology resources are currently indexed at this site. Psychology disciplines, conditions and disorders, and self-development are among the most useful.

School Psychology Resources Online
http://www.schoolpsychology.net

Numerous sites on special conditions, disorders, and disabilities, as well as other data ranging from assessment/evaluation to research, are available on this resource page for psychologists, parents, and educators.

Social Psychology Network
http://www.socialpsychology.org

The social Psychology Network is the most comprehensive source of social psychology information on the Internet, including resources, programs, and research.

UNIT 1: The Science of Psychology

Abraham A. Brill Library
http://plaza.interport.net/nypsan/service.html

Containing data on over 40,000 books, periodicals, and reprints in psychoanalysis and related fields, the Abraham A. Brill Library has holdings that span the literature of psychoanalysis from its beginning to the present day.

American Psychological Society (APS)
http://www.psychologicalscience.org/about/links.html

The APS is dedicated to advancing the best of scientific psychology in research, application, and the improvement of human conditions. Links to teaching, research, and graduate studies resources are available.

Psychological Research on the Net
http://psych.hanover.edu/Research/exponnet.html

This Net site provides psychologically related experiments. Biological psychology/neuropsychology, clinical psychology, cognition, developmental psychology, emotions, health psychology, personality, sensation/perception, and social psychology are some of the areas covered.

UNIT 2: Biological Bases of Behavior

Adolescence: Changes and Continuity
http://www.personal.psu.edu/faculty/n/x/nxd10/adolesce.htm

A discussion of puberty, sexuality, biological changes, cross-cultural differences, and nutrition for adolescents, including obesity and its effects on adolescent development, is presented here.

Division of Hereditary Diseases and Family Studies, Indiana University School of Medicine
http://www.iupui.edu/~medgen/division/hereditary/hereditary_diseases.html

The Department of Medical and Molecular Genetics is primarily concerned with determining the genetic basis of disease. It consists of a multifaceted program with a variety of interdisciplinary projects. The areas of twin studies and linkage analysis are also explored.

Institute for Behavioral Genetics
http://ibgwww.colorado.edu/index.html

Dedicated to conducting and facilitating research on the genetic and environmental bases of individual differences in behavior, this organized research unit at the University of Colorado leads to Genetic Sites, Statistical Sites, and the Biology Meta Index, as well as to search engines.

Serendip
http://serendip.brynmawr.edu/serendip/

Serendip, which is organized into five subject areas (brain and behavior, complex systems, genes and behavior, science and culture, and science education), contains interactive exhibits, articles, links to other resources, and a forum area.

UNIT 3: Perceptual Processes

Five Senses Home Page
http://www.sedl.org/scimath/pasopartners/senses/welcome.html

This elementary lesson examines the five senses and gives a list of references that may be useful.

Psychology Tutorials and Demonstrations
http://psych.hanover.edu/Krantz/tutor.html

Interactive tutorials and simulations, primarily in the area of sensation and perception, are available here.

www.dushkin.com/online/

UNIT 4: Learning and Remembering

Mind Tools
http://www.psychwww.com/mtsite/
Useful information on stress management can be found at this Web site.

The Opportunity of Adolescence
http://www.winternet.com/~webpage/adolescencepaper.html
According to this paper, adolescence is the turning point, after which the future is redirected and confirmed. The opportunities and problems of this period are presented with quotations from Erik Erikson, Jean Piaget, and others.

Project Zero
http://pzweb.harvard.edu
The Harvard Project Zero has investigated the development of learning processes in children and adults for 30 years. Today, Project Zero's mission is to understand and enhance learning, thinking, and creativity in the arts and other disciplines for individuals and institutions.

UNIT 5: Cognitive Processes

American Association for Artificial Intelligence (AAAI)
http://www.aaai.org/AITopics/index.html
This AAAI site provides a good starting point to learn about artificial intelligence (AI)--what artificial intelligence is and what AI scientists do.

Chess: Kasparov v. Deep Blue: The Rematch
http://www.chess.ibm.com/home/html/b.html
Clips from the chess rematch between Garry Kasparov and IBM's supercomputer, Deep Blue, are presented here along with commentaries on chess, computers, artificial intelligence, and what it all means.

UNIT 6: Emotion and Motivation

CYFERNET-Youth Development
http://twosocks.ces.ncsu.edu/cyfdb/browse_2.php?search=Youth
CYFERNET presents many articles on youth development, including a statement on the concept of normal adolescence and impediments to healthy development.

Emotional Intelligence Discovery
http://www.cwrl.utexas.edu/~bump/Hu305/3/3/3/
This site has been set up by students to talk about and expand on Daniel Goleman's book, *Emotional Intelligence*. There are links to many other EI sites.

John Suler's Teaching Clinical Psychology Site
http://www.rider.edu/users/suler/tcp.html
This page contains Internet resources for clinical and abnormal psychology, behavioral medicine, and mental health.

Nature vs. Nurture: Gergen Dialogue with Winifred Gallagher
http://www.pbs.org/newshour/gergen/gallagher_5-14.html
Experience modifies temperament, according to this TV interview. The author of *I.D.: How Heredity and Experience Make You Who You Are* explains a current theory about temperament.

UNIT 7: Development

American Association for Child and Adolescent Psychiatry
http://www.aacap.org
This site is designed to aid in the understanding and treatment of the developmental, behavioral, and mental disorders that could affect children and adolescents. There is a specific link just for families about common childhood problems that may or may not require professional intervention.

Behavioral Genetics
http://www.ornl.gov/hgmis/elsi/behavior.html
This government backed Web site includes helpful information on behavioral genetics.

UNIT 8: Personality Processes

The Personality Project
http://personality-project.org/personality.html
This Personality Project (by William Revelle) is meant to guide those interested in personality theory and research to the current personality research literature.

UNIT 9: Social Processes

National Clearinghouse for Alcohol and Drug Information
http://www.health.org
Information on drug and alcohol facts that might relate to adolescence and the issues of peer pressure and youth culture is presented here. Resources, referrals, research and statistics, databases, and related Net links are available.

Nonverbal Behavior and Nonverbal Communication
http://www3.usal.es/~nonverbal/
This Web site has a detailed listing of nonverbal behavior and nonverbal communication sites, including the work of historical and current researchers.

UNIT 10: Psychological Disorders

American Association of Suicidology
http://www.suicidology.org
The American Association of Suicidology is a nonprofit organization dedicated to the understanding and prevention of suicide. This site is designed as a resource to anyone concerned about suicide.

Anxiety Disorders
http://www.adaa.org/mediaroom/index.cfm
Anxiety Disorders Association of America (ADAA) reviews anxiety disorders in children, adolescents, and adults here. A detailed glossary is available.

Ask NOAH About: Mental Health
http://www.noah-health.org/english//illness/mentalhealth/mental.html
Information about child and adolescent family problems, mental conditions and disorders, suicide prevention, and much more is available here.

Mental Health Net Disorders and Treatments
http://www.mentalhelp.net/
Presented on this site are hotlinks to psychological disorders pages, which include anxiety, panic, phobic disorders, schizophrenia, and violent/self-destructive behaviors.

Mental Health Net: Eating Disorder Resources
http://www.mentalhelp.net/poc/center_index.php/id/46
This mental health Net site provides a complete list of Web references on eating disorders, including anorexia, bulimia, and obesity.

National Women's Health Resource Center (NWHRC)
http://www.healthywomen.org
NWHRC's site contains links to resources related to women's substance abuse and mental illnesses.

www.dushkin.com/online/

UNIT 11: Psychological Treatments

The C.G. Jung Page
http://www.cgjungpage.org

Dedicated to the work of Carl Jung, this is a comprehensive resource, with links to Jungian psychology, news and opinions, reference materials, graduate programs, dreams, multilingual sites, and related Jungian themes.

Knowledge Exchange Network (KEN)
http://www.mentalhealth.org

Information about mental health (prevention, treatment, and rehabilitation services) is available via toll-free telephone services, an electronic bulletin board, and publications.

NetPsychology
http://netpsych.com/index.htm

This site explores the uses of the Internet to deliver mental health services. This is a basic cybertherapy resource site.

Sigmund Freud and the Freud Archives
http://plaza.interport.net/nypsan/freudarc.html

Internet resources related to Sigmund Freud, which include a collection of libraries, museums, and biographical materials, as well as the Brill Library archives, can be found here.

We highly recommend that you review our Web site for expanded information and our other product lines. We are continually updating and adding links to our Web site in order to offer you the most usable and useful information that will support and expand the value of your Annual Editions. You can reach us at: *http://www.dushkin.com/annualeditions/*.

UNIT 1
The Science of Psychology

Unit Selections

1. **Mind Games: Psychological Warfare Between Therapists and Scientists**, Carol Tavris
2. **Teaching Skepticism via the CRITIC Acronym and the Skeptical Inquirer**, Wayne R. Bartz
3. **Causes and Correlations**, Massimo Pigliucci

Key Points to Consider

- Which area of psychology (e.g. biological psychology, social psychology, human development, etc.) do you think is the most valuable and why? Many people are aware of clinical psychology by virtue of having watched films and television where psychotherapists are depicted. Is this the most valuable area of the discipline? About which other areas of psychology do you think the public is informed? About what other areas ought the public to be informed? Why?

- How do you think psychology is related to other scientific disciplines, such as sociology, biology, and human medicine? Are there nonscience disciplines to which psychology might be related, for example, philosophy and mathematics? How so?

- What can you do when you encounter new information about which you are skeptical? Is there a way to examine the information critically? How is this method of critical thinking or critical inquiry related to psychology?

- Why is research important to psychology? What kinds of information can be gleaned from psychological research? What types of research methods do psychologists utilize? Why do psychologists employ a variety of research methods?

- What is a correlation? Does correlation prove causation? How should a correlation be interpreted? Why are correlational methods used in psychology? What other methods do psychologists utilize? Why? What is the difference between experimentation and correlation? What does a psychologist mean by the word "control"? Why does a psychologist make a statistical inference or use inferential statistics?

- Do you think editors of psychological journals should publish results "as is" or should they exclude certain types of research or results from their journals? For example, would a study showing no differences between men and women be as valuable as one that demonstrates sex differences? If you excluded a study, what factors would make you as an editor exclude it?

 **Links: www.dushkin.com/online/**
These sites are annotated in the World Wide Web pages.

Abraham A. Brill Library
    http://plaza.interport.net/nypsan/service.html
American Psychological Society (APS)
    http://www.psychologicalscience.org/about/links.html
Psychological Research on the Net
    http://psych.hanover.edu/Research/exponnet.html

Little did Wilhelm Wundt realize his monumental contribution to science when in 1879 in Germany, he opened the first psychological laboratory to examine consciousness. Wundt would barely recognize modern psychology compared to the way he practiced it.

Contemporary psychology is defined as the science or study of individual mental activity and behavior. This definition reflects the two parent disciplines from which psychology emerged: philosophy and biology. Compared to its parents, psychology is very much a new discipline. Some aspects of modern psychology are particularly biological, such as neuroscience, perception, psychophysics, and behavioral genetics. Other aspects are more philosophical such as the study of personality, while other areas within psychology approximate sociology, as does social psychology.

Today's psychologists work in a variety of settings. Many psychologists are academics, teaching and researching psychology on university campuses. Others work in applied settings such as hospitals, mental health clinics, industry, and schools. Most psychologists also specialize in psychology after graduate training. Industrial psychologists specialize in human performance in organizational settings, while clinical psychologists are concerned about the assessment, diagnosis, and treatment of individuals with a variety of mental disorders. Each specialty typically requires a graduate education and sometimes requires a license to practice.

There are some psychologists who think that psychology is still in its adolescence and that the field seems to be experiencing growing pains. Since its establishment, the field has expanded to many different areas. As mentioned above, some areas are very applied. Other areas appear to emphasize theory and research. The growing pains have resulted in conflict over what the agenda of the first national psychological association, the American Psychological Association, should be. Because academics perceived this association as mainly serving practitioners, academics and researchers established their own competing association, the American Psychological Society. Despite its varied nature and growing pains, psychology remains a viable and exciting field. The first unit of the book is designed to introduce you to the study and history of psychology.

In the first article, noted psychologist and author Carol Tavris describes the tug-of-war between academic psychologists and psychotherapists. Tavris laments the fact that the public associates psychology with therapy and knows little about the science

of psychology. It is the science that should drive the practice of psychology, so the science is very important.

In the second article, Teaching Skepticism via the CRITIC Acronym and the Skeptical Inquirer, the author helps the reader differentiate fact from fiction and science from fantasy. Using a simple procedure, anyone can better critique material he or she encounters as to its scientific merits.

A second article from the same journal differentiates cause from correlation—an important point in psychology. The author also introduces other important concepts such as control and the experimental method.

Mind Games:
Psychological Warfare Between Therapists and Scientists

By Carol Tavris

RECENTLY, while lecturing to a large group of lawyers, judges, mediators, and others involved in the family-court system in Los Angeles, I asked how many knew what a "social psychologist" was. Three people shyly raised their hands. That response was typical, and it's the reason I don't tell people anymore that I'm a social psychologist: They think I'm a therapist who gives lots of parties. If I tell them I'm a psychological scientist, they think I'm a pompous therapist, because everyone knows that "psychological science" is an oxymoron.

In fact, in many states, I cannot call myself a psychologist at all—the word is reserved for someone who has an advanced degree in clinical psychology and a license to practice psychotherapy. That immediately rules out the many other kinds of psychologists who conduct scientific research in their respective specialties, including child development, gerontology, neurobiology, emotions, sleep, behavioral genetics, memory and cognition, sexual behavior and attitudes, trauma, learning, language,... and social psychology, the study of how social situations and other people affect every human activity from love to war.

> While the public assumes, vaguely, that therapists must be "scientists" of some sort, many of the widely accepted claims promulgated by therapists are based on subjective clinical opinions and have been resoundingly disproved by empirical research conducted by psychological scientists.

For the public, however, the word "psychologist" has only one meaning: psychotherapist. It is true that *clinical* psychologists practice therapy, but many psychologists are not clinicians, and most therapists are not clinical psychologists. The word "psychotherapist" is completely unregulated. It includes people who have advanced training in psychology, along with those who get a "certification" in some therapeutic specialty; clinical social workers; marriage, family, and child counselors; psychoanalysts and psychiatrists; and countless others who have no training in anything. Starting tomorrow, I could package and market my own highly effective approach, Chocolate Immersion Therapy, and offer a weekend workshop to train neophytes ($395, chocolate included). I could carry out any kind of unvalidated, cockamamie therapy I wanted, and I would not be guilty of a single crime. Unless I described myself as a psychologist.

As a result of such proliferation of psychotherapists, the work of psychological scientists who do research and teach at colleges and universities tends to be invisible outside the academy. It is the psychotherapists who get public attention, because they turn up on talk shows, offer advice in books and newspaper columns, and are interviewed in the aftermath of every disaster or horrible crime—for example, speculating on the motives and childhoods of the Washington snipers. Our society runs on the advice of mental-health professionals, who are often called upon in legal settings to determine whether a child has been molested, a prisoner up for parole is still dangerous, a defendant is lying or insane, a mother is fit to have custody of her children, and on and on. Yet while the public assumes, vaguely, that therapists must be "scientists" of some sort, many of the widely accepted claims promulgated by therapists are based on subjective clinical opinions and have been resoundingly disproved by empirical research conducted by psychological scientists. Here are a few examples that have been shown to be false:

- Low self-esteem causes aggressiveness, drug use, prejudice, and low achievement.

- Abused children almost inevitably become abusive parents, causing a "cycle of abuse."

- Therapy is beneficial for most survivors of disasters, especially if intervention is rapid.
- Memory works like a tape recorder, clicking on at the moment of birth; memories can be accurately retrieved through hypnosis, dream analysis, or other therapeutic methods.
- Traumatic experiences, particularly of a sexual nature, are typically "repressed" from memory, or split off from consciousness through "dissociation."
- The way that parents treat a child in the first five years (three years) (one year) (five minutes) of life is crucial to the child's later intellectual and emotional success.

Indeed, the split between the research and practice wings of psychology has grown so wide that many psychologists now speak glumly of the "scientist-practitioner gap," although that is like saying there is an "Arab-Israeli gap" in the Middle East. It is a war, involving deeply held beliefs, political passions, views of human nature and the nature of knowledge, and—as all wars ultimately do—money and livelihoods. The war spilled out of academic labs and therapists' offices and into the public arena in the 1980s and '90s, when three epidemics of hysteria caught fire across the country: the rise of claims of "repressed memories" of childhood sexual abuse; the growing number of cases of "multiple-personality disorder" (MPD), from a handful before 1980 to tens of thousands by 1995; and the proliferation of day-care sex-abuse scandals, which put hundreds of nursery-school teachers in prison on the "testimony" of 3- and 4-year-old children.

The work of psychological scientists at colleges tends to be invisible outside the academy. It's the psychotherapists who get the attention.

All three epidemics were fomented and perpetuated by the mistaken beliefs of psychotherapists: that "children never lie about sexual abuse"; that childhood trauma causes the personality to "split" into several or even thousands of identities; that if you don't remember being sexually abused in childhood, that's evidence that you were; that it is possible to be raped by your father every day for 16 years and to "repress" the memory until it is "uncovered" in therapy; that hypnosis, dream analysis, and free association of fantasies are reliable methods of "uncovering" accurate memories. (On the contrary, such techniques have been shown to increase confabulation, imagination, and memory errors, while inflating the belief that the retrieved memories are accurate.) The epidemics began to subside as a result of the painstaking research of psychological scientists.

But psychotherapeutic nonsense is a Hydra: Slay one set of mistaken ideas, and others take their place. Recovered-memory therapy may be on the wane, but "rebirthing" techniques and forms of "restraint therapy"—physically abusive practices that supposedly help adopted or troubled children form attachments to their parents—are on the rise. In Colorado, 10-year-old Candace Newmaker was smothered to death during rebirthing, a procedure in which she was expected to fight her way through a "birth canal" of suffocating blankets and pillows. The two therapists convicted in Candace's death are now serving time in prison, but efforts in Colorado to prohibit all forms of "restraint therapy" were defeated by protests from "attachment therapists" in the state and throughout the country. After Candace's death, one member of the Colorado Mental Health Grievance Board noted with dismay that her hairdresser's training took 1,500 hours, whereas anyone could take a two-week course and become "certified" in rebirthing. Yet the basic premise—that children can recover from trauma, insecure attachment, or other psychological problems by "reliving" their births or being subjected to punitive and coercive restraints—has no scientific validity whatsoever.

To understand how the gap between psychological scientists and clinicians grew, it is necessary to understand a little about therapy and a little about science, and how their goals and methods diverged. For many years, the training of most clinical psychologists was based on a "scientist practitioner" model. Ideally, clinicians would study the research on human behavior and apply relevant findings to their clinical practice. Clinical psychologists who are educated at major universities are still trained in this model. They study, for example, the origins of various mental disorders and the most effective ways to treat them, such as cognitive-behavior therapy for anxiety, depression, eating disorders, anger, and obsessive-compulsive disorder.

They have also identified which interventions are unhelpful or potentially harmful. For example, independent assessments of a popular post-trauma intervention called Critical Incident Stress Debriefing have found that most survivors benefit just as much by talking with friends and other survivors as with debriefers. Sometimes CISD even slows recovery, by preventing victims from drawing on their own wellsprings of resilience. And, sometimes, it harms people—for example, by having survivors ventilate their emotions without also learning good methods of coping with them.

Good therapy depends on the therapist's insight and experience, not on knowledge of statistics, the importance of control groups, and the scientific method.

Unfortunately, the numbers of scientifically trained clinicians have been shrinking. More and more therapists are getting their degrees from "free-standing" schools, so called because they are independent of research institutions or academic psychology departments. In these schools, students are trained only to do therapy, and they do not necessarily even learn which kinds of therapy have been shown to be most effective for particular problems. Many of the schools are accredited by the American Psychological Association, and their graduates learn what they need to know to pass state licensing examinations.

But that does not mean that the graduates are scientifically knowledgeable. For example, the Rorschach Inkblot Test has been resoundingly discredited as a reliable means of diagnosing most mental disorders or emotional problems; it usually reveals more about the clinician administering it than about the individual taking it. I call it the Dracula of psychological tests, because no one has been able to drive a stake through the cursed thing's heart. Many clinicians love it; it is still widely used; and it still turns up on licensing exams.

Of course, tensions exist between researchers and practitioners in any field—medicine, engineering, education. Whenever one group is doing research and the other is working in an applied domain, their interests and training will differ. The goal of the clinician, in psychology or medicine, is to help the suffering individual; the goal of the psychological or medical researcher is to explain and predict the behavior or course of illness in people in general. That is why many clinicians argue that empirical research cannot possibly capture the complex human beings who come to their offices. Professional training, they believe, should teach students empathy and appropriate therapeutic skills. Good therapy depends on the therapist's insight and experience, not on knowledge of statistics, the importance of control groups, and the scientific method.

I agree that therapy often deals with issues on which science is silent: finding courage under adversity, accepting loss, making moral choices. My clinician friends constantly impress me with their deep understanding of the human condition, which is based on seeing the human condition sobbing in their offices many times a week. Nor am I arguing that psychological scientists, or any other kind, are white knights with a special claim to intellectual virtue. They, too, wrangle over data, dispute each other furiously in print and public, and have plenty of vested interests and biases. (For example, many scientists and consumer advocates are concerned about the growing co-optation of scientific investigators by the pharmaceutical industry—which now finances the majority of studies of treatments for mental disorders and sexual problems—because the result has been a pro-drug bias in research.)

It is not that I believe that science gives us ultimate truths about human behavior, while clinical insight is always foolish and wrong. Rather, I worry that when psychotherapists fail to keep up with basic research on matters on which they are advising their clients; when they fail to learn which methods are most appropriate for which disorders, and which might be harmful; when they fail to understand their own biases of perception and do not learn how to correct them; when they fail to test their own ideas empirically before running off to promote new therapies or wild claims—then their clients and the larger public pay the price of their ignorance.

For present purposes, I am going to do an end run around the centuries-old debate about defining science, and focus on two core elements of the scientific method. These elements are central to the training of all scientists, but they are almost entirely lacking in the training of most psychotherapists, including clinical psychologists. The first is skepticism: a willingness to

question received wisdom. The second is a reliance on gathering empirical evidence to determine whether a prediction or belief is valid. You don't get to sit in your chair and decide that autism is caused by cold, rejecting, "refrigerator" mothers, as Bruno Bettelheim did. But legions of clinicians (and mothers) accepted his cruel and unsubstantiated theory because he was, well, Bruno Bettelheim. It took skeptical scientists to compare the mothers of autistic children with those of healthy children, and to find that autism is not caused by anything parents do; it is a neurological disorder.

> The scientific method is designed to help investigators overcome the most entrenched human cognitive habit: the *confirmation bias*, the tendency to notice and remember evidence that confirms our beliefs or decisions, and to ignore, dismiss, or forget evidence that is discrepant.

The scientific method is designed to help investigators overcome the most entrenched human cognitive habit: the *confirmation bias*, the tendency to notice and remember evidence that confirms our beliefs or decisions, and to ignore, dismiss, or forget evidence that is discrepant. That's why we are all inclined to stick to a hypothesis we believe in. Science is one way of forcing us, kicking and screaming if necessary, to modify our views. Most scientists regard a central, if not defining, characteristic of the scientific method to be what Karl Popper called "the principle of falsifiability": For a theory to be scientific, it must be falsifiable—you can't show me just those observations that confirm it, but also those that might show it to be wrong, false. If you can twist any result of your research into a confirmation of your hypothesis, you aren't thinking scientifically. For that reason, many of Freud's notions were unfalsifiable. If analysts saw evidence of "castration anxiety" in their male patients, that confirmed Freud's theory of its universality; if analysts didn't see it, Freud wrote, they lacked observational skills and were just too blind or stubborn to see it. With that way of thinking, there is no way to disconfirm the belief in castration anxiety.

Yet many psychotherapists perpetuate ideas based only on confirming cases—the people they see in therapy—and do not consider the disconfirming cases. The popular belief in "the cycle of abuse" rests on cases of abusive parents who turn up in jail or therapy and who report that they were themselves victims of abuse as children. But scientists would want to know also about the disconfirming cases: children who were beaten but did not grow up to mistreat their children (and, therefore, did not end up in therapy or jail), and people who were not beaten and then did grow up to be abusive parents. When the researchers Joan Kaufman and Edward Zigler reviewed longitudinal studies of the outcomes of child abuse, they found that although being abused does considerably increase the risk of becoming an abusive parent, more than 70 percent of all abused children do not mistreat their offspring—hardly an inevitable "cycle."

Practitioners who do not learn about the confirmation bias and ways to counteract it can make devastating judgments in court cases. For example, if they are convinced that a child has been sexually molested, they are often unpersuaded by the child's repeated denials; such denials, they say, are evidence of the depth of the trauma. Sometimes, of course, that is true. But what if it isn't? In the Little Rascals day-care-abuse case in North Carolina, one mother told reporters that it took *10 months* before her child was able to "reveal" the molestation. No one at the time considered the idea that the child might have been remarkably courageous to persist in telling the truth for so long.

Because many therapists tend not to be as deeply imbued with the spirit of skepticism as scientists are (or are supposed to be), it is common for many of them to place their faith in the leader of a particular approach, and to set about trying to do what the school's founder did—rather than to raise too many questions about the founder's methods or the validity of the founder's theories. If you go off to become certified in Eye Movement Desensitization and Reprocessing (EMDR), invented by Francine Shapiro while she was walking in the woods one day, you are unlikely to ask, "Why, exactly, does waving your finger in front of someone's eyes realign the halves of the brain and reduce anxiety?" Scientific studies of this method show that the successful ingredient in EMDR is an old, tried-and-true technique from behavior therapy: exposing people to a thought or situation that makes them anxious, until the feeling subsides. The eye movements that are supposedly essential, the clinical scientist Scott O. Lilienfeld concluded, do not constitute "anything more than pseudoscientific window dressing."

Detective work is the province of scientists, who are trained *not* to automatically believe what someone says or what someone claims to remember, but to ask, "Where's the evidence?"

Similarly, most clinicians are not trained to be skeptical of what a client says or to demand corroborating evidence. Why would they be? A client comes to see you complaining that he has a terrible mother; are you going to argue? Ask to meet the mother? Some clinicians, notably those who practice cognitive-behavior therapy, would, indeed, ask you for the evidence that your mother is terrible and also invite you to consider other explanations of her behavior; but most do not. As the psychiatrist Judith Herman explained in a PBS *Frontline* special on recovered memory: "As a therapist, your job is not to be a detective; your job is not to be a fact-finder; your job is not to be a judge or a jury; and

your job is also not to make the family feel better. Your job is to help the patient make sense out of her life, make sense out of her symptoms… and make meaning out of her experience."

That remark perfectly summarizes the differing goals of most clinicians and scientists. Clinicians are certainly correct that most of the time it is not possible to corroborate a client's memory anyway, and that it isn't their job to find out what "really" happened in the client's past. Scientists, though, have shown that memories are subject to distortion. So, if the client is going to end up suing a parent for sexual abuse, or if the therapist's intervention ends up causing a devastating family rift, a little detective work seems called for. Detective work is the province of scientists, who are trained *not* to automatically believe what someone says or what someone claims to remember, but to ask, "Where's the evidence?"

For psychological scientists, clinical insight is simply not sufficient evidence. For one thing, the clinician's observations of clients will be inherently limited if they overlook comparison groups of people who are not in therapy. For example, many clinicians invent "checklists" of "indicators" of some problem or disorder—say, that "excessive" masturbation or bed-wetting are signs of sexual abuse or, my favorite, that losing track of time or becoming engrossed in a book is a sign of multiple-personality disorder. But, before you can say that bed-wetting or masturbation is an indicator that a child has been sexually abused, what must you know? Many psychotherapists cannot give you the simple answer: You must know the rates of bed-wetting and masturbation among all children, including nonabused ones. In fact, many abused children have no symptoms, and many nonabused children wet their beds, masturbate, and are fearful in new situations.

Throughout the 1980s and '90s, many therapists routinely testified in court that they could magically tell, with complete certainly, that a child had been sexually abused because of how the child played with anatomically correct dolls, or because of what the child revealed in drawings. The plausible assumption is that very young children may reveal feelings in their play or drawings that they cannot express verbally. But while such tests may have a therapeutic use, again the scientific evidence is overwhelming that they are worthless for assessment or diagnostic purposes. How do we know that? Because when scientists compared the doll play of abused children to that of control groups of nonabused children, they found that such play is not a valid way of determining whether a child has been sexually abused. The doll's genitals are pretty interesting to all kids.

Likewise, psychological scientists who study children's cognitive development empirically have examined the belief held by many psychotherapists that "children never lie" about sexual abuse. Scientists have shown in dozens of experiments that children often do tell the truth, but that they also lie, misremember, and can be influenced to make false allegations—just as adults do. Researchers have shown, too, that adults often misunderstand and misinterpret what children say, and they have identified the conditions that increase a child's suggestibility and the interviewing methods virtually guaranteed to elicit false reports. Those conditions and methods were present in the interrogations of children by social workers, therapists, and police officers in all of the sensational cases of day-care hysteria of the

1980s and '90s. And those coercive practices continue in many jurisdictions today where child-protection workers have not been trained in the latest research.

Much has been written about our scientific illiteracy, but social-scientific illiteracy is just as widespread and in some ways even more pernicious.

I fear that the scientist-therapist gap is a done deal. There are too many economic and institutional supports for it, in spite of yearly exhortations by every president of the American Psychological Association for "unity" and "cooperation." That's why, in the late 1980s, a group of psychological scientists formed their own organization, the American Psychological Society, to represent their own scientific interests. Every year, the APA does something else to rile its scientific members while placating its therapist members—like supporting prescription-writing privileges for Ph.D. psychologists and approving continuing-education programs for unvalidated methods or tests—and so, every year, more psychological scientists leave the APA for the APS.

But to the public, all this remains an internecine battle that seems to have no direct relevance. That's the danger. Much has been written about America's scientific illiteracy, but social-scientific illiteracy is just as widespread and in some ways even more pernicious. People can deny evolution or fail to learn basic physics, but such ignorance rarely affects their personal lives. The scientific illiteracy of psychotherapists has torn up families, sent innocent defendants to prison, cost people their jobs and custody of their children, and promoted worthless, even harmful, therapies. A public unable to critically assess psychotherapists' claims and methods for scientific credibility will be vulnerable to whatever hysterical epidemic comes along next. And in our psychologically oriented culture, there will be many nexts. Some will be benign; some will merely cost money; and some will cost lives.

Carol Tavris, a social psychologist, is on the board of the Council for Scientific Clinical Psychology and Psychiatry, a consulting editor of The Scientific Review of Mental Health Practice, *and a member of the editorial board of* Psychological Science in the Public Interest.

From *The Chronicle of Higher Education,* February 28, 2003, pp. B7-B9. © 2003 by Carol Tavris.

Teaching skepticism via the CRITIC acronym and the Skeptical Inquirer

Wayne R. Bartz

The CRITIC acronym provides neophyte skeptical students with an easy-to-remember, step-by-step format for applied critical thinking. Practice applying this simple method of critical analysis can include writing CRITIC reports on the feature articles found in the SKEPTICAL INQUIRER.

Most college students slouch into the first day of class assuming they already know a great deal about the world around them. As a result they may have to unlearn an accumulated wealth of misinformation in addition to absorbing the priceless new pearls of wisdom teachers toss their way. An improvement in critical thinking skills should facilitate that sometimes painful process.

When it comes to widely accepted extraordinary claims, the sources bombarding today's students are rich, the speculations boundless, and critical analysis is generally lacking. Dubious claims familiar to readers of the SKEPTICAL INQUIRER abound: Exposure to "crystal energy" improves health and mental functioning; gifted "psychics" can describe your innermost desires, divine the future, or speak with the dead; basic "personality traits" can be revealed by studying the features of an individual's face. Students routinely assume such claims to be true, or else they would not be prominently featured on radio and TV, in books, newspapers, and magazines. Rarely is the slightest critical thought demonstrated in credulous media portrayals of paranormal events (recent television network examples include NBC's The Others and Mysterious Ways). The challenge for an educator is to motivate students to critically evaluate interesting claims without having the benefit of background courses in research methodology and statistics (which most students never take).

Introductory psychology classes have always stressed a scientific approach to the study of behavior, with skeptical modes of thought being emphasized long before "critical thinking" became a buzzword in education. Some years ago a panel of psychologists assembled by the American Psychological Association concluded that the primary objective of an undergraduate psychology degree is graduates who could be described as "amiable skeptics about much of what they encounter." We in the skeptical community might hope this outcome would occur no matter what college major a young person selects, but widespread acceptance of fanciful notions by college-educated adults suggests this is a vain hope. During three decades of teaching college psychology courses and encouraging the development of "amiable skeptics," I devised a practical system of applied critical thought based upon the easy-to-remember acronym CRITIC. It could be used in a variety of courses, is readily understood by most college students, and would probably be effective even with high school and junior high school students. It is basically a simplified application of the scientific method without the complex terminology:

C Claim?
R Role of the claimant?
I Information backing the claim?
T Test?
I Independent testing?
C Cause proposed?

C—Claim: The first task is to describe exactly what is being proposed. Spell it out, define it, make it specific enough to be observable and measurable. For example, how might a claim of crystal-inspired "improved mental functioning" actually be demonstrated? What measurable mental performance would be expected and how would we determine whether or not it actually occurred? With some claims it immediately becomes apparent that we cannot pin down exactly what is being proposed, making it impossible to seriously test the claim. For example, I could assert that invisible "N-rays" emanating from Earth disturb mental functioning, but this newly discovered force cannot yet be measured. Not only that, but the effects are sporadic and influence different people in different ways, so they cannot be readily documented. The essential requirement of falsifiability can be introduced and most students will understand why a claim that cannot be falsified is worthless.

R—Role of the claimant: Who is making the claim and is there something in it for them, e.g., money, fame, power, influence, publicity? If the public accepts the claim, will the claimant profit? Does the claimant appear to be an unbiased observer or a "true believer" with something to sell? Might he or she be motivated to slant things in a specific direction for personal benefit? Some years ago Roger Smith, then president of General Motors, claimed on the Donahue show that GM manufactured the "highest quality vehicles produced in the world." Might viewers have reason to hesitate in taking his word for it? If there is some benefit for the claimant, that does not necessarily demonstrate the claim to be false, but it certainly suggests using vigilance and caution in accepting that individual as a reliable fount of knowledge.

I—Information backing the claim: What evidence is offered in support of the claim? Is it public information that can readily be verified? Or is it anecdotal or testimonial? GM's Roger Smith supported his Donahue show claim about world-beating quality by pulling a letter from his pocket and reading it aloud. The letter was purportedly received from a happy Buick owner who described driving his car more than 300,000 trouble-free miles. The common uncritical use of testimonials and anecdotal evidence in the media and in advertising can be discussed here, along with why such use should always raise a red flag. We can also question whether the information cited is genuine, who actually provided it, and for what purpose? For example, how could Donahue's viewers know for certain whether or not the Buick owner's letter was genuine? Finally, are we being provided with information that was obtained under scientific, controlled conditions and published in recognized peer-reviewed scientific journals, and why is that important?

T—Test: If there is some reason to doubt the claim, how might we design an adequate test? What would provide rigorous conditions that preclude uncontrolled variables, systematic error, or cheating from biasing the results? What is required to conclude that a claim is probably true beyond a reasonable doubt and what is reasonable doubt? The basic ideas of statistical analysis, probability, and significance can be introduced here, along with some introductory concepts of experimental design. (Beware of sudden student brain-lock when instructors begin waxing poetic about statistics and research methodology.)

I—Independent testing: Has any unbiased source actually carried out a rigorous independent test of the claim and published the results, ideally in a reputable, peer-reviewed research journal? Does it back up the claimant? If independent tests have failed to confirm the claim, was this reported by the claimant? If not, why not? Considering the General Motors quality question, a check of Consumer Reports's yearly survey of automobile owners' experiences would provide some quick, relatively unbiased data. Does it come as any surprise that Roger Smith never mentioned consumer Reports when singing GM's praise to Donahue's 8 million viewers? I wonder why?

C—Cause proposed: What is held out as a causal explanation for the claim and is it consistent with the physical laws of the universe? (It is not suggested that students can instantly make that judgment—rather, they are alerted to this being an important question that could be pursued, e.g., by asking a reputable astronomer, physicist or biologist.) For example, could there be something special about GM'S assembly line, quality control system, or workers' contract that might result in better vehicles? Perhaps, and each of these causal hypotheses is something that could be examined. But what if the proposed cause transcends the laws of physics and proposes the existence of a completely new and mysterious force or energy? What if the claim is that "General Motors has discovered a way to focus N-rays to specially harden and strengthen the metal and plastic used in all its vehicles"? If a new force or energy is proposed it is not necessarily impossible, but must be considered highly suspect and demands especially rigorous proof before being taken seriously ("extraordinary claims demand extraordinary evidence"). Often with claims about paranormal events the possible causal mechanism is simply ignored or shrugged off as something wonderful but totally unknown. This is the case when astrologers say "We don't know how the movement of the planets affects human lives, it just does." Claimed events that suggest no feasible explanation are unlikely to be true (this provides an opportunity to discuss Occam's razor).

Applying CRITIC

After outlining this CRITIC system for my students we then apply it to a variety of widely accepted claims such as those made by astrologers, mind readers, faith healers, and New Age practitioners, each accompanied by an illustrative, entertaining video example lifted from the electronic media. I encourage students to consider not whether their instructor or psychologists in general accept what is being presented, but rather how they might approach the question critically and answer it for themselves.

For students willing to try applying their CRITIC acronym skills in exchange for some extra credit, I developed a simple essay questionnaire to be filled out after reading a feature article in the SKEPTICAL INQUIRER at the college library. The questions on the report correspond to the CRITIC acronym. For example:

1. What is the claim being considered? (The student responds with a written answer: "Training in Yogic flying can allow a person to hover above the ground or move around freely in space. The training involves _____".)
2. Describe the apparent role of the person, group or organization making the claim: (etc.)

This written exercise lets them practice applying critical thinking and has the added benefit of giving most students their first exposure to the pages of the SKEPTICAL INQUIRER. The ultimate goal of the CRITIC acronym is to nudge students toward application of a more systematic and scientific approach to the fascinating world around them… as an alternative to the impressionistic, faith-based, and often authoritarian approaches that have been foisted upon them all their lives. A study involving 130 introductory psychology students found that those who had experienced the CRITIC-based course introduction were indeed more skeptical and likely to use the CRITIC terminology when evaluating controversial claims at semester's end than were students who did not receive CRITIC training.

Acknowledgment

My thanks to Richard Rasor, Bud Gallagher, and Bob Tallmon for their assistance in the study mentioned at the conclusion of this article.

Wayne R. Bartz is a recently retired college professor and clinical psychologist. He lives in Meadow Vista, California. This article is adapted from a book in preparation titled The Ultimate Liberation: From Religion and Other Popular Delusions.

THINKING ABOUT SCIENCE

Causes and Correlations

MASSIMO PIGLIUCCI

One of the most common fallacies committed by believers in the paranormal is what in philosophy is known by the Latin name of *post hoc, ergo propter hoc*, which loosely translates to "after this, therefore because of this." Surely you have heard some version of it: "I dreamed of my brother the other night, and the following morning he called me, though he rarely does." The implication here is that there is some causal connection between the dream and the phone call, that one happened because of the other. We all know what is wrong with this argument: a correlation between two events does not constitute good enough evidence of a causal connection between them. In the case of the dream as precognition, we probably dream of our relatives often enough, and most often the dream is not followed by their call; yet, because of an innate tendency of the human brain to remember hits and forget misses, we pay attention to the exceptions and charge them with special meaning.

But the good skeptic could go further and ask herself what exactly we mean by causation to begin with. If a correlation is not the hallmark of a causal relationship, what is? The modern study of causation started with the Italian physicist Galileo Galilei, who viewed causes as a set of necessary and sufficient conditions for a given effect. According to Galileo, the dream can be considered a cause of

the call only if every time the subject dreams of his brother, the following morning the brother actually does call. The problem with this idea is that it is too restrictive: many phenomena have multiple causes, a subset of which may be sufficient to generate the effect. The brother could call for other reasons than the dream, notwithstanding a true causal connection between dreaming and calling. Or, the dream may be causing the brother to have the impulse to call, but he can't do it because he is at a vacation spot where there are no phones in sight (as hard as this may seem to believe).

Scottish skeptic philosopher David Hume made the next important contribution to our understanding of causality, one that many philosophers (and a few scientists) are still grappling with. Hume argued that we never actually have any evidence that causal connections are real, we only have perceptions of the likely association between what we call a cause and an effect. Here Hume was being a good empiricist, something that a skeptic ought to appreciate. For him, talk of "causes" sounded as strange as talking of action at a distance, which in pre-Newtonian times was an exercise for mystics, not scientists. So Hume decided to settle on a very pragmatic concept of causality. He suggested that we are justified in talking about causes and effects if three conditions hold: 1) the first event (say, the dream) precedes the second one

(say, your brother's call); 2) the two events are contiguous in time, i.e., your brother called the morning after the dream, not a month or a year later; 3) there is a constant conjunction between the two events, i.e., every time you dream of your brother, he will call. As the reader will have noticed, however, the latter clause is very similar to Galileo's idea of necessary and sufficient condition, and will not actually help the scientist in real situations.

John Stuart Mill, well known as a utilitarian, proposed a concept of causation that is at the basis of much modern experimental science and, hence, of skeptical investigations. Mill argued that causality simply cannot be demonstrated without experimentation. Essentially, Mill said that in order to establish a causal connection between two phenomena, we have to be able to do experiments that allow us to manipulate the conditions so that only one factor at a time is allowed to change. A series of these experiments will eventually pinpoint the cause(s) of certain effects.

While Mill's idea has been of fundamental importance for modern science, the problem with it is that it imposes on the investigators logistic requirements that are often too restrictive. What if it is not possible to control all variables but one during an inquiry? Carefully controlled manipulative experiments are possible only in certain fields and under very taxing conditions. Should we then give up the concept of causality for the much larger number of instances in which such manipulations are not possible, unethical, or simply too expensive? That would be problematic because, for example, we could nor conclude that smoking causes cancer. It is simply not possible to do the right experiment, especially with human beings: there are too many variables, nor to mention deep ethical issues.

What then? One of the most modern conceptions of causality is the so-called probabilistic one. According to probabilistic causality we can reasonably infer that, say, cancer is caused by smoking if the probability of getting cancer is measurably higher when the subjects smoke than when they don't. Other factors here are taken into consideration statistically, not necessarily by experimental manipulation. That is, one carries out the investigation taking care of sampling individuals with different socioeconomic backgrounds, diets, exercise habits, and genetic constitution. If, when these other variables are kept in check statistically, we still detect an increase in the likelihood of getting cancer in the smokers compared to the nonsmokers, we are justified in tentatively accepting a causal connection.

Notice, however, that while the probabilistic account of causality is indeed very powerful in practice, conceptually it brings us back toward Hume: the only reason we are talking about causality is because we perceive a series of regularities, not because we know that actual causes are at play. So, in science as in skeptical investigations, we might have to admit that the most we can get is a certain probability of being right. Definitive truth is a chimera that does not belong to science after all.

Further Reading

David Hume (1739–1740). *A Treatise of Human Nature*.

Author **Massimo Pigliucci** is an associate professor in the Departments of Botany and Ecology & Evolutionary Biology at the University of Tennessee at Knoxville and author of the new book *Denying Evolution: Creationism, Scientism, and the Nature of Science* (Sinauer 2002). His earlier SKEPTICAL INQUIRER articles include "Hypothesis Testing and the Nature of Skeptical Investigations" (November/ December 2002), "Design Yes, Intelligent No" (September/October 2001), and "Where Do We Come From? A Humbling Look at the Biology of Life's Origins" (September/October 1999). His Web site is www.rationallyspeaking.org.

UNIT 2
Biological Bases of Behavior

Unit Selections

4. **What Makes You Who You Are**, Matt Ridley
5. **The Blank Slate**, Steven Pinker
6. **Neuroscience: Breaking Down Scientific Barriers to the Study of Brain and Mind**, Eric R. Kandel and Larry R. Squire

Key Points to Consider

- What do you think contributes most to our psychological makeup and behaviors: the influence of the environment, the expression of genes, evolution, or the functioning of the nervous system? Do you believe that some combination of these factors accounts for psychological characteristics and behaviors? Are all of these studied the same way; for example, under a microscope? How are these contributors to behavior studied?

- What is genetic research? Why do genetic research? How much of human behavior is influenced by genes? Do you agree with Steven Pinker that evolution and genetics account for most of our "humanness"? Can you give some examples of the influence of genes on human behavior?

- How could such research help experts in psychology and medicine predict and treat various disorders? Do you think such information could be or has been misused? How? When? What environmental factors affect genetic expression? Or do they?

- Why do psychologists study the human brain? Do you know the names and functions of the brain? Of other parts of the nervous system? What parts of the brain control various aspects of our behavior? That is, how does the brain influence human behavior and psychological characteristics? If an individual experiences brain damage, can other parts of the brain take over functions controlled by the damaged area?

- What is neuroscience? How are psychology and neuroscience related? Are there some realms of psychology that are not related to neuroscience? If yes, which ones? Are there areas of neuroscience that are not related to psychology?

 **Links: www.dushkin.com/online/**
These sites are annotated in the World Wide Web pages.

Adolescence: Changes and Continuity
http://www.personal.psu.edu/faculty/n/x/nxd10/adolesce.htm

Division of Hereditary Diseases and Family Studies, Indiana University School of Medicine
http://www.iupui.edu/~medgen/division/hereditary/hereditary_diseases.html

Institute for Behavioral Genetics
http://ibgwww.colorado.edu/index.html

Serendip
http://serendip.brynmawr.edu/serendip/

As a child, Angelina vowed she did not want to turn out like either of her parents. Angelina's mother was very passive and acquiescent about her father's drinking. When Dad was drunk, Mom always called his boss to report that Dad was "sick" and then acted as if there was nothing wrong at home. Angelina's childhood was a nightmare. Her father's behavior was erratic and unpredictable. If he drank just a little bit, most often he was happy. If he drank a lot, which was usually the case, he frequently became belligerent.

Despite vowing not to become her father, as an adult Angelina found herself in the alcohol rehabilitation unit of a large hospital. Angelina's employer could no longer tolerate her on-the-job mistakes nor her unexplained absences from work. Angelina's supervisor therefore referred her to the clinic for help. As Angelina pondered her fate, she wondered whether her genes preordained her to follow in her father's inebriated footsteps or whether the stress of her childhood had brought her to this point in her life. After all, being the child of an alcoholic is not easy.

Psychologists also are concerned with discovering the causes of human behavior. Once the cause is known, treatments for problematic behaviors can be developed. In fact, certain behaviors might even be prevented when the cause is known. But for Angelina, prevention was too late.

One of the paths to understanding humans is to understand the biological underpinnings of their behavior. Genes and chromosomes, the body's chemistry (as found in hormones, neurotransmitters, and enzymes), and the nervous system comprising the brain, spinal cord, nerve cells, and other parts are all implicated in human behavior. All represent the biological aspects of behavior and ought, therefore, to be worthy of study by psychologists.

Physiological psychologists and psychobiologists are often the ones who examine the role of biology in behavior. The neuroscientist is especially interested in brain functioning; the psychopharmacologist is interested in the effects of various pharmacological agents or psychoactive drugs on behavior.

These psychologists often utilize one of three techniques to understand the biology-behavior connection. Animal studies involving manipulation, stimulation, or destruction of certain parts of the brain offer one method of study. There is also a second available technique that includes the examination of unfortunate individuals whose brains are malfunctioning at birth or damaged later by accidents or disease.

We can also use animal models to understand genetics; with animal models we can control reproduction as well as manipulate and develop various strains of animals if necessary. Some individuals consider research with animals to be inhumane; such tactics with humans would be considered extremely unethical. However, by studying an individual's behavior in comparison to

both natural and adoptive parents or by studying identical twins reared together or apart, we can begin to understand the role of genetics versus environment in human behavior.

The articles in this unit are designed to familiarize you with the knowledge psychologists have gleaned by using these and other techniques to study physiological processes and other underlying mechanisms in human behavior. Each article should interest you and make you more curious about the role of biology in human activities.

"What Makes You Who You Are" is the first article in this important unit. Matt Ridley reviews the nagging nature-nurture controversy, the debate about whether environment or heredity plays a larger role in shaping us. Ridley introduces a rather new element into this issue—the fact that both are similarly important because each affects the other.

The second article, entitled "The Blank Slate," is also about the nature-nurture dispute. Steven Pinker, however, comes down firmly on the side of genetics and evolution in explaining our behaviors.

The final article in this section discusses the nervous system. Eric Kandel and Larry Squire claim that as time progresses, psychology and neuroscience become more and more important to one another. They highlight some of the various ways that neuroscience is informing psychological science.

WHAT MAKES YOU WHO YOU ARE

Which is stronger—nature or nurture?
The latest science says genes and your
experience interact for your whole life

By MATT RIDLEY

THE PERENNIAL DEBATE ABOUT NATURE AND NURTURE—which is the more potent shaper of the human essence?—is perennially rekindled. It flared up again in the London *Observer* of Feb. 11, 2001. REVEALED: THE SECRET OF HUMAN BEHAVIOR, read the banner headline. ENVIRONMENT, NOT GENES, KEY TO OUR ACTS. The source of the story was Craig Venter, the self-made man of genes who had built a private company to read the full sequence of the human genome in competition with an international consortium funded by taxes and charities. That sequence—a string of 3 billion letters, composed in a four-letter alphabet, containing the complete recipe for building and running a human body—was to be published the very next day (the competition ended in an arranged tie). The first analysis of it had revealed that there were just 30,000 genes in it, not the 100,000 that many had been estimating until a few months before.

Details had already been circulated to journalists under embargo. But Venter, by speaking to a reporter at a biotechnology conference in France on Feb. 9, had effectively broken the embargo. Not for the first time in the increasingly bitter rivalry over the genome project, Venter's version of the story would hit the headlines before his rivals'. "We simply do not have enough genes for this idea of biological determinism to be right," Venter told the *Observer*. "The wonderful diversity of the human species is not hard-wired in our genetic code. Our environments are critical."

In truth, the number of human genes changed nothing. Venter's remarks concealed two whopping nonsequiturs: that fewer genes implied more environmental influences and that 30,000 genes were too few to explain human nature, whereas 100,000 would have been enough. As one scientist put it to me a few weeks later, just 33 genes, each coming in two varieties (on or off), would be enough to make every human being in the world unique. There are more than 10 billion combinations that could come from flipping a coin 33 times, so 30,000 does not seem such a small number after all. Besides, if fewer genes meant more free will, fruit flies would be freer than we are, bacteria freer still and viruses the John Stuart Mill of biology.

Fortunately, there was no need to reassure the population with such sophisticated calculations. People did not weep at the humiliating news that our genome has only about twice as many genes as a worm's. Nothing had been hung on the number 100,000, which was just a bad guess.

But the human genome project—and the decades of research that preceded it—did force a much more nuanced understanding of how genes work. In the early days, scientists detailed how genes encode the various proteins that make up the cells in our bodies. Their more sophisticated and ultimately more satisfying discovery—that gene expression can be modified by experience—has been gradually emerging since the 1980s. Only now is it dawning on scientists what a big and general idea it implies: that learning itself consists of nothing more than switching genes on and off. The more we lift the lid on the genome, the more vulnerable to experience genes appear to be.

This is not some namby-pamby, middle-of-the-road compromise. This is a new understanding of the fundamental building blocks of life based on the discovery that genes are not immutable things handed down from our parents like Moses' stone tablets but are active participants in our lives, designed to take their cues from everything that happens to us from the moment of our conception.

Early Puberty
Girls raised in FATHERLESS HOUSEHOLDS experience puberty earlier. Apparently the change in timing is the reaction of a STILL MYSTERIOUS set of genes to their ENVIRONMENT. Scientists don't know how many SETS OF GENES act this way

For the time being, this new awareness has taken its strongest hold among scientists, changing how they think about everything from the way bodies develop in the womb to how new species emerge to the inevitability of homosexuality in some people. (More on all this later.) But eventually, as the general population becomes more attuned to this interdependent view, changes may well occur in areas as diverse as education, medicine, law and religion. Dieters may learn precisely which combination of fats, carbohydrates and proteins has the greatest effect on their individual waistlines. Theologians may develop a whole new theory of free will based on the observation that learning expands our capacity to choose our own path. As was true of Copernicus's observation 500 years ago that the earth orbits the sun, there is no telling how far the repercussions of this new scientific paradigm may extend.

To appreciate what has happened, you will have to abandon cherished notions and open your mind. You will have to enter a world in which your genes are not puppet masters pulling the strings of your behavior but puppets at the mercy of your behavior, in which instinct is not the opposite of learning, environmental influences are often less reversible than genetic ones, and nature is designed for nurture.

Fear of snakes, for instance, is the most common human phobia, and it makes good evolutionary sense for it to be instinctive. Learning to fear snakes the hard way would be dangerous. Yet experiments with monkeys reveal that their fear of snakes (and probably ours) must still be acquired by watching another individual react

with fear to a snake. It turns out that it is easy to teach monkeys to fear snakes but very difficult to teach them to fear flowers. What we inherit is not a fear of snakes but a predisposition to learn a fear of snakes—a nature for a certain kind of nurture.

Before we dive into some of the other scientific discoveries that have so thoroughly transformed the debate, it helps to understand how deeply entrenched in our intellectual history the false dichotomy of nature vs. nurture became. Whether human nature is born or made is an ancient conundrum discussed by Plato and Aristotle. Empiricist philosophers such as John Locke and David Hume argued that the human mind was formed by experience; nativists like Jean-Jacques Rousseau and Immanuel Kant held that there was such a thing as immutable human nature.

It was Charles Darwin's eccentric mathematician cousin Francis Galton who in 1874 ignited the nature-nurture controversy in its present form and coined the very phrase (borrowing the alliteration from Shakespeare, who had lifted it from an Elizabethan schoolmaster named Richard Mulcaster). Galton asserted that human personalities were born, not made by experience. At the same time, the philosopher William James argued that human beings have more instincts than animals, not fewer.

In the first decades of the 20th century, nature held sway over nurture in most fields. In the wake of World War I, however, three men recaptured the social sciences for nurture: John B. Watson, who set out to show how the conditioned reflex, discovered by Ivan Pavlov, could explain human learning; Sigmund Freud, who sought to explain the influence of parents and early experiences on young minds; and Franz Boas, who argued that the origin of ethnic differences lay with history, experience and circumstance, not physiology and psychology.

Homosexuality
GAY MEN are more likely to have OLDER BROTHERS than either gay women or heterosexual men. It may be that a FIRST MALE FETUS triggers an immune reaction in the mother, ALTERING THE EXPRESSION of key gender genes

Galton's insistence on innate explanations of human abilities had led him to espouse eugenics, a term he coined. Eugenics was enthusiastically adopted by the Nazis to justify their campaign of mass murder against the disabled and the Jews. Tainted by this association, the idea of innate behavior was in full retreat for most of the middle years of the century. In 1958, however, two men began the counterattack on behalf of nature. Noam Chomsky, in his review of a book by the behaviorist B.F. Skinner, argued that it was impossible to learn human language by trial and error alone; human beings must come already equipped with an innate grammatical skill. Harry Harlow did a simple experiment that showed that a baby monkey prefers a soft, cloth model of a mother to a hard, wire-frame mother, even if the wire-frame mother provides it with all its milk; some preferences are innate.

Fast-forward to the 1980s and one of the most stunning surprises to greet scientists when they first opened up animal genomes: fly geneticists found a small group of genes called the hox genes that seemed to set out the body plan of the fly during its early development—telling it roughly where to put the head, legs, wings and so on. But then colleagues studying mice found the same hox genes, in the same order, doing the same job in Mickey's world—telling the mouse where to put its various parts. And when scientists looked in our genome, they found hox genes there too.

Hox genes, like all genes, are switched on and off in different parts of the body at different times. In this way, genes can have subtly different effects, depending on where, when and how they are switched on. The switches that control this process—stretches of DNA upstream of genes—are known as promoters.

Small changes in the promoter can have profound effects on the expression of a hox gene. For example, mice have short necks and long bodies; chickens have long necks and short bodies. If you count the vertebrae in the necks and thoraxes of mice and chickens, you will find that a mouse has seven neck and 13 thoracic vertebrae, a chicken 14 and seven, respectively. The source of this difference lies in the promoter attached to HoxC8, a hox gene that helps shape the thorax of the body. The promoter is a 200-letter paragraph of DNA, and in the two species it differs by just a handful of letters. The effect is to alter the expression of the HoxC8 gene in the development of the chicken embryo. This means the chicken makes thoracic vertebrae in a different part of the body than the mouse. In the python, HoxC8 is expressed right from the head and goes on being expressed for most of the body. So pythons are one long thorax; they have ribs all down the body.

Divorce

If a FRATERNAL TWIN gets divorced, there's a 30% CHANCE that his or her twin will get divorced as well. If the twins are IDENTICAL, however, one sibling's divorce BOOSTS THE ODDS to 45% that the other will split

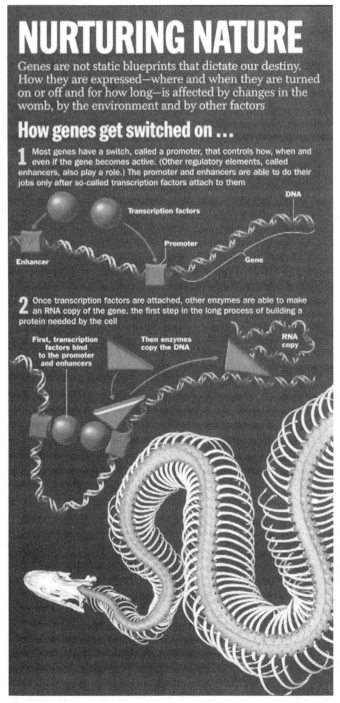

NURTURING NATURE

Genes are not static blueprints that dictate our destiny. How they are expressed—where and when they are turned on or off and for how long—is affected by changes in the womb, by the environment and by other factors

How genes get switched on …

1 Most genes have a switch, called a promoter, that controls how, when and even if the gene becomes active. (Other regulatory elements, called enhancers, also play a role.) The promoter and enhancers are able to do their jobs only after so-called transcription factors attach to them

DNA
Transcription factors
Promoter
Enhancer
Gene

2 Once transcription factors are attached, other enzymes are able to make an RNA copy of the gene, the first step in the long process of building a protein needed by the cell

First, transcription factors bind to the promoter and enhancers
Then enzymes copy the DNA
RNA copy

(continued)

To make grand changes in the body plan of animals, there is no need to invent new genes, just as there's no need to invent new words to write an original novel (unless your name is Joyce). All you need do is switch the same ones on and off in different patterns. Suddenly, here is a mechanism for creating large and small evolutionary changes from small genetic differences. Merely by adjusting the sequence of a promoter or adding a new one, you could alter the expression of a gene.

In one sense, this is a bit depressing. It means that until scientists know how to find gene promoters in the vast

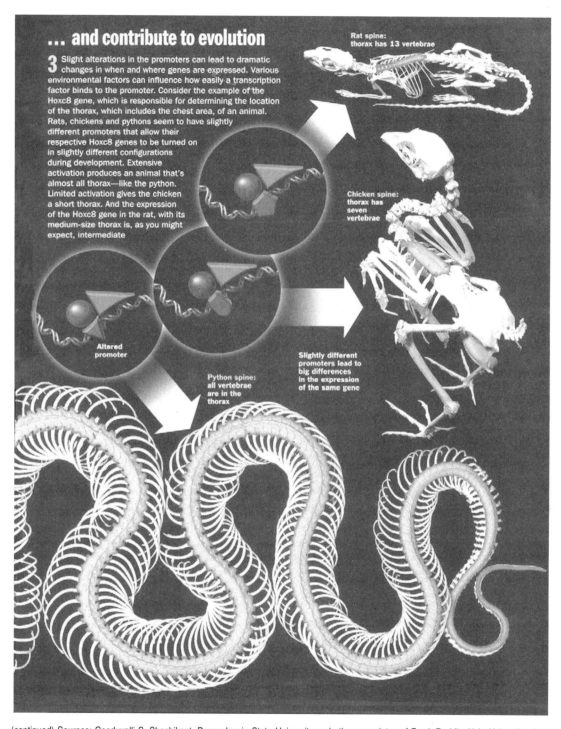

... and contribute to evolution

3 Slight alterations in the promoters can lead to dramatic changes in when and where genes are expressed. Various environmental factors can influence how easily a transcription factor binds to the promoter. Consider the example of the Hoxc8 gene, which is responsible for determining the location of the thorax, which includes the chest area, of an animal. Rats, chickens and pythons seem to have slightly different promoters that allow their respective Hoxc8 genes to be turned on in slightly different configurations during development. Extensive activation produces an animal that's almost all thorax—like the python. Limited activation gives the chicken a short thorax. And the expression of the Hoxc8 gene in the rat, with its medium-size thorax is, as you might expect, intermediate

Rat spine:
thorax has 13 vertebrae

Chicken spine:
thorax has seven vertebrae

Altered promoter

Python spine:
all vertebrae are in the thorax

Slightly different promoters lead to big differences in the expression of the same gene

(continued) Sources: Cooduvalli S. Shashikant, Pennsylvania State University and other associates of Frank Ruddle, Yale University; Anne Burke, Wesleyan University; M.J. Cohn and C. Tickle, University of Reading, Britain

Photos: TED THAI FOR TIME; TIME Graphic by Joe Lertola

text of the genome, they will not learn how the recipe for a chimpanzee differs from that for a person. But in another sense, it is also uplifting, for it reminds us more forcefully than ever of a simple truth that is all too often forgotten: bodies are not made, they grow. The genome is not a blueprint for constructing a body. It is a recipe for baking a body. You could say the chicken embryo is marinated for a shorter time in the HoxC8 sauce than the mouse embryo is. Likewise, the development of a certain human behavior takes a certain time and occurs in a certain order, just as the cooking of a perfect souffle requires not just the right ingredients but also the right amount of cooking and the right order of events.

How does this new view of genes alter our understanding of human nature? Take a look at four examples.

LANGUAGE   Human beings differ from chimpanzees in having complex, grammatical language. But language does not spring fully formed from the brain; it must be learned from other language-speaking human beings. This capacity to learn is written into the human brain by genes that open and close a critical window during which learning takes place. One of those genes, FoxP2, has recently been discovered on human chromosome 7 by Anthony Monaco and his colleagues at the Wellcome Trust Centre for Human Genetics in Oxford. Just having the FoxP2 gene, though, is not enough. If a child is not exposed to a lot of spoken language during the critical learning period, he or she will always struggle with speech.

Crime Families

GENES may influence the way people respond to a "crimogenic" ENVIRONMENT. How else to explain why the BIOLOGICAL children of criminal parents are more likely than their ADOPTED children to break the LAW?

LOVE   Some species of rodents, such as the prairie vole, form long pair bonds with their mates, as human beings do. Others, such as the montane vole, have only transitory liaisons, as do chimpanzees. The difference, according to Tom Insel and Larry Young at Emory University in Atlanta, lies in the promoter upstream of the oxytocin- and vasopressin-receptor genes. The insertion of an extra chunk of DNA text, usually about 460 letters long, into the promoter makes the animal more likely to bond with its mate. The extra text does not create love, but perhaps it creates the possibility of falling in love after the right experience.

ANTISOCIAL BEHAVIOR   It has often been suggested that childhood maltreatment can create an antisocial adult. New research by Terrie Moffitt of London's Kings College on a group of 442 New Zealand men who have been followed since birth suggests that this is true only for a genetic minority. Again, the difference lies in a promoter that alters the activity of a gene. Those with high-active monoamine oxidase A genes were virtually immune to the effects of mistreatment. Those with low-active genes were much more antisocial if maltreated, yet—if anything—slightly less antisocial if not maltreated. The low-active, mistreated men were responsible for four times their share of rapes, robberies and assaults. In other words, maltreatment is not enough; you must also have the low-active gene. And it is not enough to have the low-active gene; you must also be maltreated.

HOMOSEXUALITY   Ray Blanchard at the University of Toronto has found that gay men are more likely than either lesbians or heterosexual men to have older brothers (but not older sisters). He has since confirmed this observation in 14 samples from many places. Something about occupying a womb that has held other boys occasionally results in reduced birth weight, a larger placenta and a greater probability of homosexuality. That something, Blanchard suspects, is an immune reaction in the mother, primed by the first male fetus, that grows stronger with each male pregnancy. Perhaps the immune response affects the expression of key genes during brain development in a way that boosts a boy's attraction to his own sex. Such an explanation would not hold true for all gay men, but it might provide important clues into the origins of both homosexuality and heterosexuality.

TO BE SURE, EARLIER SCIENTIFIC DISCOVERIES HAD HINTED AT the importance of this kind of interplay between heredity and environment. The most striking example is Pavlovian conditioning. When Pavlov announced his famous experiment a century ago this year, he had apparently discovered how the brain could be changed to acquire new knowledge of the world—in the case of his dogs, knowledge that a bell foretold the arrival of food. But now we know how the brain changes: by the real-time expression of 17 genes, known as the CREB genes. They must be switched on and off to alter connections among nerve cells in the brain and thus lay down a new long-term memory. These genes are at the mercy of our behavior, not the other way around. Memory is in the genes in the sense that it uses genes, not in the sense that you inherit memories.

In this new view, genes allow the human mind to learn, remember, imitate, imprint language, absorb culture and express instincts. Genes are not puppet masters or blueprints, nor are they just the carriers of heredity. They are active during life; they switch one another on and off; they respond to the environment. They may direct the construction of the body and brain in the womb, but then almost at once, in response to experience, they set about dismantling and rebuilding what they have made. They are both the cause and the consequence of our actions.

Will this new vision of genes enable us to leave the nature-nurture argument behind, or are we doomed to reinvent it in every generation? Unlike what happened in previous eras, science is explaining in great detail precisely how genes and their environment—be it the womb, the classroom or pop culture—interact. So perhaps the pendulum swings of a now demonstrably false dichotomy may cease.

ANCIENT QUARREL

How much of who we are is learned or innate is an argument with a fruitful but fractious pedigree

Nature We may be destined to be bald, mourn our dead, seek mates, fear the dark

Nurture But we can also learn to love tea, hate polkas, invent alphabets and tell lies

IMMANUEL KANT

His philosophy sought a native morality in the mind

JOHN LOCKE

Considered the mind of an infant to be a tabula rasa, or blank slate

FRANCIS GALTON

Math geek saw mental and physical traits as innate

IVAN PAVLOV

Trained dogs to salivate at the sound of the dinner bell

KONRAD LORENZ

Studied patterns of instinctive behavior in animals

SIGMUND FREUD

Felt we are formed by mothers, fathers, sex, jokes and dreams

NOAM CHOMSKY

Argued that human beings are born with a capacity for grammar

FRANZ BOAS

Believed chance and environs are key to cultural variation

It may be in our nature, however, to seek simple, linear, cause-and-effect stories and not think in terms of circular causation, in which effects become their own causes. Perhaps the idea of nature via nurture, like the ideas of quantum mechanics and relativity, is just too counterintuitive for human minds. The urge to see ourselves in terms of nature versus nurture, like our instinctual ability to fear snakes, may be encoded in our genes.

Matt Ridley is an Oxford-trained zoologist and science writer whose latest book is Nature via Nurture *(HarperCollins)*

The Blank Slate

The long-accepted theory that parents can mold their children like clay has distorted choices faced by adults trying to balance their lives, multiplied the anguish of those whose children haven't turned out as hoped, and mangled the science of human behavior

By Steven Pinker

IF YOU READ THE PUNDITS IN NEWSPAPERS AND MAGAZINES, you may have come across some remarkable claims about the malleability of the human psyche. Here are a few from my collection of clippings:

- Little boys quarrel and fight because they are encouraged to do so.
- Children enjoy sweets because their parents use them as rewards for eating vegetables.
- Teenagers get the idea to compete in looks and fashion from spelling bees and academic prizes.
- Men think the goal of sex is an orgasm because of the way they were socialized.

If you find these assertions dubious, your skepticism is certainly justified. In all cultures, little boys quarrel, children like sweets, teens compete for status, and men pursue orgasms, without the slightest need of encouragement or socialization. In each case, the writers made their preposterous claims without a shred of evidence—without even a nod to the possibility that they were saying something common sense might call into question.

Intellectual life today is beset with a great divide. On one side is a militant denial of human nature, a conviction that the mind of a child is a blank slate that is subsequently inscribed by parents and society. For much of the past century, psychology has tried to explain all thought, feeling, and behavior with a few simple mechanisms of learning by association. Social scientists have tried to explain all customs and social arrangements as a product of the surrounding culture. A long list of concepts that

would seem natural to the human way of thinking—emotions, kinship, the sexes—are said to have been "invented" or "socially constructed."

At the same time, there is a growing realization that human nature won't go away. Anyone who has had more than one child, or been in a heterosexual relationship, or noticed that children learn language but house pets don't, has recognized that people are born with certain talents and temperaments. An acknowledgment that we humans are a species with a timeless and universal psychology pervades the writings of great political thinkers, and without it we cannot explain the recurring themes of literature, religion, and myth. Moreover, the modern sciences of mind, brain, genes, and evolution are showing that there is something to the commonsense idea of human nature. Although no scientist denies that learning and culture are crucial to every aspect of human life, these processes don't happen by magic. There must be complex innate mental faculties that enable human beings to create and learn culture.

Sometimes the contradictory attitudes toward human nature divide people into competing camps. The blank slate camp tends to have greater appeal among those in the social sciences and humanities than it does among biological scientists. And until recently, it was more popular on the political left than it was on the right.

But sometimes both attitudes coexist uneasily inside the mind of a single person. Many academics, for example, publicly deny the existence of intelligence. But privately, academics are *obsessed* with intelligence, discussing it endlessly in admissions, in hiring, and especially in their gossip about one another. And despite their protestations that it is a reactionary concept, they quickly invoke it to oppose executing a murderer with an IQ of 64 or to support laws requiring the removal of lead paint because it may lower a child's IQ by five points. Similarly, those who argue that gender differences are a reversible social construction do not treat them that way in their advice to their daughters, in their dealings with the opposite sex, or in their unguarded gossip, humor, and reflections on their lives.

No good can come from this hypocrisy. The dogma that human nature does not exist, in the face of growing evidence from science and common sense that it does, has led to contempt among many scholars in the humanities for the concepts of evidence and truth. Worse, the doctrine of the blank slate often distorts science itself by making an extreme position—that culture alone determines behavior—seem moderate, and by making the moderate position—that behavior comes from an interaction of biology and culture—seem extreme.

Although how parents treat their children can make a lot of difference in how happy they are, placing a stimulating mobile over a child's crib and playing Mozart CDs will not shape a child's intelligence.

For example, many policies on parenting come from research that finds a correlation between the behavior of parents and of their children. Loving parents have confident children, authoritative parents (neither too permissive nor too punitive) have well-behaved children, parents who talk to their children have children with better language skills, and so on. Thus everyone concludes that parents should be loving, authoritative, and talkative, and if children don't turn out well, it must be the parents' fault.

Those conclusions depend on the belief that children are blank slates. It ignores the fact that parents provide their children with genes, not just an environment. The correlations may be telling us only that the same genes that make adults loving, authoritative, and talkative make their children self-confident, well-behaved, and articulate. Until the studies are redone with adopted children (who get only their environment from their parents), the data are compatible with the possibility that genes make all the difference, that parenting makes all the difference, or anything in between. Yet the extreme position—that parents are everything—is the only one researchers entertain.

The denial of human nature has not just corrupted the world of intellectuals but has harmed ordinary people. The theory that parents can mold their children like clay has inflicted child-rearing regimes on parents that are unnatural and sometimes cruel. It has distorted the choices faced by mothers as they try to balance their lives, and it has multiplied the anguish of parents whose children haven't turned out as hoped. The belief that

human tastes are reversible cultural preferences has led social planners to write off people's enjoyment of ornament, natural light, and human scale and forced millions of people to live in drab cement boxes. And the conviction that humanity could be reshaped by massive social engineering projects has led to some of the greatest atrocities in history.

THE PHRASE "BLANK SLATE" IS A LOOSE TRANSLATION OF THE medieval Latin term tabula rasa—scraped tablet. It is often attributed to the 17th-century English philosopher John Locke, who wrote that the mind is "white paper void of all characters." But it became the official doctrine among thinking people only in the first half of the 20th century, as part of a reaction to the widespread belief in the intellectual or moral inferiority of women, Jews, nonwhite races, and non-Western cultures.

Part of the reaction was a moral repulsion from discrimination, lynchings, forced sterilizations, segregation, and the Holocaust. And part of it came from empirical observations. Waves of immigrants from southern and eastern Europe filled the cities of America and climbed the social ladder. African Americans took advantage of "Negro colleges" and migrated northward, beginning the Harlem Renaissance. The graduates of women's colleges launched the first wave of feminism. To say that women and minority groups were inferior contradicted what people could see with their own eyes.

Academics were swept along by the changing attitudes, but they also helped direct the tide. The prevailing theories of mind were refashioned to make racism and sexism as untenable as possible. The blank slate became sacred scripture. According to the doctrine, any differences we see among races, ethnic groups, sexes, and individuals come not from differences in their innate constitution but from differences in their experiences. Change the experiences—by reforming parenting, education, the media, and social rewards—and you can change the person. Also, if there is no such thing as human nature, society will not be saddled with such nasty traits as aggression, selfishness, and prejudice. In a reformed environment, people can be prevented from learning these habits.

In psychology, behaviorists like John B. Watson and B. F. Skinner simply banned notions of talent and temperament, together with all the other contents of the mind, such as beliefs, desires, and feelings. This set the stage for Watson's famous boast: "Give me a dozen healthy infants, well-formed, and my own specified world to bring them up in, and I'll guarantee to take any one at random and train him to become any type of specialist I might select—doctor, lawyer, artist, merchant-chief, and yes, even beggar-man and thief, regardless of his talents, penchants, tendencies, abilities, vocations, and race of his ancestors."

Watson also wrote an influential child-rearing manual recommending that parents give their children minimum attention and love. If you comfort a crying baby, he wrote, you will reward the baby for crying and thereby increase the frequency of crying behavior.

In anthropology, Franz Boas wrote that differences among human races and ethnic groups come not from their physical constitution but from their *culture*. Though Boas himself did not claim that people were blank slates—he only argued that all ethnic groups are endowed with the same mental abilities—his students, who came to dominate American social science, went further. They insisted not just that *differences* among ethnic groups must be explained in terms of culture (which is reasonable), but that *every aspect* of human existence must be explained in terms of culture (which is not). "Heredity cannot be allowed to have acted any part in history," wrote Alfred Kroeber. "With the exception of the instinctoid reactions in infants to sudden withdrawals of support and to sudden loud noises, the human being is entirely instinctless," wrote Ashley Montagu.

IN THE SECOND HALF OF THE 20TH CENTURY, THE IDEALS OF the social scientists of the first half enjoyed a well-deserved victory. Eugenics, social Darwinism, overt expressions of racism and sexism, and official discrimination against women and minorities were on the wane, or had been eliminated, from the political and intellectual mainstream in Western democracies.

At the same time, the doctrine of the blank slate, which had been blurred with ideals of equality and progress, began to show cracks. As new disciplines such as cognitive science, neuroscience, evolutionary psychology, and behavioral genetics flourished, it became clearer that thinking is a biological process, that the brain is not exempt from the laws of evolution, that the sexes differ above the neck as well as below it, and that people are not psychological clones. Here are some examples of the discoveries.

Hundreds of traits, from romantic love to humorous insults, can be found in every society ever documented.

Natural selection tends to homogenize a species into a standard design by concentrating the effective genes and winnowing out the ineffective ones. This suggests that the human mind evolved with a universal complex design. Beginning in the 1950s, linguist Noam Chomsky of the Massachusetts Institute of Technology argued that a language should be analyzed not in terms of the list of sentences people utter but in terms of the mental computations that enable them to handle an unlimited number of new sentences in the language. These computations have been found to conform to a universal grammar. And if this universal grammar is embodied in the circuitry that guides babies when they listen to speech, it could explain how children learn language so easily.

Similarly, some anthropologists have returned to an ethnographic record that used to trumpet differences among cultures and have found an astonishingly detailed set of aptitudes and tastes that all cultures have in common. This shared way of thinking, feeling, and living makes all of humanity look like a single tribe, which the anthropologist Donald Brown of the University of California at Santa Barbara has called the universal people. Hundreds of traits, from romantic love to humorous insults, from poetry to food taboos, from exchange of goods to

mourning the dead, can be found in every society ever documented.

One example of a stubborn universal is the tangle of emotions surrounding the act of love. In all societies, sex is at least somewhat "dirty." It is conducted in private, pondered obsessively, regulated by custom and taboo, the subject of gossip and teasing, and a trigger for jealous rage. Yet sex is the most concentrated source of physical pleasure granted by the nervous system. Why is it so fraught with conflict? For a brief period in the 1960s and 1970s, people dreamed of an erotopia in which men and women could engage in sex without hang-ups and inhibitions. "If you can't be with the one you love, love the one you're with," sang Stephen Stills. "If you love somebody, set them free," sang Sting.

But Sting also sang, "Every move you make, I'll be watching you." Even in a time when, seemingly, anything goes, most people do not partake in sex as casually as they partake in food or conversation. The reasons are as deep as anything in biology. One of the hazards of sex is a baby, and a baby is not just any seven-pound object but, from an evolutionary point of view, our reason for being. Every time a woman has sex with a man, she is taking a chance at sentencing herself to years of motherhood, and she is forgoing the opportunity to use her finite reproductive output with some other man. The man, for his part, may be either implicitly committing his sweat and toil to the incipient child or deceiving his partner about such intentions.

On rational grounds, the volatility of sex is a puzzle, because in an era with reliable contraception, these archaic entanglements should have no claim on our feelings. We should be loving the one we're with, and sex should inspire no more gossip, music, fiction, raunchy humor, or strong emotions than eating or talking does. The fact that people are tormented by the Darwinian economics of babies they are no longer having is testimony to the long reach of human nature.

ALTHOUGH THE MINDS OF NORMAL HUMAN BEINGS WORK IN pretty much the same way, they are not, of course, identical. Natural selection reduces genetic variability but never eliminates it. As a result, nearly every one of us is genetically unique. And these differences in genes make a difference in mind and behavior, at least quantitatively. The most dramatic demonstrations come from studies of the rare people who *are* genetically identical, identical twins.

Identical twins think and feel in such similar ways that they sometimes suspect they are linked by telepathy. They are similar in verbal and mathematical intelligence, in their degree of life satisfaction, and in personality traits such as introversion, agreeableness, neuroticism, conscientiousness, and openness to experience. They have similar attitudes toward controversial issues such as the death penalty, religion, and modern music. They resemble each other not just in paper-and-pencil tests but in consequential behavior such as gambling, divorcing, committing crimes, getting into accidents, and watching television. And they boast dozens of shared idiosyncrasies such as giggling incessantly, giving interminable answers to simple questions, dipping buttered toast in coffee, and, in the case of Abigail van Buren and the late Ann Landers, writing indistinguishable syndicated advice columns. The crags and valleys of their electro-encephalograms (brain waves) are as alike as those of a single person recorded on two occasions, and the wrinkles of their brains and the distribution of gray matter across cortical areas are similar as well.

Identical twins (who share all their genes) are far more similar than fraternal twins (who share just half their genes). This is as true when the twins are separated at birth and raised apart as when they are raised in the same home by the same parents. Moreover, biological siblings, who also share half their genes, are far more similar than adoptive siblings, who share no more genes than strangers. Indeed, adoptive siblings are barely similar at all. These conclusions come from massive studies employing the best instruments known to psychology. Alternative explanations that try to push the effects of the genes to zero have by now been tested and rejected.

People sometimes fear that if the genes affect the mind at all they must determine it in every detail. That is wrong, for two reasons. The first is that most effects of genes are probabilistic. If one identical twin has a trait, there is often no more than an even chance that the other twin will have it, despite having a complete genome in common (and in the case of twins raised together, most of their environment in common as well).

The second reason is that the genes' effects can vary with the environment. Although Woody Allen's fame may depend on genes that enhance a sense of humor, he once pointed out that "we live in a society that puts a big value on jokes. If I had been an Apache Indian, those guys didn't need comedians, so I'd be out of work."

Studies of the brain also show that the mind is not a blank slate. The brain, of course, has a pervasive ability to change the strengths of its connections as the result of learning and experience—if it didn't, we would all be permanent amnesiacs. But that does not mean that the structure of the brain is mostly a product of experience. The study of the brains of twins has shown that much of the variation in the amount of gray matter in the prefrontal lobes is genetically caused. And these variations are not just random differences in anatomy like fingerprints; they correlate significantly with differences in intelligence.

People born with variations in the typical brain plan can vary in the way their minds work. A study of Einstein's brain showed that he had large, unusually shaped inferior parietal lobules, which participate in spatial reasoning and intuitions about numbers. Gay men are likely to have a relatively small nucleus in the anterior hypothalamus, a nucleus known to have a role in sex differences. Convicted murderers and other violent, antisocial people are likely to have a relatively small and inactive prefrontal cortex, the part of the brain that governs decision making and inhibits impulses. These gross features of the brain are almost certainly not sculpted by information coming in from the senses. That, in turn, implies that differences in intelligence, scientific genius, sexual orientation, and impulsive violence are not entirely learned.

THE DOCTRINE OF THE BLANK SLATE HAD BEEN THOUGHT TO undergird the ideals of equal rights and social improvement, so it is no surprise that the discoveries undermining it have often been met with fear and loathing. Scientists challenging the doctrine have been libeled, picketed, shouted down, and subjected to searing invective.

This is not the first time in history that people have tried to ground moral principles in dubious factual assumptions. People used to ground moral values in the doctrine that Earth lay at the center of the universe, and that God created mankind in his own image in a day. In both cases, informed people eventually reconciled their moral values with the facts, not just because they had to give a nod to reality, but also because the supposed connections between the facts and morals—such as the belief that the arrangement of rock and gas in space has something to do with right and wrong—were spurious to begin with.

We are now living, I think, through a similar transition. The blank slate has been widely embraced as a rationale for morality, but it is under assault from science. Yet just as the supposed foundations of morality shifted in the centuries following Galileo and Darwin, our own moral sensibilities will come to terms with the scientific findings, not just because facts are facts but because the moral credentials of the blank slate are just as spurious. Once you think through the issues, the two greatest fears of an innate human endowment can be defused.

One is the fear of inequality. Blank is blank, so if we are all blank slates, the reasoning goes, we must all be equal. But if the slate of a newborn is not blank, different babies could have different things inscribed on their slates. Individuals, sexes, classes, and races might differ innately in their talents and inclinations. The fear is that if people do turn out to be different, it would open the door to discrimination, oppression, or eugenics.

But none of this follows. For one thing, in many cases the empirical basis of the fear may be misplaced. A universal human nature does not imply that *differences* among groups are innate. Confucius could have been right when he wrote, "Men's natures are alike; it is their habits that carry them far apart."

Regardless of IQ or physical strength, all human beings can be assumed to have certain traits in common.

More important, the case against bigotry is not a factual claim that people are biologically indistinguishable. It is a moral stance that condemns judging an *individual* according to the average traits of certain *groups* to which the individual belongs. Enlightened societies strive to ignore race, sex, and ethnicity in hiring, admissions, and criminal justice because the alternative is morally repugnant. Discriminating against people on the basis of race, sex, or ethnicity would be unfair, penalizing them for traits over which they have no control. It would perpetuate the injustices of the past and could rend society into hostile factions. None of these reasons depends on whether groups of people are or are not genetically indistinguishable.

Far from being conducive to discrimination, a conception of human nature is the reason we oppose it. Regardless of IQ or physical strength or any other trait that might vary among people, all human beings can be assumed to have certain traits in common. No one likes being enslaved. No one likes being humiliated. No one likes being treated unfairly. The revulsion we feel toward discrimination and slavery comes from a conviction that however much people vary on some traits, they do not vary on these.

A second fear of human nature comes from a reluctance to give up the age-old dream of the perfectibility of man. If we are forever saddled with fatal flaws and deadly sins, according to this fear, social reform would be a waste of time. Why try to make the world a better place if people are rotten to the core and will just foul it up no matter what you do?

Parents often discover that their children are immune to their rewards, punishments, and nagging. Over the long run, a child's personality and intellect are largely determined by genes, peer groups, and chance.

But this, too, does not follow. If the mind is a complex system with many faculties, an antisocial desire is just one component among others. Some faculties may endow us with greed or lust or malice, but others may endow us with sympathy, foresight, self-respect, a desire for respect from others, and an ability to learn from experience and history. Social progress can come from pitting some of these faculties against others.

For example, suppose we are endowed with a conscience that treats certain other beings as targets of sympathy and inhibits us from harming or exploiting them. The philosopher Peter Singer of Princeton University has shown that moral improvement has proceeded for millennia because people have expanded the mental dotted line that embraces the entities considered worthy of sympathy. The circle has been poked outward from the family and village to the clan, the tribe, the nation, the race, and most recently to all of humanity. This sweeping change in sensibilities did not require a blank slate. It could have arisen from a moral gadget with a single knob or slider that adjusts the size of the circle embracing the entities whose interests we treat as comparable to our own.

SOME PEOPLE WORRY THAT THESE ARGUMENTS ARE TOO FANCY for the dangerous world we live in. Since data in the social sciences are never perfect, shouldn't we err on the side of caution and stick with the null hypothesis that people are blank slates? Some people think that even if we were certain that people differed genetically, or harbored ignoble tendencies, we might still want to promulgate the fiction that they didn't.

This argument is based on the fallacy that the blank slate has nothing but good moral implications and a theory that admits a human nature has nothing but bad ones. In fact, the dangers go both ways. Take the most horrifying example of all, the abuse of biology by the Nazis, with its pseudoscientific nonsense about superior and inferior races. Historians agree that bitter memories of the Holocaust were the main reason that human nature became taboo in intellectual life after the Second World War.

But historians have also documented that Nazism was not the only ideologically inspired holocaust of the 20th century. Many atrocities were committed by Marxist regimes in the name of egalitarianism, targeting people whose success was taken as evidence of their avarice. The kulaks ("bourgeois peasants") were exterminated by Lenin and Stalin in the Soviet Union. Teachers, former landlords, and "rich peasants" were humiliated, tortured, and murdered during China's Cultural Revolution. City dwellers and literate professionals were worked to death or executed during the reign of the Khmer Rouge in Cambodia.

And here is a remarkable fact: Although both Nazi and Marxist ideologies led to industrial-scale killing, *their biological and psychological theories were opposites*. Marxists had no use for the concept of race, were averse to the notion of genetic inheritance, and were hostile to the very idea of a human nature rooted in biology. Marx did not explicitly embrace the blank slate, but he was adamant that human nature has no enduring properties: "All history is nothing but a continuous transformation of human nature," he wrote. Many of his followers did embrace it. "It is on a blank page that the most beautiful poems are written," said Mao. "Only the newborn baby is spotless," ran a Khmer Rouge slogan. This philosophy led to persecution of the successful and of those who produced more crops on their private family plots than on communal farms. And it made these regimes not just dictatorships but totalitarian dictatorships, which tried to control every aspect of life, from art and education to child rearing and sex. After all, if the mind is structureless at birth and shaped by its experience, a society that wants the right kind of minds must control the experience.

None of this is meant to impugn the blank slate as an evil doctrine, any more than a belief in human nature is an evil doctrine. Both are separated by many steps from the evil acts committed under their banners, and they must be evaluated on factual grounds. But the fact that tyranny and genocide can come from an anti-innatist belief system as readily as from an innatist one does upend the common misconception that biological approaches to behavior are uniquely sinister. And the reminder that human nature is the source of our interests and needs as well as our flaws encourages us to examine claims about the mind objectively, without putting a moral thumb on either side of the scale.

From the book The Blank Slate *by Steven Pinker. Copyright © Steven Pinker, 2002. Printed by arrangement with Viking Penguin, a member of Penguin Putman Inc. Published in September 2002.*

Neuroscience: Breaking Down Scientific Barriers to the Study of Brain and Mind

Eric R. Kandel and Larry R. Squire

During the latter part of the 20th century, the study of the brain moved from a peripheral position within both the biological and psychological sciences to become an interdisciplinary field called neuroscience that now occupies a central position within each discipline. This realignment occurred because the biological study of the brain became incorporated into a common framework with cell and molecular biology on the one side and with psychology on the other. Within this new framework, the scope of neuroscience ranges from genes to cognition, from molecules to mind.

What led to the gradual incorporation of neuroscience into the central core of biology and to its alignment with psychology? From the perspective of biology at the beginning of the 20th century, the task of neuroscience—to understand how the brain develops and then functions to perceive, think, move, and remember—seemed impossibly difficult. In addition, an intellectual barrier separated neuroscience from biology, because the language of neuroscience was based more on neuroanatomy and electrophysiology than on the universal biological language of biochemistry. During the last 2 decades this barrier has been largely removed. A molecular neuroscience became established by focusing on simple systems where anatomy and physiology were tractable. As a result, neuroscience helped delineate a general plan for neural cell function in which the cells of the nervous system are understood to be governed by variations on universal biological themes.

From the perspective of psychology, a neural approach to mental processes seemed too reductionistic to do justice to the complexity of cognition. Substantial progress was required to demonstrate that some of these reductionist goals were achievable within a psychologically meaningful framework. The work of Vernon Mountcastle, David Hubel, Torsten Wiesel, and Brenda Milner in the 1950s and 1960s, and the advent of brain imaging in the 1980s, showed what could be achieved for sensory processing, perception, and memory. As a result of these advances, the view gradually developed that only by exploring the brain could psychologists fully satisfy their interest in the cognitive processes that intervene between stimulus and response.

Here, we consider several developments that have been particularly important for the maturation of neuroscience and for the restructuring of its relationship to biology and psychology.

The Emergence of a Cellular and Molecular Neuroscience

The modern cellular science of the nervous system was founded on two important advances: the neuron doctrine and the ionic hypothesis. The neuron doctrine was established by the brilliant Spanish anatomist Santiago Ramón y Cajal[1], who showed that the brain is composed of discrete cells, called neurons, and that these likely serve as elementary signaling units. Cajal also advanced the principle of connection specificity, the central tenet of which is that neurons form highly specific connections with one another and that these connections are invariant and defining for each species. Finally, Cajal developed the principle of dynamic polarization, according to which information flows in only one direction within a neuron, usually from the dendrites (the neuron's input component) down the axon shaft to the axon terminals (the output component). Although exceptions to this principle have emerged, it has proved extremely influential, because it tied structure to function and provided guidelines for constructing circuits from the images provided in histological sections of the brain.

Cajal and his contemporary Charles Sherrington[2] further proposed that neurons contact one another only at specialized points called synapses, the sites where one neuron's processes contact and communicate with another neuron. We now know that at most synapses, there is a gap of 20 nm—the synaptic cleft—between the pre- and postsynaptic cell. In the 1930s, Otto Loewi, Henry Dale, and Wilhelm Feldberg established (at peripheral neuromuscular and autonomic synapses) that the signal that bridges the synaptic cleft is usually a small chemical, or neurotransmitter, which is released from the presynaptic terminal, diffuses across the gap, and binds to receptors on the postsynaptic target cell. Depending on the specific receptor, the postsynaptic cell can either be excited or inhibited. It took some time to establish that chemical transmission also occurs in the central nervous system, but by the 1950s the idea had become widely accepted.

Even early in the 20th century, it was already understood that nerve cells have an electrical potential, the resting membrane potential, across their membrane, and that signaling along the axon is conveyed by a propagated electrical signal, the action potential, which was thought to nullify the resting potential. In 1937 Alan Hodgkin discovered that the action potential gives rise to local current flow on its advancing edge and that this current depolarizes the adjacent region of the axonal membrane sufficiently to trigger a traveling wave of depolarization. In 1939 Hodgkin and Andrew Huxley made the surprising discovery that the action potential more than nullifies the resting potential—it reverses it. Then, in the late 1940s, Hodgkin, Huxley, and Bernard Katz explained the resting potential and the action potential in terms of the movement of specific ions—potassium (K^+), sodium (Na^+), and chloride (Cl^-)—through pores (ion channels) in the axonal membrane. This ionic hypothesis unified a large body of descriptive data and offered the first realistic promise that the nervous system could be understood in terms of physicochemical principles common to all of cell biology[3].

The next breakthrough came when Katz, Paul Fatt, and John Eccles showed that ion channels are also fundamental to signal transmission across the synapse. However, rather than being gated by voltage like the Na^+ and K^+ channels critical for action potentials, excitatory synaptic ion channels are gated chemically by ligands such as the transmitter acetylcholine. During the 1960s and 1970s, neuroscientists identified many amino acids, peptides, and other small molecules as chemical transmitters, including acetylcholine, glutamate, GABA, glycine, serotonin, dopamine, and norepinephrine. On the order of 100 chemical transmitters have been discovered to date. In the 1970s, some synapses were found to release a peptide cotransmitter that can modify the action of the classic, small-molecule transmitters. The discovery of chemical neurotransmission was followed by the remarkable discovery that transmission between neurons is sometimes electrical[4]. Electrical synapses have smaller synaptic clefts, which are bridged by gap junctions and allow current to flow between neurons.

In the late 1960s information began to become available about the biophysical and biochemical structure of ionic pores and the biophysical basis for their selectivity and gating—how they open and close. For example, transmitter binding sites and their ion channels were found to be embodied within different domains of multimeric proteins. Ion channel selectivity was found to depend on physical-chemical interaction between the channel and the ion, and channel gating was found to result from conformational changes within the channel[5].

The study of ion channels changed radically with the development of the patch-clamp method in 1976 by Erwin Neher and Bert Sakmann[6], which enabled measurement of the current flowing through a single ion channel. This powerful advance set the stage for the analysis of channels at the molecular level and for the analysis of functional and conformational change in a single membrane protein. When applied to non-neuronal cells, the method also revealed that all cells—even bacteria—express remarkably similar ion channels. Thus, neuronal signaling proved to be a special case of a signaling capability inherent in most cells.

The development of patch clamping coincided with the advent of molecular cloning, and these two methods brought neuroscientists new ideas based on the first reports of the amino acid sequences of ligand- and voltage-gated channels. One of the key insights to emerge from molecular cloning was that amino acid sequences contain clues about how receptor proteins and voltage-gated ion channel proteins are arranged across the cell membrane. The sequence data also often pointed to unexpected structural relationships (homologies) among proteins. These insights, in turn, revealed similarities between molecules found in quite different neuronal and non-neuronal contexts, suggesting that they may serve similar biological functions.

By the early 1980s, it became clear that synaptic actions were not always mediated directly by ion channels. Besides ionotropic receptors, in which ligand binding directly gates an ion channel, a second class of receptors, the metabotropic receptors, was discovered. Here the binding of the ligand initiates intracellular metabolic events and leads only indirectly, by way of "second messengers," to the gating of ion channels[7].

The cloning of metabotropic receptors revealed that many of them have seven membrane-spanning regions and are homologous to bacterial rhodopsin as well as to the photoreceptor pigment of organisms ranging from fruit flies to humans. Further, the recent cloning of receptors for the sense of smell[8] revealed that at least 1000 metabotropic receptors are expressed in the mammalian olfactory epithelium and that similar receptors are present in flies and worms. Thus, it was instantly understood that the class of receptors used for phototransduction, the initial step in visual perception, is also used for smell and aspects of taste, and that these receptors share key features with many other brain receptors that work through second-messenger signaling. These discoveries demonstrated the evolutionary conservation of receptors and emphasized the wisdom of studying a wide variety of experimental systems—vertebrates, invertebrates, even single-celled organisms—to identify broad biological principles.

The seven transmembrane-spanning receptors activate ion channels indirectly through coupling proteins (G proteins). Some G proteins have been found to activate ion channels directly. However, the majority of G proteins activate membrane enzymes that alter the level of second messengers, such as cAMP, cGMP, or inositol triphosphate, which initiate complex intracellular events leading to the activation of protein kinases and phosphatases and then to the modulation of channel perm-eability, receptor sensitivity, and transmitter release. Neuroscientists now appreciate that many of these synaptic actions are mediated intracellularly by protein phosphorylation or dephosphorylation[9]. Nerve cells use such covalent modifications to control protein activity reversibly and thereby to regulate function. Phosphorylation is also critical in other cells for the action of hormones and growth factors, and for many other processes.

Directly controlled synaptic actions are fast, lasting milliseconds, but second-messenger actions last seconds to minutes. An even slower synaptic action, lasting days or more, has been found to be important for long-term memory. In this case, protein kinases activated by second messengers translocate to the nucleus, where they phosphorylate transcription factors that alter gene expression, initiate growth of neuronal processes, and increase synaptic strength.

Ionotropic and metabotropic receptors have helped to explain the postsynaptic side of synaptic transmission. In the 1950s and 1960s, Katz and his colleagues turned to the presynaptic terminals and discovered that chemical transmitters, such as acetylcholine, are released not as single molecules but as packets of about 5000 molecules called quanta[10]. Each quantum is packaged in a synaptic vesicle and released by exocytosis at sites called active zones. The key signal that triggers this sequence is the influx of Ca^{2+} with the action potential.

In recent years, many proteins involved in transmitter release have been identified[11]. Their functions range from targeting vesicles to active zones, tethering vesicles to the cell membrane, and fusing vesicles with the cell membrane so that their contents can be released by exocytosis. These molecular studies reflect another example of evolutionary conservation: The molecules used for vesicle fusion and exocytosis at nerve terminals are variants of those used for vesicle fusion and exocytosis in all cells.

A Mechanistic View of Brain Development

The discoveries of molecular neuroscience have dramatically improved the understanding of how the brain develops its complexity. The modern molecular era of developmental neuroscience began when Rita Levi-Montalcini and Stanley Cohen isolated nerve growth factor (NGF), the first peptide growth factor to be identified in the nervous system[12]. They showed that injection of antibodies to NGF into newborn mice caused the death of neurons in sympathetic ganglia and also reduced the number of sensory ganglion cells. Thus, the survival of both sympathetic and sensory neurons depends on NGF. Indeed, many neurons depend for their survival on NGF or related molecules, which typically provide feedback signals to the neurons from their targets. Such signals are important for programmed cell death—apoptosis—a developmental strategy which has now proved to be of general importance, whereby many more cells are generated than eventually survive to become functional units with precise connectivity. In a major advance, genetic study of worms has revealed the *ced* genes and with them a universal cascade critical for apoptosis in which proteases—the caspases—are the final agents for cell death[13].

Cajal pointed out the extraordinary precision of neuronal connections. The first compelling insights into how neurons develop their precise connectivity came from Roger Sperry's studies of the visual system of frogs and salamanders beginning in the 1940s, which suggested that axon outgrowth is guided by molecular cues. Sperry's key finding was that when the nerves from the eye are cut, axons find their way back to their original targets. These seminal studies led Sperry in 1963 to formulate the chemoaffinity hypothesis[14], the idea that neurons form connections with their targets based on distinctive and matching molecular identities that they acquire early in development.

Stimulated by these early contributions, molecular biology has radically transformed the study of nervous system development from a descriptive to a mechanistic field. Three genetic systems, the worm *Caenorhabditis elegans*, the fruit fly *Drosophila melanogaster*, and the mouse, have been invaluable; some of the molecules for key developmental steps in the mouse were first characterized by genetic screens in worms and flies. In some cases, identical molecules were found to play an equivalent role throughout phylogeny. The result of this work is that neuroscientists have achieved in broad outline an understanding of the molecular basis of nervous system development[15]. A range of key molecules has been identified, including specific inducers, morphogens, and guidance molecules important for differentiation, process outgrowth, pathfinding, and synapse formation. For example, in the spinal cord, neurons achieve their identities and characteristic positions largely through two classes of inductive signaling molecules of the Hedgehog and bone morphogenic protein families. These two groups of molecules control neuronal differentiation in the ventral and dorsal halves of the spinal cord, respectively, and maintain this division of labor through most of the rostrocaudal length of the nervous system.

The process of neuronal pathfinding is mediated by both short-range and long-range cues. An axon's growth cone can encounter cell surface cues that either attract or repel it. For example, ephrins are membrane-bound, are distributed in graded fashion in many regions of the nervous system, and can repel growing axons. Other cues, such as the netrins and the semaphorins, are secreted in diffusible form and act as long-range chemoattractants or chemorepellents. Growth cones can also react to the same cues differently at different developmental phases, for example, when crossing the midline or when switching from pathfinding to synapse formation. Finally, a large number of molecules are involved in synapse formation itself. Some, such as neuregulin, erbB kinases, agrin, and MuSK, organize the assembly of the postsynaptic machinery, whereas others, such as the laminins, help to organize the presynaptic differentiation of the active zone.

These molecular signals direct differentiation, migration, process outgrowth, and synapse formation in the absence of neural activity. Neural activity is needed, however, to refine the connections further so as to forge the adult pattern of connectivity [16]. The neural activity may be generated spontaneously, especially early in development, but later depends importantly on sensory input. In this way, intrinsic activity or sensory and motor experience can help specify a precise set of functional connections.

The Impact of Neuroscience on Neurology and Psychiatry

Molecular neuroscience has also reaped substantial benefits for clinical medicine. To begin with, recent advances in the study of neural development have identified stem cells, both embryonic and adult, which offer promise in cell replacement therapy in Parkinson's disease, demyelinating diseases, and other conditions. Similarly, new insights into axon guidance molecules offer hope for nerve regeneration after spinal cord injury. Finally, because most neurological diseases are associated with cell death, the discovery in worms of a universal genetic program for cell death opens up approaches for cell rescue based on, for example, inhibition of the caspase proteases.

Next, consider the impact of molecular genetics. Huntington's disease is an autosomal dominant disease marked by progressive motor and cognitive impairment that ordinarily manifests itself in middle age. The major pathology is cell death in the basal ganglia. In 1993, the Huntington's Disease Collaborative Research Group isolated the gene responsible for the disease [17]. It is marked by an extended series of trinucleotide CAG (cytosine, adenine, guanine) repeats, thereby placing Huntington's disease in a new class of neurological disorders—the trinucleotide repeat diseases—that now constitute the largest group of dominantly transmitted neurological diseases.

The molecular genetic analysis of more complex degenerative disorders has proceeded more slowly. Still, three genes associated with familial Alzheimer's disease—those that code for the amyloid precursor protein, presenilin 1, and presenilin 2—have been identified. Molecular genetic studies have also identified the first genes that modulate the severity and risk of a degenerative disease [18]. One allele (APO E4) is a significant risk factor for late-onset Alzheimer's disease. Conversely, the APO E2 allele may actually be protective. A second risk factor is α_2-macroglobulin. All the Alzheimer's-related genes so far identified participate in either generating or scavenging a protein (the amyloid peptide), which is toxic at elevated levels. Studies directed at this peptide may lead to ways to prevent the disease or halt its progression. Similarly, the discovery of ß-secretase and perhaps γ-secretase, the enzymes involved in the processing of ß amyloid, represent dramatic advances that may also lead to new treatments.

With psychiatric disorders, progress has been slower for two reasons. First, diseases such as schizophrenia, depression, obsessive compulsive disorders, anxiety states, and drug abuse tend to be complex, polygenic disorders that are significantly modulated by environmental factors. Second, in contrast to neurological disorders, little is known about the anatomical substrates of most psychiatric diseases. Given the difficulty of penetrating the deep biology of mental illness, it is nevertheless remarkable how much progress has been made during the past 3 decades [19]. Arvid Carlsson and Julius Axelrod carried out pioneering studies of biogenic amines, which laid the foundation for psychopharmacology, and Seymour Kety pioneered the genetic study of mental illness [20]. Currently, new approaches to many conditions, such as sleep disorders, eating disorders, and drug abuse, are emerging as the result of insights into the cellular and molecular machinery that regulates specific behaviors [21]. Moreover, improvements in diagnosis, the better delineation of genetic contributions to psychiatric illness (based on twin and adoption studies as well as studies of affected families), and the discovery of specific medications for treating schizophrenia, depression, and anxiety states have transformed psychiatry into a therapeutically effective medical specialty that is now closely aligned with neuroscience.

A New Alignment of Neuroscience and Psychological Science

The brain's computational power is conferred by interactions among billions of nerve cells, which are assembled into networks or circuits that carry out specific operations in support of behavior and cognition. Whereas the molecular machinery and electrical signaling properties of neurons are widely conserved across animal species, what distinguishes one species from another, with respect to their cognitive abilities, is the number of neurons and the details of their connectivity.

Beginning in the 19th century there was great interest in how these cognitive abilities might be localized in the brain. One view, first championed by Franz Joseph Gall, was that the brain is composed of specialized parts and that aspects of perception, emotion, and language can be localized to anatomically distinct neural systems. Another view, championed by Jean-Pierre-Marie Flourens, was that cognitive functions are global properties arising from the integrated activity of the entire brain. In a sense, the history of neuroscience can be seen as a gradual ascendancy of the localizationist view.

To a large extent, the emergence of the localizationist view was built on a century-old legacy of psychological science. When psychology emerged as an experimental science in the late 19th century, its founders, Gustav Fechner and Wilhelm Wundt, focused on psychophysics—the quantitative relationship between physical stimuli and subjective sensation. The success of this endeavor encouraged psychologists to study more complex behavior, which led to a rigorous, laboratory-based tradition termed behaviorism.

Led by John Watson and later by B. F. Skinner, behaviorists argued that psychology should be concerned only with observable stimuli and responses, not with unobservable processes that intervene between stimulus and response. This tradition yielded lawful principles of behavior and learning, but it proved limiting. In the 1960s, behaviorism gave way to a broader approach concerned with cognitive processes and internal representations. This new emphasis focused on precisely those aspects of mental life—from perception to action—that had long been of interest to neurologists and other students of the nervous system.

The first cellular studies of brain systems in the 1950s illustrated dramatically how much neuroscience derived from psychology and conversely how much psychology could, in turn, inform neuroscience. In using a cellular approach, neuroscientists relied on the rigorous experimental methods of psychophysics and behaviorism to explore how a sensory stimulus resulted in a neuronal response. In so doing, they found cellular support for localization of function: Different brain regions had different cellular response properties. Thus, it became possible in the study of behavior and cognition to move beyond description to an exploration of the mechanisms underlying the internal representation of the external world.

In the late 1950s and 1960s Mountcastle, Hubel, and Wiesel began using cellular approaches to analyze sensory processing in the cerebral cortex of cats and monkeys[22]. Their work provided the most fundamental advance in understanding the organization of the brain since the work of Cajal at the turn of the century. The cellular physiological techniques revealed that the brain both filters and transforms sensory information on its way to and within the cortex, and that these transformations are critical for perception. Sensory systems analyze, decompose, and then restructure raw sensory information according to built-in connections and rules.

Mountcastle found that single nerve cells in the primary somatic sensory cortex respond to specific kinds of touch: Some respond to superficial touch and others to deep pressure, but cells almost never respond to both. The different cell types are segregated in vertical columns, which comprise thousands of neurons and extend about 2 mm from the cortical surface to the white matter below it. Mountcastle proposed that each column serves as an integrating unit, or logical module, and that these columns are the basic mode of cortical organization.

Single-cell recording was pioneered by Edgar Adrian and applied to the visual system of invertebrates by H. Keffer Hartline and to the visual system of mammals by Stephen Kuffler, the mentor of Hubel and Wiesel. In recordings from the retina, Kuffler discovered that, rather than signaling absolute levels of light, neurons signal contrast between spots of light and dark. In the visual cortex, Hubel and Wiesel found that most cells no longer respond to spots of light. For example, in area V1 at the occipital pole of the cortex, neurons respond to specific visual features such as lines or bars in a particular orientation. Moreover, cells with similar orientation preferences were found to group together in vertical columns similar to those that Mountcastle had found in somatosensory cortex. Indeed, an independent system of vertical columns—the ocular dominance columns—was found to segregate information arriving from the two eyes. These results provided an entirely new view of the anatomical organization of the cerebral cortex.

Wiesel and Hubel also investigated the effects of early sensory deprivation on newborn animals. They found that visual deprivation in one eye profoundly alters the organization of ocular dominance columns [23]. Columns receiving input from the closed eye shrink, and those receiving input from the open eye expand. These studies led to the discovery that eye closure alters the pattern of synchronous activity in the two eyes and that this neural activity is essential for fine-tuning synaptic connections during visual system development [16].

In the extrastriate cortex beyond area V1, continuing electrophysiological and anatomical studies have identified more than 30 distinct areas important for vision [24]. Further, visual information was found to be analyzed by two parallel processing streams [25]. The dorsal stream, concerned with where objects are located in space and how to reach objects, extends from area V1 to the parietal cortex. The ventral stream extends from area V1 to the inferior temporal cortex and is concerned with analyzing the visual form and quality of objects. Thus, even the apparently simple task of perceiving an object in space engages a disparate collection of specialized neural areas that represent different aspects of the visual information—what the object is, where it is located, and how to reach for it.

A Neuroscience of Cognition

The initial studies of the visual system were performed in anaesthetized cats, an experimental preparation far removed from the behaving and thinking human beings that are the focus of interest for cognitive psychologists. A pivotal advance occurred in the late 1960s when single-neuron recordings were obtained from awake, behaving monkeys that had been trained to perform sensory or motor tasks [26]. With these methods, the response of neurons in the posterior parietal cortex to a visual stimulus was found to be enhanced when the animal moved its eyes to attend to the stimulus. This moved the neurophysiological study of single neurons beyond sensory processing and showed that reductionist approaches could be applied to higher order psychological processes such as selective attention.

It is possible to correlate neuronal firing with perception rather directly. Thus, building on earlier work by Mountcastle, a monkey's ability to discriminate motion was found to closely match the performance of individual neurons in area MT, a cortical area concerned with visual motion processing. Further, electrical microstimulation of small clusters of neurons in MT shifts the monkey's motion judgments toward the direction of motion that the stimulated neurons prefer [27]. Thus, activity in area MT appears sufficient for the perception of motion and for initiating perceptual decisions.

These findings, based on recordings from small neuronal populations, have illuminated important issues in perception and action. They illustrate how retinal signals are remapped from retinotopic space into other coordinate frames that can guide behavior; how attention can modulate neuronal activity; and how meaning and context influence neuronal activity, so that the same retinal stimulus can lead to different neuronal responses depending on how the stimulus is perceived [28]. This same kind of work (relating cellular activity directly to perception and action) is currently being applied to the so-called binding problem—how the multiple features of a stimulus object, which are represented by specialized and distributed neuronal groups, are synthesized into a signal that represents a single percept or action and to the fundamental question of what aspects of neuronal activity (e.g., firing rate or spike timing) constitute the neural codes of information processing [29].

Striking parallels to the organization and function of sensory cortices have been found in the cortical motor areas supporting voluntary movement. Thus, there are several cortical areas directed to the planning and execution of voluntary movement. Primary motor cortex has columnar organization, with neurons in each column gov-

erning movements of one or a few joints. Motor areas receive input from other cortical regions, and information moves through stages to the spinal cord, where the detailed circuitry that generates motor patterns is located [30].

Although studies of single cells have been enormously informative, the functioning brain consists of multiple brain systems and many neurons operating in concert. To monitor activity in large populations of neurons, multielectrode arrays as well as cellular and whole-brain imaging techniques are now being used. These approaches are being supplemented by studying the effect of selective brain lesions on behavior and by molecular methods, such as the delivery of markers or other molecules to specific neurons by viral transfection, which promise fine-resolution tracing of anatomical connections, activity-dependent labeling of neurons, and ways to transiently inactivate specific components of neural circuits.

Invasive molecular manipulations of this kind cannot be applied to humans. However, functional neuroimaging by positron emission tomography (PET) or functional magnetic resonance imaging (fMRI) provides a way to monitor large neuronal populations in awake humans while they engage in cognitive tasks [31]. PET involves measuring regional blood flow using $H_2^{15}O$ and allows for repeated measurements on the same individual. fMRI is based on the fact that neural activity changes local oxygen levels in tissue and that oxygenated and deoxygenated hemoglobin have different magnetic properties. It is now possible to image the second-by-second time course of the brain's response to single stimuli or single events with a spatial resolution in the millimeter range. Recent success in obtaining fMRI images from awake monkeys, combined with single-cell recording, should extend the utility of functional neuroimaging by permitting parallel studies in humans and nonhuman primates.

One example of how parallel studies of humans and nonhuman primates have advanced the understanding of brain systems and cognition is in the study of memory. The neuroscience of memory came into focus in the 1950s when the noted amnesic patient H.M. was first described [32]. H.M. developed profound forgetfulness after sustaining a bilateral medial temporal lobe resection to relieve severe epilepsy. Yet he retained his intelligence, perceptual abilities, and personality. Brenda Milner's elegant studies of H.M. led to several important principles. First, acquiring new memories is a distinct cerebral function, separable from other perceptual and cognitive abilities. Second, because H.M. could retain a number or a visual image for a short time, the medial temporal lobes are not needed for immediate memory. Third, these structures are not the ultimate repository of memory, because H.M. retained his remote, childhood memories.

It subsequently became clear that only one kind of memory, declarative memory, is impaired in H.M. and other amnesic patients. Thus, memory is not a unitary faculty of the mind but is composed of multiple systems that have different logic and neuroanatomy [33]. The major dis-

A Timeline of Neuroscience

2nd Century A.D.

Galen of Pergamum identifies the brain as the organ of the mind.

17th Century

The brain becomes accepted as the substrate of mental life rather than its ventricles, as early writers had proposed.

1664

Thomas Willis publishes *Cerebri anatome*, with illustrations of the brain by Christopher Wren. It is the most comprehensive treatise on brain anatomy and function published up to that time.

1791

Luigi Galvani reveals the electric nature of nervous action by stimulating nerves and muscles of frog legs.

1808

Franz Joseph Gall proposes that specific brain regions control specific functions.

1852

Hermann von Helmholtz measures the speed of a nerve impulse in the frog.

1879

Wilhelm Wundt establishes the first laboratory of experimental psychology in Leipzig, Germany.

1891

Wilhelm von Waldeyer-Hartz introduces the term neuron.

1897

Charles Sherrington introduces the term synapse.

1898–1903

Edward Thorndike and Ivan Pavlov describe operant and classical conditioning, two fundamental types of learning.

1906

Santiago Ramón y Cajal summarizes compelling evidence for the neuron doctrine, that the nervous system is composed of discrete cells.

1906

Alois Alzheimer describes the pathology of the neurodegenerative disease that comes to bear his name.

1914

Henry Dale demonstrates the physiological action of acetylcholine, which is later identified as a neurotransmitter.

1929

In a famous program of lesion experiments in rats, Karl Lashley attempts to localize memory in the brain.

1929

Hans Berger uses human scalp electrodes to demonstrate electroencephalography.

1928–32

Edgar Adrian describes method for recording from single sensory and motor axons; H. Keffer Hartline applies this method to the recording of single-cell activity in the eye of the horseshoe crab.

1940s

Alan Hodgkin, Andrew Huxley, and Bernard Katz explain electrical activity of neurons by concentration gradients of ions and movement of ions through pores.

1946

Kenneth Cole develops the voltage-clamp technique to measure current flow across the cell membrane.

1949

Donald Hebb introduces a synaptic learning rule, which becomes known as the Hebb rule.

1930s to 1950s

The chemical nature of synaptic transmission is established by Otto Loewi, Henry Dale, Wilhelm Feldberg, Stephen Kuffler, and Bernard Katz at peripheral synapses and is extended to the spinal cord by John Eccles and others.

1930s to 1950s

Wilder Penfield and Theodore Rasmussen map the motor and sensory homunculus and illustrate localization of function in the human brain.

1950s

Karl von Frisch, Konrad Lorenz, and Nikolaas Tinbergen establish the science of ethology (animal behavior in natural contexts) and lay the foundation for neuroethology.

1955–60

Vernon Mountcastle, David Hubel, and Torsten Wiesel pioneer single-cell recording from mammalian sensory cortex; Nils-Ake Hillarp introduces fluorescent microscopic methods to study cellular distribution of biogenic amines.

1956

Rita Levi-Montalcini and Stanley Cohen isolate and purify nerve growth factor.

1957

Brenda Milner describes patient H.M. and discovers the importance of the medial temporal lobe for memory.

1958

Arvid Carlsson finds dopamine to be a transmitter in the brain and proposes that it has a role in extrapyramidal disorders such as Parkinson's disease.

(continued)

A Timeline of Neuroscience (continued)

1958
Simple invertebrate systems, including *Aplysia*, *Drosophila*, and *C. elegans*, are introduced to analyze elementary aspects of behavior and learning at the cellular and molecular level.

1962–63
Brain anatomy in rodents is found to be altered by experience; first evidence for role of protein synthesis in memory formation.

1963
Roger Sperry proposes a precise system of chemical matching between pre- and postsynaptic neuronal partners (the chemoaffinity hypothesis).

1966–69
Ed Evarts and Robert Wurtz develop methods for studying movement and perception with single-cell recordings from awake, behaving monkeys.

1970
Synaptic changes are related to learning and memory storage in *Aplysia*.

Mid-1970s
Paul Greengard shows that many neurotransmitters work by means of protein phosphorylation.

1973
Timothy Bliss and Terje Lomo discover long-term potentiation, a candidate synaptic mechanism for long-term mammalian memory.

1976
Erwin Neher and Bert Sakmann develop the patch-clamp technique for recording the activity of single ion channels.

Late 1970s
Neuroimaging by positron emission tomography is developed.

1980s
Experimental evidence becomes available for the divisibility of memory into multiple systems; an animal model of human amnesia is developed.

1986
H. Robert Horvitz discovers the *ced* genes, which are critical for programmed cell death.

1986
Patient R.B. establishes the importance of the hippocampus for human memory.

1990
Segi Ogawa and colleagues develop functional magnetic resonance imaging.

1990
Mario Capecchi and Oliver Smythies develop gene knockout technology, which is soon applied to neuroscience.

1991
Linda Buck and Richard Axel discover that the olfactory receptor family consists of over 1000 different genes. The anatomical components of the medial temporal lobe memory system are identified.

1993
The Huntington's Disease Collaborative Research Group identifies the gene responsible for Huntington's disease.

1990s
Neural development is transformed from a descriptive to a molecular discipline by Gerald Fischbach, Jack McMahan, Tom Jessell, and Corey Goodman; neuroimaging is applied to problems of human cognition, including perception, attention, and memory.

1990s
Reinhard Jahn, James Rothman, Richard Scheller, and Thomas Sudhof delineate molecules critical for exocytosis.

1998
First 3D structure of an ion channel is revealed by Rod MacKinnon.

tinction is between our capacity for conscious, declarative memory about facts and events and a collection of unconscious, nondeclarative memory abilities, such as skill and habit learning and simple forms of conditioning and sensitization. In these cases, experience modifies performance without requiring any conscious memory content or even the experience that memory is being used.

An animal model of human amnesia in the nonhuman primate was achieved in the early 1980s, leading ultimately to the identification of the medial temporal lobe structures that support declarative memory—the hippo-

campus and the adjacent entorhinal, perirhinal, and parahippocampal cortices [34]. The hippocampus has been an especially active target of study, in part because this was one of the structures damaged in patient H.M. and also because of the early discovery of hippocampal place cells, which signal the location of an animal in space [35]. This work led to the idea that, once learning occurs, the hippocampus and other medial temporal lobe structures permit the transition to long-term memory, perhaps by binding the separate cortical regions that together store memory for a whole event. Thus, long-term memory is thought to be stored in the same distributed set of cortical structures that perceive, process, and analyze what is to be remembered, and aggregate changes in large assemblies of cortical neurons are the substrate of long-term memory. The frontal lobes are also thought to influence what is selected for storage, the ability to hold information in mind for the short term, and the ability later on to retrieve it [36].

Whereas declarative memory is tied to a particular brain system, nondeclarative memory refers to a collection of learned abilities with different brain substrates. For example, many kinds of motor learning depend on the cerebellum, emotional learning and the modulation of memory strength by emotion depend on the amygdala, and habit learning depends on the basal ganglia [37]. These forms of nondeclarative memory, which provide for myriad unconscious ways of responding to the world, are evolutionarily ancient and observable in simple invertebrates such as *Aplysia* and *Drosophila*. By virtue of the unconscious status of these forms of memory, they create some of the mystery of human experience. For here arise the dispositions, habits, attitudes, and preferences that are inaccessible to conscious recollection, yet are shaped by past events, influence our behavior and our mental life, and are a fundamental part of who we are.

Bridging Cognitive Neuroscience and Molecular Biology in the Study of Memory Storage

The removal of scientific barriers at the two poles of the biological sciences—in the cell and molecular biology of nerve cells on the one hand, and in the biology of cognitive processes on the other—has raised the question: Can one anticipate an even broader unification, one that ranges from molecules to mind? A beginning of just such a synthesis may be apparent in the study of synaptic plasticity and memory storage.

For all of its diversity, one can view neuroscience as being concerned with two great themes—the brain's "hard wiring" and its capacity for plasticity. The former refers to how connections develop between cells, how cells function and communicate, and how an organism's inborn functions are organized—its sleep-wake cycles, hunger and thirst, and its ability to perceive the world. Thus, through evolution the nervous system has inherited many adaptations that are too important to be left to the vagaries of individual experience. In contrast, the capacity for plasticity refers to the fact that nervous systems can adapt or change as the result of the experiences that occur during an individual lifetime. Experience can modify the nervous system, and as a result organisms can learn and remember.

The precision of neural connections poses deep problems for the plasticity of behavior. How does one reconcile the precision and specificity of the brain's wiring with the known capability of humans and animals to acquire new knowledge? And how is knowledge, once acquired, retained as long-term memory? A key insight about synaptic transmission is that the precise connections between neurons are not fixed but are modifiable by experience. Beginning in 1970, studies in invertebrates such as *Aplysia* showed that simple forms of learning—habituation, sensitization, and classical conditioning—result in functional and structural changes at synapses between the neurons that mediate the behavior being modified. These changes can persist for days or weeks and parallel the time course of the memory process [38]. These cell biological studies have been complemented by genetic studies in *Drosophila*. As a result, studies in *Aplysia* and *Drosophila* have identified a number of proteins important for memory [39].

In his now-famous book, *The Organization of Behavior*, Donald Hebb proposed in 1949 that the synaptic strength between two neurons should increase when the neurons exhibit coincident activity [40]. In 1973, a long-lasting synaptic plasticity of this kind was discovered in the hippocampus (a key structure for declarative memory) [41]. In response to a burst of high-frequency stimuli, the major synaptic pathways in the hippocampus undergo a long-term change, known as long-term potentiation or LTP. The advent in the 1990s of the ability to genetically modify mice made it possible to relate specific genes both to synaptic plasticity and to intact animal behavior, including memory. These techniques now allow one to delete specific genes in specific brain regions and also to turn genes on and off. Such genetic and pharmacological experiments in intact animals suggest that interference with LTP at a specific synapse—the Schaffer collateral-CA1 synapse—commonly impairs memory for space and objects. Conversely, enhancing LTP at the same synapse can enhance memory in these same declarative memory tasks. The findings emerging from these new methods [42] complement those in *Aplysia* and *Drosophila* and reinforce one of Cajal's most prescient ideas: Even though the anatomical connections between neurons develop according to a definite plan, their strength and effectiveness are not predetermined and can be altered by experience.

Combined behavioral and molecular genetic studies in *Drosophila*, *Aplysia*, and mouse suggest that, despite their different logic and neuroanatomy, declarative and nondeclarative forms of memory share some common cellular and molecular features. In both systems, memory storage depends on a short-term process lasting minutes and a long-term process lasting days or longer. Short-term memory involves covalent modifications of preexisting proteins, leading to the strengthening of preexisting synaptic connections. Long-term memory involves altered gene expression, protein synthesis, and the growth of new synaptic connections. In addition, a number of key signaling molecules involved in converting transient short-term plasticity to persistent long-term memory appear to be shared by both declarative and nondeclarative memory. A striking feature of neural plasticity is that long-term memory involves structural and functional change [38, 43]. This has been shown most directly in invertebrates and is likely to apply to vertebrates as well, including primates.

It had been widely believed that the sensory and motor cortices mature early in life and thereafter have a fixed organization and connectivity. However, it is now clear that these cortices can be reshaped by experience [44]. In one experiment, monkeys learned to discriminate between two vibrating stimuli applied to one finger. After several thousand trials, the cortical representation of the trained finger became more than twice as large as the corresponding areas for other fingers. Similarly, in a neuroimaging study of right-handed string musicians the cortical representations of the fingers of the left hand (whose fingers are manipulated individually and are engaged in skillful playing) were larger than in nonmusicians. Thus, improved finger skills even involve changes in how sensory cortex represents the fingers. Because all organisms experience a different sensory environment, each brain is modified differently. This gradual creation of unique brain architecture provides a biological basis for individuality.

Coda

Physicists and chemists have often distinguished their disciplines from the field of biology, emphasizing that biology was overly descriptive, atheoretical, and lacked the coherence of the physical sciences. This is no longer quite true. In the 20th century, biology matured and became a coherent discipline as a result of the substantial achievements of molecular biology. In the second half of the century, neuroscience emerged as a discipline that concerns itself with both biology and psychology and that is beginning to achieve a similar coherence. As a result, fascinating insights into the biology of cells, and remarkable principles of evolutionary conservation, are emerging from the study of nerve cells. Similarly, entirely new insights into the nature of mental processes (perception, memory, and cognition) are emerging from the study of neurons, circuits, and brain systems, and computational studies are providing models that can guide experimental work. Despite this remarkable progress, the neuroscience of higher cognitive processes is only beginning. For neuroscience to address the most challenging problems confronting the behavioral and biological sciences, we will need to continue to search for new molecular and cellular approaches and use them in conjunction with systems neuroscience and psychological science. In this way, we will best be able to relate molecular events and specific changes within neuronal circuits to mental processes such as perception, memory, thought, and possibly consciousness itself.

References and Notes

1. S. Ramón y Cajal, Nobel Lectures: Physiology or Medicine (1901–1921) (Elsevier, Amsterdam, 1967), pp. 220–253.

2. C. S. Sherrington, The Central Nervous System, vol. 3 of A Textbook of Physiology, M. Foster, Ed. (MacMillan, London, ed. 7, 1897).

3. A. L. Hodgkin and A. F. Huxley, Nature 144, 710 (1939); A. L. Hodgkin et al., J. Physiol. (Lond.) 116, 424 (1952); A. L. Hodgkin and A. F. Huxley, J. Physiol. (Lond.) 117, 500 (1952).

4. E. J. Furshpan and D. D. Potter, Nature 180, 342 (1957); M. V. L. Bennett, in Structure and Function of Synapses, G. D. Pappas and D. P. Purpura, Eds. (Raven Press, New York, 1972), pp. 221-256.

5. C. M. Armstrong and B. Hille, Neuron 20, 371 (1998); W. A. Catterall, Neuron, in press; B. Hille et al., Nature Medicine 5, 1105 (1999); D. A. Doyle et al., Science 280, 69 (1998); J. P. Changeux and S. J. Edelstein, Neuron 21, 959 (1998); A. Karlin, Harvey Lecture Series 85, 71 (1991).

6. E. Neher and B. Sakmann, Nature 260, 799 (1976).

7. R. J. Lefkowitz, Nat. Cell Biol. 2, E133-6 (2000).

8. L. Buck and R. Axel, Cell 65, 175 (1991).

9. E. J. Nestler and P. Greengard, Protein Phosphorylation in the Nervous System (Wiley, New York, 1984).

10. J. Del Castillo and B. Katz, J. Physiol. 124, 560 (1954); B. Katz, in The Xth Sherrington Lecture (Thomas, Springfield, IL, 1969).

11. T. Sudhof, Nature 375, 645 (1995); R. Scheller, Neuron 14, 893 (1995); J. A. McNew et al., Nature 407, 153 (2000).

12. S. Cohen and R. Levi-Montalcini, Proc. Natl. Acad. Sci. U.S.A. 42, 571 (1956); W. M. Cowan, Neuron 20, 413 (1998).

13. M. M. Metzstein et al., Trends Genet. 14, 410 (1998).

14. R. W. Sperry, Proc. Natl. Acad. Sci. U.S.A. 50, 703 (1963); R. W. Hunt and W. M. Cowan, in Brain, Circuits and Functions of Mind, C. B. Trevarthen, Ed. (Cambridge Univ. Press, Cambridge, 1990), pp. 19–74.

15. M. Tessier-Lavigne and C. S. Goodman, Science 274, 1123 (1996); T. M. Jessell, Nature Rev. Genet. 1, 20 (2000); T. M. Jessell and J. R. Sanes, Curr. Opin. Neurobiol., in press.

16. L. C. Katz and C. J. Shatz, Science 274, 1133 (1996).

17. Huntington's Disease Collaborative Research Group, Cell 72, 971 (1993); H. L. Paulson and K. H. Fischbeck, Annu. Rev. Neurosci. 19, 79 (1996).

18. D. M. Walsh et al., Biochemistry 39, 10831 (2000); W. J. Strittmatter and A. D. Roses, Annu. Rev. Neurosci. 19, 53 (1996); D. L. Price, Nature 399 (6738) (Suppl), A3–5 (1999).

19. S. E. Hyman, Arch. Gen. Psychiatr. 157, 88 (2000); D. Charney et al., Eds., Neurobiology of Mental Illness (Oxford, New York, 1999); S. H. Barnodes, Molecules and Mental Illness (Scientific American Library, New York, 1993); S. Snyder, Drugs and the Brain (Scientific American Library, New York, 1986).

20. A. Carlsson, Annu. Rev. Neurosci. 10, 19 (1987); J. Axelrod, Science 173, 598 (1971); S. S. Kety, Am. J. Psychiatr. 140, 720 (1983); N. A. Hillarp et al., Pharmacol. Rev. 18, 727 (1966).

21. T. S. Kilduff and C. Peyron, Trends Neurosci. 23, 359 (2000); K. L. Houseknecht et al., J. Anim. Sci. 76, 1405 (1998); G. F. Koob, Ann. N.Y. Acad. Sci. 909, 17 (2000); E. J. Nestler, Curr. Opin. Neurobiol. 7, 713 (1997).

22. V. B. Mountcastle, J. Neurophysiol. 20, 408 (1957); D. H. Hubel and T. N. Wiesel, J. Physiol. 148, 574 (1959); D. H. Hubel and T. N. Wiesel, Neuron 20, 401 (1998).

23. T. Wiesel and D. Hubel, J. Neurophysiol. 26, 1003 (1963).

24. D. Van Essen, in Cerebral Cortex, A. Peters and E. G. Jones, Eds. (Plenum Publishing Corp., New York, 1985), vol. 3, pp. 259-327; S. Zeki, Nature 274, 423 (1978); J. Kaas and P. Garraghty, Curr. Opin. Neurobiol. 4, 522 (1992).

25. L. Ungerleider and M. Mishkin, in The Analysis of Visual Behavior, D. J. Ingle et al., Eds. (MIT Press, Cambridge, MA,

1982), pp. 549–586; A. Milner and M. Goodale, The Visual Brain in Action (Oxford, New York, 1995).

26. R. H. Wurtz, J. Neurophysiol. 32, 727 (1969); E. V. Evarts, in Methods in Medical Research, R. F. Rushman, Ed. (Year Book, Chicago, 1966), pp. 241–250.

27. W. T. Newsome et al., Nature 341, 52 (1989); C. D. Salzman et al., Nature 346, 174 (1990).

28. R. A. Andersen et al., Annu. Rev. Neurosci. 20, 303 (1997); R. Desimone and J. Duncan, Annu. Rev. Neurosci. 18, 193 (1995); M. I. Posner and C. D. Gilbert, Proc. Natl. Acad. Sci. U.S.A. 96, 2585 (1999); T. D. Albright and G. R. Stoner, Proc. Natl. Acad. Sci. U.S.A. 92, 2433 (1995); C. D. Gilbert, Physiol. Rev. 78, 467 (1998); N. K. Logothetis, Philos. Trans. R. Soc. London, Ser. B 353, 1801 (1998).

29. For the binding problem, see Neuron 24 (1) (1999); for neural codes, see M. N. Shadlen and W. T. Newsome, Curr. Opin. Neurobiol. 4, 569 (1994); W. R. Softky, Curr. Opin. Neurobiol. 5, 239 (1995).

30. S. Grillner et al., Eds., Neurobiology of Vertebrate Locomotion, Wenner-Gren Center International Symposium Series, vol. 45 (Macmillan, London, 1986); A. P. Georgopoulos, Curr. Opin. Neurobiol. 10, 238 (2000).

31. L. Sokoloff et al., J. Neurochem. 28, 897 (1977); M. Reivich et al., Circ. Res. 44 127 (1979); M. I. Posner and M. E. Raichle, Images of Mind (Scientific American Library, New York, 1994); S. Ogawa et al., Proc. Natl. Acad. Sci. U.S.A. 87, 9868 (1990); B. R. Rosen et al., Proc. Natl. Acad. Sci. U.S.A. 95, 773 (1998).

32. W. B. Scoville and B. Milner, J. Neurol., Neurosurg., Psychiatr. 20, 11 (1957); B. Milner et al., Neuron 20, 445 (1998).

33. L. R. Squire, Psychol. Rev. 99, 195 (1992); D. L. Schacter and E. Tulving, Eds., Memory Systems (MIT Press, Cambridge, MA, 1994).

34. M. Mishkin, Philos. Trans. R. Soc. London, Ser. B 298, 85 (1982); L. R. Squire and S. Zola-Morgan, Science 253, 1380 (1991).

35. J. O'Keefe and J. Dostrovsky, Brain Res. 34, 171 (1971); H. Eichenbaum et al. , Neuron 23, 209 (1999).

36. L. R. Squire and E. R. Kandel, Memory: From Mind to Molecules (Scientific American Library, New York, 1999); H. Eichenbaum, Nature Rev. Neurosci. 1, 1 (2000); P. Goldman-Rakic, Philos. Trans. R. Soc. London, Ser. B 351, 1445 (1996); R. Desimone, Proc. Natl. Acad. Sci. U.S.A. 93, 13494 (1996); S. Higuchi and Y. Miyashita, Proc. Natl. Acad. Sci. U.S.A. 93, 739 (1996).

37. R. F. Thompson and D. J. Krupa, Annu. Rev. Neurosci. 17, 519 (1994); J. LeDoux, The Emotional Brain (Simon & Schuster, New York, 1996); J. L. McGaugh, Science 287, 248 (2000); M. Mishkin et al., in Neurobiology of Learning and Memory, G. Lynch et al., Eds. (Guilford, New York, 1984),

pp. 65–77; D. L. Schacter and R. L. Buckner, Neuron 20, 185 (1998).

38. V. Castellucci et al., Science 167, 1745 (1970); M. Brunelli et al., Science 194, 1178 (1976); C. Bailey et al., Proc. Nat. Acad. Sci. U.S.A. 93, 13445 (1996).

39. S. Benzer, Sci. Am. 229, 24 (1973); W. G. Quinn and R. J. Greenspan, Annu. Rev. Neurosci. 7, 67 (1984); R. L. Davis, Physiol. Rev. 76, 299 (1996); J. Yin and T. Tully, Curr. Opin. Neurobiol. 6, 264 (1996).

40. D. O. Hebb, The Organization of Behavior: A Neuropsychological Theory (Wiley, New York, 1949).

41. T. V. P. Bliss and T. Lomo, J. Physiol. (Lond.) 232, 331 (1973).

42. M. Mayford et al., Science 274, 1678 (1996); J. Tsien et al., Cell 87, 1327 (1996); A. Silva et al., Annu. Rev. Neurosci. 21, 127 (1998); S. Martin et al., Annu. Rev. Neurosci. 23, 613 (2000); E. P. Huang and C. F. Stevens, Essays Biochem. 33, 165 (1998); R. C. Malenka and R. A. Nicoll, Science 285, 1870 (1999); H. Korn and D. Faber, CR Acad. Sci. III 321, 125 (1998).

43. W. T. Greenough and C. H. Bailey, Trends Neurosci. 11, 142 (1998).

44. D. V. Buonomano and M. M. Merzenich, Annu. Rev. Neurosci. 21, 149 (1998); C. Gilbert, Proc. Nat. Acad. Sci. U.S.A. 93 10546 (1996); T. Elbert et al., Science 270, 305 (1995).

The work of E.R.K. is supported by NIMH, the G. Harold and Leila Y. Mathers Foundation, the Lieber Center for Research on Schizophrenia, and the Howard Hughes Medical Institute. The work of L.R.S. is supported by the Medical Research Service of the Department of Veterans Affairs, NIMH, and the Metropolitan Life Foundation. We thank Thomas Jessell and Thomas Albright for their helpful comments on the manuscript.

Eric R. Kandel is University Professor, Columbia University, New York, and Senior Investigator at the Howard Hughes Medical Institute. He is a member of the National Academy of Sciences and the Institute of Medicine and a past president of the Society for Neuroscience. This past October, he was named a co-recipient of the Nobel Prize in physiology or medicine.

Larry R. Squire is Research Career Scientist at the Veterans Affairs San Diego Healthcare System and Professor of Psychiatry, Neurosciences, and Psychology, University of California, San Diego. He is a member of the National Academy of Sciences and the Institute of Medicine and a past president of the Society for Neuroscience.

UNIT 3
Perceptual Processes

Unit Selections

Key Points to Consider

- Do you think vision is the most important human sense? Is it the dominant sense in all other animals? How is the brain involved in vision? Does stem cell transplantation help blind people to see? Why or why not? If you were blind, would you want a stem cell transplant? What are the controversies swirling around stem cell transplants? Which side of the controversy do you take?

- Why do psychologists study language? Does language influence our perception? Does language influence how we think? How so? Can you give some concrete examples of how language influences thought and perception?

- What is deafness; is it complete hearing loss? What are some of the causes of deafness? Are Americans at risk for deafness? How much noise is too much noise? What can be done to reduce noise levels so that they are not detrimental to us?

- Why is it important to study pain? Why are psychologists interested in pain and pain management? How can pain be better managed?

- What is REM sleep? What is NREM sleep? What are some of the problems dream researchers encounter? What do dreams mean? Was Freud correct that dreams are repressed wishes? On the other hand, are dreams about events we would rather remember? What are some of the other theories that attempt to explain why we dream?

 **Links: www.dushkin.com/online/**
These sites are annotated in the World Wide Web pages.

Five Senses Home Page
http://www.sedl.org/scimath/pasopartners/senses/welcome.html
Psychology Tutorials and Demonstrations
http://psych.hanover.edu/Krantz/tutor.html

Marina and her roommate have been friends since freshman year. Because they share so much in common, they decided to become roommates in their sophomore year. They both want to travel abroad one day. Both date men from the same college, are education majors, and want to work with young children after graduation from college. Today they are at the local art museum. As they walk around the galleries, Marina is astonished at her roommate's taste in art. Whatever her roommate likes, Marina hates. The paintings and sculptures that Marina admires are the very ones to which her roommate turns up her nose. "How can our tastes in art be so different when we share so much in common?" Marina wonders.

What Marina and her roommate are experiencing is a difference in perception or the interpretation of the sensory stimulation provided by the artwork. Perception and its sister area of psychology, sensation, are the foci of this unit.

For many years, it was popular for psychologists to consider sensation and perception as two distinct processes. Sensation was defined in passive terms as the simple event of some stimulus energy (e.g. a sound wave) impinging on the body or on a specific sense organ that then reflexively transmitted appropriate information to the central nervous system. With regard to the concept of sensation, in the past both passivity and simple reflexes were stressed. Perception, on the other hand, was defined as an integrative and interpretive process that the higher centers of the brain supposedly accomplish based on sensory information and available memories for similar events.

The Gestalt psychologists, early German researchers, were convinced that perception was a higher order function compared to sensation. The Gestalt psychologists believed that the whole stimulus was more than the sum of its individual sensory parts; Gestalt psychologists believed this statement was made true by the process of perception.

For example, some of you listen to a song and hear the words, the loudness, and the harmony as well as the main melody. However, you do not really hear each of these units; what you hear is a whole song. If the song is pleasant to you, you may exclaim that you like the song and even buy the CD. If the song is raucous to you, you may perceive that you do not like it and hope it ends soon. However, even the songs you first hear and do not like may become liked after repeated exposure. Hence perception, according to these early Gestalt psychologists, was a more advanced and complicated process than sensation.

This dichotomy of sensation and perception is no longer widely accepted. The revolution came in the mid-1960s when a psychologist published a then-radical treatise in which he reasoned that perceptual processes included all sensory events

that he believed were directed by an actively searching central nervous system. Also, this view provided that certain perceptual patterns, such as recognition of a piece of artwork, may be species-specific. That is, all humans, independent of learning history, should share some of the same perceptual repertoires. This unit on perceptual processes is designed to further your understanding of these complex and interesting processes.

The first article in this unit, "Sight Unseen," explores one of the most important senses in humans—vision. The author, Michael Abrams, guides us through the journey of a man, blind from childhood, in a quest to restore his vision. Even after surgery that should have assured good vision, the man still cannot see. Abrams explains why.

A companion article, "Different Shades of Perception," addresses color perception. Interestingly, the author claims, the study of language has demonstrated that some people perceive colors differently from the way other people perceive them. The cause is probably the language they learned and the way they use it.

One of the other dominant senses in humans is audition or hearing. In the next article, "It's a Noisy, Noisy World Out There!," Richard Carmen discloses information about just how much noise Americans are exposed to and why certain noises can be detrimental. With enough exposure to certain sounds, individuals can become deaf. The article also reveals what can be done to save Americans' hearing.

In the article that follows, Marni Jackson describes how and why scientists are studying pain and what they have learned thus far. One important factor is that scientists now know better how to control pain.

The final selection of this unit relates to an altered state of perception or altered state of consciousness (something outside of normal sensation and perception). This last article is about sleeping and dreaming, something we all do and something that fascinates most individuals. By studying sleep, especially dream or REM sleep, researchers are beginning to understand why we dream and what dreams may mean. Freud's was the first theory to address these issues, but newer theories are making headway on the nature and causes of dreaming. Author Bruce Bower explores both Freud's theory and other theories in a search for a better understanding of the function of dreams.

Sight Unseen

Mike May was blind most of his life until surgery gave him his sight back.
But two years later he still can't recognize his own wife.
By learning why, psychologists are revealing the very origins of vision

BY MICHAEL ABRAMS

MIKE MAY HOLDS THE WORLD SPEED RECORD FOR downhill skiing by a blind person. In his competitive days he would slalom down the steepest black-diamond slopes at 65 miles an hour, with a guide 10 feet ahead to shout "left" and "right." The directions were just obvious cues. The rest came from the feel of the wind racing against his cheeks and the sound of the guide's skis snicking over the snow. But May's days as a world-class blind athlete are behind him. He's no longer blind.

May lost his vision at the age of 3, when a jar of fuel for a miner's lantern exploded in his face. It destroyed his left eye and scarred the cornea of his right, but over the next 43 years he never let those disabilities slow him down. He played flag football in elementary school, soccer in college, and nearly any activity that didn't involve projectiles as an adult. He earned a master's degree in international affairs from Johns Hopkins, took a job with the CIA, and became the president and CEO of the Sendero Group, a company that makes talking Global Positioning Systems for the blind. Along the way, he found time to help develop the first laser turntable, marry, have two children, and buy a house in Davis, California. "Someone once asked me if I could have vision or fly to the moon, what would I choose," he once wrote. "No question—I would fly to the moon. Lots of people have sight, few have gone to the moon."

Then one November day in 1999, he came back to his senses. At St. Mary's Hospital in San Francisco, surgeon Daniel Goodman dropped a doughnut of corneal stem cells onto May's right eye (his left was too severely damaged to be repaired). The cells replaced scar tissue and rebuilt the ocular surface, preparing the eye for a corneal transplant. On March 7, 2000, when the wraps were removed, May got his first look at his wife, his children, and for the first time since he was a toddler, himself.

Sight restoration is a periodic miracle both for its recipients and for the scientists who have the privilege of studying them. As early as the fifth century B.C., Egyptian surgeons used a needle to push their patients' cataract-covered lenses away from their pupils, affording them some degree of sight. More recently, in the late 1960s, surgeons learned to remove cataracts with ultrasound. The stem-cell surgery performed on May was developed in Japan and introduced in 1999. Since then hundreds of people have benefited from it. But of all those who have had their sight restored throughout history, only about 20 recorded cases were blind since childhood, and of those, most had less-than-perfect corneas after surgery. When Goodman peered into May's eye after the surgery, he saw a lens that ought to provide crystal-clear vision.

It doesn't—far from it. Pristine as his optical hardware is, May's brain has never been programmed to process the visual information it receives. May still travels with his dog, Josh, or taps the sidewalk with a cane, and refers to himself as "a blind man with vision." And that paradox fascinates Don MacLeod and Ione Fine, experimental psychologists at the University of California at San Diego. The speed with which babies learn to understand the world suggests that they're born with the ability to process some aspects of vision. But which aspects, exactly? What is learned and what is hardwired? During the past year and a half, Fine and MacLeod have put May through a battery of physical and psychological tests, including functional magnetic resonance imaging, or fMRI, which tracks blood flow in the brain. The results are opening the first clear view into how we learn to see.

MacLEOD'S LABORATORY AT THE UNIVERSITY IS A LABYRINTH of filing cabinets, optical equipment, and oddly placed desks. "It's well booby-trapped," he says, steering May toward the first of many tests one afternoon. "But May has an uncanny ability to navigate complicated arrangements." Tall and athletic, with features that look boyishly handsome despite his graying black hair, May would make a good James Bond if not for a few side effects of his blindness. Unlike the rest of his body, his eyelids haven't had a lifelong workout. Perpetually half closed, they lend a stoic blankness to his face that's relieved only by the occasional smile. He has yet to learn facial expressions.

A blind man who is suddenly given vision, Molyneux suggested, wouldn't be able to tell the difference between a cube and a sphere

Sitting obligingly in front of an ancient computer monitor, May watches as thick black-and-orange bars appear on the screen. MacLeod and Fine are testing his ability to see detail. His job is to adjust the contrast with a trackball until he can just see the bars. A click on a mouse brings up another set of bars, thinner than the last, and he plays around with those until he can see them too. Although his right eye ought to provide 20/20 vision, in reality it's closer to 20/500. Instead of discerning the letter *E* on an eye chart from 25 feet, May can see it only from two. In the past the blurred vision of people with restored sight was blamed on scar tissue from surgery. But stem-cell surgery leaves no scars. The signals are reaching May's brain, but they are not being interpreted very well.

More than 300 years ago, in a famous letter to the philosopher John Locke, the Irish thinker William Molyneux anticipated what May sees. A blind man who is suddenly given vision, Molyneux suggested, wouldn't be able to tell the difference between a cube and a sphere. Sight is one kind of perception and touch another; they can be linked only through experience.

The most dramatic proof of this theory came in an experiment published in 1963 by Richard Held and Alan Hein, who were then professors at Brandeis University in Waltham, Massachusetts. Held and Hein raised two kittens in total darkness. But every so often they would place the kittens in separate baskets, suspend the baskets from a single circular track, and turn on the lights. Both baskets hung just above the floor, but one had holes for the kitten's legs to poke through; the other did not. The free-limbed cat ran in circles on the floor, pulling the other basket along behind it; the other kitten had no choice but to sit and watch. While the active kitten learned to see normally, the passive kitten stayed effectively blind: Its eyes could see, but its brain never learned to interpret the sensory input.

Held and Hein's experiment has never been duplicated. But in the past half century, studies of sight restoration, most notably by Oliver Sacks and Richard Gregory, have verified that some things can't be understood without experience. Objects, faces, depth—just about everything that helps us function in the world—are meaningless when a person who has never seen before gets sight. "Babies are born into a bright, buzzing confusion, but we can't ask them what it's like," Fine says. "In some ways talking to Mike May is like getting to talk to a 7-month-old."

IN THE FIRST MONTHS AFTER HIS SURGERY, MAY FULFILLED Molyneux's prediction: He couldn't distinguish a sphere from a cube. Since then his sight has improved, but only slightly. He has a better grasp of spheres and squares ("We've shown him an awful lot of them," Fine says), and with practice he can understand things he's seen again and again. But this is only a workaround: He's past the critical period for learning to recognize objects instantly.

"Two of the major clues I have are color and context," May says. "When I see an orange thing on a basketball court, I assume it's round. But I may not be really seeing the roundness of it." Faces give him even more trouble. Although he has seen faces everywhere since the first day his vision was restored, they simply don't coalesce into recognizable people. Their expressions—their moods and personalities—elude him entirely. Even his wife is familiar to him only by the quality of her gait, the length of her hair, and the clothes she wears. "If a face has no hair and a fake moustache, we can still tell the gender," Fine says. "But he can't deal with it. The bit of the brain that does that isn't working."

The best proof of this can be seen in the basement, where MacLeod's interferometer sits. Designed to test the brain's ability to process visual information, the machine works by shining a split laser beam into a subject's eye. As the beams travel, their light waves interfere with each other, bypassing the optics of the cornea and projecting a pattern onto the retina. Most subjects who sit in front of the interferometer will see light and dark stripes, regardless of the quality of their optics. But when May opens his eyes to receive the beams, he sees nothing at all.

The interferometer results are backed by fMRI scans, which track May's brain activity as it's occurring. The scans show that when May sees faces and objects, the part of his brain that should be used to recognize them is inactive. But there's a catch. When he sees an object in motion, the motion-detection part of his brain lights up like a disco ball. He can interpret

Do You See What I See?

May ought to have 20/20 vision since his right eye was restored by stem-cell surgery and a corneal transplant. Instead, his vision is closer to 20/500—or about as blurry as the example to the right. "Basically, the results say that you can only get precise vision early in life at the critical period, " Don Macload says. "We don't really know where May will end up, but he isn't approaching normal vision at a quick rate."

Above: A lifetime of blindness has left May insusceptible to visual illusions. Most people would say that the top of the dark cube is darker than the front of the light cube. To May they're the same exact shade. It's only when MacLeod explains the illusion that May can even see that squares are supposed to look three-dimensional.

movement on a computer screen as well as any normal-sighted adult and seems to have the same skill in real life. "We were driving along, and a minivan came up to us pretty fast on his side," Fine remembers. "It whizzed by him, and he mentioned that it was going fast. That's a complicated calculation. The motion on the retina depends on how big the car is, how close, and how fast it's going."

It's hard to escape the conclusion that motion detection, unlike every other visual experience aside from color, is largely hardwired. The best illustration of this may be offered, once again, by cats. "If you roll a ball along a floor, the cat will chase it as long as it's moving," Fine says. "As soon as its stationary, the cat will have a hard time seeing it and will ignore it." That's why mice freeze when they're afraid. It may also explain why May, who can barely recognize a stationary ball, is pretty good at catching a moving one. It's his favorite use of his new sense. "I don't know who has more fun," he says, "my 8-year-old or me."

BLIND PEOPLE SPEND THEIR ENTIRE LIVES UNDERSTANDING THE world through their hands. Their memories, their mental maps of the places they know, their understanding of Labradors, doorknobs, and the moguls on a ski slope are all tactile. The sudden introduction of a new sense can't alter that fundamental way of experiencing the universe. Instead, any new information gleaned from light is simply graphed onto the original, tactile map. "The old idea that there is one picture of the world on the surface of the cortex is way too simple," MacLeod says. "In fact, we have a couple dozen complete maps." For someone just learning how to merge all that information, this can make for a great deal of confusion. But it might also offer a richer, truer sense of the world than the one perceived by those of us who have never been blind.

Sitting in the lab one day, MacLeod, smirking like a schoolboy who's hatching a prank, slides a drawing across the table to May. On the paper are four cubes. The top right cube and the bottom left cube are dark; the other two are light. The drawing is shaded as if light were coming from above, so the tops of the squares are lighter than their fronts. This makes the top of the dark square the same shade as the front of the light square. Experience tells us that the top of the dark cube has been brightened by a hidden light, but it still seems darker than the front of a light cube. It's an illusion based on knowledge. Naturally, May doesn't fall for it.

"He's actually closer to reality," Fine says. "We once showed him two circles—a small one close to him and a larger one farther away. To you or me they would have appeared to be the same size. But when we asked, 'What's the apparent size?' he couldn't understand. He kept saying, 'I know it's bigger because it's far away.'" Similarly, May's tactile experience with hallways and highways tells him that their sides are parallel, so he simply can't perceive converging lines of perspective. "A hallway doesn't look like it closes in at all," he says. "I see the lines on either side of the path, but I don't really think of them as coming closer in the distance." He pauses to mull this over. "Or maybe my mind doesn't believe what my mind is perceiving. When I see an object, it doesn't look different to me as I circle around it. I know orange cones around vehicles are cones because of context, not because I'm seeing the shape. If I picture looking down on a cone, it still looks like a cone."

Only a handful of adults have ever seen the world through the eyes of a newborn, and many who did came away wishing they were still blind

Learning to see, for May, is really about learning to fall for the same illusions we all do, to call a certain mass of colors and lines his son, to call another group of them a ball.

ONE APRIL MORNING, ONLY WEEKS AFTER HIS EYE SURGERY, may took his skis and his family up to the Kirkwood Mountain Resort in the Sierra Nevadas—a place he knew like the texture on the back of his hand. This was where he had first learned to ski and where he had later met his wife. The sun was out, the trees were green (greener than he'd imagined), and the slopes were surrounded by gorgeous cliffs (were they miles away or just a few hundred yards?). As the lift churned above, skiers in puffy parkas flitted by, popping into his field of vision. His wife, acting as a guide, had to remind him to stop gawking and ski.

With only one working eye, May already lacked depth perception. But he also had little experience reading the shades and contours of a landscape. Heading down the mountain, he could hardly distinguish shadows from people, poles, or rocks. At first, he tried to compute the lay of the land consciously: If a certain slope was being lit from the side and a shadow fell in such a way, then the slope must be convex. But once he hit his first bump, he was tempted to close his eyes and ski the way he knew and loved.

Only a handful of adults have ever seen the world through the eyes of a newborn, and many who did came away wishing they were still blind. Their family and friends had convinced them that vision would offer a miraculous new appreciation and understanding of the world. Instead, even the simplest actions—walking down stairs, crossing the street—became terrifyingly difficult. Dispirited and depressed, about a third of them reverted back to the world of the blind, preferring dark rooms and walking with their eyes shut.

If May feels differently, it may be because his expectations were so low. For a man who used to enjoy windsurfing blind and alone, able more often than not to return to the pier from which he'd started, sight is just another adventure in a life of invigorating obstacles. Two years after his return to Kirkwood Mountain, May has learned to match what he sees on a ski slope with his repeated physical experience of it. "He has jury-rigged himself quite a functional little system," Fine says. "He knows that this kind of shadow makes this bump, this kind makes another." Instead of closing his eyes on even the easiest slopes, he can now negotiate moguls without a guide.

"People have this idea that it's so overwhelmingly practical to have sight," May says. "I say it's great from an entertainment point of view. I'm constantly looking for things that are unique to vision. Running and catching a ball is one of them—I've been chasing balls my whole life. Seeing the difference between the blue of my two sons' eyes is another. Or if you drop something, you can find it."

The gift of sight may seem most miraculous, in the end, to those who have never been blind. But May still finds things in the world to entrance him. Sitting in the passenger seat of Fine's car one day, with his dog, Josh, panting at his feet, he ignores the blue Pacific to the left, the towering, top-heavy eucalyptus trees lining the road like something out of Dr. Seuss. Instead, he gazes at the beam of sunlight filtering through the window onto his lap. "I can't believe the dust is just floating in the air like this," he says. Oceans and trees, Seussean or otherwise, he has known all his life through touch. But this glitter of dust, suspended in the bright La Jolla sun, is an entirely new awareness. He waves his hand through the sparkling beam. "It's like having little stars all around you."

Different shades of perception

A new study shows how learning—and possibly language—
can influence color perception.

BY ETIENNE BENSON
Monitor staff

Color categories make the world easier to live in. Granny Smith (green) and Red Delicious (red) apples belong in different bins; so do violets (blue) and roses (red).

"Color perception is not as rigid and inflexible as was thought before."

Emre Özgen,
University of Surrey

To most of us, those categories seem natural, but in many other languages the categories differ. Some African languages have five primary color words or fewer; Russian has as many as English, plus an additional kind of blue. Often the boundaries between two colors shift as one moves from one language community to another.

Now, a new study by researchers at the University of Surrey suggests that the process of learning new color categories produces subtle but significant changes in how people actually perceive those colors.

The findings, published in the *Journal of Experimental Psychology:* *General* (Vol. 131, No. 4), support the linguistic relativity hypothesis—the idea that the language one speaks can affect the way one thinks about and perceives the world.

"The main conclusions of the study are basic: that color perception is not as rigid and inflexible as was thought before," says the study's lead author, Emre Özgen, PhD. "This is the first time that it's been shown that a new perceptual color category boundary can actually be induced through laboratory training."

The experiment

Previous studies have shown that people find it easier to distinguish between similar hues that belong to different color categories than between hues that fall within a single color category. A bluish green and a greenish blue, for example, are easier to tell apart than a bluish green and a yellowish green.

The central question of the current study was whether these improvements in performance at the boundaries of color categories—an effect known as "categorical perception"—are fixed or changeable. Can training enhance the effect, making people more sensitive to color differences across boundaries? Can new boundaries be created, even ones that lie right in the middle of conventional color categories?

In their first experiment, Özgen and Ian Davies, PhD, sought to answer the more basic question: whether training could improve participants' ability to distinguish between similar hues of a single color. The answer was yes: Participants became increasingly accurate over the course of three days of training.

Özgen and Davies then moved to the second, critical question: whether novel categorical perception effects could be acquired in the laboratory. Participants were trained to divide a basic color category, blue or green, into two new categories. The boundaries of the new categories lay at the focal points of the old categories—the greenest greens, for example, now lay at the boundary between a category of yellowish greens and a category of bluish greens.

After three days of training, participants were better able to distinguish between hues that fell on either side of the novel color boundaries than between hues within a single category, even when the absolute difference between the two hues was the same—a classic categorical perception effect. At the same time, participants effectively unlearned their pre-existing color categories: They stopped showing categorical perception effects as "natural" boundaries that lay within the range of hues on which they had trained.

A follow-up experiment showed that the change in categorical perception could be produced after a single training session of 500 trials, though the improved performance was not evident until the next day—perhaps, the researchers speculate, because improvement at the end of the first session was masked by fatigue.

In their final experiment, Özgen and Davies explored whether participants would learn new categories based on differences in lightness, just as participants in the previous experiments had learned categories based on differences in hue. They found that lightness training produced the same kinds of categorical perception effects that hue training did, but they also found an interesting asymmetry: Participants who trained on hue-based categories showed no new categorical perception effects when later tested on lightness, whereas participants trained on lightness-based categories showed categorical perception effects for hue. The results suggest that lightness can be ignored when it is irrelevant to a task, but hue is processed automatically.

"People have shown categorical perception effects for color before, but there's been a large number of people who've argued that these are innate color categories," says Robert Goldstone, PhD, a professor of psychology at Indiana University. "What the current study shows is that you can get acquired categorical perception."

Linguistic relativity

The study also offers a new spin on the work of University of California, Berkeley, psychologist Eleanor Rosch, PhD, who suggested in the 1970s that linguistic differences have little effect on how people actually perceive colors. She reported that speakers of a New Guinean language with only two color words— one for cold, dark colors and one for warm, light colors—learned and remembered colors more easily when they were prototypical examples of colors identified in English, such as red, green and blue, than when they were not. The results were a blow to the linguistic relativity hypothesis, also known as the Sapir-Whorf hypothesis, which suggests that cognition is shaped by the languages people speak.

In recent years, however, University of Essex psychologist Debi Roberson, PhD, and others have tried to replicate Rosch's work among other tribes with few color words, and have found results that appear to contradict hers. Their findings suggest that there are differences— small but nonetheless significant—in the color perception of speakers of different languages.

"These kinds of categorical perception effects seem to be language-dependent," says Davies, who has collaborated with Roberson on some of those studies. "If an African language doesn't mark a blue-green boundary, then adult speakers don't seem to show categorical perception across that boundary, whereas English speakers do."

The current study is partly motivated by the cross-cultural research. But as MIT psychologist Lera Boroditsky, PhD, points out, unlike the cross-cultural studies, it does not directly address the linguistic relativity hypotheses. It does not, for instance, provide evidence that learning a new linguistic distinction can produce a new categorical perception effect.

What the study does provide, says Özgen, is evidence that categorical perception can change quickly as well as a plausible mechanism for how it changes. It is a small leap from there to being able to show how a distinction that starts off as merely linguistic—this sort of color goes in category A; that sort goes in category B—can become deeply ingrained in perception.

"Linguistic relativity may work with similar principles, in that as a child grows up, he or she will have to continually learn a category boundary just as our subjects learn in the lab," says Özgen. But he cautions, "neither the linguistic relativity nor the universal hypotheses would hold if we were to take an extreme position. To say that language completely shapes thought would be as extreme as saying that thought is entirely hardwired."

IT'S A NOISY, NOISY WORLD OUT THERE!

From the acoustic trauma of airbag deployment to the blast of personal stereos, we must stop turning a deaf ear to the daily menace of noise in our environment.

by Dr. Richard Carmen

The 80-decibel (dB) alarm clock (two feet from my head) shatters the silence at 6:45 a.m. and does bad things to nice dreams. Anything less noisy risks not waking me up.

Moments later, the electric shaver mows precariously near my ears at 85 dB. After the shower, it's time for the hair-blower endurance test of 112 dB. If decibels were converted to wind velocity, the hair dryer could self-propel. This new dryer—a "Turbo-Rocket Torque-357"—should require special handling and be reclassified as a leaf blower. On days when I'm short on time, I move it closer to my hair and therefore nearer to my ears. Not a good idea.

This racket signals my four-year-old daughter that my day has begun. She bolts into the bathroom shouting louder than the dryer, sometimes toting her toy megaphone to amplify her morning song, "Fe Fi Fo Fum!" (135 dB one foot away) If this cacophony were to occur outside, my neighbors could have me fined and, in some cities, even arrested!

By the time I make it to my quiet morning coffee, a short but heartfelt reprieve, the doorbell is intermittently emitting sounds that remind me of an Alfred Hitchcock movie. Each 115 dB buzz (just below my auditory discomfort but exceeding my annoyance level) reminds me I have to get rid of it.

It's my daughter's ride to school. She dashes out the door, and I'm right behind her. We're greeted with a blare of the horn. It feels like dual five-inch cannons against our foreheads. Reflexively, I raise my arms and drop her lunchbox. Ears slightly ringing, I accept the driver's wave of apology and hobble back to my tepid coffee. I would normally use the microwave to reheat it, but the "Ready" alarm is just more than I can handle this morning. And the day has just begun.

I escape momentarily into the TV room, when my wife walks in. "How can you stand it that loud?" she queries. "You better check your hearing, honey!" she adds as she leaves.

I follow her into the kitchen where a high-speed blender prepares her morning nutritional drink. Military assault weapons make less noise.

"How can you stand it that loud?" I shout, wondering if the noise does as much mixing as the blades.

"What?" she asks. At least I think that's what she says; it was the right lip movement. I don't answer her because she can't read lips, and besides, she's turned on the disposal (94 dB)—loud, but inconsequential, considering the blender. I blow her a kiss, and I'm off to work.

The slam of the door on my old truck, metal to metal, surely has acoustic peaks exceeding 120 dB. It hurts, but if I don't slam it, the door remains ajar. I've noticed ringing in that left ear lately.

On the highway, I wave to a physician friend riding his motorcycle without a helmet, and wonder if he knows that riding at 80 mph for just one hour puts him at risk for hearing loss.

And so it goes for families all across America.

Despite the Occupational Safety and Health Administration's (OSHA) decree stating that workers should not be exposed to more than 90 dB for an eight-hour period, these limits

How's Your Hearing?

The following questions can help you determine if you have a hearing loss and need to have your hearing evaluated.

- ❏ Do you have a problem hearing over the telephone?
- ❏ Do you hear better with one ear than the other when you are on the telephone?
- ❏ Do you have trouble following the conversation when two or more people are talking at the same time?
- ❏ Do people complain that you turn the TV volume up too high?
- ❏ Do you have to strain to understand conversation?
- ❏ Do you have trouble hearing in a noisy background?
- ❏ Do you have trouble hearing in restaurants?
- ❏ Do you have dizziness, pain, or ringing in your ears?
- ❏ Do you find yourself asking people to repeat themselves?
- ❏ Do family members or coworkers remark about your missing what has been said?
- ❏ Do many people you talk to seem to mumble (or not speak clearly)?
- ❏ Do you misunderstand what others are saying and respond inappropriately?
- ❏ Do you have trouble understanding the speech of women and children?
- ❏ Do people get annoyed because you misunderstand what they say?

If you answer yes to more than two of these questions, you should have your hearing tested by a licensed audiologist.

ear protection, you're not supposed to hear well. The solution is to provide ear defenders that incorporate telecommunication ability, like the kind pit crews wear at auto races so coworkers can share essential information. Although this technology works, it's expensive. Nevertheless, corporations should realize that protection is in their best interest; the average annual cost of medical management for hearing loss is $56 billion.

Unfortunately, government-approved noise levels for an eight-hour day are not proven to be safe. Furthermore, for many of us, dangerously loud noise levels may not even end at work. And if you happen to work around certain chemicals (e.g., lacquer or varnish containing toluene) while exposed to high-level noise, you have a significantly increased risk for hearing loss.

Noise holds a certain "prestige" for some. "Manly" men who model themselves after the character Tim Allen played on his TV show are proud to show off their latest power mowers (105 dB), sandblasters (110 dB), power drills (115 dB), or chain saws that can V-cut right into the hardest knot of an oak tree (135 dB)!

Recreational "boy toys" (yes, and "girl toys," too) range from snowmobiles (110 dB) to rifles and guns (120 to 140 dB). Then there are those kids with boom boxes (better identified as "bomb boxes") in their cars. The average continuous output of these devices exceeds 120 dB; these kids' window-rattling "music" will surely come back to haunt them one day.

Because women aren't typically exposed to as much noise as men, they may think they're safe from noise hazards. Not so. That sweet bundle of joy sleeping peacefully in your arms is capable of hurling cries at 120-plus dB. The toys that accompany such bundles can put not only children but also caretakers at risk.

Every year, children's toys are removed from the market because of their intolerably dangerous noise levels. Some peaks reach 150 dB. Despite the watchful eye of OSHA,

Noise Levels

dBA*	NOISE SOURCE
190 ...	105mm howitzer
170 ...	deployed auto airbag
163 ...	bazooka at one foot
155 ...	assault rifles 13 feet from the muzzle
150 ...	child's toy mimicking an assault rifle
145 ...	U.S. Army Sergeant missile at 100 feet
140 ...	threshold of pain; military assault rifle; toy cap gun; siren at 100 feet
135 ...	U.S. Army tactical launcher at 400 feet; jet taking off; child's voice-amplified toy; amplified music
130 ...	miniature rifles; air-raid siren
125 ...	child's toy phone
120 ...	threshold of discomfort; auto horn; chain saw; jackhammer; snowmobile (driver's seat); child's musical instruments
110 ...	MRI (at head location in the isocenter); inboard motorboat; sandblaster; baby rattle; films in movie theaters
105 ...	power saw; helicopter
100 ...	subway train; tractor; farm equipment
95 ...	ride in a convertible car on freeway
90 ...	industrial noise
80 ...	live piano music
70 ...	dog bark
60 ...	vacuum cleaner
50 ...	conversation; some vowels in conversation
40 ...	soft music
30 ...	some high-frequency consonants
20 ...	dripping water
10 ...	soft whisper
5 ...	soft rustling leaves
0 ...	the best hearing threshold

* Sound pressure levels as measured on the A scale.

This table was compiled by the author from a variety of scientific sources.

are exceeded every day throughout U.S. industry. I've been in paper mills and factories where hard hats and earplugs are required upon entry.

The workers' biggest complaint about hearing protection is that they can't hear one another or potentially lifesaving warnings, like backup signals of heavy equipment. With good some toys sneak through, even by brand-name companies we've come to trust.

A couple of years ago, one toy manufacturer's trendy slogan flashed through our industry like a thunderbolt: "Play It Loud." After much opposition from the hearing industry, this company backed down and eliminated the banner line. Yet, toy cellular telephones and walkie-talkies at clearly hazardous levels are still marketed to our children.

Although the polls say that women continue to shoulder the load when it comes to housework, heavy cleaning can be an equal-opportunity noise hazard. A manufacturer once put a quiet vacuum cleaner on the market, a product that was proven to be as effective as its competition. It died quietly in stores throughout the country. Consumers didn't believe it; noise is equated with power and effectiveness. We like it loud!

A front-row seat at a rock concert or in a bar with a live band can easily carry acoustic peaks exceeding 130 dB. This sound level can wreak the same results as excessive drinking: nausea and vomiting.

With the advent of CD-quality TVs, stereos, telephones, and the like, the tremendous enhancement in fidelity requires less volume. Improved signal-to-noise ratios produce less internal noise; however, we still demand louder volume levels. The problem is that we've grown accustomed to it, and the misperception that "louder is better" persists.

Current statistics suggest that about a third of all hearing loss is attributable to noise. From health club fitness classes, where bombardment of music is maintained at 110 dB for 30 minutes or more, to movie theaters that exceed 130 dB (actually replicating the sound pressure level of a gun!), you as a willing participant are at risk. In a sure sign of progress, the associations for both these groups, The International Association of Fitness Professionals and the National Association of Theater Owners, are at long last recommending sound-level reductions, indicating that maybe "softer is better."

We all differ in our sensitivities. Some people have a more highly developed sense of smell, taste, vision, touch, or hearing. While there may be established norms, individual variability can be great. Some people with more acute hearing have an increased susceptibility to noise-induced hearing loss. Research data have shown that people with light-colored eyes (vs. dark eyes) run an increased risk of hearing loss when around high-level noise.

Furthermore, *The Lancet* (Jan. 2, 1999) reported on a French study among 1,208 men aged 18 to 24. They found that those who had regularly used personal stereo headsets for at least an hour daily and who also had a history of ear infections had significantly greater incidence of hearing loss.

Permanent, irreversible, instantaneous hearing loss occurs every day. Acoustic trauma is inflicted upon people in seemingly innocuous situations such as air-bag deployment, where sound-pressure levels can reach 170 dB. An estimated 30 million construction workers are at risk. Many airport workers are losing their hearing. And data now implicate MRIs as a factor in hearing loss, a situation that can be solved by wearing earplugs during the test. Dentists and dental hygienists are at risk due to daily exposure to dental equipment such as blasters, drills, ultrasonic scalers, and so forth.

This is to name but a few of the culprits.

What are we doing to ourselves? While we don't have to buy products that emit toxic noise, sometimes we cannot escape, it, particularly when the noise is part of the work environment. Most of us can't just quit our jobs, but we can influence change.

Writing letters to manufacturers can make a difference. Professionals who use equipment with high noise levels (like dentists) must exert pressure on their suppliers. If we simply stopped purchasing their goods, manufacturers would respond accordingly. Nearly all products have noise reduction capability.

As parents, we must not support toy manufacturers that place our kids at risk. Stop buying their toys.

It has been said that one letter of complaint represents a hundred voices. Write one. When enough of us do, manufacturers will listen. Complain to theater managers and workout instructors. Noise will come down.

One person can make a difference. But in today's world, you may need to shout to be heard.

Richard Carmen, Au.D., FAAA, is a clinical audiologist and editor of the book *The Consumer Handbook on Hearing Loss & Hearing Aids: A Bridge to Healing*. His article appeared originally in *Hearing Health* magazine.

PAIN AND ITS MYSTERIES

Genetic and psychological factors help determine how well we withstand it

BY MARNI JACKSON

I was riding a bike in the Rockies, near Banff, when a bee flew into my mouth, and I felt a slim, unambiguous lance of pain, like a splinter of glass. Right away, I noticed, this sensation began to sprout a narrative. It wasn't just bad luck that the bee had stumbled into me; I saw the sting as punishment for biking "the wrong way"—distracted, churning along too fast, panting with open mouth. I had not been paying attention. Then pain had come along and rinsed the morning clear of small deceptions.

The next day, apart from having fabulous Angelina Jolie lips, I was back to normal. Unlike the chronic ache of arthritis or the lightning stab of trigeminal neuralgia, a bee sting is a wonderfully minor, finite form of pain. But the experience had nevertheless raised a swarm of questions about the mysterious nature of pain, and our relationship to it. For instance, why do we still talk about mental pain versus physical pain, when pain is always an emotional experience? How has it come about that something so universal remains so poorly understood, especially in an age of relentless self-scrutiny? And why hasn't anyone noticed the embarrassing fact that science is about to clone a human being, but it still can't cure the pain of a bad back?

The U.S. National Pain Foundation says more than four out of 10

American adults experience pain every day. The situation is likely much the same in Canada. North Americans consume four tons of ASA, a year, while chronic pain is on the rise. It's almost as if pain flourishes on our diet of analgesics. And it seems the more science learns how pain behaves (a quantum leap in the last 50 years), the less doctors want to do to treat it. To try to understand how we got ourselves in this pickle, I embarked on a four-year inquiry that zigzagged between art and science, doctor and patient. I talked to pain experts, and people who have learned to live with chronic pain. I tried to integrate the migrainish portrait of pain in Emily Dickinson's poetry or Virginia Woolf's novels with the latest MRI images of pain in the brain. I went back into the history of ideas about pain, where I encountered eccentric thinkers and unsung heroes, and forward into the genetic research into pain—where, once again, I ran into bees.

The inability to feel any pain at all is something that is inherited. Imagine: no hangovers, no sore pitching arm, no tremors in the dentist's chair. But congenital analgesia (as it's known) turns out to be both a nuisance and a life-threatening peril. Dr. Ron Melzack of McGill Univer-

sity and his British colleague, Dr. Patrick Wall—the two researchers whose "gate-control theory" revolutionized the way science now views pain—describe the consequences of a pain free life in their classic study, *The Challenge of Pain*. One girl with this condition suffered third-degree burns on her knees after climbing up on a hot radiator. And because there was no discomfort to let her know when she should shift her weight or posture, she eventually developed an inflammation in her joints and died at the age of 29.

Be glad it hurts when you stub your toe, because pain plays a vital role in our lives

Another woman with congenital analgesia felt nothing but a "funny, feathery feeling" when she delivered the first of her two children. But one of the best known examples of this rare inherited disorder was an American vaudeville performer in the 1920s, Edward H. Gibson, known as the Human Pincushion. His act involved sticking 50 to 60 pins into his body and then slowly removing them. It seems that for those born incapable of feeling pain, the career options are narrow, and life is short. Be glad it hurts when you stub your toe, because pain plays a vital, protective role in our lives.

Congenital analgesia is at the far end of a wide spectrum of inherited pain disorders. Genetic factors are involved in 39 to 55 per cent of migraines, 55 per cent of menstrual pain, and half of the back-pain population. Gender also has an influence, which will come as a surprise to no one. Men appear to suffer less pain, but require more pain relievers. There's no proof that women tolerate pain better than men, but they are three times more likely to suffer migraines, and six times more vulnerable to fibromyalgia. In a 1999 Gallup survey, 46 per cent of American women said they felt daily pain, compared to 37 per cent of men. And whether it's gene-related or stiletto-induced, one in four women also reported that their feet hurt.

"For a long time, people have accepted that there are wide variations in the way people respond to pain or to analgesics, but no one ever seriously considered attributing it to genetics, until now."

I was talking to Jeff Mogil, the first person in the world to put together training in psychology, genetics and pain. Mogil studied under psychologist and pain science pioneer John Liebeskind in California. After postdoctoral training in genetics, he joined the faculty at the University of Illinois in 1996. In 2001, Melzack lured him up to McGill University, where Mogil has succeeded him as the E. P. Taylor professor of pain research in psychology. This suggests that the pendulum is swinging back: science has moved away from seeing pain as a slippery psychological interpretation of something that only happens to the body, to approaching it as an experience that is at once neural, emotional and deeply rooted in our cells and genes.

"Pain genetics is where all the action is now, but it was a totally empty field when I moved into it," says Mogil, who is 35. "Nobody thought that pain had anything to do

with genes. But then other people started working with knock-out mice, figuring out what happens when you remove this or that protein from a gene, and now knock-out mice are everywhere."

"Knock-out mice" always sounded to me like something you could order by the dozen at 3 a.m., from an infomercial. The sea monkeys of science. These mice are bred to lack a particular gene, and the protein it produces. "Then you look for what's wrong with the knock-out mouse when it doesn't have this or that protein any more," said Mogil. "It's the hottest technique in biology right now, and in pain research, too." It used to be that scientists didn't concern themselves with whatever strain of mouse they used in their studies, he added. But with knock-out mice "they discovered that the genetic background of the mouse was affecting their outcomes. It turned out that I was the only person paying attention to this sort of information."

When it comes to pain, he found, there is no such thing as a "universal rat." Pain sensitivity varies widely from strain to strain of rats and mice. Mogil also discovered that some mice are born either "doubly unlucky"—both over-sensitive to pain and under-responsive to analgesics—or vice versa, the lucky ones who feel less pain and require less painkiller.

"What the study of knock-out mice means for humans," Mogil said, "is that it helps explain individual sensitivities to pain and to drugs, as well as the fact that while most people will recover from an injury, some five per cent won't. They'll go on to develop chronic pain. Obviously, the factors that determine this are both environmental and genetic, and it's very tricky to sort these out. But if we know that some people have a propensity to chronic pain, then we might be able to find ways to keep it from developing in the first place. And as we learn more about pharmacogenetics, we can target their treatment with more precision. It also means that people who com-

plain more about pain aren't necessarily whiners—they may actually feel more than other people. If humans really are like mice, then roughly half of that variability in pain response is due to their inherited genes."

Mogil has also studied the variety of ways people respond to painkillers. Indeed, the world seems to be divided into "responders" and "nonresponders," since morphine is only successful with about 65 per cent of the population. This explains why pain doctors have to fiddle with a variety of pain medications before they get it right. Among Caucasians, about seven to 10 per cent are known as "poor metabolizers" who won't respond to codeine. They end up getting all the side effects, but none of the pain relief.

I asked Mogil whether this news would encourage more magic-bullet thinking—the notion that we can simply zero in on these "pain genes," knock them out, and throw away the Tylenol.

Genes don't work like that, he replied. "Just as there is no pain centre, there is no single pain gene that controls it. But it doesn't look like there's a hundred of them either. We're looking for a particular type of gene that exists in different forms that can be inherited—and of those genes, there are five to 10, maybe 20 tops."

But people are so eager to blame their genes for everything now, I said. Doesn't this new focus on the genetic aspect downplay the way cultural, political and social forces shape our perception of pain?

"But that's the thing about pain—the cortical stuff is really, really important," he said. Mogil automatically translates the word "culture" as "cortical activity," but I got his drift. He was referring to the emotions, ideas and attitudes that are the result of our memory, learning, and experience. And in Melzack and Wall's gate-control theory of pain, it is the "cortical stuff" that descends to the spinal cord, amplifying or muting the pain signals coming in from the periphery of the body. In other words sensory data travels up; "culture" moves down. And for both Mogil and Melzack, "everything is equally biological."

Melding neuroscience and psychology, Mogil (like Melzack before him) seems to be describing culture not as something "out there" but embodied in the way the brain shapes our experience of pain. It's interesting, I said to Mogil, that he and Melzack are both psychologists, sometimes seen as low men on the totem pole when the hard-science boys get together.

"Pain *is* psychological," Mogil emphasized. "There's all this neural activity going on, but it can always be trumped by culture, attitudes and behaviour. Being a psychologist lets me do work with a high level of variability in my tests. Most scientists don't want to see variability in their results. They're looking for consistency. But I get happy when I see messy data."

Then the bee came back into the picture. It turns out that pain researchers will sometimes use bee venom to induce what Ron Melzack calls a "good, classic pain, the type we can learn a lot from." Although bee venom has a long list of active ingredients, the main toxin is a peptide called melittin. This can produce chemicals known as cytokines that play an important role in painkilling.

(Tests on beekeepers who have been stung repeatedly have revealed elevated levels of cytokines.) In fact, bee venom has been popular in treating the pain of arthritis for centuries, especially in Europe. Now it's also being touted as helpful therapy for autoimmune conditions like multiple sclerosis, and a protective agent against X-irridiation in cancer patients. The alternative-network literature for BVT (bee venom therapy) is vast, and that's only one aspect of apitherapy, which uses everything from bee pollen, royal jelly and honey to the wax and venom to treat an array of disorders.

So my original suspicion that a bee sting is a complicated thing was not entirely off-base. It turns out that everything involved in the orchestration of the event we call pain—the swelling, inflammation, redness, heat and stinging sensation—may, under different, controlled circumstances, also offer pain relief. In other words, better pain treatment may not lie in our efforts to suppress it or surgically excise it, but in a deeper understanding of how the body can use aspects of the pain process to promote healing and recovery. The answer to pain may lie inside pain itself.

As science looks beyond the role of pain as symptom, its hidden narrative will continue to unfold. If Jeff Mogil is right, 50 years from now we will look at pain quite differently. Tylenol tablets will seem as quaint to us as sarsaparilla tonic. Instead, we'll take our ID bracelet to the local pharmacologist to order some bespoke analgesics, tailored to gender and genotype. Some of us may rise at 4 a.m. to meditate, and feel the struggle against pain lighten. We'll carry geno-cards that list our inherited predispositions: photosensitivity, osteoporosis and poor response to codeine.

Addiction might be redefined not as a character flaw but as "biochemical deficit management." Medical schools will actually teach doctors about the way pain behaves, and how to treat it. Our emotional habits will become an accepted factor of good health, and we'll know whether we're at risk for depression or rheumatoid arthritis in the same way we know that we're Scottish, or hazel-eyed. How we live with this new information, of course, will still be our choice. But we will understand that pain is sometimes history, in the body.

Adapted from Pain: The Fifth Vital Sign *by Marni Jackson. Copyright 2002 Marni Jackson. Reproduced by permission of the publisher, Random House Canada.*

Brains in Dreamland

Scientists hope to raise the neural curtain on sleep's virtual theater

By BRUCE BOWER

After his father's death in 1896, Viennese neurologist Sigmund Freud made a momentous career change. He decided to study the mind instead of the brain. Freud began by probing his own mind. Intrigued by his conflicted feelings toward his late father, the scientist analyzed his own dreams, slips of the tongue, childhood memories, and episodes of forgetfulness.

Freud's efforts culminated in the 1900 publication of *The Interpretation of Dreams*. In that book, he depicted dreams as symbolic stories in which sleepers' unconscious sexual and aggressive desires play out in disguised forms.

Later in his life, Freud acknowledged that dreams don't always gratify wishes. For instance, he noted that some dreams represent attempts to master a past traumatic experience. Yet the father of psychoanalysis always held that dreams contain both surface events and subterranean themes of great personal importance. For that reason, he wrote, "the interpretation of dreams is the royal road to a knowledge of the unconscious activities of the mind."

Freud's theory of how dreams work has had a huge cultural impact over the past century, even as it attracted intense criticism. Now, brain scientists—members of the discipline that Freud left behind—have stepped to the forefront of this passionate dream dispute.

One prominent group of scientists asserts that Freud profoundly misunderstood dreams. In their view, the act of dreaming yields a guileless collage of strange but heartfelt images that carry no hidden meanings.

These scientists say that dreaming occurs when a primitive structure called the brain stem stirs up strong emotions, espe-cially anxiety, elation, and anger. At the same time, neural gateways to the external world shut down, as do centers of memory and rational thought. The brain then creates bizarre, internal visions that strongly resonate for the dreamer.

An opposing view corresponds in many ways to Freud's ideas. Its supporters portray dreams as products of a complex frontal-brain system that seeks out objects of intense interest or desire. When provoked during sleep, this brain system depicts deep-seated goals in veiled ways so as not to rouse the dreamer.

A third group of investigators regards the brain data as intriguing but inconclusive. Dreams may serve any of a variety of functions, they argue. Depending on the society, these uses include simulating potential threats, grappling with personal and community problems, sparking artistic creativity, and diagnosing and healing physical illnesses.

"It is striking that 100 years after Freud [published *The Interpretation of Dreams*], there is absolutely no agreement as to the nature of, function of, or brain mechanism underlying dreaming," says neuroscientist Robert Stickgold of Harvard Medical School in Boston.

A broad consensus exists on one point, though. If neuroscientists hope to understand the vexing relationship of brain and mind, they need to get a handle on dreams.

Freud's royal road to the unconscious looks like a scientific dead-end to psychiatrist J. Allan Hobson. Neuroscientific evidence indicates that the sleeping brain churns out dreams as an afterthought to its other duties, argue Hobson, Stickgold, and Edward F. Pace-Schott, also of Harvard Medical School.

"Unconscious wishes play little or no part in dream instigation, dream emotion is uncensored and undisguised, sleep is not protected by dreaming, and dream interpretation has no scientific status," Hobson says.

Hobson's assault on Freudian dream theory began more than a decade ago. At that time, he proposed that dreams result from random bursts of activity in a brain stem area that regulates breathing and other basic bodily functions. These brain stem blasts zip to the frontal brain during periods of rapid eye movement (REM) sleep, when the entire brain becomes nearly as active as when a person is awake.

Dreams most often occur during REM sleep. A slumbering individual enters REM sleep about every 90 minutes.

Hobson's group published a revision of this theory in the December 2000 BEHAVIORAL AND BRAIN SCIENCES. Their new approach grants that dreams harbor emotional significance, but not in the way Freud posited.

Brain imaging and sleep-laboratory data clearly delineate among wakefulness, REM sleep, and non-REM sleep, the Harvard scientists note.

Three essential processes during REM sleep make it the prime time for dreaming, they say. First, brain stem activity surges and sets off responses in emotional and visual parts of the brain. Second, brain regions that handle sensations from the outside world, control movement, and carry out logical analysis shut down. Third, brain stem cells pump out acetylcholine, a chemical messenger that jacks up activity in emotional centers.

At the same time, two neurotransmitters essential for waking activity—noradrenaline and serotonin—take a snooze.

The result, in Hobson's view: a vivid hallucination, informed by strong emotions, that takes bizarre twists and turns. REM sleep's biological makeup fosters the mistaken belief that one is awake while dreaming, saps the ability to reflect on the weirdness of dreams as they occur, and makes it difficult to recall dreams after waking up.

REM sleep conducts far more important business than dreaming, Hobson argues. Its central functions may include supporting brain development, regulating body temperature, fortifying the immune system, and fostering memories of recently learned information. The last possibility evokes heated scientific debate (SN: 7/22/00, p. 55).

Hobson's theoretical focus on brain stems and REMs doesn't do dreams justice, argues neuropsychologist Mark Solms of St. Bartholomew's and Royal London (England) School of Medicine.

"Dreaming is generated under the direction of a highly motivated, wishful state of mind," Solms holds. "I won't be at all surprised if we find that Freud's understanding of [dream] mechanisms was basically on the right track."

To dream, the brain—both in and out of REM sleep—stimulates a frontal-lobe system that orchestrates motivation and the pursuit of goals and cravings, the British scientist proposes. A neurotransmitter called dopamine ferries messages in the brain's motivation system.

The crux of Solms' argument rests on studies of brain-damaged patients. In rare instances where people incur injuries only to their brain stem, dreaming continues despite severe disruptions of REM sleep. In contrast, people who suffer damage to frontal-brain regions involved in motivation report that they no longer dream but still have nightly REM sleep. These individuals also become apathetic and lose much of their initiative, imagination, and ability to plan. This group includes several hundred mental patients who decades ago, as a therapy, had some of their frontal-brain nerve fibers surgically cut.

Additional support for Solms' view comes from brain-imaging studies indicating that frontal areas involved in motivation, emotion, and memory exhibit elevated activity during REM sleep.

Various forms of cerebral activation can trigger the motivation system and lead to dreaming, Solms suggests. This explains why vivid dreams occur shortly after falling asleep and in the morning, not just in the depths of REM sleep, he says.

Brain data can't yet confirm or disprove Freud's idea that dreams play a symbolic game of hide-and-seek with unconscious desires, Solms adds.

For now, something of a standoff exists between the dreaming-brain theories of Hobson and Solms.

Hobson and his coworkers welcome the possibility, raised by neuroscientist Tore A. Nielsen of the University of Montreal, that crucial elements of REM sleep operate in non-REM states as well. For instance, as people fall asleep they display slow eye movements and electrical activity in the brain and muscles that may constitute a kind of "covert REM activity," Nielsen says.

If the REM state in one form or another saturates much of sleep, then the brain stem and related emotional centers create dreams throughout the night, Hobson asserts.

Solms regards "covert REM" as a hazy concept. REM sleep consists of diverse physiological changes in the brain and body. This sleep stage can't be equated with a few of its biological components that may appear at other times during the night, he contends.

Haziness also afflicts attempts to decipher dreams with recordings of brain activity, remarks neuroscientist Allen Braun of the National Institutes of Health in Bethesda, Md. These images of neural tissue show where the brain is stirring during specific sleep stages, Braun says, but not how those areas operate or whether they play a direct role in dreaming.

Brain-imaging reports generally support Solms' theory that dreams derive from a frontal-brain motivation system, Braun notes (SN: 1/17/98, p. 44). However, a frontal-brain area considered pivotal for self-monitoring and abstract thought naps throughout sleep. Braun considers this finding to clash with the Freudian notion of dreams as hotbeds of disguised meaning.

Freud's emphasis on wish fulfillment in dreams needs revision too, according to neuroscientist Antti Revonsuo of the University of Turku in Finland. Dreaming instead enables people to simulate threatening events so that they can rehearse ways to either deal with or avoid them, Revonsuo theorizes.

Threatening incidents of various kinds and degrees frequently appear in the dream reports of adults and children around the world, the Finnish scientist says. They also show up in descriptions of recurrent dreams, nightmares, and post-traumatic dreams.

Hunter-gatherer populations, such as the Mehinaku Indians in Brazil, report many dreams about threatening events, he adds. Mehinaku men's dreams range from fending off an attacking jaguar to dealing with an angry wife.

Revensuo's theory faces threats of its own, though. Evidence from contemporary hunter-gatherers indicates that dreaming functions in a variety of ways, argues psychologist Harry T. Hunt of Brock University in St. Catharines, Ontario. Members of these groups generally view dreams as real events in which a person's soul carries out activities while the person sleeps.

Hunter-gatherers' dreams sometimes depict encounters with supernatural beings who provide guidance in pressing community matters, aid in healing physical illnesses, or give information about the future, Hunt says. Individuals who are adept at manipulating their own conscious states may engage in lucid dreaming, in which the dreamer reasons clearly, remembers the conditions of waking life, and acts according to a predetermined plan.

Dreaming represents a basic orienting response of the brain to novel information, ideas, and situations, Hunt proposes. It occurs at varying intensities in different conscious states, including REM sleep, bouts of reverie or daydreaming, and episodes of spirit possession that individuals in some cultures enter while awake (SN: 2/17/01, p. 104).

Scientists, musicians, inventors, artists, and writers often use dreaming of one kind or another to solve problems and spark creativity, Hunt notes.

Whatever purposes dreaming serves, Hobson's group and many other researchers underestimate the extent to which the brain tunes in to the external world during sleep, says neuroscientist Chiara M. Portas of University College London. Several studies indicate that sensory areas of the brain respond to relevant sounds and other sensations during REM and non-REM sleep.

No conclusive results support any theory of dreaming or sleep, in her view.

Ironically, dreams are attracting growing scientific interest as they fade into the background of modern life. Artificial lighting and society's focus on daytime achievements have fueled this trend (SN: 9/25/99, p. 205).

Sleep now typically occurs in single chunks of 7 hours or less. Yet as recently as 200 years ago in Europe, people slept in two nightly phases of 4 to 5 hours each. Shortly after midnight, individuals awoke for 1 to 2 hours and frequently reflected on their dreams or talked about them with others.

Well before Freud's time, Europeans prized dreams for their personal insights, and particularly for what they revealed about a dreamer's relationship with God, says historian A. Roger Ekirch of Virginia Polytechnic Institute and State University in Blacksburg.

Organizing sleep into two segments encouraged people to remember dreams and to use them as paths to self-discovery, Ekirch contended in the April AMERICAN HISTORICAL REVIEW.

Dreams have lost their allure even for the psychoanalytic theorists and clinicians who are the heirs to Freud's ideas, remarks Paul Lippmann of the William Alanson White Psychoanalytic Institute in Stockbridge, Mass. These days, psychoanalysts show far more interest in dissecting the emotional nature of their dealings with patients than in eliciting and interpreting dreams, according to Lippmann, himself a psychoanalytic clinician.

Like Ekirch, Lippmann suspects that modern culture has eroded interest in dreaming. "The American Dream has little room for the nighttime variety," he said in the Fall 2000 PSYCHOANALYTIC PSYCHOLOGY.

Yet many neuroscientists seem determined to swim against that cultural tide. Even the researchers who see little psychological significance in sleep's visions want to explain how and why the brain produces them.

They can dream, can't they?

UNIT 4
Learning and Remembering

Unit Selections

Key Points to Consider

- What is implicit learning? Can you give some examples of information or behaviors that you learned implicitly this week? How does implicit learning differ from intentional learning? Which do you think is more important—implicit learning or intentional learning?

- What is a reward? What is punishment? Why is it better to reward than punish behaviors? Do most American parents use spanking to alter their child's behavior? Do you think spanking a child is the best recourse? What are some of the side effects of using spanking to modify children's behaviors?

- Why is memory important? What is forgetting? Why do psychologists want to know about the various mechanisms that underlie learning and remembering? To what use can we put this information? Why do we forget? Are there methods we can use to improve memory? What are they; can you give an example of each?

- What types of memory lapses are normal? What memory mistakes signal problems?

- What are the seven sins of memory? Can you provide an example of each? What role does biology play in remembering, if any?

- How do our minds play memory tricks on us? What are some of the ways we alter material so as to remember it differently? Can you provide concrete examples of some of the memory games that affect us?

 **Links: www.dushkin.com/online/**
These sites are annotated in the World Wide Web pages.

Mind Tools
   http://www.psychwww.com/mtsite/
The Opportunity of Adolescence
   http://www.winternet.com/~webpage/adolescencepaper.html
Project Zero
   http://pzweb.harvard.edu

Do you remember your first week of classes at college? There were so many new buildings and so many people's names to remember. And you had to recall accurately where all your classes were as well as your professors' names. Just remembering your class schedule was problematic enough. For those of you who lived in residence halls, the difficulties multiplied. You had to remember where your residence was, recall the names of individuals living on your floor, and learn how to navigate from your room to other places on campus, such as the dining halls and library. Then came examination time. Did you ever think you would survive college exams? The material, in terms of difficulty level and amount, was perhaps more than you thought you could manage.

What a stressful time you experienced when you first came to campus! Much of what created the stress was the strain on your learning and memory systems, two complicated processes unto themselves. Indeed, most of you survived just fine and with your memories, learning strategies, and mental health intact.

Two of the processes you depended on when you first came to college are the processes of learning and memorizing, some of the oldest psychological processes studied by psychologists. Today, with their sophisticated experimental techniques, psychologists have distinguished several types of memory processes and have discovered what makes learning more complete so that subsequent memory is more accurate. We also have discovered that humans aren't the only organisms capable of these processes. All types of animals can learn, even if the organism is as simple as an earthworm or amoebae.

Psychologists know, too, that rote learning and practice are not the only forms of learning. For instance, at this point in time in your introductory psychology class, you might be studying operant and classical conditioning, two very simple but nonetheless important forms of learning of which both humans and simple organisms are capable. Both types of conditioning can occur without our awareness or active participation in them. The articles in this unit examine the processes of learning and remembering (or its reciprocal, forgetting) in some detail.

The authors of the first article examine implicit learning, learning that takes place without our awareness. This type of learning is important to understand because it accounts for a large amount of our knowledge base. Peter Frensch and Dennis Runger, the authors, discuss the mechanisms that likely underlie this learning.

In "New Evidence for the Benefits of Never Spanking," learning is again examined. However, one specific form of learning, childhood behavior change, is emphasized. The author discusses the ramifications of the use of spanking (punishment) by parents and concludes that this might not always be the best tactic for developing cooperative, well-behaved children.

We next turn our attention to memory, because once something is learned, it needs to be remembered to be useful. In "The Seven Sins of Memory: How the Mind Forgets and Remembers," Daniel Schacter discusses common memory problems and what causes them. He also elucidates several memory techniques from which we can all benefit, even if we don't have serious memory disorders such as Alzheimer's disease, which he also mentions.

The final selection of this unit describes how memory plays "tricks" on us. There are a variety of "games" that our minds play, including blocking, misattribution, and persistence that cause memory distortion. Sharon Begley, the author, provides some good examples, too; for instance a divorcing couple remembers only the bad times together, not the good.

Article 12

Implicit Learning

Peter A. Frensch[1] and Dennis Rünger
Department of Psychology, Humboldt University, Berlin, Germany

Abstract
Implicit learning appears to be a fundamental and ubiquitous process in cognition. Although defining and operationalizing implicit learning remains a central theoretical challenge, scientists' understanding of implicit learning has progressed significantly. Beyond establishing the existence of "learning without awareness," current research seeks to identify the cognitive processes that support implicit learning and addresses the relationship between learning and awareness of what was learned. The emerging view of implicit learning emphasizes the role of associative learning mechanisms that exploit statistical dependencies in the environment in order to generate highly specific knowledge representations.

Keywords
cognitive psychology; learning; consciousness; awareness

Have you ever wondered why it is that you can speak your native language so well without making any grammatical errors although you do not know many of the grammatical rules you follow? Have you ever wondered how it is that you can walk properly although you cannot describe the rules of mechanics your body must certainly follow? These two examples point to an important human property, namely, the ability to adapt to environmental constraints—to learn—in the absence of any knowledge about how the adaptation is achieved. *Implicit learning*—laxly defined as learning without awareness—is seemingly ubiquitous in everyday life.

In this article, we try to provide an overview of the difficulties research on implicit learning has been facing and of the advances that have been made in scientists' understanding of the concept. More specifically, we discuss three separate issues. First, we address what is meant by implicit learning and how the concept has been empirically approached in the recent past. Second, we summarize what is currently known with some certainty about the cognitive processes underlying implicit learning and the mental representations that are acquired through it. Third, we discuss some of the most important current topics of investigation.

DEFINITION AND OPERATIONALIZATION

The one basic theoretical issue that reigns supreme among the difficulties facing researchers concerns the definition and operationalization of implicit learning. Although it seems clear that implicit learning needs to be viewed in opposition to learning that is not implicit (often called explicit, hypothesis-driven learning), it has so far proven extremely difficult to provide a satisfactory definition of implicit learning. At least a dozen different definitions have been offered in the field.

One important consequence of the heterogeneity of definitions is that different researchers have operationalized implicit learning in different ways. For example, Arthur Reber, whose early work in the 1960s rekindled interest in implicit learning, has done most of his empirical work with artificial-grammar-learning tasks. In these tasks, participants are asked to memorize a set of letter strings, such as "XXRTRXV" and "QQWMWQP," that are, unbeknownst to the participants, generated by some rules. After the memorization phase, participants are told that the strings they memorized followed certain rules, and are asked to classify new strings as grammatical (i.e., following the rules) or not. Typically, participants can perform this classification task with accuracy better than would be expected by chance, despite remaining unable to verbally describe the rules.

Thus, in a grammar-learning task, participants learn about permissible and nonpermissible combinations of letters that are presented simultaneously. By comparison, in another task often used to investigate implicit learning, the serial reaction time task (SRTT), participants learn about permissible and nonpermissible combinations of spatial locations that occur over time. In the SRTT, participants are asked to select and depress a key that matches each of the locations at which a stimulus appears on a screen. The sequence of locations at which the stimulus appears is fixed. In general, participants seem to be able to learn the sequence of spatial locations even when they are not able to verbally describe it.

Divergent definitions of implicit learning entail divergent operationalizations of the concept, but even researchers who agree in their definitions might use experimental tasks that differ in what exactly participants might learn. Therefore, it remains an open empirical issue to what extent results from a given task that has been used to probe implicit learning can be generalized to other tasks. This point leads to our first conclusion:

- *Conclusion 1.* Implicit learning of Task A is not necessarily comparable to implicit learning of Task B. Neither the properties of the learning mechanisms involved nor the acquired mental representations need be the same. It is even conceivable that implicit learning of Task A might be possible, but implicit learning of Task B might not.

THE KEY ISSUE

Regardless of how implicit learning is defined and operationalized, the key empirical issue that research needs to address is whether or not learning that is "implicit" is possible, and if it is, whether implicit learning is different from learning that is "not implicit." Many researchers have for practical reasons adopted as their definition of implicit learning "the capacity to learn without awareness of the products of learning." Thus, learning is assumed to be "implicit" when participants are unaware of what they learned. Alternatively, learning is assumed not to be implicit when participants are aware of what they learned. In other words, implicit learning is defined in terms of its product rather than the properties of the learning process.

Various measures have been proposed to assess awareness of the products of learning. The most notable measures are verbal reports and forced-choice tests (such as recognition tests).

Participants in implicit-learning experiments have consistently been shown to be able to acquire knowledge that they cannot verbally describe. This appears to be true for a wide variety of tasks, including the grammar-learning and sequence-learning tasks we described earlier. Thus, if verbal report is used to assess awareness of acquired knowledge, many experimental findings appear to support the conclusion that implicit learning is possible.

However, many authors have argued that verbal reports may have poor validity. First, it has been argued that the verbal-report

data do not pass the information criterion; that is, the information assessed by verbal recall tests is not always the same information that has led to the demonstrated learning. Second, verbal recall tests might not pass the sensitivity criterion; that is, they may not provide a level of sensitivity that is comparable to that of tests demonstrating learning in the first place. Many researchers have therefore suggested that awareness should be assessed by forced-choice tests, such as recognition tests, rather than verbal recall.

In the grammar-learning paradigm, participants are sometimes asked to complete recognition tests after they have categorized letter strings as grammatical or nongrammatical. For example, in some studies participants were asked to indicate for each letter string which particular letters they thought made the string grammatical or not. It was found that participants' markings correlated with their classification performance, suggesting at least partial awareness of the knowledge learned.

Similar findings have been obtained in studies that have used other implicit-learning paradigms. For example, after participants had completed the SRTT, they were presented sequence patterns of varying lengths in numerical form. Each sequence (e.g., 123432) denoted a series of locations on the computer screen. Participants were asked to mark patterns that they had encountered during the experiment as true and patterns that they had not seen as false. It was found that participants' recognition scores correlated with their learning scores for the SRTT. In general, many different studies using different experimental paradigms have used forced-choice tests to assess awareness of the acquired knowledge, and these studies appear not to support the existence of implicit learning.

However, it has been argued that this particular interpretation rests on the assumption that the forced-choice tests are pure assessments of awareness (i.e., are process pure). This is almost certainly not the case. Indeed, participants might choose a correct answer on a forced-choice test not because they are aware of the fact that it is the correct answer but because they rely on some intuition that they are not able to express. The growing understanding that tests are rarely process pure has fostered the use of new methodologies that are not based on this assumption. For example, Jacoby's process dissociation procedure offers a measure of awareness that is derived from experimental conditions that are believed to trigger both implicit and nonimplicit processes simultaneously. This consideration of how awareness should be assessed leads to our second conclusion:

- *Conclusion 2.* Many researchers have tried to avoid the difficult issue of how to define implicit learning and have, often without stating so explicitly, adopted the stance that implicit learning is the capacity to learn without awareness of the products of learning. However, it has become clear that the amount of support for implicit learning varies considerably with the specific measure that is selected to assess awareness of what was learned. Thus, by avoiding the issue of how to define implicit learning, researchers have introduced the problem of how to define awareness. In the end, the definitional question has not been resolved, but has merely been transferred from one concept to another.

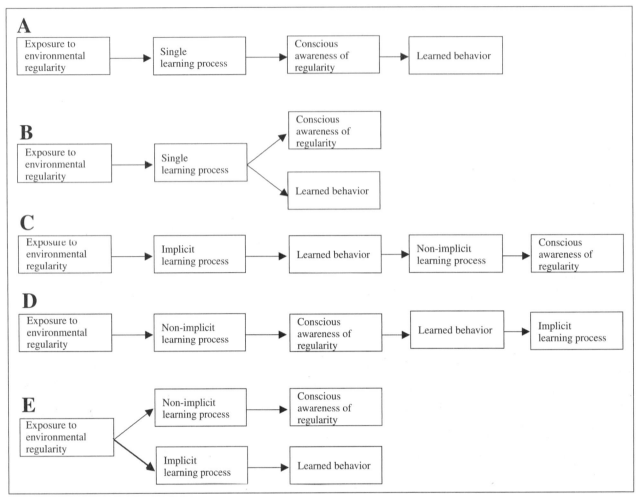

Fig. 1 Possible relations between learning and awareness of what was learned.

MECHANISMS OF LEARNING AND AWARENESS

Even when implicit learning (in the sense of learning that yields knowledge the learner is not aware of) is demonstrated conclusively, one learns little about the mechanisms underlying implicit learning. It is helpful to consider the different ways in which, in principle, learning and awareness of the products of learning might be related. Figure 1 depicts five of the many distinct possibilities that have been proposed.

First, it is, of course, conceivable that learning and awareness of what has been learned are perfectly correlated. According to this proposal, implicit learning does not exist. As is shown in Figure 1a, learning might be achieved by a single mechanism that generates memory representations a learner is always aware of.

According to the four remaining possibilities, learning and awareness need not be—but might be—perfectly correlated. According to the second possibility, depicted in Figure 1b, a single learning mechanism is assumed to create memory representations that control behavior. Some of the learned memory representations might be open to awareness; some might not be.

The last three possibilities (Figs. 1c–1e) allow for truly implicit learning. According to the third possibility, an implicit-learning mechanism might generate memory representations that control behavior. The perception of one's own behavior, in turn, might lead to nonimplicit (i.e., hypothesis-testing) learning that might generate awareness of what was learned (Fig. 1c). Under this view, the effects of implicit learning are an important trigger for nonimplicit learning. For example, a tennis player might perceive an increased accuracy of her serve. She might then conclude that the reason for this improvement is to be found in a slightly higher toss of the ball.

The fourth possibility is that nonimplicit learning might lead to awareness of what was learned, and might control behavior. The expression of behavior, in turn, might provide the input for the operation of an implicit-learning mechanism (Fig. 1d). For example, most tennis players know that solid ground strokes require a player to move toward the approaching ball instead of away from it. The conscious effort to engage in a forward movement may lead to learning within the motor systems that lies largely outside of conscious awareness.

The fifth possibility, shown in Figure 1e, is that there exist two distinct learning mechanisms, with one of the mechanisms generating memory representations that a learner is aware of, and the other mechanism generating representations that a learner is not aware of but that nevertheless control behavior.

Most of the research that has been concerned with the difference between implicit and nonimplicit learning has not addressed which possibility in Figure 1 describes the nature of implicit learning, but rather has tried to demonstrate that learning is possible in the absence of learners' awareness of the acquired knowledge. However, several attempts have been made to distinguish the two-systems hypothesis (i.e., that there are separate systems for implicit and nonimplicit learning), represented by the possibilities depicted in 1c through 1e, from the single-system hypothesis, represented by the possibilities depicted in 1a and 1b. The relative adequacy of these two hypotheses can be assessed by exploring the potentially differing influence of variables such as intention to learn, attention, age of participants, individual differences in intelligence, stimulus complexity, and task demands on learning with awareness and on learning without awareness.

For example, researchers have explored the possibility that implicit and nonimplicit learning might be differentially affected by age. With the SRTT, it has been found that implicit learning is less affected by age than is learning that is based on hypothesis testing. Indeed, implicit learning in the SRTT does not appear to begin to decline until relatively old age, and even then, the elderly display performance levels that are much closer to those of younger adults for implicit-learning tasks than for nonimplicit-learning tasks involving, for example, problem solving, reasoning, and long-term memory. On the whole, this research therefore lends some credibility to the multiple-systems view.

Also, both neuropsychological studies and neuroimaging studies have addressed the adequacy of the multiple-systems and single-system hypotheses. For example, early studies suggested that even densely amnesic patients can show near-normal implicit learning in both the grammar-learning and the sequence-learning paradigms, although they are specifically impaired on recognition and prediction tasks. More recent critical reexaminations have, however, demonstrated that amnesic patients do seem to show a deficit in implicit learning compared with normal control participants; it is therefore unclear whether or not the findings, on the whole, support the multiple-systems view.

Brain-imaging techniques have increasingly been used to study implicit learning in the SRTT. Although some results suggest that partially distinctive brain areas are involved in implicit and nonimplicit forms of learning, it is, at present, not clear whether these findings should be interpreted as evidence supporting the multiple-systems view or as evidence supporting a "single-system plus awareness" view (depicted in Fig. 1b).

Consideration of the cognitive mechanisms that might be involved in implicit learning leads to our third conclusion:

• *Conclusion 3.* Defining implicit learning with respect to awareness of the products of learning has drawn attention away from the mechanisms that are responsible for the generation of different forms of knowledge. Despite a continuously increasing amount of empirical data, the debate between multiple-systems proponents and single-system

proponents has not been settled yet. Furthermore, the question of how exactly awareness and learning might be interrelated has only recently begun to be addressed empirically.

IMPORTANT ADVANCES MADE

If one agrees with the use of verbal-report measures to assess awareness, then recent research on implicit learning has modified earlier theoretical beliefs in important ways. Earlier work had characterized implicit learning as a mechanism by which abstract knowledge of regularities that are present in the environment is acquired automatically and unintentionally by mere exposure to relevant instances. The proposal of a smart unconscious was based, to a large extent, on empirical findings with the grammar-learning task that appeared to show that participants possessed abstract knowledge about the rules of the grammar that went beyond the surface characteristics of the information encountered. This claim seemed further supported by findings indicating that implicitly acquired knowledge may transfer across modalities; for example, learning from a task involving written letters (visual stimuli) can transfer to performance in a task involving letter sounds (auditory stimuli).

This view has been challenged, however, by many recent findings. For example, it has been repeatedly shown that implicitly acquired knowledge might consist of little more than short fragments or chunks of the materials encountered in an implicit-learning situation. In the wake of these findings, neural-network models and fragment-based models that are capable of simulating a great deal of the available experimental findings have been developed. These models utilize representations of elementary stimuli in the learning situation (e.g., representations of letters in a grammar-learning task) and associations between the representations. Learning consists of a continuous, incremental change in the associative pattern that is sensitive to the statistical features of the set of items or events encountered. Thus, a representation of the implicit-learning situation that is shaped by statistical constraints gradually evolves. Although the characterization of implicitly acquired knowledge is still a matter of debate, the current trend is to assume that abstract knowledge might not be implicitly generated.

Many recent studies have explored whether implicit learning, unlike nonimplicit learning (i.e., explicit hypothesis testing), proceeds automatically, without the use of attentional resources. By far, most of these studies have used the SRTT, often manipulating the amount of attentional resources available to participants by asking them to perform the SRTT either by itself or together with a secondary task (typically a tone-counting task).

In general, it has been found that implicit learning takes place both in the presence and in the absence of a secondary task. What remains unclear, at present, is the extent to which implicit learning is affected by the attention manipulation. Some researchers argue that the secondary task interferes with task performance rather than with implicit learning proper (i.e., that the secondary task impedes the expression of what has been learned). Under this view, implicit learning does not depend on the availability of attentional resources. Others take the stance that the learning process itself is adversely affected by the presence of a secondary task and thus requires attentional resources.

On the whole, the experiments that have been conducted all suffer from the problem that attention itself is an ill-defined concept that might refer to both mental capacity and selection. In the latter sense, "attention" points to the problem of allocating cognitive resources to a specific item or event. When "attention" is used synonymously with "mental capacity," it instead refers to a limitation of cognitive resources that becomes apparent when resources have to be shared by concurrent cognitive processes. When these two factors are separately and experimentally manipulated, it appears that implicit learning occurs only when stimuli are relevant to the task and are attended to, but that implicit learning may require no or very little mental capacity.

Recent advances in researchers' understanding of implicit learning lead to our fourth conclusion:

- *Conclusion 4.* The early proposal of a smart unconscious capable of acquiring abstract knowledge in an effortless, automatic manner has been replaced recently by the assumption of one or more implicit learning mechanisms that operate mostly associatively. These mechanisms pick up statistical dependencies encountered in the environment and generate highly specific knowledge representations. It is likely that the mechanisms operate only on information that is attended to and that is relevant to the response to be made.

CONCLUSIONS

Researchers' understanding of implicit learning has come a long way. Today, many believe that implicit learning exists, and furthermore that it is based on relatively simple learning mechanisms. These mechanisms associate environmental stimuli that are attended to and that are relevant for behavior. Despite the recent advances, however, the field still suffers from a number of unresolved empirical and theoretical issues. First, there exist conflicting results regarding the role of attention in implicit learning. Second, the exact relation between learning and awareness (see Fig. 1) is very much unknown. Third, the key theoretical issue of how to define implicit learning has still not been resolved.

We strongly believe that progress on the former two (empirical) issues will be made soon and will be based on improved methodology and the joint use of computational modeling and functional brain-imaging techniques. Progress on the key theoretical issue can come, however, only from theoretical advances in understanding of the concepts of "consciousness," "awareness," and "intention." To achieve this progress might require the joint efforts of philosophers, neuroscientists, and cognitive psychologists.

Recommended reading

Berry, D.C., & Dienes, Z. (1993). *Implicit learning: Theoretical and empirical issues.* Hove, England: Erlbaum.

Cleeremans, A. (1993). *Mechanisms of implicit learning: Connectionist models of sequence processing.* Cambridge, MA: MIT Press.

Reber, A.S. (1993). *Implicit learning and tacit knowledge: An essay on the cognitive unconscious.* New York: Oxford University Press.

Stadler, M.A., & Frensch, P.A. (Eds.). (1998). *Handbook of implicit learning.* Thousand Oaks, CA: Sage.

Note

1. Address correspondence to Peter A. Frensch, Department of Psychology, Humboldt University, Hausvogteiplatz 5-7, D-10177 Berlin, Germany; e-mail: peter.frensch@psychologie. hu-berlin.de.

From *Current Directions in Psychological Science*, February 2003, pp. 13-18. © 2003 by Blackwell Publishing Ltd., Oxford, UK. Reprinted by permission.

Social Science and Public Policy

NEW EVIDENCE FOR THE BENEFITS OF NEVER SPANKING

Murray A. Straus

Virtually a revolution has occurred in the last four years in the state of scientific knowledge about the long-term effects of corporal punishment. This article summarizes the results of that research and explains why the new research shows, more clearly than ever before, the benefits of avoiding corporal punishment.

Somewhat ironically, at the same time as these new studies were appearing, voices arose in state legislatures, the mass media, and in social science journals to defend corporal punishment. Consequently, a second purpose is to put these recent defenses of corporal punishment in perspective.

This is followed by a section explaining a paradox concerning trends in corporal punishment. Public belief in the necessity of corporal punishment and the percentage of parents who hit teenagers is about half of what it was only 30 years ago. Despite these dramatic changes, 94 percent of parents of toddlers in a recent national survey reported spanking, which is about the same as it was in 1975 (Straus and Stewart, 1999).

The article concludes with an estimate of the benefits to children, to parents, and to society as a whole that could occur if corporal punishment were to cease.

Defenders of corporal punishment say or imply that no-corporal punishment is the same as no-discipline or "permissiveness." Consequently, before discussing the new research, it is important to emphasize that no-corporal punishment does not mean no-discipline. Writers and organizations leading the movement away from corporal

punishment believe that rules and discipline are necessary, but that they will be *more* effective without corporal punishment. Their goal is to inform parents about these more effective disciplinary strategies, as exemplified in the very name of one such organization—the Center for Effective Discipline (see their web site: *http://www.stophitting.com;* see also the web site of Positive Parenting program *http://parenting.umn.edu*).

Previous Research on Corporal Punishment

In order to grasp the importance of the new research, the limitations of the previous 45 years of research need to be understood. These 45 years saw the publication of more than 80 studies linking corporal punishment to child behavior problems such as physical violence. A meta-analysis of these studies by Gershoff (in press) found that almost all showed that the more corporal punishment a child had experienced, the worse the behavior of the child. Gershoff's review reveals a consistency of findings that is rare in social science research. Thompson concluded that "Although... corporal punishment does secure children's immediate compliance, it also increases the likelihood of eleven [types of] negative outcomes [such as increased physical aggression by the child and depression later in life]. Moreover, even studies conducted by defenders of corporal punishment show that, even when the criterion is immediate compliance, non-corporal discipline strategies work just as well as corporal punishment.

The studies in my book *Beating the Devil Out of Them* are examples of the type of negative outcome reviewed by Thompson. For example, the more corporal punishment experienced, the greater the probability of hitting a wife or husband later in life. Another study of kindergarten children used data on corporal punishment obtained by interviews with the mothers of the children. Six months later the children were observed in school. Instances of physical aggression were tallied for each child. The children of mothers who used corporal punishment attacked other children twice as often as the children whose mothers did not. The children of mothers who went beyond ordinary corporal punishment had four times the rate of attacking other children. This illustrates another principle: that the psychologically harmful effects of corporal punishment are parallel to the harmful effects of physical abuse, except that the magnitude of the effect is less.

Despite the unusually high constancy in the findings of research on corporal punishment, there is a serious problem with all the previous research, these studies do not indicate which is cause and which is effect. That is, they do not take into account the fact that aggression and other behavior problems of the child lead parents to spank. Consequently, although there is clear evidence that the more corporal punishment, the greater the probability of hitting a spouse later in life, that finding could simply indicate that the parents were responding to a high level of aggression by the child at Time 1. For example, they might have spanked because the child repeatedly grabbed toys from or hit a brother or sister. Since aggression is a relatively stable trait, it is not surprising that the most aggressive children at Time 1 are still the most aggressive at Time 2 and are now hitting their wives or husbands. To deal with that problem, the research needs to take into account the child's aggression or other antisocial behavior at Time 1 (the time of the spanking). Studies using that design can examine whether, in the months or years following, the behavior of children who were spanked improves (as most people in the USA think will be the case) or gets worse. There are finally new studies that use this design and provide information on long term change in the child's behavior.

Five New Landmark Studies

In the three-year period 1997–1999 five studies became available that can be considered "landmark" studies because they overcame this serious defect in 45 years of previous research on the long-term effects of corporal punishment. All five of the new studies took into account the child's behavior at Time 1, and all five were based on large and nationally representative samples of American children. None of them depended on adults recalling what happened when they were children.

Study 1: Corporal Punishment and Subsequent Antisocial Behavior

This research studied over 3,000 children in the National Longitudinal Survey of Youth (Straus, et al., 1997). The children were in three age groups: 3–5, 6–9, and 10–14. The mothers of all three groups of children were interviewed at the start of the study in 1988, and then again in 1990 and 1992. The findings were very similar for all three age groups and for change after two years and four years. To avoid excess detail only the results for the 6–9 year old children and for the change in antisocial behavior two years after the first interview will be described here.

Measure of corporal punishment. To measure corporal punishment, the mothers were told "Sometimes kids mind pretty well and sometimes they don't," and asked "About how many times, if any, have you had to spank your child in the past week?"

Measure of Antisocial Behavior. To measure Antisocial Behavior the mothers were asked whether, in the past three months, the child frequently "cheats or tells lies," "bullies or is cruel/mean to others," "does not feel sorry after misbehaving," "breaks things deliberately," "is disobedient at school," "has trouble getting along with teachers." This was used to create a measure of the number of antisocial behaviors frequently engaged in by the child.

Other Variables. We also took into account several other variables that could affect antisocial behavior by the child. These include the sex of child, cognitive stimulation provided by the parents, emotional support by the mother, ethnic group of the mother, and socioeconomic status of the family.

Findings. The more corporal punishment used during the first year of the study, the greater the tendency for Antisocial Behavior to *increase* subsequent to the corporal punishment. It also shows that this effect applied to both Euro American children and children of other ethnic groups. Of course, other things also influence Antisocial Behavior. For example, girls have lower rates of Antisocial Behavior than boys, and children whose mothers are warm and supportive are less likely to behave in antisocial ways. Although these other variables do lessen the effect of corporal punishment, we found that the tendency for corporal punishment to make things worse over the long run applies regardless of race, socioeconomic status, gender of the child, and regardless of the extent to which the mother provides cognitive stimulation and emotional support.

Study 2: A Second Study of Corporal Punishment and Antisocial Behavior

Sample and Measures. Gunnoe and Mariner (1997) analyzed data from another large and representative sample of American children—the National Survey of Families and Households. They studied 1,112 children in two age groups: 4–7 and 8–11. In half of the cases the mother was interviewed and in the other half the father provided the information. The parents were first interviewed in 1987–88, and then five years later. Gunnoe and Mariner's measure of corporal punishment was the same as in the Straus et al. study just described; that is, how often the parent spanked in the previous week.

Gunnoe and Mariner examined the effect of corporal punishment on two aspects of the child's behavior: fighting at school and antisocial behavior. Their Antisocial Behavior measure was also the same as in the Straus et al. study.

Findings on Fighting. Gunnoe and Mariner found that the more corporal punishment in 1987–88, the greater the amount of fighting at school five years later. This is consistent with the theory that in the long run corporal punishment is counter-productive. However, for toddlers and for African-American children, they found the opposite, i.e. that corporal punishment is associated with *less* fighting 5 years later. Gunnoe and Mariner suggest that this occurs because younger children and African-American children tend to regard corporal punishment as a legitimate parental behavior rather than as an aggressive act. However, corporal punishment by parents of young children and by African-American parents is so nearly universal (for example, 94 percent of parents of toddlers) that it suggests an alternative explanation: that no-corporal punishment means no-discipline. If that is the case, it is no wonder that children whose parents exercise no-discipline are less well behaved. Corporal punishment may not be good for children, but failure to properly supervise and control is even worse.

Findings on Antisocial Behavior. The findings on the relation of corporal punishment to Antisocial Behavior show that the more corporal punishment experienced by the children in Year 1, the *higher* the level of Antisocial Behavior five years later. Moreover, they found that the harmful effect of corporal punishment applies to all the categories of children they studied—that is, to children in each age group, to all races, and to both boys and girls. Thus, both of these major long-term prospective studies resulted in evidence that, although corporal punishment may work in the short run, in the long run it tends to boomerang and make things worse.

An important sidelight of the Gunnoe and Mariner study is that it illustrates the way inconvenient findings can be ignored to give a desired "spin." The findings section includes one brief sentence acknowledging that their study "replicates the Straus et al. findings." This crucial finding is never again mentioned. The extensive discussion and conclusion sections omit mentioning the results showing that corporal punishment at Time 1 was associated with more antisocial behavior subsequently for children of all ages and all ethnic groups. Marjorie Gunnoe told me that she is opposed to spanking and has never spanked her own children. So the spin she put on the findings is not a reflection of personal values or behavior.

Perhaps it reflects teaching at a college affiliated with a church which teaches that God expects parents to spank.

Study 3: Corporal Punishment and Child-to-Parent Violence

Timothy Brezina (1999) analyzed data on a nationally representative sample of 1,519 adolescent boys who participated in the Youth in Transition study. This is a three-wave panel study that was begun in 1966. Although the data refer to a previous generation of high school students, there is no reason to think that the relationship between corporal punishment and children hitting parents is different now that it was then, except that the rate may have decreased because fewer parents now slap teen-agers.

Measure of Corporal Punishment. Corporal punishment was measured by asking the boys "How often do your parents actually slap you?" The response categories ranged from 1 (never) to 5 (always). Twenty eight percent of the boys reported being slapped by their parents during the year of the first wave of the study when their average age was 15, and 19 percent were slapped during the wave 2 year (a year and half later).

Measure of Child Aggression. The boys were asked similar questions about how often they hit their father and their mother. Eleven percent reported hitting a parent the first year, and 7 percent reported hitting a parent at Time 2 of the study.

Findings. Brezina found that corporal punishment at Time 1 was associated with an *increased* probability of a child assaulting the parent a year and a half later. Thus, while it is true that corporal punishment teaches the child a lesson, it is certainly not the lesson intended by the parents.

As with the other four studies, the data analysis took into account some of the many other factors that affect the probability of child-to-parent violence. These include the socioeconomic status and race of the family, the age of the parents, the child's attachment to the parent, child's attitude toward aggression, and child's physical size.

Study 4: Corporal Punishment and Dating Violence

Simons, Lin, and Gordon (1998) tested the theory that corporal punishment by the parents increases the probability of later hitting a partner in a dating relationship. They studied 113 boys in a rural area of the state of Iowa, beginning when they were in the 7th grade or about age 13.

Measure of Corporal Punishment. The mothers and the fathers of these boys were asked how often they spanked or slapped the child when he did something wrong, and how often they used a belt or paddle for corporal punishment. These questions were repeated in waves 2 and 3 of this 5-year study. The scores for the mother and the father for each of the three years were combined to create an overall measure of corporal punishment. More than half of the boys experienced corporal punishment during those years. Consequently, the findings about corporal punishment apply to the majority of boys in that community, not just to the children of a small group of violent parents.

Measure of Dating Violence. The information on dating violence came from the boys, so it is not influenced by whether the parents viewed the boy as aggressive. The boys were asked whether, in the last year, "When you had a disagreement with your girlfriend, how often did you hit, push, shove her?"

Measure of Delinquency at Time 1. As explained earlier, it is critical to take into account the misbehavior that leads parents to use corporal punishment. In this study, that was done by asking the boys at Time 1 how often they had engaged in each of 24 delinquent acts such as skipping school, stealing, and physically attacking someone with a weapon; and also how often they had used drugs and alcohol.

Parental involvement and support. Finally the study also took into account the extent to which the parents showed warmth and affection, were consistent in their discipline, monitored and supervised the child, and explained rules and expectations. In addition, it also controlled for witnessing parental violence.

Findings. Simons and his colleagues found that the more corporal punishment experienced by these boys, the greater the probability of their physically assaulting a girlfriend. Moreover, like the other prospective studies, the analysis took into account the misbehavior that led parents to use corporal punishment, and also the quality of parenting. This means that the relation of corporal punishment to violence against a girlfriend is very unlikely to be due to poor parenting. Rather, it is another study showing that the long run effect of corporal punishment is to engender more rather than less misbehavior. In short, spanking boomerangs.

Study 5: Corporal Punishment and Child's Cognitive Development

The last of these five studies (Straus and Paschall, 1999) was prompted by studies showing that talking to children (including pre-speech infants) is associated with an increase in neural connections in the brain and in cognitive performance. Those findings led us to theorize that if parents avoid corporal punishment, they are more likely to engage in verbal methods of behavior control such as explaining to the child, and that the increased verbal interaction with the child will in turn enhance the child's cognitive ability.

This theory was tested on 806 children of mothers in the National Longitudinal Study of Youth who were age 2 to 4 in the first year of our analysis, and the tests were repeated for an additional 704 children who were age 5 to 9 in the first year. Corporal punishment was measured by whether the mother was observed hitting the child during the interview and by a question on frequency of spanking in the past week. A corporal punishment scale was created by adding the number of times the parent spanked in two sample weeks. Cognitive ability was measured in Year 1 and two years later by tests appropriate for the age of the child at the time of testing such as the Peabody Picture Vocabulary Test.

The study took into account the mother's age and education, whether the father was present in the household, number of children in the family, mother's supportiveness and cognitive stimulation, ethnic group, and the child's age, gender, and child's birth weight.

The less corporal punishment parents use on toddlers, the greater the probability that the child will have an above average cognitive growth. The greater benefit of avoiding corporal punishment for the younger children is consistent with the research showing the most rapid growth of neural connections in the brain of early ages. It is also consistent with the theory that what the child learns as an infant and toddler is crucial because it provides the necessary basis for subsequent cognitive development. The greater adverse effect on cognitive development for toddlers has an extremely important practical implication because the defenders of corporal punishment have now retreated to limiting their advocacy to toddlers. Their recommendation is not based on empirical evidence. The evidence from this study suggests that, at least in so far as cognitive development is concerned, supporters of corporal punishment have unwittingly advised parents to use corporal punishment at the ages when it will have the most adverse effect.

The Message Of The Five Studies: "Don't Spank"

Each of the five studies I briefly summarized is far from perfect. They can be picked apart one by one, as can just about every epidemiological study. This is what the tobacco industry did for many years. The Surgeon General's committee on smoking did the opposite. Their review of the research acknowledged the limitations of the studies when taken one-by-one. But they concluded that despite the defects of the individual studies, the cumulative evidence indicated that smoking does cause lung cancer and other diseases, and they called for an end to smoking. With respect to spanking, I believe that the cumulative weight of the evidence, and especially the five prospective studies provides sufficient evidence for a new Surgeon General's warning. A start in that direction was made by the American Academy of Pediatrics, which in 1998 published "Guidelines for Effective Discipline" (*Pediatrics* 101: 723–728) that advises parents to avoid spanking.

Is There a Backlash?

It is ironic that during the same period as the new and more definitive research was appearing, there were hostile or ridiculing articles in newspapers and magazines on the idea of never spanking a child. In 1999, Arizona and Arkansas passed laws to remind parents and teachers that they have the right to use corporal punishment and to urge them to do so. There has also been a contentious debate in scientific journals on the appropriateness of corporal punishment. These developments made some advocates for children concerned that there is a backlash against the idea of no-spanking. However, there are several reasons for doubting the existence of a backlash in the sense of a reversal in the trend of decreasing public support for corporal punishment, or in the sense of non-spanking parents reverting to using corporal punishment.

One reason for doubting the existence of a backlash is that, each year, a larger and larger proportion of the American population opposes corporal punishment. In 1968, which was only a generation ago, almost everyone (94 percent) believed that corporal punishment is sometimes necessary. But in the last 30 years public support for corporal punishment has been decreasing. By 1999, almost half of US adults rejected the idea that spanking is necessary.

The Advocates Are Long-Time Supporters

In 1968, those who favored corporal punishment did not need to speak out to defend their view because, as just indicated, almost everyone believed it was necessary. The dramatic decrease in support for corporal punishment means that long time advocates of corporal punishment now have reason to be worried, and they are speaking out. Consequently, their recent publications do not indicate a backlash in the sense of a change from being opposed to corporal punishment to favoring it. I suggest that it is more like dying gasps of support for an ancient mode of bringing up children that is heading towards extinction.

The efforts of those who favor corporal punishment have also been spurred on by the increase in crime in many countries. The rise in youth crime in the United States, although recently reversed, is a very disturbing trend, and it has prompted a search for causes and corrective steps. It should be no surprise that people who have always believed in the use of corporal punishment believe that a return to their favored mode of bringing up children will help cure the crime problem. They argue that children need "discipline," which is correct. However, they equate discipline with corporal punishment, which is not correct. No-corporal punishment does not mean no-discipline. Delinquency prevention does require, among other things, discipline in the sense of clear rules and standards for behavior and parental supervision and monitoring and enforcement. To the extent that part of the explanation for crime, especially crime by youth, is the lack of discipline, the appropriate step is not a return to corporal punishment but parental standards, monitoring, and enforcement by non-violent methods. In fact, as the studies reviewed here indicate, if discipline takes the form of more corporal punishment, the problem will be exacerbated because, while corporal punishment does work with some children, more typically it boomer-

angs and increases the level of juvenile delinquency and other behavior problems.

The criticism in scientific journals of research on corporal punishment is also not a backlash. It has to be viewed in the light of the norms of science. A standard aspect of science is to examine research critically, to raise questions, and to suggest alternative interpretations of findings. This results in a somewhat paradoxical tendency for criticism to increase as the amount of research goes up. There has recently been an increase in research showing long-term harmful effects of corporal punishment. Given the critical ethos of science, it is only to be expected that the increased research has elicited more commentary and criticism, especially on the part of those who believed in corporal punishment in the first place.

Three Paradoxes About Corporal Punishment

Three paradoxical aspects of the movement away from corporal punishment are worth noting. The first is that, although approval of corporal punishment had declined precipitously in the last generation, almost all parents continue to spank toddlers. The second paradox is that professionals advising parents, including those who are opposed to spanking, generally fail to tell parents not to spank. They call this avoiding a "negative approach." Finally, and most paradoxically of all, focusing almost exclusively on a so-called "positive approach," unwittingly contributes to perpetuating corporal punishment and helps explain the first paradox.

Paradox 1: Contradictory Trends. Some aspects of corporal punishment have changed in major ways. A smaller and smaller percent of the public favors spanking (Straus and Mathur, 1996). Fewer parents now use belts, hairbrushes and paddles. The percent of parents who hit adolescents has dropped by half since 1975. Nevertheless, other aspects of corporal punishment continue to be prevalent, chronic, and severe. The 1995 Gallup national survey of parents (Straus and Stewart, 1999) found that:

- Almost all parents of toddlers (94 percent) used corporal punishment that year
- Parents who spanked a toddler, did it an average of about three times a week
- 28 percent of parents of children age 5–12 used an object such as a belt or hairbrush
- Over a third of parents of 13-year-old children hit them that year

The myths about corporal punishment in *Beating The Devil Out Of Them* provide important clues to understanding why parents who "don't believe in spanking" continue to do so. These myths also undermine the ability of professionals who advise parents to do what is needed to end corporal punishment.

Paradox 2: Opposing Spanking but Failing to Say Don't Spank. Many pediatricians, developmental psychologists, and parent educators are now opposed to corporal punishment, at least in principle. But most also continue to believe that there may be a situation where spanking by parents is necessary or acceptable (Schenck, 2000). This is based on cultural myths. One myth is that spanking works when other things do not. Another is that "mild" corporal punishment is harmless. All but a small minority of parents and professionals continue to believe these myths despite the experimental and other evidence showing that other disciplinary strategies work just as well as spanking, even in the short run and are more effective in the long run as shown by the first four of the studies described earlier in this article.

Consequently, when I suggest to pediatricians, parent educators, or social scientists that it is essential to tell parents that they should never spank or use any other type of corporal punishment, with rare exception, that idea has been rejected. Some, like one of America's leading developmental psychologists, object because of the unproven belief that it would turn off parents. Some object on the false belief that it could be harmful because parents do not know what else to do. They argue for a "positive approach" by which they mean teaching parents alternative disciplinary strategies, as compared to what they call the "negative approach" of advising to never spank. As a result, the typical pattern is to say nothing about spanking. Fortunately, that is slowly changing. Although they are still the exception, an increasing number of books for parents, parent education programs, and guidelines for professionals advise never-spanking.

Both the movement away from spanking, and an important limitation of that movement are illustrated by publication of the "Guidelines For Effective Discipline" of the American Academy of Pediatrics. This was an important step forward, but it also reflects the same problem. It recommends that parents avoid corporal punishment. However, it also carefully avoids saying that parents should *never* spank. This may seem like splitting hairs, but because of the typical sequence of parent-child interaction that eventuates in corporal punishment described in the next paragraph, it is a major obstacle to ending corporal punishment. Omitting a never-spank message is a serious obstacle because, in the absence of a commitment to never-spank, even parents who are against spanking continue to spank. It is important to understand what underlies the paradox of parents who are opposed to spanking, nonetheless spanking.

Paradox 3: Failing To Be Explicit Against Spanking Results in More Spanking. The paradox that fewer and fewer parents are in favor of spanking, but almost all spank toddlers reflects a combination of needing to cope with the typical behavior of toddlers and perceiving those behaviors through the lens of the myth that spanking works when other things do not.

When toddlers are corrected for misbehavior (such as hitting another child or disobeying), the "recidivism" rate is about 80 percent within the same day and about 50 percent within two hours. For some children it is within two minutes. One researcher (who is a defender of corporal punishment) found that these "time to failure" rates apply equally to corporal punishment and to other disciplinary strategies (Larzelere, et al., 1996). Consequently, on any given day, a parent is almost certain to find that so-called alternative disciplinary strategies such as explaining, deprivation of privileges and time out, "do not work." When that happens, they turn to spanking. So, as pointed out previously, just about everyone (at least 94 percent) spanks toddlers.

The difference between spanking and other disciplinary strategies is that, when spanking does not work, parents do not question its effectiveness. The idea that spanking works when other methods do not is so ingrained in American culture that, when the child repeats the misbehavior an hour or two later (or sometimes a few minutes later) parents fail to perceive that spanking has the same high failure rate as other modes of discipline. So they spank again, and for as many times as it takes to ultimately secure compliance. That is the correct strategy because, with consistency and perseverance, the child will eventually learn. What so many parents miss is that it is also the correct strategy for non-spanking methods. Thus, unless there is an absolute prohibition on spanking, parents will "see with their own eyes" that alternatives do not work and continue to find it is necessary to spank.

"Never-Spank" Must Be The Message

Because of the typical behavior of toddlers and the almost inevitable information processing errors just described, teaching alternative disciplinary techniques by itself is not sufficient. There must also be an unambiguous "never-spank" message, which is needed to increase the chances that parents who disapprove of spanking will act on their beliefs. Consequently, it is essential for pediatricians and others who advise parents to abandon their reluctance to say "never-spank." To achieve this, parent-educators must themselves be educated. They need to understand why, what they now consider a "negative approach," is such an important part of ending the use of corporal punishment. Moreover, because they believe that a "negative approach" does not work, they also need to know about the experience of Sweden. The Swedish experience shows that, contrary to the currently prevailing opinion, a never-spank approach has worked (Durrant, 1999).

In short, the first priority step to end or reduce spanking may be to educate professionals who advise parents. Once professionals are ready to move, the key steps are relatively easy to implement and inexpensive.

> Parent-education programs, such as STEP, which are now silent on spanking, can be revised to include the evidence that spanking does *not* work better than other disciplinary tactics, even in the short run; and to specifically say "*never* spank."

The Public Health Service can follow the Swedish model and sponsor no-spanking public service announcements on TV and on milk cartons.

There can be a "No-Spanking" poster and pamphlets in every pediatrician's office and every maternity ward.

There could be a notice on birth certificates such as:

WARNING: SPANKING HAS BEEN DETERMINED TO BE DANGEROUS TO THE HEALTH AND WELL BEING OF YOUR CHILD—**DO NOT EVER, UNDER ANY CIRCUMSTANCES, SPANK OR HIT YOUR CHILD**

Until professionals who advise parents start advising parents to *never* spank, the paradox of parents becoming less and less favorable to spanking while at the same continuing to spank toddlers will continue. Fortunately, that is starting to happen.

The benefits of avoiding corporal punishment are many, but they are virtually impossible for parents to perceive by observing their children. The situation with spanking is parallel to that of smoking. Smokers could perceive the short run satisfaction from a cigarette, but had no way to see the adverse health consequences down the road. Similarly, parents can perceive the beneficial effects of a slap (and, for the reasons explained in the previous section, fail to see the equal effectiveness of alternatives), they have no way of looking a year or more into the future to see if there is a harmful side effect of having hit their child to correct misbehavior. The only way parents can know this would be if there were a public policy to publicize the results of research such as the studies summarized in this article.

Another reason the benefits of avoiding spanking are difficult to see is that they are not dramatic in any one case. This is illustrated by the average increase of 3 or 4 points in mental ability associated with no-corporal punishment. An increase of that size would hardly be noticed in an individual case. However, it is a well established principle in public health and epidemiology that a widely prevalent risk factor with small effect size, for example spanking, can have a much greater impact on public health than a risk factor with a large effect size, but low prevalence, for example, physical abuse. For example, assume that: (1) 50 million US children experienced CP and 1 million experienced physical abuse. (2) The probability of being depressed as an adult is increased by 2 percent for children who experienced CP and by 25 percent for children who experienced physical abuse. Given these assumptions, the additional cases of depression caused by CP is 1.02 times 50 million, or 1 million. The additional cases of depression caused by physical abuse is 1.25 time 1 million or 250,000. Thus CP is associated with a four

times greater increase in depression than is physical abuse.

Another example of a major benefit resulting from reducing a risk factor that has a small effect, but for a large proportion of the population, might be the increase in scores on intelligence tests that has been occurring worldwide. Corporal punishment has also been decreasing worldwide. The decrease in use of corporal punishment and the increase in scores in IQ tests could be just a coincidence. However, the results of the study described earlier in this article which showed that less spanking is associated with faster cognitive development suggest that the trend away from corporal punishment may be one of a number of social changes (especially, better educated parents) that explain the increase in IQ scores in so many nations.

The other four prospective studies reviewed in this article and the studies in *Beating the Devil Out of Them* show that ending corporal punishment is likely to also reduce juvenile violence, wife-beating, and masochistic sex, and increase the probability of completing higher education, holding a high income job, and lower rates of depression and alcohol abuse. Those are not only humanitarian benefits, they can also result in huge monetary savings in public and private costs for dealing with mental health problems, and crime.

I concluded the first edition of *Beating the Devil Out of Them* in 1994 by suggesting that ending corporal punishment by parents "portends profound and far reaching benefits for humanity." The new research summarized in this article makes those words even more appropriate. We can look forward to the day when children in almost all countries have the benefit of being brought up without being hit by their parents; and just as important, to the day when many nations have the benefit of the healthier, wealthier, and wiser citizens who were brought up free from the violence that is now a part of their earliest and most influential life experiences.

Suggested Further Readings

Brezina, Timothy. 1999. "Teenage violence toward parents as an adaptation to family strain: Evidence from a national survey of male adolescents." *Youth & Society* 30: 416–444.

Durrant, Joan E. 1999. "Evaluating the success of Sweden's corporal punishment ban." *Child Abuse & Neglect* 23: 435–448.

Gershoff, Elizabeth Thompson. In press. "Corporal punishment by parents and associated child behaviors and experiences: A meta-analytic and theoretical review." *Psychological Bulletin.*

Gunnoe, Marjorie L., and Carrie L. Mariner. 1997. "Toward a developmental-contextual model of the effects of parental spanking on children's aggression." *Archives of Pediatric and Adolescent Medicine* 151: 768–775.

Larzelere, Robert E., William N. Schneider, David B. Larson, and Patricia L. Pike. 1996. "The effects of discipline responses in delaying toddler misbehavior recurrences." *Child and Family Therapy* 18: 35–37.

Neisser, Ulric. 1997. "Rising scores on intelligence tests: Test scores are certainly going up all over the world, but whether intelligence itself has risen remains controversial." *American Scientist* 85: 440–447.

Schenck, Eliza R., Robert D. Lyman, and S. Douglas Bodin. 2000. "Ethical beliefs, attitudes, and professional practices of psychologists regarding parental use of corporal punishment: A survey." *Children's Services: Social Policy, Research, and Practice* 3: 23–38.

Simons, Ronald L., Kuei-Hsiu Lin, and Leslie C. Gordon. 1998. "Socialization in the Family of origin and male dating violence: A prospective study." *Journal of Marriage and the Family* 60: 467–478.

Straus, Murray A., and Anitia K. Mathur. 1996. "Social change and change in approval of corporal punishment by parents from 1968 to 1994." Pp. 91–105 in *Family violence against children: A challenge for society.*, edited by D. Frehsee, W. Horn, and K-D Bussmann, New York: Walter deGruyter.

Straus, Murray A., and Mallie J. Paschall. 1999. "Corporal punishment by mothers and children's cognitive development: A longitudinal study of two age cohorts." in *6th International Family Violence Research Conference.* Durham, NH: Family Research Laboratory, University of New Hampshire.

Straus, Murray A., and Julie H. Stewart. 1999. "Corporal punishment by American parents: National data on prevalence, chronicity, severity, and duration, in relation to child, and family characteristics." *Clinical Child and Family Psychology Review* 2: 55–70.

Straus, Murray A., David B. Sugarman, and Jean Giles-Sims. 1997. "Spanking by parents and subsequent antisocial behavior of children." *Archives of pediatric and adolescent medicine* 151: 761–767.

Murray A. Straus is professor of sociology and co-director of the Family Research Laboratory at the University of New Hampshire. He is the author or co-author or editor of 18 books including Stress, Culture, and Aggression. *This article is adapted from Chapter 12 of* Beating the Devil Out of Them: Corporal Punishment in American Families and Its Effects on Children, *2nd edition, published by Transaction.*

The Seven Sins of Memory:

How the Mind Forgets and Remembers

Memory's errors are as fascinating as they are important

By Daniel Schacter, Ph.D.

In Yasunari Kawabata's unsettling short story, "Yumi-ura," a novelist receives an unexpected visit from a woman who says she knew him 30 years earlier. They met when he visited the town of Yumiura during a harbor festival, the woman explains. But the novelist cannot remember her. Plagued recently by other troublesome memory lapses, he sees this latest incident as a further sign of mental decline. His discomfort turns to alarm when the woman offers more revelations about what happened on a day when he visited her room. "You asked me to marry you," she recalls wistfully. The novelist reels while contemplating the magnitude of what he had forgotten. The woman explains that she had never forgotten their time together and felt continually burdened by her memories of him.

After she finally leaves, the shaken novelist searches maps for the town of Yumiura with the hope of triggering recall of the place and the reasons why he had gone there. But no maps or books list a town called Yumiura. The novelist then realizes that he could not have been in the part of the country the woman described at the time she remembered. Her detailed, heart-felt and convincing memories were entirely false.

Kawabata's story dramatically illustrates different ways in which memory can get us into trouble. Sometimes we forget the past and at other times we distort it; some disturbing memories haunt us for years. Yet we also rely on memory to perform an astonishing variety of tasks in our everyday lives. Recalling conversations with friends or recollecting family vacations; remembering appointments and errands we need to run; calling up words that allow us to speak and understand others; remembering foods we like and dislike; acquiring the knowledge needed for a new job—all depend, in one way or another, on memory. Memory plays such a pervasive role in our daily lives that we often take it for granted until an incident of forgetting or distortion demands our attention.

Memory's errors have long fascinated scientists, and during the past decade they have come to occupy a prominent place in our society. Forgotten encounters, misplaced eyeglasses and failures to recall the names of familiar faces are becoming common occurrences for many adults who are busily trying to juggle the demands of work and family, and cope with the bewildering array of new communications technologies. How many passwords and "PINs" do you have to remember just to manage your affairs on the Internet, not to mention your voice mail at the office or on your cell phone?

In addition to dealing with the frustration of memory failures in daily life, the awful specter of Alzheimer's disease looms large on the horizon. As the general public becomes ever more aware of its horrors through such high-profile cases as Ronald Reagan's battle with the disorder, the prospects of a life dominated by catastrophic forgetting further increase our preoccupations with memory.

Although the magnitude of the woman's memory distortion in Yumiura seems to stretch the bounds of credulity, it has been equaled and even exceeded in everyday life. Consider the story of Binjimin Wikomirski, whose 1996 Holocaust memoir, *Fragments,* won worldwide acclaim for portraying life in a concentration camp from the perspective of a child. Wilkomirski presented readers with raw, vivid recollections of the unspeakable terrors he witnessed as a young boy. Even more remarkable, Wilkomirski had spent much of his adult life unaware of these traumatic childhood memories, only becoming aware of them in therapy. Because his story and memories inspired countless others, Wilkomirski became a sought-after international figure and a hero to Holocaust survivors.

The story began to unravel, however, in late August 1998, when Daniel Ganzfried, a Swiss journalist and himself the son of a Holocaust survivor, published a stunning article in a Zurich newspaper. Ganzfried revealed that Wilkomirski is actually Bruno Dossekker, a Swiss native born in 1941 to a young woman named Yvone Berthe Grosjean, who later gave him up for adoption to an orphanage. His foster parents, the Dossekkers, found him there. Young Bruno spent all of the war years in the safe confines of his native Switzerland. Whatever the basis for his traumatic "memories" of Nazi horrors, they did not come from childhood experiences in a concentration camp. Is Dossekker/Wilkomirski simply a liar? Probably not: he still strongly believes his recollections are real.

Memory's errors are as fascinating as they are important. They can be divided into seven fundamental transgressions or "sins," which I call transience, absentmindedness, blocking, misattribution, suggestibility, bias and persistence. Just like the ancient seven deadly sins—pride, anger, envy, greed, gluttony, lust and sloth—the memory sins occur frequently in everyday life and can have serious consequences for all of us.

Transience, absentmindedness and blocking are sins of omission: we fail to bring to mind a desired fact, event or idea. Transience refers to a weakening or loss of memory over time. It is a basic feature of memory, and the culprit in many memory problems. Absentmindedness involves a breakdown at the interface between attention and memory. Absentminded memory errors—misplacing your keys or eyeglasses, or forgetting a lunch appointment—typically occur because we are preoccupied with distracting issues or concerns, and don't focus attention on what we need to remember.

The third sin, blocking, entails a thwarted search for information we may be desperately trying to retrieve. We've all had the experience of failing to produce a name to a familiar face. This frustrating experience happens even though we are attending carefully to the task at hand, and even though the desired name has not faded from our minds—as we become acutely aware when we unexpectedly retrieve the blocked name hours or days later.

The next four sins of misattribution, suggestibility, bias and persistence are all sins of commission: some form of memory is present, but it is either incorrect or unwanted. The sin of misattribution involves assigning a memory to the wrong source: mistaking fantasy for reality, or incorrectly remembering that a friend told you a bit of trivia that you actually read about in a newspaper. Misattribution is far more common than most people realize, and has potentially profound implications in legal settings. The related sin of suggestibility refers to memories that are implanted as a result of leading questions, comments or suggestions when a person is trying to call up a past experience. Like misattribution, suggestibility is especially relevant to—and sometimes can wreak havoc within—the legal system.

The sin of bias reflects the powerful influences of our current knowledge and beliefs on how we remember our pasts. We often edit or entirely rewrite our previous experiences—unknowingly and unconsciously—in light of what we now know or believe. The result can be a skewed rendering of a specific incident, or even of an extended period in our lives, that says more about how we feel now than about what happened then.

The seventh sin—persistence—entails repeated recall of disturbing information or events that we would prefer to banish from our minds altogether: remembering what we cannot forget, even though we wish that we could. Everyone is familiar with persistence to some degree: Recall the last time you suddenly awoke at 3 a.m., unable to keep out of your mind a painful blunder on the job or a disappointing result on an important exam. In more extreme cases of serious depression or traumatic experience, persistence can be disabling and even life-threatening.

"Two regions of the brain showed greater activity when people made abstract/concrete judgments about words they later remembered compared with those they later forgot."

New discoveries, some based on recent breakthroughs in neuroscience that allow us to see the brain in action as it learns and remembers, are beginning to illuminate the basis of the seven sins. These studies allow us to see in a new light what's going on inside our heads during the frustrating incidents of memory failure or error that can have a significant impact on our everyday lives. But to understand the seven sins more deeply, we also need to ask why our memory systems have come to exhibit these bothersome and sometimes dangerous properties: Do the seven sins represent mistakes made by Mother Nature during the course of evolution? Is memory flawed in a way that has placed our species at unnecessary risk? I don't think so. To the contrary, I contend that each of the seven sins is a byproduct of otherwise desirable and adaptive features of the human mind. Let's consider two of the most common memory sins: transience and absentmindedness.

TRANSIENCE

On October 3, 1995 the most sensational criminal trial of our time reached a stunning conclusion: a jury acquitted O. J. Simpson of murder. Word of the verdict spread quickly, nearly everyone reacted with either outrage or jubilation, and many people could talk about little else for days and weeks afterward. The Simpson verdict seemed like just the sort of momentous event that most of us would always remember vividly: how we reacted to it, and where we were when we heard the news.

Now, can you recall how you found out that Simpson had been acquitted? Chances are that you don't remember, or that what you remember is wrong. Several days after the verdict, a group of California undergraduates provided researchers with detailed accounts of how they learned about the jury's decision. When the researchers probed students' memories again 15 months later, only half recalled accurately how they found out about the decision. When asked again nearly three years after the verdict, less than 30% of students' recollections were accurate; nearly half were dotted with major errors.

The culprit in this incident is the sin of transience: forgetting that occurs with the passage of time. Research has shown that minutes, hours or days after an experience, memory preserves a relatively detailed record, allowing us to reproduce the past with reasonable if not perfect accuracy. But with the passing of time, the particulars fade and opportunities multiply for interference—generated by later, similar experiences—to blur our recollections.

Consider the following question: If I measure activity in your brain while you are learning a list of words, can I tell from this activity which words you will later remember having studied, and which words you will later forget? In other words, do measurements of brain activity at the moment when a perception is being transformed into a memory allow scientists to predict future remembering and forgetting of that particular event? If so, exactly which regions allow us to do the predicting?

In 1997, our group at the imaging center of Massachusetts General Hospital came up with an experiment to answer the question. Holding still in this cacophonous tunnel [the magnetic resonance imaging or MRI scanner], participants in our experiment saw several hundred words, one every few seconds, flashed to them from a computer by specially arranged mirrors. To make sure that they paid attention to every word, we asked our volunteers to indicate whether each word refers to something abstract, such as "thought," or concrete, such as "garden." Twenty minutes after the scan, we showed subjects the words they had seen in the scanner, intermixed with an equal number of words they hadn't seen, and asked them to indicate which ones they did and did not remember seeing in the scanner. We knew, based on preliminary work, that people would remember some words and forget others. Could we tell from the strength of the signal when participants were making abstract/concrete judgments which words they would later remember and which ones they would later forget?

We could. Two regions of the brain showed greater activity when people made abstract/concrete judgments about words they later remembered compared with those they later forgot. One was in the inner part of the temporal lobe, a part of the brain that, when damaged, can result in severe memory loss. The other region whose activity predicted subsequent memory was located further forward, in the lower left part of the vast territory known as the frontal lobes.

This finding was not entirely unexpected, because previous neuroimaging studies indicated that the lower left part of the frontal lobe works especially hard when people elaborate on incoming information by associating it to what they already know.

These results were exciting because there is something fascinating, almost science fiction-like, about peering into a person's brain in the present and foretelling what she will likely remember and forget in the future. But beyond an exercise in scientific fortune-telling, these studies managed to trace some of the roots of transience to the split-second encoding operations that take place during the birth of a memory. What happens in frontal and temporal regions during those critical moments determines, at least in part, whether an experience will be remembered for a lifetime, or drop off into the oblivion of the forgotten.

ABSENTMINDEDNESS

On a brutally cold day in February 1999, 17 people gathered in the 19th floor office of a Manhattan skyscraper to compete for a title known to few others outside that room: National Memory Champion. The winner of the U.S. competition would go on to challenge for the world memory championship several months later in London.

The participants were asked to memorize thousands of numbers and words, pages of faces and names, lengthy poems and decks of cards. The victor in this battle of mnemonic virtuosos, a 27-year-old administrative assistant named Tatiana Cooley, relied on classic encoding techniques: generating visual images, stories and associations that link incoming information to what she already knows. Given her proven ability to commit vast amounts of information to memory, one might also expect that Cooley's everyday life would be free from the kinds of memory problems that plague others. Yet this memory champion considers herself dangerously forgetful. "I'm incredibly absentminded," Cooley told a reporter. Fearful that she will forget to carry out everyday tasks, Cooley depends on to-do lists and notes scribbled on sticky pads. "I live by Post-its," she admitted ruefully.

The image of a National Memory Champion dependent on Post-its in her everyday life has a paradoxical, even surreal quality: Why does someone with a capacity for prodigious recall need to write down anything at all? Can't Tatiana Cooley call on the same memory abilities and strategies that she uses to memorize hundreds of words or thousands of numbers to help remember that she needs to pick up a jug of milk at the store? Apparently not: The gulf that separates Cooley's championship memory performance from her forgetful everyday life illustrates the distinction between transience and absentmindedness.

The kinds of everyday memory failures that Cooley seeks to remedy with Post-it notes—errands to run, appointments to keep and the like—have little to do with transience. These kinds of memory failures instead reflect the sin of absentmindedness: lapses of attention that result in failing to remember information that was either never encoded property (if at all) or is available in memory but is overlooked at the time we need to retrieve it.

To appreciate the distinction between transience and absentmindedness, consider the following three examples:

A man tees up a golf ball and hits it straight down the fairway. After waiting a few moments for his partner to hit, the man tees up his ball again, having forgotten that he hit the first drive.

A man puts his glasses down on the edge of a couch. Several minutes later, he realizes he can't find the glasses, and spends a half-hour searching his home before locating them.

"Memory's errors have long fascinated scientists, and during the past decade they have come to occupy a prominent place in our society."

A man temporarily places a violin on the top of his car. Forgetting that he has done so, he drives off with the violin still perched on the roof.

Superficially, all three examples appear to reflect a similar type of rapid forgetting. To the contrary, it is likely that each occurred for very different reasons.

The first incident took place back in the early 1980s, when I played golf with a patient who had been taking part in memory research conducted in my laboratory. The patient was in the early stage of Alzheimer's disease, and he had severe difficulties remembering recent events. Immediately after hitting his tee shot, the patient was excited because he had knocked it straight down the middle; he realized he would now have an easy approach shot to the green. In other words, he had encoded this event in a relatively elaborate manner that would ordinarily yield excellent memory. But when he started teeing up again and I asked him about his first shot, he expressed no recollection of it whatsoever. This patient was victimized by transience: he was incapable of retaining the information he had encoded, and no amount of cueing or prodding could bring it forth.

In the second incident, involving misplaced glasses, entirely different processes are at work. Sad to say, this example comes from my own experience—and happens more often than I would care to admit. Without attending to what I was doing, I placed my glasses in a spot where I usually do not put them. Because I hadn't fully encoded

this action to begin with—my mind was preoccupied with a scientific article I had been reading—I was at a loss when I realized that my glasses were missing. When I finally found them on the couch, I had no particular recollection of having put them there. But unlike the golfing Alzheimer's patient, transience was not the culprit: I never adequately encoded the information about where I put my glasses and so had no chance to retrieve it later.

The third example, featuring the misplaced violin, turned into far more than just a momentary frustration. In August 1967, David Margetts played second violin in the Roth String Quartet at UCLA. He had been entrusted with the care of a vintage Stradivarius that was owned by the department of music. After Margetts put the violin on his car's roof and drove off without removing it, UCLA made massive efforts to recover the instrument. Nonetheless, it went missing for 27 years before resurfacing in 1994 when the Stradivarius was brought in for repair and a dealer recognized the instrument. After a lengthy court battle, the violin was returned to UCLA in 1998.

There is, of course, no way to know exactly what Margetts was thinking about when he put the violin on his car's roof. Perhaps he was preoccupied with other things, just as I was when I misplaced my glasses. But because one probably does not set down a priceless Stradivarius without attending carefully to one's actions, I suspect that had Margetts been reminded before driving off, he would have remembered perfectly well where he had just placed the violin. In other words, Margetts was probably not sabotaged by transience, or even by failure to encode the event initially. Rather, forgetting in Margett's case was likely attributable to an absent-minded failure to notice the violin at the moment he needed to recall where he had put it. He missed a retrieval cue—the violin on the car's roof—which surely would have reminded him that he needed to remove the instrument.

Even though they often seem like our enemies, the seven sins are an integral part of the mind's heritage because they are so closely connected to features of memory that make it work well. The seven sins are not merely nuisances to minimize or avoid. They illuminate how memory draws on the past to inform the present, preserves elements of present experience for future reference, and allows us to revisit the past at will. Memory's vices are also its virtues, elements of a bridge across time that allows us to link the mind with the world.

Adapted from Daniel Schacter, Ph.D.'s *The Seven Sins of Memory: How the Mind Forgets and Remembers* (Houghton-Mifflin, 2001)

Daniel L. Schacter, Ph.D., is chairman of the psychology department at Harvard University and also author of "Searching for Memory" (HarperCollins, 1997).

Memory's Mind Games

Absent-mindedness is just the start of memory problems. When the brain distorts the past, our view of who we are suffers.

By Sharon Begley

As slide shows go, it wasn't even in the same league as your aunt's vacation snapshots, but the audience was paying close attention: there was going to be a quiz. In one sequence a student sitting in a packed lecture hall topples onto the floor. In others, a hand retrieves oranges that have rolled all over a supermarket, and a woman picks up groceries scattered across a floor. Between 15 minutes and 48 hours later, the Boston University undergrads—volunteers in this psychology experiment—scrutinize more photos and, for each one, decide whether they ever saw it before. Yup, saw the student carelessly leaning back in his chair. Yeah, also saw the guy stupidly take an orange from the bottom of the pile. Uh-huh, saw the grocery bag rip. In all, 68 percent of the time the students remembered seeing the "cause" picture (a ripping bag) whose effect (spilled groceries) had been part of the show.

There was only one problem. The slides did not include a single such cause photo. "When people saw the effect photo but not the cause photo, they 'filled in the blank' by saying they *had* seen the cause with their own two eyes," says psychologist Mark Reinitz of the University of Puget Sound. Writing in the July issue of the Journal of Experimental Psychology, he and Sharon Hannigan of Bard College conclude that the mind's drive to infer causes can fool people into "remembering" something they never saw. In other words, says Reinitz, "memories can be illusions."

When it comes to memory problems, forgetting is only the tip of the iceberg. The failures and failings of memory run much deeper than an inability to recall your neighbor's name, the capital of Illinois or the location of your keys. Much recent memory research has focused on why we forget, shedding light on tragedies like Alzheimer's as well as puzzles like why we often know the first letter of a name or word we're trying to remember, but not the rest of it. But unlike absent-mindedness and other "sins of omission," as psychologist Daniel Schacter of Harvard University calls them in his new book, "The Seven Sins of

Memory," memory's "sins of commission" shape—and often distort—our view of reality and relationships. Some of the sins:

Blocking. Somewhere between remembering and forgetting lies blocking. You *know* that the word for an oration at a funeral begins with a vowel, maybe even a "u"… but it just won't spring into consciousness. You *know* the name of the longtime neighbor who's approaching as you talk to the new people next door, but as the seconds tick down until you'll have to make the introduction, the best you can come up with is that his name begins with an "R." Proper names are blocked more than any other words, memory researchers find, and more in old people than young. The problem with names is that they are (in Western cultures, at least) completely arbitrary: that guy looks no more like a Richard than he does a Paul. Also, the sound of a word is encoded in the brain in a different place from its meaning. If the links from concept (the context in which you know a person) to visual representation (aha, that face belongs to my neighbor!) to the word itself (Paulie Walnuts) are weak, then we can't get to the word even though we may remember everything about it. You may tickle neurons here, but the reverberations never reach those deeper in the circuit.

Sometimes we get to the first sound in the word but no further: the phonemes of words are apparently encoded separately, too, and coming up with that "eu-" sound doesn't guarantee that you'll move on to "-lo." Words we use infrequently are especially subject to this tip-of-the-tongue phenomenon. If you need to remember which medicine to take for a common ailment, you'll probably come up easily with "aspirin" for a headache or "antacid" for a stomach upset. But you might well struggle before remembering what's needed to treat a sudden allergic reaction: "antihistamine."

Misattribution. The El Al cargo flight had smashed into an apartment building outside Amsterdam, killing 39 residents and all four crew members in a fiery explo-

BIAS:

YOUR BRAIN REWRITES THE PAST UNDER THE INFLUENCE OF CURRENT EVENTS… E.G., A DIVORCING COUPLE REMEMBER ONLY THE BAD TIMES TOGETHER, NOT THE GOOD

SUGGESTIBILITY:

LEADING QUESTIONS/REMARKS COLOR YOUR MEMORIES OR EVEN "CREATE" THEM… E.G., PARENT TO CHILD: REMEMBER WE TOOK YOU TO DISNEYLAND AND YOU TALKED TO MICKEY MOUSE? REMEMBER? AND CHILD "REMEMBERS."

MISATTRIBUTION:

YOU MISATTRIBUTE THE SOURCE OF YOUR MEMORY… E.G., JOE REMEMBERS SAYING SOMETHING TO SALLY WHEN IN FACT HE SAID IT TO SUE

BLOCKING:

YOU CAN'T REMEMBER A NAME OR WORD, BUT YOU CAN REMEMBER THE FIRST LETTER

PERSISTENCE:

YOU WANT TO FORGET TRAUMAS, TRAGEDIES, ETC., BUT CAN'T… THE UNWANTED MEMORIES PERSIST

sion. Ten months after the 1992 disaster, Dutch psychologists quizzed colleagues about how well they remembered television footage of the crash. Most remembered it so well that they could describe whether the fuselage was aflame before it hit, where the plane fell after impact and other details. But there was no such footage: people attributed to video what they had inferred from newspapers, discussions with friends and other sources.

In misattribution, people unconsciously transfer a memory from one mental category to another—from imagination to reality, from this time and place to that one, from hearsay to personal experience. The brain has made what psychologists call a "binding error," incorrectly linking the content of a memory with its context. The fault may lie in the hippocampus, a seahorse-shaped structure deep in the brain's temporal lobe, whose job includes binding together all facets of a memory. When the hippocampus is damaged, patients are more prone to binding errors. So next time you believe that you experienced something you only imagined, or that you mentioned your impending business trip to your wife when in fact you told only your secretary, blame a hiccup in your hippocampus.

Suggestibility. In this memory error, people confuse personal recollection with outside sources of information. Suggestibility is therefore a form of misattribution, but an especially pernicious one. "Leading questions or even encouraging feedback can result in 'memories' of events that never happened," says Schacter. In one recent case, Korean War veteran Edward Daly became convinced that he participated in the horrific massacre of civilians at No Gun Ri. Military records show he was nowhere near the site at the time, suggesting that he had confused hearing rumors of the massacre with witnessing it. (Some reporters, though, believe he was outright lying.) But that wasn't the end of it. As Daly talked to vets who were present at the massacre, "reminding" them of his deeds that day, several became convinced, as one told The New York Times, that "Daly was there. I know that. I know that."

Suggestibility can lead to false eyewitness IDs because even seemingly innocuous feedback can distort recall. In one study, psychologist Gary Wells of Iowa State University and colleagues showed volunteers a security video of a man entering a Target store. Moments later, Wells told them, the man murdered a guard. He then showed them photos and asked them to identify the gunman (who actually appeared in none of the snapshots). Good, you identified the actual suspect, the scientists told some of the volunteers.

Those who received this encouragement later told Wells they were more confident in their recall and had had a better view of the man on the video than those who did not get a verbal pat on the back for their "correct" ID. Certainty and your assurance that you got a good look at the suspect are the kinds of details a jury uses when weighing eyewitness testimony. Positive feedback seems to cement memory and even erase any original uncertainty.

Persistence. Memories that refuse to fade tend to involve regret, trauma and other potent negative emotions. All emotions strengthen a memory, but negative ones seem to write on the brain in indelible ink, Schacter finds. That's especially true if the memory reinforces your self-image: if you think of yourself as a screw-up, you'll have a hard time erasing the memory of the time you spilled wine all over your boss. Blame your amygdala. When you experience a threatening event like the approach of a menacing stranger, the level of activity in this clutch of brain neurons predicts how well you will remember the experience. Stress hormones seem to strengthen the neuronal circuit that embodies a traumatic memory.

Bias. It is a cliché that couples in love recall their courtship as a time of bliss, while unhappy pairs recall that "I never really loved him [or her]." But the cliché is true. "We rewrite our memories of the past to fit our present views and needs," says Schacter. That may be an outgrowth of forgetting: we can't recall how we felt in the past, so we assume it must be how we feel today. But often bias arises when more powerful mental systems bully poor little memory. The left brain, driven to keep thoughts of yesterday and today from conflicting, reconciles past and present as boldly as the Ministry of Truth in Orwell's "1984."

Linda Levine of UC, Irvine, showed exactly this when she interviewed supporters of Ross Perot right after he unexpectedly dropped out of the 1992 presidential race that July. How did they feel about his decision? she asked. Soon after Perot re-entered in October, Levine revisited the same supporters, asking again how they had felt about the July drop-out. Those who'd never wavered in their support remembered feeling less sad about Perot's quitting than they had claimed in July: their happiness over his return had overwritten their unhappy memory. Disgruntled support-

ers who had initially switched to another candidate but had gone back to Perot recalled feeling less anger in October than they reported in July. Their relief over his return to the race trumped their ire at feeling abandoned.

Stereotyping can also bias memory. Researchers at Yale University led by Mahzarin Banaji asked students which names on a list they recalled as those of criminals recently in the news. The students were twice as likely to "remember" the stereotypically black names ("Tyrone Washington") as they were the stereotypically white ones ("Adam McCarthy"). None of the names had been in the news as criminal suspects or anything else, the scientists reported in 1999. When memory conflicts with what you're convinced is true, it often comes out on the losing end. And that can make forgetting where you put your keys seem trivial indeed.

From *Newsweek*, July 16, 2001, pp. 52-54. © 2001 by Newsweek, Inc. All rights reserved. Reprinted by permission.

UNIT 5
Cognitive Processes

Unit Selections

16. **Mind in a Mirror**, Rachel K. Sobel
17. **Intelligent Intelligence Testing**, Etienne Benson
18. **The Inner Savant**, Douglas S. Fox

Key Points to Consider

• What is brain mapping? How does it help us understand the human mind? Is the mind as complex as we think it is? What is morality? What is "self"? What is awareness? Does the brain play a role in each? How far advanced is the science of understanding the interrelationship between neurology and cognition?

• What is intelligence? Are learning and thinking central to our concepts of intelligence? How so? Is intelligence central to our concept of cognition. Why is the concept of intelligence so criticized? Why have IQ tests been criticized? Do you think the criticism is merited? What changes would you recommend to make intelligence tests more acceptable?

• What are the newer theories of intelligence? How do they contrast with older theories of intelligence? Can you think of people whom you would call "bright" by standards other than the traditional definitions of intelligence?

• What is a savant? Are you a savant, or do you know someone who might be classified as one? Are savants common in the general population? From where does this special cognitive functioning come? What are some examples of the kinds of abilities savants possess? What practical purpose could these abilities serve?

 **Links: www.dushkin.com/online/**
These sites are annotated in the World Wide Web pages.

American Association for Artificial Intelligence (AAAI)
http://www.aaai.org/AITopics/index.html
Chess: Kasparov v. Deep Blue: The Rematch
http://www.chess.ibm.com/home/html/b.html

76

As Rashad watches his 4-month-old, he is convinced that the baby possesses a degree of understanding of the world around her. In fact, Rashad is sure he has one of the smartest babies in the neighborhood. Although he is indeed a proud father, he keeps these thoughts to himself so as not to alienate his neighbors whom he perceives as having less intelligent babies.

Gustav lives in the same neighborhood as Rashad. However, Gustav doesn't have any children, but he does own two fox terriers. Despite Gustav's most concerted efforts, the dogs never come to him when he calls them. In fact, the dogs have been known to run in the opposite direction on occasion. Instead of being furious, Gustav accepts his dogs' disobedience because he is sure the dogs are just dumb beasts and don't know any better.

Both of these vignettes illustrate important and interesting ideas about cognition or thought processes. In the first vignette, Rashad ascribes cognitive abilities and high intelligence to his child; in fact, Rashad perhaps ascribes too much cognitive ability to his 4-month-old. On the other hand, Gustav assumes that his dogs are incapable of thought, more specifically incapable of premeditated disobedience, and therefore he forgives them.

Few adults would deny the existence of their cognitive abilities. Some adults, in fact, think about thinking, something which psychologists call metacognition. Cognition is critical to our survival as adults. But are there differences in mentation in adults? And what about other organisms? Can young children—infants for example—think? If they can, do they think like adults? And what about animals; can they think and solve problems? These and other questions are related to cognitive psychology and cognitive science, which is showcased in this unit.

Cognitive psychology has grown faster than most other specialties in psychology in the past 30 years. Much of this has occurred in response to new computer technology as well as to the growth of psycholinguistics. Computer technology has prompted an interest in artificial intelligence, the mimicking of human intelligence by machines. Similarly the study of psycholinguistics has prompted the examination of the influence of language on thought and vice versa.

While interest in these two developments has eclipsed interest in more traditional areas of cognition such as intelligence, we cannot ignore these traditional areas in this anthology. With regard to intelligence, one persistent problem has been the difficulty of defining just what intelligence is. David Wechsler, author of several of the most popular intelligence tests in current clinical use, defines intelligence as the global capacity of the individual to act purposefully, to think rationally, and to deal effectively with the environment. Other psychologists have proposed more complex definitions. The definitional problem arises when we try to develop tests that validly and reliably measure such abstract, intangible concepts. A valid test is one that measures what it purports to measure. A reliable test yields the same score for the same individual over and over again. Because defining and assessing intelligence have been so controversial and so difficult,

historian Edward Boring once suggested that we define intelligence as whatever it is that an intelligence test measures!

In "Mind in a Mirror," the role of the brain in cognition is examined. Specifically, the role brain functioning plays in the development of morality, awareness, and the formation of self-concept are revealed. The science, however, is rudimentary because the research on brain and cognition is still in its preliminary stages, according to this article.

We next continue with a discussion of intelligence—an important underpinning of cognitive ability. In "Intelligent Intelligence Testing," Etienne Benson puts forth the various definitions of intelligence and the ways intelligence is measured. She also explains how intelligence develops and related issues.

"Savant" may be a new word to you. Savants are those individuals who possess extraordinary ability, usually in one aspect of cognitive functioning. What causes someone to be a savant and whether we all have this potential are thoughtfully explored in this article by Douglas Fox.

Mind in a Mirror

Mapping morality, awareness, and 'self' in the brain

BY RACHEL K. SOBEL

So you're looking for your keys. You can't find them, but you keep looking and... all of a sudden, there they are, right where you already looked. Your eyes had rolled right over those keys. Then something happened and you *saw*. What explains that click, that sudden shift from looking to seeing?

Güven Güzeldere wants to find out. The Duke University researcher is a philosopher and a neuroscientist, and his work straddles both worlds. He has turned to functional magnetic resonance imaging (fMRI), an imaging tool that highlights regions of brain activity, to get a snapshot of the neural circuitry that supports this sudden flash of awareness. His work has just begun, but he hopes that what he learns about awareness will offer a peek into larger issues. "I'm ultimately interested in philosophical questions," he says. "Like what is the nature of consciousness? What is it for? And what makes us different than animals and machines?"

In the past, Güzeldere could have approached those questions only as a philosopher, not as a scientist. But after decades of refining their tools and techniques, brain imagers are trying to glimpse the seemingly unglimpseable. By challenging subjects with cleverly designed problems while using an fMRI scanner to map the ebb and flow of brain activity, these researchers are trying to learn how our 3-pound mass of gray flesh gives rise to the mind. So far, the data may resemble crude cartography. But neuroscientists think they will one day be able to unravel many of the

intricate neural systems underlying our most elusive traits, including consciousness, morality, and empathy.

Until recently, brain mappers mostly charted more basic functions, such as memory, language, and vision. Even there, no one claims to have all the details. But neuroscientists believe they have enough of a blueprint to begin probing the biological underpinnings of more complex activities. Take a new study on the nature of moral decisions. Scientists asked subjects to contemplate a variety of moral dilemmas and imaged their brains while they were doing so. The researchers then used earlier data about where emotions are processed in the brain to interpret the scans. The results showed that even when people think they are making rational judgments, their emotions may actually be driving the outcome.

The findings, published in a September issue of *Science*, offer a glimpse of a process that philosophers have speculated about for centuries. "To start understanding the mechanisms of something as essentially human as the moral judgments we make," says Joshua Greene, a philosophy doctoral candidate at Princeton University and the lead author of the study, "we're really getting at the nuts and bolts of who we are."

You and me. Another trait thought to be at the core of who we are is our sense of "self." Marcus Raichle, a professor of radiology and neurology at Washington University in St. Louis, is trying to learn how the brain generates this sense that "you're you and I'm me and we know that." He and

his colleagues suspected that some of the brain's frenetic "resting" activity—it consumes about 20 percent of the body's entire energy budget even when not engaged in any particular task—might be supporting self-awareness. A hint of where this might be happening in the brain came from scans of people tackling challenges that seem to lie outside the self, such as math problems. Baseline resting activity dropped off in a portion of the brain's prefrontal cortex, a couple of inches behind the center of the forehead.

To investigate further, Raichle's team designed a new experiment that compared brain activity in situations that were identical except in the self-involvement they demanded. In one, the subjects had to say whether pictures of mundane objects, such as picnic scenes and kittens, belonged indoors or outdoors. This task—which required the subjects to step outside of themselves—caused activity in the prefrontal area to decrease. In the other, they were asked to consider whether the same pictures had pleasant or unpleasant associations. Activity in the supposed "self" networks surged as the viewers considered their own response to the pictures. The contrast, the researchers argued last March in *Proceedings of the National Academy of Sciences*, suggests that at least part of our sense of self depends on knots of neurons elaborately intertwined in the prefrontal cortex.

Other thoughts. At the other end of the spectrum, some researchers are looking for the underpinnings of "other"—our ability to put ourselves in other people's shoes and imagine their beliefs and desires. In one telling study, Chris Frith and his team at University College London asked subjects in the scanner to think about the following incident: A burglar robs a shop, walks down the street, and unknowingly drops his glove. A policeman coming from behind stops him to tell him about the glove. The burglar turns around and gives himself up. Why does he do this?

The answer—that the burglar thinks the policeman is about to arrest him—requires thinking about the "other": the thief and his mental state. Frith's team scanned subjects' brains at this moment of empathy. The data showed intriguing parallels between the neural circuits that lit up and the ones typically activated when thinking about one's self. "Thinking about yourself in a situation may be the way you think about other people," says Frith.

Researchers trying to image the mind are quick to hedge their claims. Dartmouth University's Michael Gazzaniga, the first scientist to secure an fMRI machine for a psychology department, admits that it is a somewhat crude tool. It traces brain activity by tracking blood flow, which rises wherever there's a surge in metabolism. It's possible, Gazzaniga says, that elements of certain tasks "may be so automatic that they require no increase in metabolism," which would allow active brain regions to slip past the technique undetected. Other sober scientists note that interpreting brain maps can get hairy. "If a number of areas show activation, we don't know whether they are causally involved or going along for the ride," says Eric Kandel, professor of neurobiology at Columbia University College of Physicians and Surgeons.

In the end, no one claims that the work will point to a single brain area for, say, morality or consciousness. Indeed, the brain mappers are careful to distance themselves from 19th-century phrenologists, who believed that every ability had its own brain compartment. "Everything that happens in the brain is based on the work of systems, like music in an orchestra performed from a score," says Antonio Damasio, professor of neurology at the University of Iowa. "It all sounds like one thing, but it's coming from 100 or more individual parts. What we're doing is finding out those little parts."

Intelligent intelligence testing

Psychologists are broadening the concept of intelligence and how to test it.

BY ETIENNE BENSON
Monitor staff

Standardized intelligence testing, now almost 100 years old, has been called one of psychology's greatest successes. It is certainly one of the field's most persistent and widely used inventions.

Since Alfred Binet first used a standardized test to identify learning-impaired Parisian children in the early 1900s, it has become one of the primary tools for identifying children with mental retardation and learning disabilities. It has helped the U.S. military place its new recruits in positions that suit their skills and abilities. And, since the administration of the original Scholastic Aptitude Test (SAT)—adapted in 1926 from an intelligence test developed for the U.S. Army during World War I—it has spawned a variety of aptitude and achievement tests that shape the educational choices of millions of students each year.

But intelligence testing has also been accused of unfairly stratifying test-takers by race, gender, class and culture; of minimizing the importance of creativity, character and practical know-how; and of propagating the idea that people are born with an unchangeable endowment of intellectual potential that determines their success in life.

Since the 1970s, intelligence researchers have been trying to preserve the usefulness of intelligence tests while addressing those concerns. They have done so in a number of ways, including updating the Wechsler Intelligence Scale for Children (WISC) and the Stanford-Binet Intelligence Scale so they better reflect the abilities of test-takers from diverse cultural and linguistic backgrounds. They have developed new, more sophisticated ways of creating, administering and interpreting those tests. And they have produced new theories and tests that broaden the concept of intelligence beyond its traditional boundaries.

As a result, many of the biases identified by critics of intelligence testing have been reduced, and new tests are available that, unlike traditional intelligence tests, are based on modern theories of brain function, says Alan Kaufman, PhD, a clinical professor of psychology at the Yale School of Medicine.

For example, in the early 1980s, Kaufman and his wife, Nadeen Kaufman, EdD, a lecturer at the Yale School of Medicine, published the Kaufman Assessment Battery for Children (K-ABC), then one of the only alternatives to the WISC and the Stanford-Binet. Together with the Woodcock-Johnson Tests of Cognitive Ability, first published in the late 1970s, and later tests, such as the Differential Ability Scales and the Cognitive Assessment System (CAS), the K-ABC helped expand the field of intelligence testing beyond the traditional tests.

Nonetheless, says Kaufman, there remains a major gap between the theories and tests that have been developed in the past 20 years and the way intelligence tests are actually used. Narrowing that gap remains a major challenge for intelligence researchers as the field approaches its 100th anniversary.

King of the hill

Among intelligence tests for children, one test currently dominates the field: the WISC-III, the third revision of psychologist David Wechsler's classic 1949 test for children, which was modeled after Army intelligence tests developed during World War I.

Since the 1970s, says Kaufman, "the field has advanced in terms of incorporating new, more sophisticated methods of interpretation, and it has very much advanced in terms of statistics and methodological sophistication in development and construction of tests. But the field of practice has lagged woefully behind."

Nonetheless, people are itching for change, says Jack Naglieri, PhD, a psychologist at George Mason University who has spent the past two decades developing the CAS in collaboration with University of Alberta psychologist J.P. Das, PhD. Practitioners want tests that can help them design interventions that will actually improve children's learning; that can distinguish between children with different conditions, such as a learning disability or attention deficit disorder; and that will accurately measure the abilities of children from different linguistic and cultural backgrounds.

Naglieri's own test, the CAS, is based on the theories of Soviet neuropsychologist A.R. Luria, as is Kaufman's K-ABC. Unlike traditional intelligence tests, says Naglieri, the CAS helps teachers choose interventions for children with learning problems, identifies children with learning disabilities and attention deficit disorder and fairly assesses children from diverse backgrounds. Now, he says, the challenge is to convince people to give up the traditional scales, such as the WISC, with which they are most comfortable.

According to Nadeen Kaufman, that might not be easy to do. She believes that the practice of intelligence testing is divided between those with a neuropsychological bent, who have little interest in the subtleties of new quantitative tests, and those with an educational bent, who are increasingly shifting their interest away from intelligence and toward achievement. Neither group, in her opinion, is eager to adopt new intelligence tests.

For Naglieri, however, it is clear that there is still a great demand for intelligence tests that can help teachers better instruct children with learning problems. The challenge is convincing people that tests such as the CAS—which do not correlate highly with traditional tests—still measure something worth knowing. In fact, Naglieri believes that they measure something even more worth knowing than what the traditional tests measure. "I think we're at a really good point in our profession, where change can occur," he says, "and I think that what it's going to take is good data."

Pushing the envelope

The Kaufmans and Naglieri have worked within the testing community to effect change; their main concern is with the way tests are used, not with the basic philosophy of testing. But other reformers have launched more fundamental criticisms, ranging from "Emotional Intelligence" (Bantam Books, 1995), by Daniel Goleman, PhD, which suggested that "EI" can matter more than IQ, to the multiple intelligences theory of Harvard University psychologist Howard Gardner, PhD, and the triarchic theory of successful intelligence of APA President Robert J. Sternberg, PhD, of Yale University. These very different theories have one thing in common: the assumption that traditional theories and tests fail to capture essential aspects of intelligence.

But would-be reformers face significant challenges in convincing the testing community that theories that sound great on paper—and may even work well in the laboratory—will fly in the classroom, says Nadeen Kaufman. "A lot of these scientists have not been able to operationalize their contributions in a meaningful way for practice," she explains.

In the early 1980s, for example, Gardner attacked the idea that there was a single, immutable intelligence, instead suggesting that there were at least seven distinct intelligences: linguistic, logical-mathematical, musical, bodily-kinesthetic, spatial, interpersonal and intrapersonal. (He has since added existential and naturalist intelligences.) But that formulation has had little impact on testing, in part because the kinds of quantitative factor-analytic studies that might validate the theory in the eyes of the testing community have never been conducted.

Sternberg, in contrast, has taken a more direct approach to changing the practice of testing. His Sternberg Triarchic Abilities Test (STAT) is a battery of multiple-choice questions that tap into the three independent aspects of intelligence—analytic, practical and creative—proposed in his triarchic theory.

Recently, Sternberg and his collaborators from around the United States completed the first phase of a College Board-sponsored Rainbow Project to put the triarchic theory into practice. The goal of the project was to enhance prediction of college success and increase equity among ethnic groups in college admissions. About 800 college students took the STAT along with performance-based measures of creativity and practical intelligence.

Sternberg and his collaborators found that triarchic measures predicted a significant portion of the variance in college grade point average (GPA), even after SAT scores and high school GPA had been accounted for. The test also produced smaller differences between ethnic groups than did the SAT. In the next phase of the project, the researchers will fine-tune the test and administer it to a much larger sample of students, with the ultimate goal of producing a test that could serve as a supplement to the SAT.

Questioning the test

Beyond the task of developing better theories and tests of intelligence lies a more fundamental question: Should we even be using intelligence tests in the first place?

In certain situations where intelligence tests are currently being used, the consensus answer appears to be "no." A recent report of the President's Commission on Excellence in Special Education (PCESE), for example, suggests that the use of intelligence tests to diagnose learning disabilities should be discontinued.

For decades, learning disabilities have been diagnosed using the "IQ-achievement discrepancy model," according to which children whose achievement scores are a standard deviation or more below their IQ scores are identified as learning disabled.

The problem with that model, says Patti Harrison, PhD, a professor of school psychology at the University of Alabama, is that the discrepancy doesn't tell you anything about what kind of intervention might help the child learn. Furthermore, the child's actual behavior in the classroom and at home is often a better indicator of a child's ability than an abstract intelligence test, so children might get educational services that are more appropriate to their needs if IQ tests were discouraged, she says.

Even staunch supporters of intelligence testing, such as Naglieri and the Kaufmans, believe that the IQ-achievement discrepancy model is flawed. But, unlike the PCESE, they don't see that as a reason for getting rid of intelligence tests altogether.

For them, the problem with the discrepancy model is that it is based on a fundamental misunderstanding of the Wechsler scores, which were never intended to be used as a single, summed number. So the criticism of the discrepancy model is correct, says Alan Kaufman, but it misses the real issue: whether or not intelligence tests, when properly administered and interpreted, can be useful.

"The movement that's trying to get rid of IQ tests is failing to understand that these tests are valid in the hands of a competent practitioner who can go beyond the numbers—or at least use the numbers to understand what makes the person tick, to integrate those test scores with the kind of child you're looking at, and to blend those behaviors with the scores to make useful recommendations," he says.

Intelligence tests help psychologists make recommendations about the kind of teaching that will benefit a child most, according to Ron Palomares, PhD, assistant executive director in the APA Practice Directorate's Office of Policy and Advocacy in the Schools. Psychologists are taught to assess patterns of performance on intelligence tests and to obtain clinical observations of the child during the testing session. That, he says, removes the focus from a single IQ score and allows for an assessment of the child as a whole, which can then be used to develop individualized teaching strategies.

Critics of intelligence testing often fail to consider that most of the alternatives are even more prone to problems of fairness and validity than the measures that are currently used, says APA President-elect Diane F. Halpern, PhD, of Claremont McKenna College.

"We will always need some way of making intelligent decisions about people," says Halpern. "We're not all the same; we have different skills and abilities. What's wrong is thinking of intelligence as a fixed, innate ability, instead of something that develops in a context."

From *Monitor on Psychology*, February 2003, pp. 48-51. © 2003 by American Psychological Association.

The Inner Savant

ARE YOU CAPABLE OF MULTIPLYING 147,631,789 BY 23,674 IN YOUR HEAD, INSTANTLY? PHYSICIST ALLAN SNYDER SAYS YOU PROBABLY CAN, BASED ON HIS NEW THEORY ABOUT THE ORIGIN OF THE EXTRAORDINARY SKILLS OF AUTISTIC SAVANTS

BY DOUGLAS S. FOX

DRAWINGS BY NORMAL 4-YEAR-OLDS
When 4-year-old children draw a horse, they typically choose to establish its contour and familiar features such as head, eyes, legs, and tail. Allan Snyder believes that these kids draw on a concept of the horse to re-create it rather than recalling the precise physical details, as savants do.

NADIA APPEARED HEALTHY AT BIRTH, BUT BY THE time she was 2, her parents knew something was amiss. She avoided eye contact and didn't respond when her mother smiled or cooed. She didn't even seem to recognize her mother. At 6 months she still had not spoken a word. She was unusually clumsy and spent hours in repetitive play, such as tearing paper into strips.

But at 3 1/2, she picked up a pen and began to draw—not scribble, *draw*. Without any training, she created from memory sketches of galloping horses that only a trained adult could equal. Unlike the way most people might draw a horse, beginning with its outline, Nadia began with random details. First a hoof, then the horse's mane, then its harness. Only later did she lay down firm lines connecting these floating features. And when she did connect them, they were always in the correct position relative to one another.

Nadia is an autistic savant, a rare condition marked by severe mental and social deficits but also by a mysterious talent that appears spontaneously—usually before age 6.

Sometimes the ability of a savant is so striking, it eventually makes news. The most famous savant was a man called Joseph, the individual Dustin Hoffman drew upon for his character in the 1988 movie *Rain Man*. Joseph could immediately answer this question: "What number times what number gives 1,234,567,890?" His answer was "Nine times 137,174,210." Another savant could double 8,388,628 up to 24 times within several seconds, yielding the sum 140,737,488,355,328. A 6-year-old savant named Trevor listened to his older brother play the piano one day, then climbed onto the piano stool himself and played it better. A savant named Eric could find what he called the "sweet spot" in a room full of speakers playing music, the spot where sound waves from the different sources hit his ears at exactly the same time.

Most researchers have offered a simple explanation for these extraordinary gifts: compulsive learning. But Allan Snyder, a vision researcher and award-winning physicist who is director of the Center for the Mind at the University of Sydney and the Australian National University, has advanced a new explanation of such talents. "Each of us has the innate capacity for savantlike skills," says Snyder, "but that mental machinery is unconscious in most people."

Savants, he believes, can tap into the human mind's remarkable processing abilities. Even something as simple as seeing, he explains, requires phenomenally complex information processing. When a person looks at an object, for example, the brain immediately estimates an object's distance by calculating the subtle differences between the two images on each retina (computers programmed to do this require extreme memory and speed). During the process of face recognition, the brain analyzes countless details, such as the texture of skin and the shape of the eyes, jawbone, and lips. Most people are not aware of these calculations. In savants, says Snyder, the top layer of mental processing—conceptual

thinking, making conclusions—is somehow stripped away. Without it, savants can access a startling capacity for recalling endless detail or for performing lightning-quick calculations. Snyder's theory has a radical conclusion of its own: He believes it may be possible someday to create technologies that will allow any nonautistic person to exploit these abilities.

THE ORIGINS OF AUTISM ARE THOUGHT TO LIE IN EARLY brain development. During the first three years of life, the brain grows at a tremendous rate. In autistic children, neurons seem to connect haphazardly, causing widespread abnormalities, especially in the cerebellum, which integrates thinking and movement, and the limbic region, which integrates experience with specific emotions. Abnormalities in these regions seem to stunt interest in the environment and in social interaction. Autistic children have narrowed fields of attention and a poor ability to recognize faces. They are more likely to view a face, for example, as individual components rather than as a whole. Imaging studies have shown that when autistic children see a familiar face, their pattern of brain activation is different from that of normal children.

That narrowed focus may explain the autistic child's ability to concentrate endlessly on a single repetitive activity, such as rocking in a chair or watching clothes tumble in a dryer. Only one out of 10 autistic children show special skills.

In a 1999 paper, Snyder and his colleague John Mitchell challenged the compulsive-practice explanation for savant abilities, arguing that the same skills are biologically latent in all of us. "Everyone in the world was skeptical," says Vilayanur Ramachandran, director of the Center for Brain and Cognition at the University of California at San Diego. "Snyder deserves credit for making it clear that savant abilities might be extremely important for understanding aspects of human nature and creativity."

SNYDER'S OFFICE AT THE UNIVERSITY OF SYDNEY IS IN A Gothic building, complete with pointed towers and notched battlements. Inside, Nadia's drawings of horses adorn the walls; artwork by other savants hangs in nearby rooms.

Snyder's interest in autism evolved from his studies of light and vision. Trained as a physicist, he spent several years studying fiber optics and how light beams can guide their own path. At one time he was interested in studying the natural fiber optics in insects' eyes. The question that carried him from vision research to autism had to do with what happens after light hits the human retina: How are the incoming signals transformed into data that is ultimately processed as images in the brain? Snyder was fascinated by the processing power required to accomplish such a feat.

During a sabbatical to Cambridge in 1987, Snyder devoured Ramachandran's careful studies of perception and optical illusions. One showed how the brain derives an object's three-dimensional shape: Falling light creates a shadow pattern on the object, and by interpreting the shading, the brain grasps the object's shape. "You're not aware how your mind comes to those conclusions," says Snyder. "When you look at a ball, you don't know why you see it as a ball and not a circle. The reason is your brain is extracting the shape from the subtle shading around the ball's surface." Every brain possesses that innate ability, yet only artists can do it backward, using shading to portray volume.

"Then," says Snyder, speaking slowly for emphasis, "I asked the question that put me on a 10-year quest"—how can we bypass the mind's conceptual thinking and gain conscious access to the raw, uninterpreted information of our basic perceptions? Can we shed the assumptions built into our visual processing system?

A few years later, he read about Nadia and other savant artists in Oliver Sacks's *The Man Who Mistook His Wife for a Hat and Other Clinical Tales*. As he sat in his Sydney apartment one afternoon with the book in hand, an idea surfaced. Perhaps someone like Nadia who lacked the ability to organize sensory input into concepts might provide a window into the fundamental features of perception.

IF SOMEONE CAN BECOME AN INSTANT SAVANT, SNYDER WONDERED, DOESN'T THAT SUGGEST WE ALL HAVE SAVANTLIKE POTENTIAL LOCKED AWAY IN OUR BRAINS?

Snyder's theory began with art, but he came to believe that all savant skills, whether in music, calculation, math, or spatial relationships, derive from a lightning-fast processor in the brain that divides things—time, space, or an object—into equal parts. Dividing time might allow a savant child to know the exact time when he's awakened, and it might help Eric find the sweet spot by allowing him to sense millisecond differences in the sounds hitting his right and left ears. Dividing space might allow Nadia to place a disembodied hoof and mane on a page precisely where they belong. It might also allow two savant twins to instantaneously count matches spilled on the floor (one said "111"; the other said "37, 37, 37"). Meanwhile, splitting numbers might allow math savants to factor 10-digit numbers or easily identify large prime numbers—which are impossible to split.

Compulsive practice might enhance these skills over time, but Snyder contends that practice alone cannot explain the phenomenon. As evidence, he cites rare cases of sudden-onset savantism. Orlando Serrell, for example, was hit on the head by a baseball at the age of 10. A few months later, he began recalling an endless barrage of license-plate numbers, song lyrics, and weather reports.

If someone can become an instant savant, Snyder thought, doesn't that suggest we all have the potential locked away in our brains? "Snyder's ideas sound very New Age. This is why people are skeptical," says Ramachandran. "But I have a more open mind than many of my colleagues simply because I've seen [sudden-onset cases] happen."

Bruce Miller, a neurologist at the University of California at San Francisco, has seen similar transformations in patients with frontotemporal dementia, a degenerative brain disease that strikes people in their fifties and sixties. Some of these patients, he says, spontaneously develop both interest and skill in art and music. Brain-imaging studies have shown that most patients with frontotemporal dementia who develop skills have abnormally low blood flow or low metabolic activity in their left temporal lobe. Because language abilities are concentrated in the left side of the brain, these people gradually lose the ability to speak, read, and write. They also lose face recognition. Meanwhile, the right side of the brain, which supports visual and spatial processing, is better preserved.

"They really do lose the linguistic meaning of things," says Miller, who believes Snyder's ideas about latent abilities complement his own observations about frontotemporal dementia. "There's a loss of higher-order processing that goes on in the anterior temporal lobe." In particular, frontotemporal dementia damages the ventral stream, a brain region that is associated with naming objects. Patients with damage in this area can't name what they're looking at, but they can often paint it beautifully. Miller has also seen physiological similarities in the brains of autistic savants and patients with frontotemporal dementia. When he performed brain-imaging studies on an autistic savant artist who started drawing horses at 18 months, he saw abnormalities similar to those of artists with frontotemporal dementia: decreased blood flow and slowed neuronal firing in the left temporal lobe.

ONE BLUSTERY, RAINY MORNING I DROVE TO MANSFIELD, a small farm town 180 miles northeast of Melbourne. I was heading to a day clinic for autistic adults, where I hoped to meet a savant. The three-hour drive pitched and rolled through hills, occasionally cutting through dense eucalyptus forests punctuated with yellow koala-crossing signs. From time to time, I saw large, white-crested

A DRAWING BY A 3-YEAR OLD SAVANT
A 3-year-old child named Nadia became famous for her ability to sketch spectacularly detailed horses and riders from memory. Savants like Nadia show the ability to perform unusual feats of illustration or calculation when they are younger than 6. Snyder wants to figure out how they do it.

parrots; in one spot, a flock of a thousand or more in flight wheeled about like a galaxy.

I finally spotted my destination: Acorn Outdoor Ornaments. Within this one-story house, autistic adults learn how to live independently. They also create inexpensive lawn decorations, like the cement dwarf I see on the roof.

Joan Curtis, a physician who runs Acorn and a related follow-up program, explained that while true savants are rare, many people with autism have significant talents. Nurturing their gifts, she said, helps draw them into social interaction. Guy was one of the participants I met at Acorn. Although he was uncomfortable shaking my hand, all things electronic fascinated him, and he questioned me intently about my tape recorder.

Every horizontal surface in Guy's room was covered with his creations. One was an electric fan with a metal alligator mouth on the front that opened and closed as it rotated from side to side. On another fan a metal fisherman raised and lowered his pole with each revolution. And

then I saw the sheep. Viewed from the left, it was covered in wool. Viewed from the right, it was a skeleton, which I learned Guy had assembled without any help. Guy didn't say much about himself. He cannot read nor do arithmetic, but he has built an electric dog that barks, pants, wags its tail, and urinates.

During my visit, another Acorn participant, Tim, blew into the room like a surprise guest on *The Tonight Show*. He was in a hurry to leave again, but asked me my birthday—July 15, 1970.

"Born on a Wednesday, eh?" he responded nonchalantly—and correctly.

"How did you do that?" I asked.

"I did it well," he replied.

"But how?" I asked.

"*Very* well," he replied, with obvious pleasure. Then he was out the door and gone.

HOW DO CALENDAR SAVANTS DO IT? SEVERAL YEARS AGO Timothy Rickard, a cognitive psychologist at the University of California at San Diego, evaluated a 40-year-old man with a mental age of 5 who could assign a day of the week to a date with 70 percent accuracy. Because the man was blind from birth, he couldn't study calendars or even imagine calendars. He couldn't do simple arithmetic either, so he couldn't use a mathematical algorithm. But he could only do dates falling within his lifetime, which suggests that he used memory.

He could, however, do some arithmetic, such as answer this question: If today is Wednesday, what day is two days from now? Rickard suspects that memorizing 2,000 dates and using such arithmetic would allow 70 percent accuracy. "That doesn't reduce it to a trivial skill, but it's not inconceivable that someone could acquire this performance with a lot of effort," he says. It's especially plausible given the single-minded drive with which autistics pursue interests.

Yet Tim, the savant at Acorn, can calculate dates as far back as 1900, as well as into the future. And there are reports of twins who could calculate dates 40,000 years in the past or future. Still, practice may be part of it. Robyn Young, an autism researcher at Flinders University in Adelaide, Australia, says some calendar savants study perpetual calendars several days a week (there are only 14 different calendar configurations; perpetual calendars cross-reference them to years).

But even if savants practice, they may still tap into that universal ability Snyder has proposed. Here it helps to consider art savants. That Nadia began drawings with minor features rather than overall outlines suggests that she tended to perceive individual details more prominently than she did the whole—or the concept—of what she was drawing. Other savant artists draw the same way.

DRAWING BY A SAVANT CHILD
As a child, Stephen Wiltshire did not communicate with the world except through drawing. At 10, he sketched London's Natural History Museum from memory. He is now, at 27, an accomplished artist.

PHOTOGRAPH FROM *NATURAL HISTORY MUSEUM*, J. M. DENT & SONS LTD., 1987, COPYRIGHT STEPHEN WILTSHIRE.

THERE ARE REPORTS OF TWINS WHO COULD CALCULATE DATES UP TO 40,000 YEARS IN THE PAST OR FUTURE

Autistic children differ from nonautistic children in another way. Normal kids find it frustrating to copy a picture containing a visual illusion, such as M. C. Escher's drawing in which water flows uphill. Autistic children don't. That fits with Snyder's idea that they're recording what they see without interpretation and reproducing it with ease in their own drawings.

Even accomplished artists sometimes employ strategies to shake up their preconceptions about what they're seeing. Guy Diehl is not a savant, but he is known for his series of crystal-clear still lifes of stacked books, drafting implements, and fruit. When Diehl finds that he's hit a sticking point on a painting, for example, he may actually view it in a mirror or upside down. "It reveals things you otherwise wouldn't see, because you're seeing it differ-

ently," he says. "You're almost seeing it for the first time again."

Diehl showed me how art students use this technique to learn to draw. He put a pair of scissors on a table and told me to draw the negative space around the scissors, not the scissors themselves. The result: I felt I was drawing individual lines, not an object, and my drawing wasn't half bad, either.

Drawing exercises are one way of coaxing conceptual machinery to take five, but Snyder is pursuing a more direct method. He has suggested that a technique called transcranial magnetic stimulation, which uses magnetic fields to disrupt neuronal firing, could knock out a normal person's conceptual brain machinery, temporarily rendering him savantlike.

Young and her colleague Michael Ridding of the University of Adelaide tried it. Using transcranial magnetic stimulation on 17 volunteers, they inhibited neural activity in the frontotemporal area. This language and concept-supporting brain region is affected in patients with frontotemporal dementia and in the art savant whom Miller studied. In this altered state, the volunteers performed savantlike tasks—horse drawing, calendar calculating, and multiplying.

Five of the 17 volunteers improved—not to savant levels, but no one expected that, because savants practice. Furthermore, transcranial magnetic stimulation isn't a precise tool for targeting brain regions. But the five volunteers who improved were those in whom separate neurological assessments indicated that the fronto-temporal area was successfully targeted. "Obviously I don't think the idea is so outlandish anymore," says Young. "I think it is a plausible hypothesis. It always was, but I didn't expect we'd actually find the things we did."

Snyder himself is experimenting with grander ideas. "We want to enhance conceptual abilities," he says, "and on the other hand remove them and enhance objectivity."

He imagines a combination of training and hardware that might, for example, help an engineer get past a sticking point on a design project by offering a fresh angle on the problem. One method would involve learning to monitor one's own brain waves. By watching one's own brain waves during drawing exercises, Snyder imagines it may be possible to learn to control them in a way that shuts down their concept-making machinery—even the left temporal lobe itself.

Even if further research never fully reveals why savants have extraordinary skills, we may at least learn from their potential. Snyder is optimistic. "I envisage the day," he says, "when the way to get out of a [mental rut] is you pick up this thing—those of us with jobs that demand a certain type of creativity—and you stimulate your brain. I'm very serious about this."

From *Discover*, February 2002, pp. 42-49. © 2002. Reprinted with permission of the author, Douglas S. Fox.

UNIT 6
Emotion and Motivation

Unit Selections

19. **Fundamental Feelings**, Antonio Damasio
20. **Medical Detection of False Witness**, Brandon Spun
21. **Emotions and the Brain: Laughter**, Steven Johnson
22. **How to Multitask**, Catherine Bush

Key Points to Consider

- What is motivation? What is an emotion? How are the two related to each other? Do you think they always affect one another?

- From where do emotions originate, nature or nurture? Why did you give the answer you did? Are various emotions controlled by different factors? For example, does the brain control some emotions while other emotions are controlled by the situation? What role does the nervous system play in emotionality?

- What are some positive emotions? What are some examples of negative emotions? Do you think there is an "appropriate" emotion for every situation? Why are some people unemotional and others very expressive?

- Are humans the only creatures that experience humor, joy, and laughter? Why did you answer as you did? How does neuroscience contribute to our understanding of humor and laughter?

- Do you sometimes feel unmotivated or overwhelmed by too much to do? When you have to multitask, how do you usually respond to the challenge? Do you think you can improve your ability to juggle several tasks at the same time? If a friend asked you how she could improve her ability to multitask, what advice would you offer?

 **Links: www.dushkin.com/online/**
These sites are annotated in the World Wide Web pages.

CYFERNET-Youth Development
http://twosocks.ces.ncsu.edu/cyfdb/browse_2.php?search=Youth

Emotional Intelligence Discovery
http://www.cwrl.utexas.edu/~bump/Hu305/3/3/3/

John Suler's Teaching Clinical Psychology Site
http://www.rider.edu/users/suler/tcp.html

Nature vs. Nurture: Gergen Dialogue with Winifred Gallagher
http://www.pbs.org/newshour/gergen/gallagher_5-14.html

Jasmine's sister was a working mother and always reminded Jasmine about how exciting life on the road as a sales representative was. Jasmine stayed home because she loved her children, two-year-old Min, four-year-old Chi'Ming, and newborn Yuan. On the day of the particular incident described below, Jasmine was having a difficult time with the children. The baby, Yuan, had been crying all day from colic. The other two children had been bickering over their toys. Jasmine, realizing that it was already 5:15 and her husband would be home any minute, frantically started preparing dinner. She wanted to fix a nice dinner so that she and her husband could eat after the children went to bed, then relax and enjoy each other.

This was not to be. Jasmine sat waiting for her no-show husband. When he finally walked in the door at 10:15, Jasmine was furious. His excuse that his boss had invited the whole office for dinner didn't reduce Jasmine's ire. Jasmine reasoned that her husband could have called to say that he wouldn't be home for dinner; he could have taken five minutes to do that. He said he did but the phone was busy. Jasmine berated her husband. Her face was taut and red with rage. Her voice wavered as she escalated her decibel level. Suddenly, bursting into tears, she ran into the living room. Her husband retreated to the safety of their bedroom.

Exhausted and disappointed, Jasmine sat alone and pondered why she was so angry with her husband. Was she just tired? Was she frustrated by negotiating with young children all day and simply want another adult around once in a while? Was she secretly worried and jealous that her husband was seeing another woman and had lied about his whereabouts? Was she combative because her husband's and her sister's lives seemed so much fuller than her own life? Jasmine was unsure just how she felt and why she exploded in such rage at her husband, someone she loved dearly.

This story, while sad and gender stereotypical, is not necessarily unrealistic when it comes to emotions. There are times when we are moved to deep emotion. On other occasions when we expect waterfalls of tears, we find that our eyes are dry or simply a little misty. What are these strange things we call emotions? What motivates us to rage at someone we love? And why do we pick apart our every mood?

These questions and others have inspired psychologists to study emotions and motivation. The above episode about Jasmine, besides introducing these topics to you, also illustrates why these two topics are usually interrelated in psychology. Some emotions are pleasant, so pleasant that we are motivated to keep them going. Pleasant emotions are exemplified by love, pride, and joy. Other emotions are terribly draining and oppressive—so negative that we hope they will be over as soon as possible. Negative emotions are exemplified by anger, grief, and jealousy. Emotions and motivation and their relationship to each other are the focus of this unit.

Four articles round out this unit. "Fundamental Feelings" is the first article and was written by noted scientist, Antonio Damasio. Damasio is famous for his studies linking emotions to the nervous system. In this brief article he introduces us to his research and his ideas regarding emotionality.

A companion article, "Medical Detection of False Witness," also discusses emotions. The slant of the article, though, is not how we experience emotions but rather whether we can detect false emotions in others. The polygraph, used in the past to detect guilt and lying, has received much criticism in the literature and from the courts. In the present article, new methods for uncovering deceit are discussed.

The next article examines emotions and the brain. In the article by Steven Johnson entitled "Emotions and the Brain: Laughter," both humor and laughter are discussed. An interesting question addressed by Johnson is whether humans are the only creatures to experience humor and laughter. Again, neuroscience is pointing to the answer.

One article on motivation is included in this unit—"How to Multitask." Multitasking is a term frequently associated with computers, but it also is an apt description of what most of us are asked to do daily—undertake multiple tasks at the same time. Multitasking can divide our attention, demand more time than it ought, and make us complete each responsibility less well than if we attempted it singly. How to be more successful at daily life—especially when confronted with the challenge of completing multiple jobs at the same time—is reviewed here.

Fundamental feelings

Antonio Damasio

The groundwork for the science of emotion was laid down most auspiciously over a century ago, but neuroscience has given the problem a resolute cold shoulder until recently. By the time that Charles Darwin had remarked on the continuity of emotional phenomena from non-human species to humans; William James had proposed an insightful mechanism for its production; Sigmund Freud had noted the central role of emotions in psychopathological states; and Charles Sherrington had begun the physiological investigation of the neural circuits involved in emotion, one might have expected neuroscience to be poised for an all-out attack on the problem. It is not usually appreciated that the probable cause of the neglect of the topic was the improper distinction between the concepts of emotion and feelings.

Some traits of feelings—their subjective nature, the fact that they are private, hidden from view, and often difficult to analyse—were projected onto emotions, so that they too were deemed subjective, private, hidden and elusive. Not surprisingly, neuroscientists were disinclined to give their best efforts to a problem that did not seem to be amenable to proper hypothesizing and measurement. Somewhat alarmingly, this conflation of the two concepts persists, as does the idea that the neurobiology of feelings is out of reach. A clarification is in order.

An emotion, be it happiness or sadness, embarrassment or pride, is a patterned collection of chemical and neural responses that is produced by the brain when it detects the presence of an emotionally competent stimulus—an object or situation, for example. The processing of the stimulus may be conscious but it need not be, as the responses are engendered automatically.

Emotional responses are a mode of reaction of brains that are prepared by evolution to respond to certain classes of objects and events with certain repertoires of action. Eventually, the brain associates other objects and events that occur in individual experience with those that are innately set to cause emotions, so that another set of emotionally competent stimuli arises.

The main target of the emotional responses is the body—the internal milieu, the viscera and the musculoskeletal system—but there are also targets within the brain itself, for example, monoaminergic nuclei in the brainstem tegmentum. The result of the body-targeting responses is the creation of an emotional state—involving adjustments in homeostatic balance—as well as the enactment of specific behaviours, such as freezing or fight-or-flight, and the production of particular facial expressions. The result of the brain-targeting responses is an alteration in the mode of brain operation during the emotional body adjustments, the consequence of which is, for example, a change in the attention accorded to stimuli.

Emotion

Emotion and feelings are closely related but separable phenomena; their elucidation, at long last, is now proceeding in earnest.

Emotions allow organisms to cope successfully with objects and situations that are potentially dangerous or advantageous. They are just the most visible part of a huge edifice of undeliberated biological regulation that includes the homeostatic reactions that maintain metabolism; pain signalling; and drives such as hunger and thirst. Most emotional responses are directly observable either with the naked eye or with scientific probes such as psychophysiological and neurophysiological measurements and endocrine assays. Thus, emotions are not subjective, private, elusive or undefinable. Their neurobiology can be investigated objectively, not just in humans but in laboratory species, from *Drosophila* and *Aplysia* to rodents and non-human primates.

A working definition of feelings is a different matter. Feelings are the mental representation of the physiological changes that characterize emotions. Unlike emotions, which are scientifically public, feelings are indeed private, although no more subjective than any other aspect of the mind, for example my planning of this sentence, or the mental solving of a mathematical problem. Feelings are as amenable to scientific analysis as any other cognitive phenomenon, provided that appropriate methods are used. Moreover, because feelings are the direct consequences of emotions, the elucidation of emotional neurobiology opens the way to elucidating the neurobiology of feelings.

If emotions provide an immediate response to certain challenges and opportunities faced by an organism, the feeling of those emotions provides it with a mental alert. Feelings amplify the impact of a given situation, enhance learning, and increase the probability that comparable situations can be anticipated.

The neural systems that are involved in the production of emotions are being identified through studies of humans and other animals. Various structures, such as the amygdala and the ventromedial prefrontal cortices, trigger emotions by functioning as interfaces between the processing of emotionally competent stimuli and the execution of emotions. But the real executors of emotions are structures in the hypothalamus, in the basal forebrain (for example, the nucleus accumbens) and in the brainstem (for example, the nuclei in the periaqueductal grey). These are the structures that directly signal, chemically and neurally, to the body and brain targets at which alterations constitute an emotional state.

No less importantly, recent functional imaging studies reveal that body-sensing areas, such as the cortices in the insula, the second somatosensory region (S2) and the cingulate region of the brain, show a statistically significant pattern of activation or deactivation when normal individuals experience the emotions of sadness, happiness, fear and anger. Moreover, these patterns vary between different emotions. Those body-related patterns are tangible neural correlates of feelings, meaning that we know where to look further to unravel the remaining neurophysiological mysteries behind one of the most critical aspects of human experience.

FURTHER READING

Damasio, A. R. *The Feeling of What Happens: Body and Emotion in the Making of Consciousness* (Harcourt Brace, New York, 1999).

Davidson, R. J. & Irwin, W. *Trends Cogn. Neurosci.* **3**, 11–22 (1999).

Panksepp, J. *Affective Neuroscience: The Foundations of Human and Animal Emotions* (Oxford Univ. Press, New York, 1998).

Vuillemier, P., Driver, J., Armony, J. & Dolan, R. J. *Neuron* **30**, 829–841 (2000).

Antonio Damasio is in the Department of Neurology, University of Iowa College of Medicine, 200 Hawkins Drive, Iowa City, Iowa 52242, USA.

Medical detection of false witness

High-tech lie detectors one day may be impossible to fool, but so far the only guarantee is that they will stir up as much controversy as the original polygraph.

By Brandon Spun

Try this scenario: Zacarias Moussaoui is led out of a dark cell into a silent room at an undisclosed location. An electrode headset is fitted to his skull while his lawyer watches disapprovingly. After nearly an hour of flicking switches and flashing lights, the procedure concludes. An investigator reviews the results and determines exactly what role Moussaoui played in the Sept. 11 terrorist attacks. You cannot hide your memories from the machine.

Some say this no longer is science fiction. In the months following Sept. 11, articles about techno-security have appeared in the popular press and in professional journals promising just such a result from high-tech lie detectors. One of these machines was featured in the *New York Times Magazine's* "2001 Encyclopedia of Innovations, Conceptual Leaps and Harebrained Schemes." An INSIGHT review of new polygraph technologies suggests that most of them fit all three categories.

"When one uses any kind of lie detector, one is saying 'ask the body, not the person,'" says Mike Gazzaniga, director of the Center for Cognitive Neuroscience based at Dartmouth College. "One assumes with autonomic studies [polygraphs] that the body can't lie," Gazzaniga says. The assumption is that the body's autonomic reactions—such as blood pressure, breathing and heart rate—cannot be manipulated to support deception. "They assume that lies are mental constructs," Gazzaniga continues. "Among those things that separate man from animal is his capacity for deception. The question is how to make a science and not folk psychology out of this."

One investigative method established for autonomic research is the "guilty-knowledge test," which consists of confronting a suspect with a series of items, some relevant to a crime and others irrelevant. It is believed that a subject who has "guilty knowledge" will react most strongly to relevant or target items, while an innocent person will not.

Such tests have been disputed since the first polygraph was invented by William Marston in 1917. A polygraph can be an effective tool, but high-profile cases such as those of Aldrich

Ames and Robert Hanssen, spies who beat the machine, frequently are cited to show its fallibility. Critics point out that data gathered from these tests are indicative of physiological response rather than veracity, with the latter being distinguished from the former. They say there is no necessary connection between a subject's verbal and physical report.

Polygraph expert Drew Richardson, a former FBI special agent at Quantico Laboratories, says "the test is generally not admissible in court because it is largely not accepted as a valid scientific technique."

But what if a better mousetrap were to become available? What if there were a machine that could not be fooled? What if an autonomic response to lying were to be identified that could not be suppressed? Recently, some have made such claims. Here is a look at those claims and what is being said about them.

Brain fingerprinting: According to Larry Farwell, an independent psychophysiologist at Human Brain Research Laboratory in Fairfield, Iowa, the fundamental difference between a guilty and innocent person is a record of the crime stored in the brain. "The difference between a terrorist who has been through a training camp and an Afghan student is the memory," Farwell says. Brain fingerprinting identifies memories, he claims.

This examination consists of a modified guilty-knowledge test that uses targets and irrelevants, but adds probes that are unique details of a crime that only the culprit could know. All subjects are familiarized with the targets in order actively to identify them during the test. A guilty subject is expected to have the same response to the probes as to the targets.

When one is exposed to something that already is stored in memory, the brain emits an electrical response called a p300 wave. This phenomenon occurs approximately 300 milliseconds after a meaningful stimulus. The "p" stands for positive electrical voltage (certain speech processes emit a negative 400). Electrodes on the parietal zero (the top of the back of the head) record this activity.

Brain fingerprinting has been tested on FBI agents and in field situations. Farwell reports a 99 percent success rate, though he estimates the process is applicable for only 70 percent of investigations. What has attracted attention is his claim that Sept. 11 may be a good fit. He proposes sorting suspects into three groups through his method for lie detecting: those involved in the planning of the attacks, terrorists from different cells and the innocent. "We were able to detect whether someone was an FBI agent by using information from their training manuals," Farwell says. "We could use the same method with al-Qaeda's manual for terrorists."

One of the first things other scientists familiar with Farwell's proposal for lie detection point out is that the last peer-reviewed paper he published on this was in 1991. Emanuel Donchin, a professor of psychology at the University of South Florida, contributed to the federal evaluation of Farwell's techniques. He also was Farwell's teacher and 1991 research partner. "Larry does a nice demonstration, but it needs much more research," Donchin says. "It is not ready as a practical tool." Donchin raises three major problems with the Farwell approach: stimuli, the oddball paradigm and interpretation.

The stimuli problem is that a probe is chosen by subjective analysis. "An investigator, not science, makes the decision," Donchin says.

The oddball paradigm involves the order of stimuli. Apparently probes change the environment of the brain. "A p300 is enormously sensitive to the order of events," Donchin says. It can occur because something is infrequent as well as meaningful. So detecting a p300 is equivalent to detecting that a memory has been distinguished by the brain. Thus, as Donchin succinctly puts it, "response to a probe ensures nothing."

Interpretation is a standard problem for lie detection. Donchin is not convinced that Farwell has overcome it. "Larry's interpretation of what must be remembered as significant is invalid and subjective," he says. "Larry is an entrepreneur, a businessman advertising a product. If you get people gullible enough to buy your product, that's all that is required."

A pre-eminent figure in psychophysiology had more to say on the subject. J.P. Rosenfeld, a professor at the University of Utah, says evaluators should look at the distribution of several p300s recorded from an individual subject while Farwell uses only one or two. "Farwell arbitrarily selected a wave," Rosenfeld says. "I am sure his data would be discounted by impartial psychophysiologists."

Rosenfeld also is concerned about Farwell's choice of subjects. "It turns out he has done extremely well using highly motivated, paid subjects from his labs," Rosenfeld says.

Conflict resolution: What first interested Daniel Langleben, assistant professor of psychiatry at the University of Pennsylvania, in lie detection was not terrorism but the behavior of drug addicts. "A substance abuser lies with no protective value," Langleben says. "For instance, you are practically suicidal if you don't tell an emergency doctor you take insulin," and yet they often don't.

Langleben, a psychiatrist as well as a self-taught anthropologist, says his mother, a linguistics professor, is an enthusiast for the works of St. Augustine and Immanuel Kant. He believes all this has been good preparation for studying the willful lie as opposed to philosophical truth. "That is, I am not interested in what philosophy would call objective truth," Langleben says. "My notion of a lie, what I explore, is remarkably similar to Augustine's."

Langleben has performed magnetic resonance imaging (MRI) on the brains of subjects as they underwent guilty-knowledge tests. While p300s provided information regarding quantity of activity, Langleben looked for blood flow and spatial resolution. He found what he says is the part of the brain active during a lie.

A normal or bold MRI is used to locate unusual activity, such as tumors, in the brain. It works by placing the body within a strong magnetic field while a weak, perpendicular magnetic field is turned on and off. This causes magnetic resonance, like flicking a car antenna. An fMRI, a bit less accurate, reads changes in blood flow up to 4 millimeters. However, by overlaying scans from fMRIs and bold MRIs, Langleben located blood flow at 6 to 8 millimeters even on the worst day.

When a person thinks, parts of the brain need more oxygen. Having performed fMRIs on people engaged in guilty-knowledge tests, Langleben claims to have isolated the location in the brain active during willful deception. He believes it is the anterior cingulate cortex, a part of the brain often associated with conflict. Though a subject might control supposed autonomic responses, this discovery is promising because we could pinpoint the very act of deception.

Langleben has not contacted the Department of Justice and was reluctant to comment on what should have been done to check the veracity of those arrested and interrogated for terrorism. However, he says, any tool to speed up the process of identifying lies in such circumstances is important. "Unlike most endless scientific questions, this one is solvable," he says.

But admittedly there are problems with this lie detector, says Langleben assistant Ruben Gur. "For one thing, you need a cooperative individual, as one must remain very still during these tests." Any movement invites error, and a subject also must remain relatively relaxed as emotional arousal can alter results.

Gur suggests the next step in research should be to perform fMRIs in conjunction with other bioindicators. And Langleben is aware of the need for more study. "If this is the Manhattan Project we are at 1941, not 1944," he says.

Other experts note problems. Rosenfeld suggests the theory may be flawed because it involves averaging multiple results, preventing case-by-case examination. He also points out that fMRIs are extremely expensive.

And, though the anterior cingulate cortex may be related to conflict and lying, not everyone is certain. This is a frontier subject. "Some say it is responsible for almost anything," says P.J. Casey, professor of psychology at Cornell University in New York. Others see it as a homunculus, or a little brain running the bigger show. "But most do say it has to do with conflict or conflict resolution," Casey says.

The foremost expert in this area, psychiatrist John Cohen of Princeton University, is of the opinion that activity in the anterior cingulate cortex is indicative of conflict but not resolution.

If so, Langleben's method may not always tell us what we want to know.

Casey explains this in a paper in which she says "paradigms of affective processing often require the subject to induce an affective state or think of emotional information that is contrary or in conflict with the subject's current state of affairs." This is crucial because, in other words, a person can consider an option without actually choosing that option, thereby inducing conflict but not producing it. This would leave investigators wondering whether a subject lied or merely considered lying.

The eye detector: Lying eyes are the latest addition to the list of science wizardry. Fox News and Science Daily are among those that have claimed that thermal-imaging lie detectors soon may be in place at airport-security checkpoints. They are referring to camera studies by James Levine, an endocrinologist at the Mayo Clinic's Honeywell Laboratories.

Levine and his collaborators theorized that subjects blush just before lying. They tested this theory using high-definition thermal-imaging cameras originally designed to see through heavy makeup and disguises.

Tests were conducted at Fort Jackson, S.C., as new recruits tried to fool the camera during an interrogation after some of them stole $20 from a mannequin they stabbed. Levine reported that in these tests the camera identified a lie with 80 percent accuracy. Advantages of the technology include quick investigations, real-time results, noninvasive screening and unskilled operation.

Levine says more testing is necessary and that the equipment must be refined for airport use, but he claims his lie detectors soon will be in commercial use. Other scientists tell INSIGHT that the "lying eye" needs more than refinement. In fact, some call the Levine system a mere blush detector. "Big Brother? More like special brother," commented one.

While Levine talks about his work as both "new" and "potentially accurate," critics say it is neither. Here are excerpts from a letter to the prestigious journal Nature that John Furedy, a professor of psychology at the University of Toronto, is preparing in response to Levine's lie-detector research:

"The procedure was only 'validated' against polygraph examination by experts (at the Department of Defense Polygraph Institute). There was no mention of a considerable body of scientific, psychophysiological literature that casts grave doubt on the scientific basis of this purported application of psychophysiology.

"The fundamental problem with the polygraph, even when administered by 'experts,' is that the measures it uses, such as electrodermal response, are virtually useless for differentiating the anxious but innocent person from the anxious and guilty one. Why should we think that thermal-imaging measures will be any more discriminating?

"It is disturbing not only for Americans, but also the world, that the national security of the world's only remaining superpower appears to depend on this modern flight of superstitious technological fancy, the only effect of which is to spread distrust within those organizations that employ it."

Or, as Rosenfeld says of the currently excited state of lie detection, "people were excited after 9/11, but that didn't advance knowledge at all, just funding."

BRANDON SPUN IS A REPORTER FOR Insight.

Emotions and the Brain:

Laughter

IF EVOLUTION COMES DOWN TO SURVIVAL OF THE FITTEST, THEN WHY DO WE JOKE AROUND SO MUCH? NEW BRAIN RESEARCH SUGGESTS THAT THE URGE TO LAUGH IS THE LUBRICANT THAT MAKES HUMANS HIGHER SOCIAL BEINGS

BY STEVEN JOHNSON

ROBERT PROVINE WANTS ME TO SEE HIS TICKLE Me Elmo doll. Wants me to hold it, as a matter of fact. It's not an unusual request for Provine. A professor of psychology and neuroscience at the University of Maryland, he has been engaged for a decade in a wide-ranging intellectual pursuit that has taken him from the panting play of young chimpanzees to the history of American sitcoms—all in search of a scientific understanding of that most unscientific of human customs: laughter.

The Elmo doll happens to incorporate two of his primary obsessions: tickling and contagious laughter. "You ever fiddled with one of these?" Provine says, as he pulls the doll out of a small canvas tote bag. He holds it up, and after a second or two, the doll begins to shriek with laughter. There's something undeniably comic in the scene: a burly, bearded man in his mid-fifties cradling a red Muppet. Provine hands Elmo to me to demonstrate the doll's vibration effect. "It brings up two interesting things," he explains, as I hold Elmo in my arms. "You have a best-selling toy that's a glorified laugh box. And when it shakes, you're getting feedback as if you're tickling."

Provine's relationship to laughter reminds me of the dramatic technique that Bertolt Brecht called the distanciation effect. Radical theater, in Brecht's vision, was supposed to distance us from our too-familiar social structures, make us see those structures with fresh eyes. In his study of laughter, Provine has been up to something comparably enlightening, helping us to recognize the strangeness of one of our most familiar emotional states. Think about that Tickle Me Elmo doll: We take it for granted that tickling causes laughter and that one person's laughter will easily "infect" other people within earshot. Even a child knows these things. (Tickling and contagious laughter are two of the distinguishing characteristics of childhood.) But when you think about them from a distance, they are strange conventions. We can understand readily enough why natural selection would have implanted the fight-or-flight response in us or endowed us with sex drives. But the tendency to laugh when others laugh in our presence or to laugh when someone strokes our belly with a feather—what's the evolutionary advantage of that? And yet a quick glance at the Nielsen ratings or the personal ads will tell you that laughter is one of the most satisfying and sought-after states available to us.

Funnily enough, the closer Provine got to understanding why we laugh, the farther he got from humor. To appreciate the roots of laughter, you have to stop thinking about jokes.

THERE IS A LONG, SEMI-ILLUSTRIOUS HISTORY OF SCHOLARLY investigation into the nature of humor, from Freud's *Jokes and Their Relation to the Unconscious,* which may well be the least funny book about humor ever written, to a British research group that announced last year that they had determined the World's Funniest Joke. Despite the fact that the researchers said they had sampled a massive international audience in making this discovery, the winning joke revolved around New Jersey residents:

A couple of New Jersey hunters are out in the woods when one of them falls to the ground. He doesn't seem to be breathing; his eyes are rolled back in his head. The other guy whips out his cell phone and calls the emergency services. He gasps to the operator: "My friend is dead! What can I do?"

The operator says: "Take it easy. I can help. First, let's make sure he's dead." There is silence, then a shot is heard. The guy's voice comes back on the line. He says, "OK, now what?"

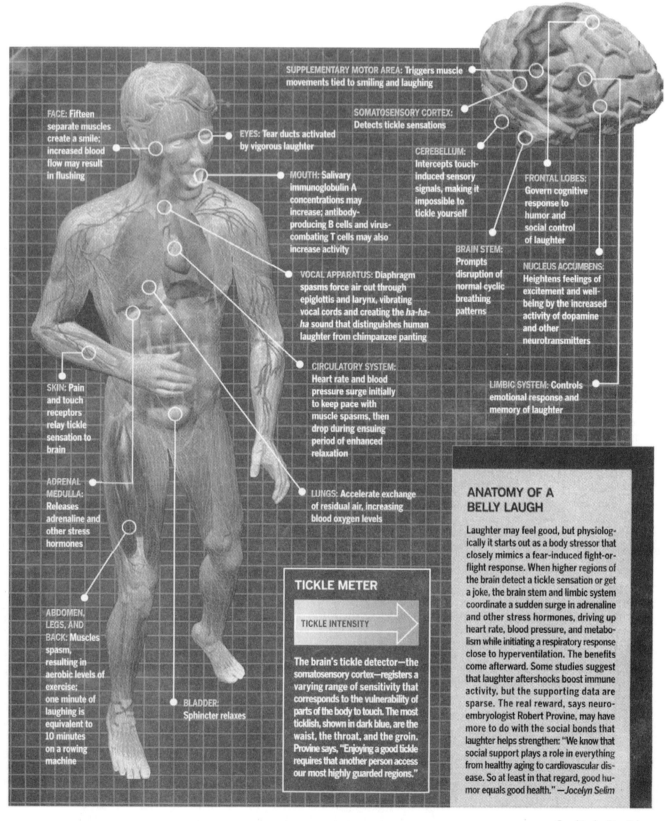

SUPPLEMENTARY MOTOR AREA: Triggers muscle movements tied to smiling and laughing

SOMATOSENSORY CORTEX: Detects tickle sensations

FACE: Fifteen separate muscles create a smile; increased blood flow may result in flushing

EYES: Tear ducts activated by vigorous laughter

MOUTH: Salivary immunoglobulin A concentrations may increase; antibody-producing B cells and virus-combating T cells may also increase activity

CEREBELLUM: Intercepts touch-induced sensory signals, making it impossible to tickle yourself

FRONTAL LOBES: Govern cognitive response to humor and social control of laughter

VOCAL APPARATUS: Diaphragm spasms force air out through epiglottis and larynx, vibrating vocal cords and creating the *ha-ha-ha* sound that distinguishes human laughter from chimpanzee panting

BRAIN STEM: Prompts disruption of normal cyclic breathing patterns

NUCLEUS ACCUMBENS: Heightens feelings of excitement and well-being by the increased activity of dopamine and other neurotransmitters

SKIN: Pain and touch receptors relay tickle sensation to brain

CIRCULATORY SYSTEM: Heart rate and blood pressure surge initially to keep pace with muscle spasms, then drop during ensuing period of enhanced relaxation

LIMBIC SYSTEM: Controls emotional response and memory of laughter

ADRENAL MEDULLA: Releases adrenaline and other stress hormones

LUNGS: Accelerate exchange of residual air, increasing blood oxygen levels

ABDOMEN, LEGS, AND BACK: Muscles spasm, resulting in aerobic levels of exercise; one minute of laughing is equivalent to 10 minutes on a rowing machine

BLADDER: Sphincter relaxes

TICKLE METER

TICKLE INTENSITY

The brain's tickle detector—the somatosensory cortex—registers a varying range of sensitivity that corresponds to the vulnerability of parts of the body to touch. The most ticklish, shown in dark blue, are the waist, the throat, and the groin. Provine says, "Enjoying a good tickle requires that another person access our most highly guarded regions."

ANATOMY OF A BELLY LAUGH

Laughter may feel good, but physiologically it starts out as a body stressor that closely mimics a fear-induced fight-or-flight response. When higher regions of the brain detect a tickle sensation or get a joke, the brain stem and limbic system coordinate a sudden surge in adrenaline and other stress hormones, driving up heart rate, blood pressure, and metabolism while initiating a respiratory response close to hyperventilation. The benefits come afterward. Some studies suggest that laughter aftershocks boost immune activity, but the supporting data are sparse. The real reward, says neuro-embryologist Robert Provine, may have more to do with the social bonds that laughter helps strengthen: "We know that social support plays a role in everything from healthy aging to cardiovascular disease. So at least in that regard, good humor equals good health." —*Jocelyn Selim*

Graphics by Don Foley

This joke illustrates that most assessments of humor's underlying structure gravitate to the notion of controlled incongruity: You're expecting x, and you get y. For the joke to work, it has to be readable on both levels. In the hunting joke there are two plausible ways to interpret the 911 operator's instructions—either the hunter checks his friend's pulse or he shoots him. The context sets you up to expect that he'll check his friend's pulse, so the—admittedly dark—humor arrives when he takes the more unlikely path. That incongruity has limits, of course: If the hunter chooses to do something utterly nonsensical—untie his shoelaces or climb a tree—the joke wouldn't be funny.

A number of studies in recent years have looked at brain activity while subjects were chuckling over a good joke—an attempt to locate a neurological funny bone. There is evidence that the frontal lobes are implicated in "getting" the joke while the brain regions associated with motor control execute the physical response of laughter. One 1999 study analyzed patients with damage to the right frontal lobes, an integrative region of the brain where emotional, logical, and perceptual data converge. The brain-damaged patients had far more difficulty than control subjects in choosing the proper punch line to a series of jokes, usually opting for absurdist, slapstick-style endings rather than traditional ones. Humor can often come in coarse, lowest-common-denominator packages, but actually getting the joke draws upon our higher brain functions.

When Provine set out to study laughter, he imagined that he would approach the problem along the lines of these humor studies: Investigating laughter meant having people listen to jokes and other witticisms and watching what happened. He began by simply observing casual conversations, counting the number of times that people laughed while listening to someone speaking. But very quickly he realized that there was a fundamental flaw in his assumptions about how laughter worked. "I started recording all these conversations," Provine says, "and the numbers I was getting—I didn't believe them when I saw them. The speakers were laughing more than the listeners. Every time that would happen, I would think, 'OK, I have to go back and start over again because that can't be right.'"

Speakers, it turned out, were 46 percent more likely to laugh than listeners—and what they were laughing at, more often than not, wasn't remotely funny. Provine and his team of undergrad students recorded the ostensible "punch lines" that triggered laughter in ordinary conversation. They found that only around 15 percent of the sentences that triggered laughter were traditionally humorous. In his book, *Laughter: A Scientific Investigation*, Provine lists some of the laugh-producing quotes:

I'll see you guys later./Put those cigarettes away./I hope we all do well./It was nice meeting you too./We can handle this./I see your point./I should do that, but I'm too lazy./I try to lead a normal life./I think I'm done./I told you so!

The few studies of laughter to date had assumed that laughing and humor were inextricably linked, but Provine's early research suggested that the connection was only an occasional one. "There's a dark side to laughter that we are too quick to overlook," he says. "The kids at Columbine were laughing as they walked through the school shooting their peers."

As his research progressed, Provine began to suspect that laughter was in fact about something else—not hu-

mor or gags or incongruity but our social interactions. He found support for this assumption in a study that had already been conducted, analyzing people's laughing patterns in social and solitary contexts. "You're 30 times more likely to laugh when you're with other people than you are when you're alone—if you don't count simulated social environments like laugh tracks on television," Provine says. "In fact, when you're alone, you're more likely to talk out loud to yourself than you are to laugh out loud. Much more." Think how rarely you'll laugh out loud at a funny passage in a book but how quick you'll be to make a friendly laugh when greeting an old acquaintance. Laughing is not an instinctive physical response to humor, the way a flinch responds to pain or a shiver to cold. It's a form of instinctive social bonding that humor is crafted to exploit.

PROVINE'S LAB AT THE BALTIMORE COUNTY CAMPUS OF THE University of Maryland looks like the back room at a stereo repair store—long tables cluttered with old equipment, tubes and wires everywhere. The walls are decorated with brightly colored pictures of tangled neurons, most of which were painted by Provine. (Add some Day-Glo typography and they might pass for signs promoting a Dead show at the Fillmore.) Provine's old mentor, the neuroembryologist Viktor Hamburger, glowers down from a picture hung above a battered Silicon Graphics workstation. His expression suggests a sense of concerned bafflement: "I trained you as a scientist, and here you are playing with dolls!"

The more technical parts of Provine's work—exploring the neuromuscular control of laughter and its relationship to the human and chimp respiratory systems—draw on his training at Washington University in St. Louis under Hamburger and Nobel laureate Rita Levi-Montalcini. But the most immediate way to grasp his insights into the evolution of laughter is to watch video footage of his informal fieldwork, which consists of Provine and a cameraman prowling Baltimore's inner harbor, asking people to laugh for the camera. The overall effect is like a color story for the local news, but as Provine and I watch the tapes together in his lab, I find myself looking at the laughters with fresh eyes. Again and again, a pattern repeats on the screen. Provine asks someone to laugh, and they demur, look puzzled for a second, and say something like, "I can't just laugh." Then they turn to their friends or family, and the laughter rolls out of them as though it were as natural as breathing. The pattern stays the same even as the subjects change: a group of high school students on a field trip, a married couple, a pair of college freshmen.

At one point Provine—dressed in a plaid shirt and khakis, looking something like the comedian Robert Klein—stops two waste-disposal workers driving a golf cart loaded up with trash bags. When they fail to guffaw on cue, Provine asks them why they can't muster one up.

97

"Because you're not funny," one of them says. They turn to each other and share a hearty laugh.

"See, you two just made each other laugh," Provine says.

"Yeah, well, we're coworkers," one of them replies.

The insistent focus on laughter patterns has a strange effect on me as Provine runs through the footage. By the time we get to the cluster of high school kids, I've stopped hearing their spoken words at all, just the rhythmic peals of laughter breaking out every 10 seconds or so. Sonically, the laughter dominates the speech; you can barely hear the dialogue underneath the hysterics. If you were an alien encountering humans for the first time, you'd have to assume that the laughing served as the primary communication method, with the spoken words interspersed as afterthoughts. After one particularly loud outbreak, Provine turns to me and says, "Now, do you think they're all individually making a conscious decision to laugh?" He shakes his head dismissively. "Of course not. In fact, we're often not aware that we're even laughing in the first place. We've vastly overrated our conscious control of laughter."

The limits of our voluntary control of laughter are most clearly exposed in studies of stroke victims who suffer from a disturbing condition known as central facial paralysis, which prevents them from voluntarily moving either the left side or the right side of their faces, depending on the location of the neurological damage. When these individuals are asked to smile or laugh on command, they produce lopsided grins: One side of the mouth curls up, the other remains frozen. But when they're told a joke or they're tickled, traditional smiles and laughs animate their entire faces. There is evidence that the physical mechanism of laughter itself is generated in the brain stem, the most ancient region of the nervous system, which is also responsible for fundamental functions like breathing. Sufferers of amyotrophic lateral sclerosis—Lou Gehrig's disease—which targets the brain stem, often experience spontaneous bursts of uncontrollable laughter, without feeling mirth. (They often undergo a comparable experience with crying as well.) Sometimes called the reptilian brain because its basic structure dates back to our reptile ancestors, the brain stem is largely devoted to our most primal instincts, far removed from our complex, higher-brain skills in understanding humor. And yet somehow, in this primitive region of the brain, we find the urge to laugh.

We're accustomed to thinking of common-but-unconscious instincts as being essential adaptations, like the startle reflex or the suckling of newborns. Why would we have an unconscious propensity for something as frivolous as laughter? As I watch them on the screen, Provine's teenagers remind me of an old Carl Sagan riff, which begins with his describing "a species of primate" that likes to gather in packs of 50 or 60 individuals, cram together in a darkened cave, and hyperventilate in unison, to the point of almost passing out. The behavior is described in such a way as to make it sound exotic and somewhat foolish, like salmon swimming furiously upstream to their deaths or butterflies traveling thousands of miles to rendezvous once a year. The joke, of course, is that the primate is *Homo sapiens,* and the group hyperventilation is our fondness for laughing together at comedy clubs or theaters, or with the virtual crowds of television laugh tracks.

I'm thinking about the Sagan quote when another burst of laughter arrives through the TV speakers, and without realizing what I'm doing, I find myself laughing along with the kids on the screen, I can't help it—their laughter is contagious.

WE MAY BE THE ONLY SPECIES ON THE PLANET THAT LAUGHS together in such large groups, but we are not alone in our appetite for laughter. Not surprisingly, our near relatives, the chimpanzees, are also avid laughers, although differences in their vocal apparatus cause the laugher to sound somewhat more like panting. "The chimpanzee's laughter is rapid and breathy, whereas ours is punctuated with glottal stops," says legendary chimp researcher Roger Fouts. "Also, the chimpanzee laughter occurs on the inhale and exhale, while ours is primarily done on our exhales. But other than these small differences, chimpanzee laughter seems to me to be just like ours in most respects."

Chimps don't do stand-up routines, of course, but they do share a laugh-related obsession with humans, one that Provine believes is central to the roots of laughter itself: Chimps love tickling. Back in his lab, Provine shows me video footage of a pair of young chimps named Josh and Lizzie playing with a human caretaker. It's a full-on ticklefest, with the chimps panting away hysterically when their bellies are scratched. "That's chimpanzee laughter you're hearing," Provine says. It's close enough to human laughter that I find myself chuckling along.

Parents will testify that ticklefests are often the first elaborate play routine they engage in with their children and one of the most reliable laugh inducers. According to Fouts, who helped teach sign language to Washoe, perhaps the world's most famous chimpanzee, the practice is just as common, and perhaps more long lived, among the chimps. "Tickling… seems to be very important to chimpanzees because it continues throughout their lives," he says. "Even Washoe at the age of 37 still enjoys tickling and being tickled by her adult family members." Among young chimpanzees that have been taught sign language, tickling is a frequent topic of conversation.

Like laughter, tickling is almost by definition a social activity. Like the incongruity theory of humor, tickling relies on a certain element of surprise, which is why it's impossible to tickle yourself. Predictable touch doesn't elicit the laughter and squirming of tickling—it's unpredictable touch that does the trick. A number of tickle-related studies have convincingly shown that tickling exploits the sensorimotor system's awareness of the difference between self and other: If the system orders your hand to move toward your belly, it doesn't register surprise when the nerve endings on your belly report being stroked. But if the touch is being generated by another sensorimotor system, the belly stroking will come as a surprise. The pleasant laughter of tickle is the way the brain responds to that touch. In both human and chimpanzee societies, that touch usually first appears in parent-child interactions and has an essential role in creating those initial bonds. "The reason [tickling and laughter] are so important," Roger Fouts says, "is because they play a role in maintaining the affinitive bonds of friendship within the family and community."

A few years ago, Jared Diamond wrote a short book with the provocative title *Why Is Sex Fun?* These recent studies suggest an evolutionary answer to the question of why tickling is fun: It encourages us to play well with others. Young children are so receptive to the rough-and-tumble play of tickle that even pretend tickling will often send them into peals of laughter. (Fouts reports that the threat of tickle has a similar effect on his chimps.) In his book, Provine suggests that "feigned tickle" can be thought of as the Original Joke, the first deliberate behavior designed to exploit the tickling-laughter circuit. Our comedy clubs and our sitcoms are culturally enhanced versions of those original playful childhood exchanges. Along with the suckling and smiling instincts, the laughter of tickle evolved as a way of cementing the bond between parents and children, laying the foundation for a behavior that then carried over into the social lives of adults. While we once laughed at the surprise touch of a parent or sibling, we now laugh at the surprise twist of a punch line.

Bowling Green State University professor Jaak Panksepp suggests that there is a dedicated "play" circuitry in the brain, equivalent to the more extensively studied fear and love circuits. Panksepp has studied the role of rough-and-tumble play in cementing social connections between juvenile rats. The play instinct is not easily suppressed. Rats that have been denied the opportunity to engage in this kind of play—which has a distinct choreography, as well as a chirping vocalization that may be the rat equivalent of laughter—will nonetheless immediately engage in play behavior given the chance. Panksepp compares it to a bird's instinct for flying. "Probably the most powerful positive emotion of all—once your tummy is full and you don't have bodily needs—is vigorous social engagement among the young," Panksepp says. "The largest amount of human laughter seems to occur in the midst of early childhood—rough-and-tumble play, chasing, all the stuff they love."

Playing is what young mammals do, and in humans and chimpanzees, laughter is the way the brain expresses the pleasure of that play. "Since laughter seems to be ritualized panting, basically what you do in laughing is replicate the sound of rough-and-tumble play," Provine says. "And you know, that's where I think it came from. Tickle is an important part of our primate heritage.

Touching and being touched is an important part of what it means to be a mammal."

THERE IS MUCH THAT WE DON'T KNOW YET ABOUT THE NEU-rological underpinnings of laughter. We do not yet know precisely why laughing feels so good; one recent study detected evidence that stimulating the nucleus accumbens, one of the brain's pleasure centers, triggered laughter. Panksepp has performed studies that indicate opiate antagonists significantly reduce the urge to play in rats, which implies that the brain's endorphin system may be involved in the pleasure of laughter. Some anecdotal and clinical evidence suggest that laughing makes you healthier by suppressing stress hormones and elevating immune system antibodies. If you think of laughter as a form of behavior that is basically synonymous with the detection of humor, the laughing-makes-you-healthier premise seems bizarre. Why would natural selection make our immune system respond to jokes? Provine's approach helps solve the mystery. Our bodies aren't responding to wisecracks and punch lines; they're responding to social connection.

In this respect, laughter reminds us that our emotional lives are as much outward bound as they are inner directed. We tend to think of emotions as private affairs, feelings that wash over our subjective worlds. But emotions are also social acts, laughter perhaps most of all. It's no accident that we have so many delicately choreographed gestures and facial expressions—many of which appear to be innate to our species—to convey our emotions. Our emotional systems are designed to share our feelings and not just represent them internally—an insight that Darwin first grasped more than a century ago in his book *The Expression of the Emotions in Man and Animals.* "The movements of expression in the face and body, whatever their origin may have been, are in themselves of much importance for our welfare. They serve as the first means of communication between mother and infant; she smiles approval, and thus encourages her child on the right path.… The free expression by outward signs of an emotion intensifies it."

And even if we don't yet understand the neurological basis of the pleasure that laughing brings us, it makes sense that we should seek out the connectedness of infectious laughter. We are social animals, after all. And if that laughter often involves some pretty childish behavior, so be it. "I mean, this is why we're not like lizards," Provine says, holding the Tickle Me Elmo doll on his lap. "Lizards don't play, and they're not social the way we are. When you start to see play, you're starting to see mammals. So when we get together and have a good time and laugh, we're going back to our roots. It's ironic in a way: Some of the things that give us the most pleasure in life are really the most ancient."

From *Discover* magazine, April 2003, pp. 63-69. © 2003 by Steven Johnson.

How to Multitask

By Catherine Bush

Who can remember life before multitasking? These days we all do it: mothers, air-traffic controllers, ambidextrous athletes, high-flying executives who manage to eat, take conference calls, write e-mail and conduct board meetings all at the same time. We lionize those who appear to multitask effortlessly and despair at our own haphazard attempts to juggle even two tasks, secretly wondering if there exists a race of superior beings whose brains are hard-wired for multitasking feats. Only recently have neurologists begun to understand what our brains are up to when we do it. What they've learned offers hope to all multitasking delinquents out there.

1. Don't think you can actually do two things at once.

Even when you think you're doing more than one thing simultaneously—say, driving and talking on a cell phone—you aren't. Unlike a computer, the brain isn't structured as a parallel processor. It performs actions, even very simple actions, in a strict linear sequence. You must complete the first task, or part of that task, before moving on to the next. What we call multitasking is actually task switching.

Hal Pashler, a professor of psychology at the University of California at San Diego, conducted an experiment in which he tested the brain's ability to respond to two different sounds in quick succession. What he found is that the brain stalls fractionally before responding to the second stimulus. The second sound is heard (the brain can take in information simultaneously), but it requires time, if only milliseconds, to organize a response. "When you really study precisely what people's brains are doing at any moment, there's less concurrent processing than you might think," Pashler explains. "The brain is more of a time-share operation." He adds, "When fractions of a second matter, we're better off not doing another task."

2. Prioritize.

To know when to switch tasks, you must distinguish between the tasks you must perform and those you can afford to blow off.

Consider the experiment that Jordan Grafman developed at the National Institute of Neurological Disorders and Stroke (N.I.N.D.S.) in Bethesda, Md. It's a driving simulation in which you must avoid errant cars and jaywalkers, all while reciting sequences of numbers called out to you. Typically, your driving skills will grow more erratic as you pay attention to the numbers (although, frighteningly, you may not be aware of this). But when a virtual pedestrian dashes into the road, you'll most likely abandon the recitation. That's because in a driving simulation, avoiding killing people is the one challenge that outranks all others.

Before approaching multiple tasks, recommends Grafman, clearly establish which tasks are more important than others. "Mentally rehearsing," he says, "definitely improves performance."

3. Immerse yourself in your immediate task, but don't forget what remains to be done next.

To switch tasks successfully, the brain must marshal the resources required to perform the new task while shutting off, or inhibiting, the demands of the previous one. At the same time, you must maintain the intention to break off at a certain point and switch to another activity. During such moments of mental juggling, a section of the brain called Brodmann's Area 10 comes alive. (Area 10 is located in the fronto-polar prefrontal cortex—at the very front of the brain.)

The crucial role played by Area 10 in multitasking was documented in a 1999 study that Grafman helped conduct; the results were published in the journal Nature. Functional magnetic resonance imaging scans (functional M.R.I.'s) were given to subjects at the Institute of Neurological Disorders while they performed simple multitasking experiments. Blood flow to Area 10 increased when people kept a principal goal in mind while temporarily engaged in secondary tasks. "This is presumably the last part of the brain to evolve, the most mysterious and exciting part," Grafman says. "It's what makes us most human."

Paul Burgess, who researches multitasking at University College, London, has also been focusing on the role of Area 10. "If you're missing it due to injury or a birth defect," he explains, "you keep forgetting to do things." He points out that successful multitasking requires that you not continuously think about switching tasks. That is, the activation of Area 10 does not require constant, conscious rehearsing of the need to switch tasks. For instance, if you have to make an important phone call at the end of the day, you don't tend to make an explicit mental note of this fact every five minutes. Rather, you engage in a less explicit act of remembrance—a kind of low-level arousal, Burgess speculates, in which blood flow increases to Area 10.

4. Depend on routines—and compare new tasks with old ones. Multitasking becomes easier, scientists believe, when you make parts of the process routine. For example, driving, a familiar activity for many of us, becomes largely automatic—the parts of the prefrontal cortex involved in cognition surrender to the regions deeper in the brain that govern visual and motor control. Once a task has been learned, the brain will try to shift the load for performance to its deeper structures, freeing up the cortex for other tasks requiring active cognition. That way, if something unexpected happens (like a pedestrian bolting into the road), you'll have the resources to deal with it.

When you are thrown into a new task, it's helpful to search for a comparison to something you've done before. The brain thrives on analogies. If you're suddenly forced to fly a crashing plane, you might want to draw on your PlayStation skills. "We solve task-switching dilemmas by trying to retrieve similar circum-

stances, similar situations being represented in similar regions of the prefrontal cortex," Grafman says. "If we don't, our experience will be totally chaotic, and we will clearly fail." He then laughs. "This cannot explain Art Tatum." The jazz pianist's wild two-handed improvising was pouring from his CD player when I entered his office. "With Tatum, nothing was routine. He must have had a great prefrontal cortex."

5. Make schedules, not to-do lists. And whatever you do, don't answer the phone. For those of us who find multitasking difficult, Burgess claims that the simplest aids—like timers and alarms—are the most effective. When the American astronaut Jerry Linenger was working aboard the space station Mir, he wore three or four watches with alarms set to notify him when to switch tasks.

"The alarm does not have to carry any information, just be a reminder that something has to be done," Burgess says. Studies have shown that neurologically impaired patients have been helped at multitasking by nothing more than someone clapping their hands at random intervals. An interruption breaks your train of thought and initiates a recall of what else needs to be done.

It's important, however, that the interruption itself not entail a task. For example, if the phone rings, don't answer it. Dealing with whatever the call is about will distract your brain from what you've already set out to do. Instead, use the in-

terruption to see if you're on track with other activities. "Make calling others one of the things that needs to be scheduled," Burgess advises. "And if you have to answer the call, don't go straight back to what you were doing before the call arrived. Very deliberately check the time, and ask yourself if there was something else you should have been doing."

By following such an approach, you can actually change your brain. Visualizing the circumstances in which you need to switch tasks will establish a mental pathway that will be available when you really need it. As functional brain scans suggest, just by thinking about what we need to do and when we need to do it, we can increase blood flow to Area 10, our multitasking hot spot.

Age also improves us. Children are easily distracted from tasks by competing signals, and younger adults, with their maturing prefrontal cortexes, are best at learning and combining new tasks. As we age (and our brains atrophy), learning new tasks becomes harder, but we get better at extracting themes and prioritizing tasks.

"For tasks performed in a short period of time, the younger tend to do better," Burgess says. "Older people learn from their mistakes and begin to compensate over time. This is very encouraging science for those of us not 20 years old."

Catherine Bush is the author of the novel "The Rules of Engagement."

UNIT 7
Development

Unit Selections

Key Points to Consider

- What are the various milestones or developmental landmarks that signal stages in human development? What purpose do various developmental events serve? Can you give examples of some of these events?

- Why is embryonic and fetal life so important? How do the experiences of the fetus affect the child after it is born? What factors deter the fetus from achieving its full potential? What advice would you give a pregnant woman to help her understand how important prenatal life is?

- Do parents matter, or do you think that genes mostly dictate child development? Do you think that both nature and nurture affect development? Do you think one of these factors is more important than the other? Which one and why? Do you think it is important for both parents to be present during their child's formative years? Do you think fathers and mothers differ in their interactions with their children? How so? Why do some claim that parenting is a "lost art"? How and why are parents and schools at odds with each other?

- What is adolescence? How are today's teens different from teens in the past, for example, from their parents' generation? What societal factors influence teens today? If you had to rank these factors, which are most influential, which are least influential? Do you think teens actively search for identity? Do you think today's teens look forward to adulthood? What can parents do to help guide their teens toward a healthy identity and positive adulthood?

- Is there any such thing as a midlife crisis? What changes occur during middle adulthood? Are there sex differences in the way men and women age as they develop during midlife? Which do you think are most problematic for individuals at midlife— physiological, psychological, or social changes?

- Why is death a stigmatized topic in America? Do you think people should discuss it more often and more openly? Do you think they ever will? How can we make dying easier for the dying person and for those close to the dying person? What in general can Americans do to help those with terminal illnesses?

 **Links: www.dushkin.com/online/**
These sites are annotated in the World Wide Web pages.

American Association for Child and Adolescent Psychiatry
http://www.aacap.org
Behavioral Genetics
http://www.ornl.gov/hgmis/elsi/behavior.html

The Garcias and the Szubas are parents of newborns. Both sets of parents wander down to the hospital's neonatal nursery where pediatric nurses care for both babies—Jose Garcia and Kimberly Szuba—when the babies are not in their mothers' rooms. Kimberly is alert, active, and often crying and squirming when her parents watch her. On the other hand, Jose is quiet, often asleep, and less attentive to external stimuli when his parents monitor him in the nursery.

Why are these babies so different? Are the differences gender related? Will these differences disappear as the children develop, or will the differences become exaggerated? What does the future hold for each child? Will Kimberly excel at sports and Jose excel at English? Can Kimberly overcome her parents' poverty and succeed in a professional career? Will Jose become a doctor like his mother or a pharmacist like his father? Will both of these children escape childhood disease, abuse, and the other misfortunes sometimes visited upon children?

Developmental psychologists are concerned with all of the Kimberlys and Joses of our world. Developmental psychologists study age-related changes in language, motoric and social skills, cognition, and physical health. Developmental psychologists are interested in the common skills shared by all children as well as the differences between children and the events that create these differences.

In general, developmental psychologists are concerned with the forces that guide and direct development. Some developmental theorists argue that the forces that shape a child are found in the environment in such factors as social class, quality of available stimulation, parenting style, and so on. Other theorists insist that genetics and related physiological factors such as hormones underlie the development of humans. A third set of psychologists, in fact many psychologists, believe that some combination or interaction of all these factors, physiology and environment (or nature and nurture), are responsible for development.

In this unit, we are going to look at issues of development in a chronological fashion. In the first article, "The Biology of Aging," an overview of human development is given.

The very first stage is fetal development, which is crucial to the physical and psychological growth of the child after it is born. Various environmental factors can deter development of or even damage the fetus. In "Inside the Womb," Madeleine Nash writes about these potential threats to the unborn child along each step of uterine development.

In the next article, "Parenting: The Lost Art," Kay Hymowitz discusses children's misconduct and academic failure. She attempts to disentangle the blaming that occurs by schools and parents in order to discover the real cause. Part of the problem, she advises, is that today's parents want to be friends with, rather than parents to, their children.

We move next to some information about adolescence. Adolescence may be a time when children concertedly search for a self-identity and head toward adulthood. This passage to adulthood can sometimes be stormy and difficult. Despite more risks and demands on them, this generation of teens is coping well with the challenges.

The next article in this unit is about adulthood and aging. Middle age is stereotyped as a time of trouble for the individual. In an article on midlife changes, the authors discuss physiological, psychological, and social changes at midlife. They attend to sex differences while enlightening the reader.

The final article in this series looks at the ultimate stage in development—death. Death is stigmatized in America; few people openly discuss it. This article claims that we ought to be more open and is therefore designed to stimulate dialogue on this subject. There is much information contained in "Start the Conversation" about issues surrounding death such as hospice care, how to be with a dying person, and so forth.

The Biology of Aging

Why, after being so exquisitely assembled, do we fall apart so predictably? Why do we outlive dogs, only to be outlived by turtles? Could we catch up with them? Living to 200 is not a realistic goal for this generation, but a clearer picture of how we grow old is already within our reach.

By Geoffrey Cowley

IF ONLY GOD HAD FOUND A more reliable messenger. Back around the beginning of time, according to east African legend, he dispatched a scavenging bird known as the halawaka to give us the instructions for endless self-renewal. The secret was simple. Whenever age or infirmity started creeping up on us, we were to shed our skins like tattered shirts. We would emerge with our youth and our health intact. Unfortunately, the halawaka got hungry during his journey, and happened upon a snake who was eating a freshly killed wildebeest. In the bartering that ensued, the bird got a satisfying meal, the snake learned to molt and humankind lost its shot at immortality. People have been growing old and dying ever since.

The mystery of aging runs almost as deep as the mystery of life. During the past century, life expectancy has nearly doubled in developed countries, thanks to improvements in nutrition, sanitation and medical science. Yet the potential life span of a human being has not changed significantly since the halawaka met the snake. By the age of 50 every one of us, no matter how fit, will begin a slow decline in organ function and sensory acuity. And though some will enjoy another half century of robust health, our odds of living past 120 are virtually zero. Why, after being so exquisitely assembled, do we fall apart so predictably? Why do we outlive dogs, only to be outlived by turtles? And what are our prospects for catching up with them?

Until recently, all we could do was guess. But as the developed world's population grows grayer, scientists are bearing down on the dynamics of aging, and they're amassing crucial insights. Much of the new understanding has come from the study of worms, flies, mice and monkeys—species whose life cycles can be manipulated and observed in a laboratory. How exactly the findings apply to people is still a matter of conjecture. Could calorie restriction extend our lives by half? It would take generations to find out for sure. But the big questions of why we age—and which parts of the experience we can change—are already coming into focus.

The starkest way to see how time changes us (aside from hauling out an old photo album) is to compare death rates for people of different ages. In Europe and North America the annual rate among 15-year-olds is roughly .05 percent, or one death for every 2,000 kids. Fifty-year-olds are far less likely to ride their skateboards down banisters, yet they die at 30 times that rate (1.5 percent annually). The yearly death rate among 105-year-olds is 50 percent, 1,000 times that of the adolescents. The rise in mortality is due mainly to heart disease, cancer and stroke—diseases that anyone over 50 is right to worry about. But here's the rub. Eradicating these scourges would add only 15 years to U.S. life expectancy (half the gain we achieved during the 20th century), for unlike children spared of smallpox, octogenarians without cancer soon die of something else. As the biologist Leonard Hayflick observes, what ultimately does us in is not disease per se, but our declining ability to resist it.

Biologists once regarded senescence as nature's way of pushing one generation aside to make way for the next. But under natural conditions, virtually no creature lives long enough to experience decrepitude. Our own ancestors typically starved, froze or got eaten long before they reached old age. As a result, the genes that leave us vulnerable to chronic illness in later life rarely had adverse consequences. As long as they didn't hinder reproduction, natural selection had no occasion to weed them out. Natural selection may even *favor* a gene that causes cancer late in life if it makes young adults more fertile.

But why should "later life" mean 50 instead of 150? Try thinking of the body as a vehicle, designed by a group of genes to transport them through time. You might expect durable bodies to have an inherent advantage. But if a mouse is sure to become a cat's dinner within five years, a body that could last twice that long is a waste of resources. A 5-year-old mouse that can produce eight litters annually will leave twice the legacy of a 10-year-old mouse that delivers only four each year. Under those conditions, mice will evolve to live roughly five years. A sudden disappearance of cats may improve their odds of completing that life cycle, but it won't change their basic genetic makeup.

That is the predicament we face. Our bodies are nicely adapted to the harsh conditions our Stone Age ancestors faced, but often poorly adapted to the cushy ones we've created. There is no question that we can age better by exercising, eating healthfully, avoiding cigarettes and staying socially and mentally active. But can we realistically expect to extend our maximum life spans?

The First Years of Growth

In childhood the body is wonderfully resilient, and **sound sleep** supports the growth of tissues and bones. During the teenage years, **hormonal changes** trigger the development of sexual organs. Boys add **muscle mass**. Even the muscles in their voice box lengthen, causing voices to deepen. In girls, fat is redistributed to hips and breasts.

Researchers have already accomplished that feat in lab experiments. In the species studied so far, the surest way to increase life span has been to cut back on calories—way back. In studies dating back to the 1930s, researchers have found that species as varied as rats, monkeys and baker's yeast age more slowly if they're given 30 to 60 percent fewer calories than they would normally consume. No one has attempted such a trial among humans, but some researchers have already embraced the regimen themselves. Dr. Roy Walford, a 77-year-old pathologist at the University of California, Los Angeles, has survived for years on 1,200 calories a day and expects to be doing the same when he's 120. That may be optimistic, but he looks as spry as any 60-year-old in the photo he posts on the Web, and the animal studies suggest at least a partial explanation. Besides delaying death, caloric restriction seems to preserve bone mass, skin thickness, brain function and immune function, while providing superior resistance to heat, toxic chemicals and traumatic injury.

How could something so perverse be so good for you? Scientists once theorized that caloric restriction extended life by delaying development, or by reducing body fat, or by slowing metabolic rate. None of these explanations survived scrutiny, but studies have identified several likely mechanisms. The first involves oxidation. As mitochondria (the power plants in our cells) release the energy in food, they generate corrosive, unpaired electrons known as free radicals. By reacting with nearby fats, proteins and nucleic acids, these tiny terrorists foster everything from cataracts to vascular disease. It appears that caloric restriction not only slows the production of free radicals but helps the body counter them more efficiently.

Food restriction may also shield tissues from the damaging effects of glucose, the sugar that enters our bloodstreams when we eat carbohydrates. Ideally, our bodies respond to any rise in blood glucose by releasing insulin, which shuttles the sugar into fat and muscle cells for storage. But age or obesity can make our

cells resistant to insulin. And when glucose molecules linger in the bloodstream, they link up with collagen and other proteins to wreak havoc on nerves, organs and blood vessels. When rats or monkeys are allowed to eat at will, their cells become less sensitive to insulin over time, just as ours do. But according to Dr. Mark Lane of the National Institute on Aging, older animals on calorie-restricted diets exhibit the high insulin sensitivity, low blood glucose and robust health of youngsters. No one knows whether people's bodies will respond the same way. But the finding suggests that life extension could prove as simple, or rather as complicated, as preserving the insulin response.

Another possible approach is to manipulate hormones. No one has shown conclusively that any of these substances can alter life span, but there are plenty of tantalizing hints. Consider human growth hormone, a pituitary protein that helps drive our physical development. Enthusiasts tout the prescription-only synthetic version as an antidote to all aspects of aging, but mounting evidence suggests that it could make the clock tick faster. The first indication came in the mid-1980s, when physiologist Andrzej Bartke outfitted lab mice with human or bovine genes for growth hormone. These mighty mice grew to twice the size of normal ones, but they aged early and died young. Bartke, now based at Southern Illinois University, witnessed something very different in 1996, when he began studying a strain of rodents called Ames dwarf mice. Due to a congenital lack of growth hormone, these creatures reach only a third the size of normal mice. But they live 50 to 60 percent longer.

As it happens, the mini-mice aren't the only ones carrying this auspicious gene. The island of Krk, a Croatian outpost in the eastern Adriatic, is home to a group of people who harbor essentially the same mutation. The "little people of Krk" reach an adult height of just 4 feet 5 inches. But like the mini-mice, they're exceptionally long-lived. Bartke's mouse studies suggest that besides stifling growth hormone, the gene that causes this stunting may also improve sensitivity to—you guessed it—insulin. If so, the mini-mice, the Croatian dwarfs and the half-starved rats and monkeys have more than their longevity in common. No one is suggesting that we stunt people's growth in the hope of extending their lives. But if you've been pestering your doctor for a vial of growth hormone, you may want to reconsider.

The Early Years of Adulthood

In many ways, the 20s are the prime of life. We're blessed with an efficient metabolism, **strong bones** and **good flexibility**. As early as the 30s, however, metabolism begins to slow and women's **hormone levels** start to dip. Bones may start to lose density in people who don't exercise or who don't get the vitamin D required for calcium absorption.

Growth hormone is just one of several that decline as we age. The sex hormones estrogen and testosterone follow the same pattern, and replacing them can rejuvenate skin, bone and muscle. But like growth hormone, these tonics can have costs as well as benefits. They evolved not to make us more durable but to make us more fertile. As the British biologist Roger Gosden observed in his 1996 book, "Cheating Time," "sex hormones are required for fertility and for making biological gender distinctions, but they do not prolong life. On the contrary, a price may have to be paid for living as a sexual being." Anyone suffering from breast or prostate cancer would surely agree.

The Joys of Middle Age

Around 40, people often start noticing gray hairs, mild **memory lapses** and difficulty focusing their eyes on small type. Around 51, most women will experience **menopause**. Estrogen levels plummet, making the skin thinner and bones less dense. Men suffer more **heart disease** than women at this age. Metabolism slows down in both sexes.

In most of the species biologists have studied, fertility and longevity have a seesaw relationship, each rising as the other declines. Bodies designed for maximum fertility have fewer resources for self-repair, some perishing as soon as they reproduce (think of spawning salmon). By contrast, those with extraordinary life spans are typically slow to bear offspring. Do these rules apply to people? The evidence is sketchy but provocative. In a 1998 study, researchers at the University of Manchester analyzed genealogical records of 32,000 British aristocrats born during the 1,135-year period between 740 and 1875 (long before modern contraceptives). Among men and women who made it to 60, the least fertile were the most likely to survive beyond that age. A whopping 50 percent of the women who reached 81 were childless.

Eunuchs seem to enjoy (if that's the word) a similar advantage in longevity. During the 1940s and '50s, anatomist James Hamilton studied a group of mentally handicapped men who had been castrated at a state institution in Kansas. Life expectancy was just 56 in this institution, but the neutered men lived to an average age of 69—a 23 percent advantage—and not one of them went bald. No one knows exactly how testosterone speeds aging, but athletes who abuse it are prone to ailments ranging from hypertension to kidney failure.

All of this research holds a fairly obvious lesson. Life itself is lethal, and the things that make it sweet make it *more* lethal. Chances are that by starving and castrating ourselves, we really could secure some extra years. But most of us would gladly trade a lonely decade of stubborn survival for a richer middle age. Our bodies are designed to last only so long. But with care and maintenance, they'll live out their warranties in style.

With RACHEL DAVIS

Inside The Womb

What scientists have learned about those amazing first nine months—
and what it means for mothers

By J. Madeleine Nash

As THE CRYSTAL PROBE SLIDES ACROSS HER BELLY, HILDA Manzo, 33, stares wide-eyed at the video monitor mounted on the wall. She can make out a head with a mouth and two eyes. She can see pairs of arms and legs that end in tiny hands and feet. She can see the curve of a backbone, the bridge of a nose. And best of all, she can see movement. The mouth of her child-to-be yawns. Its feet kick. Its hands wave.

Dr. Jacques Abramowicz, director of the University of Chicago's ultrasound unit, turns up the audio so Manzo can hear the gush of blood through the umbilical cord and the fast thump, thump, thump of a miniature heart. "Oh, my!" she exclaims as he adjusts the sonic scanner to peer under her fetus' skin. "The heart is on the left side, as it should be," he says, "and it has four chambers. Look—one, two, three, four!"

Such images of life stirring in the womb—in this case, of a 17-week-old fetus no bigger than a newborn kitten—are at the forefront of a biomedical revolution that is rapidly transforming the way we think about the prenatal world. For although it takes nine months to make a baby, we now know that the most important developmental steps—including laying the foundation for such major organs as the heart, lungs and brain—occur before the end of the first three. We also know that long before a child is born its genes engage the environment of the womb in an elaborate conversation, a two-way dialogue that involves not only the air its mother breathes and the water she drinks but also what drugs she takes, what diseases she contracts and what hardships she suffers.

One reason we know this is a series of remarkable advances in MRIs, sonograms and other imaging technologies that allow us to peer into the developmental process at virtually every stage—from the fusion of sperm and egg to the emergence, some 40 weeks later, of a miniature human being. The extraordinary pictures on these pages come from a new book that captures some of the color and excitement of this research: *From Conception to Birth: A Life Unfolds* (Doubleday), by photographer Alexander Tsiaras and writer Barry Werth. Their com-puter-enhanced images are reminiscent of the remarkable fetal portraits taken by medical photographer Lennart Nilsson, which appeared in Life magazine in 1965. Like Nilsson's work, these images will probably spark controversy. Antiabortion activists may interpret them as evidence that a fetus is a viable human being earlier than generally believed, while pro-choice advocates may argue that the new technology allows doctors to detect serious fetal defects at a stage when abortion is a reasonable option.

The other reason we know so much about what goes on inside the womb is the remarkable progress researchers have made in teasing apart the sequence of chemical signals and switches that drive fetal development. Scientists can now describe at the level of individual genes and molecules many of the steps involved in building a human, from the establishment of a head-to-tail growth axis and the budding of limbs to the sculpting of a four-chambered heart and the weaving together of trillions of neural connections. Scientists are beginning to unroll the genetic blueprint of life and identify the precise molecular tools required for assembly. Human development no longer seems impossibly complex, says Stanford University biologist Matthew Scott. "It just seems marvelous."

How is it, we are invited to wonder, that a fertilized egg—a mere speck of protoplasm and DNA encased in a spherical shell—can generate such complexity? The answers, while elusive and incomplete, are beginning to come into focus.

Only 20 years ago, most developmental biologists thought that different organisms grew according to different sets of rules, so that understanding how a fly or a worm develops—or even a vertebrate like a chicken or a fish—would do little to illuminate the process in humans. Then, in the 1980s, researchers found remarkable similarities in the molecular tool kit used by organisms that span the breadth of the animal kingdom, and those similarities have proved serendipitous beyond imagining. No matter what the species, nature uses virtually the same nails

How They Did It

With just a few keystrokes, Alexander Tsiaras does the impossible. He takes the image of a 56-day-old human embryo and peers through its skin, revealing liver, lungs, a bulblike brain and the tiny, exquisite vertebrae of a developing spine.

These are no ordinary baby pictures. What Tsiaras and his colleagues are manipulating are layers of data gathered by CT scans, micro magnetic resonance imaging (MRI) and other visualization techniques. When Lennart Nilsson took his groundbreaking photographs in the 1960s, he was limited to what he could innovatively capture with a flash camera. Since then, says Tsiaras, "there's been a revolution in imaging."

What's changed is that development can now be viewed through a wide variety of prisms, using different forms of energy to illuminate different aspects of the fetus. CT scans, for example, are especially good at showing bone, and MRI is excellent for soft tissue. These two-dimensional layers of information are assembled, using sophisticated computer software, into a three-dimensional whole.

The results are painstakingly accurate and aesthetically stunning. Tsiaras, who trained as a painter and sculptor, used medical specimens from the Carnegie Human Embryology Collection at the National Museum of Health and Medicine in Washington as models for all but a few images. The specimens came from a variety of sources, according to museum director Adrianne Noe, including miscarriages and medically necessary procedures. None were acquired from elective abortions.

—By David Bjerklie

and screws, the same hammers and power tools to put an embryo together.

Among the by-products of the torrent of information pouring out of the laboratory are new prospects for treating a broad range of late-in-life diseases. Just last month, for example, three biologists won the Nobel Prize for Medicine for their work on the nematode *Caenorhabditis elegans*, which has a few more than 1,000 cells, compared with a human's 50 trillion. The three winners helped establish that a fundamental mechanism that *C. elegans* embryos employ to get rid of redundant or abnormal cells also exists in humans and may play a role in AIDS, heart disease and cancer. Even more exciting, if considerably more controversial, is the understanding that embryonic cells harbor untapped therapeutic potential. These cells, of course, are stem cells, and they are the progenitors of more specialized cells that make up organs and tissues. By harnessing their generative powers, medical researchers believe, it may one day be possible to repair the damage wrought by injury and disease. (That prospect suffered a political setback last week when a federal advisory committee recommended that embryos be considered the same as human subjects in clinical trials.)

To be sure, the marvel of an embryo transcends the collection of genes and cells that compose it. For unlike strands of DNA floating in a test tube or stem cells dividing in a Petri dish, an embryo is capable of building not just a protein or a patch of tissue but a living entity in which every cell functions as an integrated part of the whole. "Imagine yourself as the world's tallest skyscraper, built in nine months and germinating from a single brick," suggest Tsiaras and Werth in the opening of their book. "As that brick divides, it gives rise to every other type of material needed to construct and operate the finished tower—a million tons of steel, concrete, mortar, insulation, tile, wood, granite, solvents, carpet, cable, pipe and glass as well as all furniture, phone systems, heating and cooling units, plumbing, electrical wiring, artwork and computer networks, including software."

Given the number of steps in the process, it will perhaps forever seem miraculous that life ever comes into being without a major hitch. "Whenever you look from one embryo to another," observes Columbia University developmental neurobiologist Thomas Jessell, "what strikes you is the fidelity of the process."

Sometimes, though, that fidelity is compromised, and the reasons why this happens are coming under intense scrutiny. In laboratory organisms, birth defects occur for purely genetic reasons when scientists purposely mutate or knock out specific sequences of DNA to establish their function. But when development goes off track in real life, the cause can often be traced to a lengthening list of external factors that disrupt some aspect of the genetic program. For an embryo does not develop in a vacuum but depends on the environment that surrounds it. When a human embryo is deprived of essential nutrients or exposed to a toxin, such as alcohol, tobacco or crack cocaine, the consequences can range from readily apparent abnormalities—spina bifida, fetal alcohol syndrome—to subtler metabolic defects that may not become apparent until much later.

IRONICALLY, EVEN AS SOCIETY AT LARGE CONTINUES TO WORRY almost obsessively about the genetic origins of disease, the biologists and medical researchers who study development are mounting an impressive case for the role played by the prenatal environment. A growing body of evidence suggests that a number of serious maladies—among them, atherosclerosis, hypertension and diabetes—trace their origins to detrimental prenatal conditions. As New York University Medical School's Dr. Peter Nathanielsz puts it, "What goes on in the womb before you are born is just as important to who you are as your genes."

Most adults, not to mention most teenagers, are by now thoroughly familiar with the mechanics of how the sperm in a man's semen and the egg in a woman's oviduct connect, and it is at this point that the story of development begins. For the sperm and the egg each contain only 23 chromosomes, half the amount of DNA needed to make a human. Only when the sperm and the egg fuse their chromosomes does the tiny zygote, as a fertilized egg is called, receive its instructions to grow. And grow it does, replicating its DNA each time it divides—into two cells, then four, then eight and so on.

If cell division continued in this fashion, then nine months later the hapless mother would give birth to a tumorous ball of literally astronomical proportions. But instead of endlessly dividing, the zygote's cells progressively take form. The first striking change is apparent four days after conception, when a 32-cell clump called the morula (which means "mulberry" in Latin) gives rise to two distinct layers wrapped around a fluid-filled core. Now known as a blastocyst, this spherical mass will proceed to burrow into the wall of the uterus. A short time later, the outer layer of cells will begin turning into the placenta and amniotic sac, while the inner layer will become the embryo.

The formation of the blastocyst signals the start of a sequence of changes that are as precisely choreographed as a ballet. At the end of Week One, the inner cell layer of the blastocyst balloons into two more layers. From the first layer, known as the endoderm, will come the cells that line the gastrointestinal tract. From the second, the ectoderm, will arise the neurons that make up the brain and spinal cord along with the epithelial cells that make up the skin. At the end of Week Two, the ectoderm spins off a thin line of cells known as the primitive streak, which forms a new cell layer called the mesoderm. From it will come the cells destined to make the heart, the lungs and all the other internal organs.

At this point, the embryo resembles a stack of Lilliputian pancakes—circular, flat and horizontal. But as the mesoderm forms, it interacts with cells in the ectoderm to trigger yet another transformation. Very soon these cells will roll up to become the neural tube, a rudimentary precursor of the spinal cord and brain. Already the embryo has a distinct cluster of cells at each end, one destined to become the mouth and the other the anus. The embryo, no larger at this point than a grain of rice, has determined the head-to-tail axis along which all its body parts will be arrayed.

How on earth does this little, barely animate cluster of cells "know" what to do? The answer is as simple as it is startling. A human embryo knows how to lay out its body axis in the same way that fruit-fly embryos know and *C. elegans* embryos and the embryos of myriad other creatures large and small know. In all cases, scientists have found, in charge of establishing this axis is a special set of genes, especially the so-called homeotic homeobox, or HOX, genes.

HOX genes were first discovered in fruit flies in the early 1980s when scientists noticed that their absence caused striking mutations. Heads, for example, grew feet instead of antennae, and thoraxes grew an extra pair of wings. HOX genes have been found in virtually every type of animal, and while their number varies—fruit flies have nine, humans have 39—they are invariably arrayed along chromosomes in the order along the body in which they are supposed to turn on.

Many other genes interact with the HOX system, including the aptly named Hedgehog and Tinman genes, without which fruit flies grow a dense covering of bristles or fail to make a heart. And scientists are learning in exquisite detail what each does at various stages of the developmental process. Thus one of the three Hedgehog genes—Sonic Hedgehog, named in honor of the cartoon and video-game character—has been shown to play a role in making at least half a dozen types of spinal-cord neurons. As it happens, cells in different places in the neural tube are exposed to different levels of the protein encoded by this gene; cells drenched in significant quantities of protein mature into one type of neuron, and those that receive the barest sprinkling mature into another. Indeed, it was by using a particular concentration of Sonic Hedgehog that neurobiologist Jessell and his research team at Columbia recently coaxed stem cells from a mouse embryo to mature into seemingly functional motor neurons.

At the University of California, San Francisco, a team led by biologist Didier Stainier is working on genes important in cardiovascular formation. Removing one of them, called Miles Apart, from zebra-fish embryos results in a mutant with two nonviable hearts. Why? In all vertebrate embryos, including humans, the heart forms as twin buds. In order to function, these buds must join. The way the Miles Apart gene appears to work, says Stainier, is by detecting a chemical attractant that, like the smell of dinner cooking in the kitchen, entices the pieces to move toward each other.

The crafting of a human from a single fertilized egg is a vastly complicated affair, and at any step, something can go wrong. When the heart fails to develop properly, a baby can be born with a hole in the heart or even missing valves and chambers. When the neural tube fails to develop properly, a baby can be born with a brain not fully developed (anencephaly) or with an incompletely formed spine (spina bifida). Neural-tube defects, it has been firmly established, are often due to insufficient levels of the water-soluble B vitamin folic acid. Reason: folic acid is essential to a dividing cell's ability to replicate its DNA.

Vitamin A, which a developing embryo turns into retinoids, is another nutrient that is critical to the nervous system. But watch out, because too much vitamin A can be toxic. In another newly released book, *Before Your Pregnancy* (Ballantine Books), nutritionist Amy Ogle and obstetrician Dr. Lisa Mazzullo caution would-be mothers to limit foods that are overly rich in vitamin A, especially liver and food products that contain lots of it, like foie gras and cod-liver oil. An excess of vitamin A, they note, can cause damage to the skull, eyes, brain and spinal cord of a developing fetus, probably because retinoids directly interact with DNA, affecting the activity of critical genes.

Folic acid, vitamin A and other nutrients reach developing embryos and fetuses by crossing the placenta, the remarkable temporary organ produced by the blastocyst that develops from the fertilized egg. The outer ring of cells that compose the placenta are extremely aggressive, behaving very much like tumor cells as they invade the uterine wall and tap into the pregnant woman's blood vessels. In fact, these cells actually go in and replace the maternal cells that form the lining of the uterine arteries, says Susan Fisher, a developmental biologist at the University of California, San Francisco. They trick the pregnant woman's immune system into tolerating the embryo's presence rather than rejecting it like the lump of foreign tissue it is.

In essence, says Fisher, "the placenta is a traffic cop," and its main job is to let good things in and keep bad things out. To this

9 months

This series showing how a baby emerges from the birth canal began with an unusual delivery that required doctors to place the mother in a spiral CT scanner. The images were merged with CT and ultrasound data from other babies to create this re-enacted birth

end, the placenta marshals platoons of natural killer cells to patrol its perimeters and engages millions of tiny molecular pumps that expel poisons before they can damage the vulnerable embryo.

ALAS, THE PLACENTA'S DEFENSES ARE SOMETIMES BREACHED— by microbes like rubella and cytomegalovirus, by drugs like thalidomide and alcohol, by heavy metals like lead and mercury, and by organic pollutants like dioxin and PCBs. Pathogens and poisons contained in certain foods are also able to cross the placenta, which may explain why placental tissues secrete a nausea-inducing hormone that has been tentatively linked to morning sickness. One provocative if unproved hypothesis says morning sickness may simply be nature's crude way of making sure that potentially harmful substances do not reach the womb, particularly during the critical first trimester of development.

Timing is decisive where toxins are concerned. Air pollutants like carbon monoxide and ozone, for example, have been linked to heart defects when exposure coincided with the second month of pregnancy, the window of time during which the heart forms. Similarly, the nervous system is particularly vulnerable to damage while neurons are migrating from the part of the brain where they are made to the area where they will ultimately reside. "A tiny, tiny exposure at a key moment when a certain process is beginning to unfold can have an effect that is not only quantitatively larger but qualitatively different than it would be on an adult whose body has finished forming," observes Sandra Steingraber, an ecologist at Cornell University.

Among the substances Steingraber is most worried about are environmentally persistent neurotoxins like mercury and lead (which directly interfere with the migration of neurons formed during the first trimester) and PCBs (which, some evidence suggests, block the activity of thyroid hormone). "Thyroid hormone plays a noble role in the fetus," says Steingraber. "It actually goes into the fetal brain and serves as kind of a conductor of the orchestra."

PCBs are no longer manufactured in the U.S., but other chemicals potentially harmful to developing embryos and fetuses are. Theo Colborn, director of the World Wildlife Fund's contaminants program, says at least 150 chemicals pose possible risks for fetal development, and some of them can interfere with the naturally occurring sex hormones critical to the development of a fetus. Antiandrogens, for example, are widely found in fungicides and plastics. One in particular—DDE, a breakdown product of DDT—has been shown to cause hypospadias in laboratory mice, a birth defect in which the urethra fails to extend to the end of the penis. In humans, however, notes Dr. Allen Wilcox, editor of the journal *Epidemiology*, the link between hormone-like chemicals and birth defects remains elusive.

THE LIST OF POTENTIAL THREATS TO EMBRYONIC LIFE IS LONG. It includes not only what the mother eats, drinks or inhales, explains N.Y.U.'s Nathanielsz, but also the hormones that surge through her body. Pregnant rats with high blood-glucose levels (chemically induced by wiping out their insulin) give birth to female offspring that are unusually susceptible to developing gestational diabetes. These daughter rats are able to produce enough insulin to keep their blood glucose in check, says Nathanielsz, but only until they become pregnant. At that point, their glucose level soars, because their pancreases were damaged by prenatal exposure to their mother's sugar-spiked blood. The next generation of daughters is, in turn, more susceptible to gestational diabetes, and the transgenerational chain goes on.

In similar fashion, atherosclerosis may sometimes develop because of prenatal exposure to chronically high cholesterol levels. According to Dr. Wulf Palinski, an endocrinologist at the University of California at San Diego, there appears to be a kind of metabolic memory of prenatal life that is permanently retained. In genetically similar groups of rabbits and kittens, at least, those born to mothers on fatty diets were far more likely to develop arterial plaques than those whose mothers ate lean.

But of all the long-term health threats, maternal undernourishment—which stunts growth even when babies are born full term—may top the list. "People who are small at birth have, for life, fewer kidney cells, and so they are more likely to go into renal failure when they get sick," observes Dr. David Barker, director of the environmental epidemiology unit at England's University of Southampton. The same is true of insulin-producing cells in the pancreas, so that low-birth-weight babies stand a higher chance of developing diabetes later in life because their pancreases—where insulin is produced—have to work that much harder. Barker, whose research has linked low birth weight to heart disease, points out that undernourishment can trigger lifelong metabolic changes. In adulthood, for example, obesity may become a problem because food scarcity in prenatal life causes the body to shift the rate at which calories are turned into glucose for immediate use or stored as reservoirs of fat.

But just how does undernourishment reprogram metabolism? Does it perhaps prevent certain genes from turning on, or does it turn on those that should stay silent? Scientists are racing to answer those questions, along with a host of others. If they succeed, many more infants will find safe passage through the critical first months of prenatal development. Indeed, our expanding knowledge about the interplay between genes and the prenatal environment is cause for both concern and hope. Concern because maternal and prenatal health care often ranks last on the political agenda. Hope because by changing our priorities, we might be able to reduce the incidence of both birth defects and serious adult diseases.

—***With reporting by David Bjerklie and Alice Park/New York and Dan Cray/Los Angeles***

PARENTING: THE LOST ART

BY KAY S. HYMOWITZ

LAST FALL the Federal Trade Commission released a report showing what most parents already knew from every trip down the aisle of Toys R Us and every look at prime time television: Entertainment companies routinely market R-rated movies, computer games, and music to children. The highly publicized report detailed many of the abuses of these companies—one particularly egregious example was the use of focus groups of 9- and 10-year-olds to test market violent films—and it unleashed a frenzied week of headlines and political grandstanding, all of it speaking to Americans' alarm over their children's exposure to an increasingly foul-mouthed, vicious, and tawdry media.

But are parents really so alarmed? A more careful reading of the FTC report considerably complicates the fairy tale picture of big, bad wolves tempting unsuspecting, innocent children with ads for *Scream* and *Doom* and inevitably raises the question: "Where were the parents?" As it turns out, many youngsters saw the offending ads not when they were reading *Nickelodeon Magazine* or watching *Seventh Heaven* but when they were leafing through *Cosmo Girl*, a junior version of Helen Gurley Brown's sex manual *Cosmopolitan*, or lounging in front of *Smackdown!*—a production of the World Wrestling Federation where wrestlers saunter out, grab their crotches, and bellow "Suck It!" to their "ho's" standing by. Other kids came across the ads when they were watching the WB's infamous teen sex soap opera *Dawson's Creek* or MTV, whose most recent hit, "Undressed," includes plots involving whipped cream, silk teddies, and a tutor who agrees to strip every time her student gets an answer right. All of these venues, the report noted without irony, are "especially popular among 11- to 18-year-olds." Oh, and those focus groups of 9- and 10-year-olds? It turns out that all of the children who attended the meetings had permission from their parents. To muddy the picture even further, only a short time before the FTC report, the Kaiser Family Foundation released a study entitled *Kids and Media: The New Millennium*

showing that half of all parents have no rules about what their kids watch on television, a number that is probably low given that the survey also found that two-thirds of American children between the ages of eight and eighteen have televisions in their bedrooms; and even more shocking, one-third of all under the age of seven.

In other words, one conclusion you could draw from the FTC report is that entertainment companies are willing to tempt children with the raunchiest, bloodiest, crudest media imaginable if it means expanding their audience and their profits. An additional conclusion, especially when considered alongside *Kids and the Media*, would be that there are a lot of parents out there who don't mind enough to do much about it. After all, protesting that your 10-year-old son was subjected to a trailer for the R-rated *Scream* while watching *Smackdown!* is a little like complaining that he was bitten by a rat while scavenging at the local dump.

Neither the FTC report nor *Kids and the Media* makes a big point of it, but their findings do begin to bring into focus a troubling sense felt by many Americans—and no one more than teachers—that parenting is becoming a lost art. This is not to accuse adults of being neglectful or abusive in any conventional sense. Like always, today's boomer parents love their children; they know their responsibility to provide for them and in fact, as *Kids and the Media* suggests, they are doing so more lavishly than ever before in human history. But throughout that history adults have understood something that perplexes many of today's parents: That they are not only obliged to feed and shelter the young, but to teach them self-control, civility, and a meaningful way of understanding the world. Of course, most parents care a great deal about their children's social and moral development. Most are doing their best to hang on to their sense of what really matters while they attempt to steer their children through a dizzyingly stressful, temptation-filled, and in many ways unfamiliar world. Yet these parents know they often cannot count on the support of their peers. The parents of their 10-year-old's friend let the girls watch an R-rated movie until 2 a.m. during a sleepover; other parents are nowhere to be found when beer is passed around at a party attended by their 14-year-old. These AWOL parents have redefined the meaning of the term. As their children gobble down their own microwaved dinners, then go on to watch their own televisions or surf the Internet on their own computers in wired bedrooms where they set their own bedtimes, these parents and their children seem more like housemates and friends than experienced adults guiding and shaping the young. Such parent-peers may be warm companions and in the short run effective advocates for their children, but they remain deeply uncertain about how to teach them to lead meaningful lives.

If anyone is familiar with the fallout from the lost art of parenting, it is educators. About a year ago, while researching an article about school discipline, I spoke to teachers, administrators, and school lawyers around the country and asked what is making their job more difficult today. Their top answer was almost always the same: parents. Sometimes they describe overworked, overburdened parents who have simply checked out: "I work 10 hours a day, and I can't come home and deal with this stuff. He's *your* problem," they might say. But more often teachers find parents who rather than accepting their role as partners with educators in an effort to civilize the next generation come in with a "my-child-right-or-wrong" attitude. These are parent-advocates.

Everyone's heard about the growing number of suspensions in middle and high schools around the country. Now the state of Connecticut has released a report on an alarming increase in the number of young children—first-graders, kindergartners, and *preschoolers*—suspended for persistent biting, kicking, hitting, and cursing. Is it any wonder? Parent-advocates have little patience for the shared rules of behavior required to turn a school into a civil community, not to mention those who would teach their own children the necessary limits to self-expression. "'You and your stupid rules.' I've heard that a hundred times," sighs Cathy Collins, counsel to the School Administrators of Iowa, speaking not, as it might sound, of 16-year-olds, but of their parents. Even 10 years ago when a child got into trouble, parents assumed the teacher or principal was in the right. "Now we're always being second-guessed," says a 25-year veteran of suburban New Jersey elementary schools. "I know my child, and he wouldn't do this," or, proudly, "He has a mind of his own," are lines many educators repeat hearing.

In the most extreme cases, parent-advocates show (and teach their children) their contempt for school rules by going to court. Several years ago, a St. Charles, Mo., high schooler running for student council was suspended for distributing condoms on the day of the election as a way of soliciting votes. His family promptly turned around and sued on the grounds that the boy's free speech rights were being violated because other candidates had handed out candy during student council elections without any repercussions. Sometimes principals are surprised to see a lawyer trailing behind an angry parent arriving for a conference over a minor infraction. Parents threaten teachers with lawsuits, and kids repeat after them: "I'll sue you," or "My mother's

going to get a lawyer." Surveys may show a large number of parents in favor of school uniforms, but for parent-advocates, dress codes that limit their child's self-expression are a particular source of outrage. In Northumberland County, Pa., parents threatened to sue their children's *elementary* school over its new dress code. "I have a little girl who likes to express herself with how she dresses," one mother of a fourth-grader said. "They ruined my daughter's first day of school," another mother of a kindergartner whined.

Parent-advocates may make life difficult for teachers and soccer coaches. But the truth is things aren't so great at home either. Educators report parents of second- and third-graders saying things like: "I can't control what she wears to school," or "I can't make him read." It's not surprising. At home, parent-advocates aspire to be friends and equals, hoping to maintain the happy affection they think of as a "good relationship." It rarely seems to happen that way. Unable to balance warmth with discipline and affirmation with limit-setting, these parents are puzzled to find their 4-year-old ordering them around like he's Louis XIV or their 8-year-old screaming, "I hate you!" when they balk at letting her go to a sleepover party for the second night in a row. These buddy adults are not only incapable of helping their children resist the siren call of a sensational, glamorous media; in a desperate effort to confirm their "good relationship" with their kids, they actively reinforce it. They buy them their own televisions, they give them "guilt money," as market researchers call it, to go shopping, and they plan endless entertainments. A recent article in *Time* magazine on the Britney Spears fad began by describing a party that parents in Westchester, N.Y., gave their 9-year-old complete with a Britney impersonator boogying in silver hip-huggers and tube top. Doubtless such peer-parents tell themselves they are making their children happy and, anyway, what's the harm. They shouldn't count on it. "When one of our teenagers comes in looking like Britney Spears, they carry with them an attitude," one school principal was quoted as saying. There's a reason that some of the clothing lines that sell the Britney look adopt names such as "Brat" or "No Boundaries."

Of course, dressing like a Las Vegas chorus girl at 8 years old does not automatically mean a child is headed for juvenile hall when she turns 14. But it's reasonable to assume that parent-friends who don't know how to get their third-graders to stop calling them names, never mind covering their midriffs before going to school, are going to be pretty helpless when faced with the more serious challenges of adolescence. Some parents simply give up. They've done all they can, they say to themselves; the kids have to figure it out for themselves. "I feel if [my son] hasn't learned the proper values by 16, then we haven't done our job," announces the mother of a 16-year-old in a fascinating 1999 *Time* magazine series, "Diary of a High School." Others continue the charade of peer friendship by endorsing their adolescent's risk-taking as if they were one of the in-crowd. In a recent article in *Education Week*, Anne W. Weeks, the director of college guidance at a Maryland high school, tells how when police broke up a party on the field of a nearby college, they discovered that most of the kids were actually local high schoolers. High school officials called parents to express their concern, but they were having none of it; it seems parents were the ones providing the alcohol and dropping their kids off at what they knew to be a popular (and unchaperoned) party spot. So great is the need of some parents to keep up the pretense of their equality that they refuse to heed their own children's cry for adult help. A while back, the *New York Times* ran a story on Wesleyan University's "naked dorm" where, as one 19-year-old male student told the reporter: "If I feel the need to take my pants off, I take my pants off," something he evidently felt the need to do during the interview. More striking than the dorm itself—after all, when kids are in charge, as they are in many colleges, what would we expect?—was the phone call a worried female student made to her parents when she first realized she had been assigned to a "naked dorm." She may have been alarmed, but her father, she reports, simply "laughed."

Perhaps more common than parents who laugh at naked dorms or who supply booze for their kids' parties, are those who dimly realize the failure of their experiment in peer-parenting. These parents reduce their role to exercising damage control over kids they assume "are going to do it anyway." For them, there is only one value left they are comfortable fighting for: safety. One mother in *Time*'s "Diary of a High School" replenishes a pile of condoms for her own child and his friends once a month, doubtless congratulating herself that she is protecting the young. Safety also appears to be the logic behind the new fad of co-ed sleepover parties as it was described recently in the *Washington Post*. "I just feel it's definitely better than going to hotels, and this way you know all the kids who are coming over, you know who they are with," explains the mother of one high schooler. Kids know exactly how to reach a generation of parents who, though they waffled on whether their 8-year-old could call them "idiot," suddenly became tyrants when it came to seat belts and helmets. The article describes how one boy talked his parents into allowing him to give a co-ed sleepover party. "It's too dangerous for us to be out late at night with all the drunk drivers. Better that we are home. It's better than us lying about where we are and renting some sleazy motel room." The father found the "parental logic," as the reporter puts it, so irresistible that he allowed the boy to have not one, but two co-ed sleepover parties.

Nothing gives a better picture of the anemic principles of peer-parenting—and their sorry impact on kids—than a 1999 PBS *Frontline* show entitled "The Lost Children of Rockdale County." The occasion for the show was an outbreak of syphilis in an affluent Atlanta suburb that ultimately led health officials to treat 200 teenagers. What was so remarkable was not that 200 teenagers in a large suburban area were having sex and that they have overlapping partners. It was the way they were having sex. This was teen sex as *Lord of the Flies* author William Golding might have imagined it—a heart of darkness tribal rite of such degradation that it makes a collegiate "hook up" look like splendor in the grass. Group sex was commonplace, as were 13-year-old participants. Kids would gather together after school and watch the Playboy cable TV channel, making a game of imitating everything they saw. They tried almost every permutation of

sexual activity imaginable—vaginal, oral, anal, girl-on-girl, several boys with a single girl, or several girls with a boy. During some drunken parties, one boy or girl might be "passed around" in a game. A number of the kids had upwards of 50 partners.

To be sure, the Rockdale teens are the extreme case. The same could not be said of their parents. As the *Frontline* producers show them, these are ordinary, suburban soccer moms and dads, more affluent than most, perhaps, and in some cases overly caught up in their work. But a good number were doing everything the books tell you to do: coaching their children's teams, cooking dinner with them, going on vacations together. It wasn't enough. Devoid of strong beliefs, seemingly bereft of meaningful experience to pass on to their young, these parents project a bland emptiness that seems the exact inverse of the meticulous opulence of their homes and that lets the kids know there are no values worth fighting for. "They have to make decisions, whether to take drugs, to have sex," the mother of one of the boys intones expressionlessly when asked for her view of her son's after-school activity. "I can give them my opinion, tell them how I feel. But they have to decide for themselves." These lost adults of Rockdale County have abdicated the age-old distinction between parents and children, and the kids know it. "We're pretty much like best friends or something," one girl said of her parents. "I mean I can pretty much tell 'em how I feel, what I wanna do and they'll let me do it." Another girl pretty well sums up the persona of many contemporary parents when she says of her own mother. "I don't really consider her a mom all that much. She takes care of me and such, but I consider her a friend more."

So what happened to the lost art of parenting? Why is it that so many adults have reinvented their traditional role and turned themselves into advocates, friends, and copious providers of entertainment?

For one thing, this generation of parents has grown up in a culture that devotedly worships youth. It's true that America, a nation of immigrants fleeing the old world, has always been a youthful country with its eye on the future. But for the "I-hope-I-die-before-I-get-old" generation, aging, with its threat of sexual irrelevance and being out of the loop, has been especially painful. Boomers are the eternal teenagers—hip, sexy, and aware—and when their children suggest otherwise, they're paralyzed with confusion. In an op-ed published in the *New York Times* entitled "Am I a Cool Mother?" Susan Borowitz, co-creator of *Fresh Prince of Bel-Air*, describes her struggle with her role as parent-adult that one suspects is all too common. On a shopping expedition, she is shocked when her 10-year-old daughter rolls her eyes at the outfits she has chosen for her. "There is nothing more withering and crushing," she writes. "I stood there stunned. 'This can't be happening to me. I'm a cool mom.'" Determined to hang on to her youthful identity, she buys a pair of bell-bottom pants to take her daughter to DJ Disco Night at her school where she spots other "cool moms... pumping their fist and doing the Arsenio woof." Finally Borowitz comes to her senses. "This was a party for the kids. I am not a kid. I am a mom." No one could quarrel with her there, but the telling point is that it took 10 years for her to notice.

The Parent as Career Coach

There is one exception to today's parents' overall vagueness about their job description: They *know* they want their children to develop impressive résumés. This is what William Doherty, professor of family science at the University of Minnesota, calls "parenting as product development."

As early as the preschool years, parent-product developers begin a demanding schedule of gymnastics, soccer, language, and music lessons. In New York City, parents take their children to "Language for Tots," beginning at six months—that is, before they can even speak. Doherty cites the example of one Minnesota town where, until some cooler—or more sleep-deprived—heads prevailed, a team of 4-year-olds was scheduled for hockey practice the only time the rink was available—at 5 A.M. By the time children are ready for Little League, some parents hire hitting and pitching coaches from companies like Grand Slam USA. So many kids are training like professionals in a single sport instead of the more casual three or four activities of childhood past that doctors report a high rate of debilitating and sometimes even permanent sports injuries.

Of course, there's nothing wrong with wanting to enrich your children's experience by introducing them to sports and the arts. But as children's list-worthy achievements take on disproportionate and even frenzied significance, parents often lose sight of some of the other things they want to pass down—such as kindness, moral clarity, and a family identity. One Manhattan nursery school director reports that if a child receives a high score on the ERB (the IQ test required to get into private kindergarten), parents often conclude that the child's brilliance excuses him or her from social niceties. "If he can't pass the juice or look you in the eye, it's 'Oh, he's bored.'" Douglas Goetsch, a teacher at Stuyvesant High School, the ultra-competitive school in New York City, recently wrote an article in the school newspaper about the prevalence of cheating; in every case, he says, cheating is related to an "excessively demanding parent." Other educators are seeing even young children complaining about stress-related headaches and stomachaches.

Katherine Tarbox, a Fairfield, Conn., teen, describes all this from the point of view of the child-product in her recently published memoir *Katie.com*. At 13, Katie was an "A" student, an accomplished pianist who also sang with the school choir, and a nationally ranked swimmer. Impressive as they were, Katie's achievements loomed too large. "I always felt like my self-worth was determined by how well I placed. And I think my parents felt the same way—their status among the team parents depended on how well their child placed." Like many middle-class children today, the combination of school, extracurricular activities, and her parents' work schedule reduced family time so much that, "Home was a place I always felt alone." Aching to be loved for herself rather than her swim times and grade point average, she develops an intense relationship with a man on the Internet who very nearly rapes her when they arrange to meet at an out-of-town swim meet.

Even after their daughter's isolation stands revealed, Katie's parents are so hooked on achievement they still don't really notice their daughter. Katie complains to her therapist that her mother is always either at the office or working on papers at home. The woman has a helpful suggestion that epitomizes the overly schematized, hyper-efficient lives that come with parenting as product development: She suggests that Katie schedule appointments with her mother.

Related to this youth worship is the boomer parents' intense ambivalence about authority. The current generation of parents came of age at a time when parents, teachers, the police, and the army represented an authority to be questioned and resisted. Authority was associated with *Father Knows Best*, the Vietnam War, Bull Connor, and their own distant fathers. These associations linger in boomer parents' subconscious minds and make them squirm uncomfortably when their own children beg for firm guidance. Evelyn Bassoff, a Colorado therapist, reports that when she asks the women in her mothers' groups what happens when they discipline their daughters, they give answers such as "I feel mean," "I feel guilty," and "I quake all over; it's almost like having dry heaves inside." A survey by Public Agenda confirms that parents feel "tentative and uncertain in matters of discipline and authority." And no wonder. Notice the way *Time* describes the dilemma faced by parents of Britney Spears wannabes; these parents, the writers explain, are "trying to walk the line between fashion and fascism." The message is clear; the opposite of letting your child do what she wants is, well, becoming Hitler.

It would be difficult to overstate how deep this queasiness over authority runs in the boomer mind. Running so hard from outmoded models of authority that stressed absolute obedience, today's parents have slipped past all recognition of the child's longing for a structure he can believe in. In some cases, their fear not only inhibits them from disciplining their children, it can actually make them view the rebellious child as a figure to be respected. (Oddly enough, this is true even when, as is almost always the case these days, that rebellion takes the form of piercings and heavy metal music vigorously marketed by entertainment companies.) It's as if parents believe children learn individuality and self-respect in the act of defiance, or at the very least through aggressive self-assertion. Some experts reinforce their thinking. Take Barbara Mackoff, author of *Growing a Girl* (with a chapter tellingly entitled "Make Her the Authority"). Mackoff approvingly cites a father who encourages a child "to be comfortable arguing or being mad at me. I figure if she has lots of practice getting mad at a six-foot-one male, she'll be able to say what she thinks to anyone." The author agrees; the parent who tells the angry child "calm down, we don't hit people," she writes, "is engaging in silencing." In other words, to engage in civilization's oldest parental task—teaching children self-control—is to risk turning your child into an automaton ripe for abuse.

But the biggest problem for boomer peer-parents is that many of them are not really sure whether there are values important enough to pursue with any real conviction. In his book *One Nation After All*, the sociologist Alan Wolfe argues that although Americans are concerned about moral decline, they are also opposed to people who get too excited about it. This inherent contradiction—people simultaneously judge and refuse to judge—explains how it is that parents can both dislike their children watching *Smackdown!* on TV, talking back to them, drinking, or for that matter, engaging in group sex, but also fail to protest very loudly. Having absorbed an ethos of nonjudgmentalism, the parents' beliefs on these matters have been drained of all feeling and force. The Rockdale mother who blandly repeats "her opinion" about drugs and sex to her son is a perfect example; perhaps she is concerned about moral decline, but because her concern lacks all gravity or passion, it can't possibly have much effect. All in all, Wolfe seems to find the combination of concern and nonjudgmentalism a fairly hopeful state of affairs—and surely he is right that tolerance is a key value in a pluralistic society—but refusing to judge is one thing when it comes to your neighbor's divorce and quite another when it comes to your 13-year-old child's attitudes toward, say, cheating on a test or cursing out his soccer coach.

WHEN PARENTS fail to firmly define a moral universe for their children, it leaves them vulnerable to the amoral world evoked by their peers and a sensational media. As the Rockdale story makes clear, the saddest consequences appear in the sex lives of today's teenagers. Recently in an iVillage chat room, a distraught mother wrote to ask for advice after she learned that her 15-year-old daughter had sex with a boy. The responses she got rehearsed many of the principles of peer-parenting. Several mothers stressed safety and told the woman to get her daughter on the pill. Others acted out the usual boomer uneasiness over the power they have with their children. "Let your daughter know you trust her to make the 'right' decision when the time comes," wrote one. "Tell her that you are not 'giving your permission,'" another suggested, "but that you are also very aware that she will not 'ask for permission' either when the time comes." But it was the one teenager who joined in that showed how little these apparently hip mothers understood about the pressures on kids today; when she lost her virginity at 14, the girl writes: "it was because of a yearning to be loved, to be accepted." Indeed, the same need for acceptance appears to be driving the trend among middle-schoolers as young as seventh grade engaging in oral sex. According to the December 2000 *Family Planning Perspectives*, some middle school girls view fellatio as the unpleasant price they have to pay to hang on to a boyfriend or to seem hip and sophisticated among their friends. The awful irony is that in their reluctance to evoke meaningful values, parent advocates and peers have produced not the free-thinking, self-expressive, confident children they had hoped, but kids so conforming and obedient they'll follow their friends almost anywhere.

And so in the end, it is children who pay the price of the refusal of parents to seriously engage their predicament in a media-saturated and shadowy adult world. And what a price it is. When parenting becomes a lost art, children are not only deprived of the clarity and sound judgment they crave. They are deprived of childhood.

Kay S. Hymowitz, a senior fellow at the Manhattan Institute and contributing editor at City Journal, *is the author of* Ready or Not: What Happens When We Treat Children as Small Adults *(Encounter Books, 2000).*

The Future of Adolescence:
Lengthening Ladders to Adulthood

BY REED LARSON

Navigating the social and economic complexities of adult life requires more savvy and education than ever.

The life stage of adolescence is a crucial link in the future of society. It is a period when young people either become prepared for and enthusiastic about taking over adult roles, or they rebel against the expectations and responsibilities of adulthood. When things go right, adolescents enter adulthood with new energy and ideas that revitalize society and its institutions.

As we move into the twenty-first century, this life stage is changing rapidly across the world due to globalization, shifting job markets, and transformations in the family, among other things. It is crucial to learn how these changes affect young people's preparedness for the social and economic complexities of the adult world. The Study Group on Adolescence in the 21st Century, composed of a consortium of international scholars, examined the various contours of adolescents' preparation for the years ahead. The Group found that, although the demands on adolescents and the hazards they face in reaching adulthood are increasing, many young people are rising to the challenge.

A Raised Bar for Adulthood

What we expect of young people is extraordinary. First, we expect them to attend school for 12 to 18 years or longer without any guarantee that this education will match what they will need for career success. We ask them to make a leap of trust based on the assumption that the skills they are learning will be relevant when they eventually enter adulthood. Furthermore, we expect them to study without financial remuneration, accept a generic identity defined by their student role, and delay starting a family while in school. These circumstances put young people in a kind of limbo status for years.

As society evolves, this period of limbo continues to lengthen. Young people around the world are being expected to delay entry into adulthood ever longer. This is happening, in large part, because the platform one needs to reach for suc-

cessful adulthood is getting higher. An information society requires that young people learn more to become full members.

In postindustrial societies, we expect people to attend school until they're at least 22 years old—with no guarantee that their studies will lead to future employment, says author Reed Larson.

Education tops the list of new demands for adulthood, as more and more jobs, including manufacturing and service jobs, require literacy, numeracy, and computer skills. Brains are increasingly valued over brawn: In the United States, entry-level wages for people with only a high-school education have fallen by more than 20% since the 1970s. Job prospects are bleaker than ever for youths who do not continue their education after high school, and while there are exceptions—like the teenager who starts a basement computer business and becomes a multimillionaire—working a string of low-paying service jobs with no medical insurance is a much more common scenario for those with limited education.

The growing need for literacy skills in adult life extends beyond the workplace. Literacy is required to navigate complex insurance papers, retirement packages, legal regulations, and countless other complicated bureaucracies that are part of everyday life. Adults must be literate just to keep up with their own health care. Whereas 40 years ago patients were simply told what to do by their doctors, today patients are expected to be partners in their health management and to keep up with ever-changing research on diet, exercise, and disease prevention and treatment.

In addition to literacy, adolescents need to develop more versatile interpersonal skills to navigate the different worlds of home, work, and school—worlds of increasing complexity and diversity. Adult relationships are becoming less scripted and more transient, and teens need to develop skills for negotiating more *ad hoc* associations. Adults also must be able to operate in more-diverse social worlds. On the job, around the neighborhood, even within families, there is an increased likelihood that young people will need to know how to relate with people from different cultural and religious backgrounds. In developing the knowledge and vernaculars to move smoothly and communicate effectively across various social worlds, adolescents will need to acquire skills to change language, posture, tone, and negotiation strategies to adapt to multiple milieus. The adolescent who is able to function in only one world is increasingly ill-prepared for adult life.

Obstacles to Adulthood

As the platform of adulthood rises, the ladders required to get there lengthen. These boosted demands and longer ladders can increase the precariousness of adolescence, since a longer climb to adulthood creates new disadvantages for those who lack the financial means, emotional support, or mental capacity to keep climbing.

At work, at home, and at play, the human landscape increasingly features the co-mingling of individuals from different cultural, religious, and economic backgrounds. It is crucial for teens to develop social skills that will enable them to be comfortable and effective communicating with a variety of people in multiple milieus, suggests the author.

Acquiring advanced education and opportunities for learning diverse life skills often requires family wealth. In the United States, for example, annual college tuition generally ranges from $16,000 to $36,000—a full year's salary for many parents. Even when tuition is covered by grants and scholarships, families must have sufficient wealth to be able to forgo the income their college-bound children would otherwise provide; many poor families, especially in developing countries, cannot afford this sacrifice. By contrast, middle- and upper-class youths throughout the world are gaining access to new resources, such as after-school programs, camps, tutors, travel opportunities,

computers and new technologies, which will prepare them for both the literacy and life skills of modern adulthood.

Education and Earnings in the United States

High School	$1.2 million
Bachelor's	$2.1 million
Master's	$2.5 million
Ph.D.	$3.4 million
Professional	$4.4 million

Average lifetime work earnings by educational degree, based on 1999 earnings projected over a typical adult work life from age 25 to 64.

Source: U.S. Census Bureau

Girls are at a particular disadvantage in many nations, facing sex discrimination as an obstacle to obtaining even basic education and social skills. In the Middle East and South Asia, girls are more likely to be pulled from school at an early age and are thus less likely to develop critical literacy skills. Across most of the world, girls face more demands for work in the home and restrictions on movement that constrain their opportunities to gain direct experience with diverse social worlds. As rates of divorce and abandonment rise worldwide, so do the risks for young women who fail to obtain skills to function independently. As they reach adulthood, uneducated women are increasingly vulnerable to poverty and exploitation.

Even academically skilled youths from middle-class families are subject to new perils on the climb to adulthood. The rapidly changing job market makes it difficult to predict what opportunities will be available when these adolescents finally seek employment. Entire sectors can disappear on short notice when industries move their operations abroad or close shop altogether.

High school and college curricula in the United States, many critics argue, provide a poor fit to the job market. Schools in many developing countries in South Asia and Africa are using curricula that have changed little since they were colonies of Western nations, focusing on memorization rather than critical thinking and on areas such as classics rather than marketable skills in computer technology or business. The result is growing numbers of youths who are educated but unemployed.

Backlash against Limbo

It is also the case that a longer climb to adulthood, resulting in a longer period of limbo, can increase the stress experienced by adolescents. Even worse, it can lead to behaviors that arrest their process of preparation. In the United States, the experience of stress among young people has been steadily increasing. In 1999, 30% of college freshmen reported being "frequently overwhelmed," up from 16% in 1985.

The lengthening of ladders, then, increases the risk that more youths will "fall off." Adolescents who, for whatever reason, do not continue in education increasingly find themselves stuck in a low-paying and unstable labor pool.

Young people tend to live in the present moment and find immediate attractions much more appealing than long-term goals—especially when the achievement of those goals is abstract and being pushed further and further away. There is increasing possibility that adolescents will respond to the high-pressure, competitive worlds they are being asked to take on by turning off or turning away.

Societies must be concerned with a major unknown: whether young people, as a group, might rebel against the increasing demands placed upon them and the longer period of limbo they must endure. This result is increasingly probable as adolescents are spending more time with peers than they did in the past, which is creating distinct youth cultures in many societies. These youth cultures might become vehicles of mass resistance to adult society, like the hippie culture of the 1960s.

In New Zealand, Maori adolescents have drawn on American rap and hip-hop culture to resist assimilation into the mainstream. The attraction of radical Islam to many youths reflects a reaction against the competition and materialism of the new global world. In some cases these adolescents' resistance may lead to their joining militant groups, while in others it may simply mean that they enter adulthood unprepared to hold a job and raise a family.

However, we should not be too alarmist. Resistance is most likely when the ladders to adulthood are uninviting, poorly marked, and when the outcomes are uncertain—all things we can do something about. There is also a strong likelihood that the new youth cultures in the twenty-first century will lead society in positive directions. Often youth movements are inspired by pursuit of core human values: compassion, authenticity, and renewal of meaning. It is possible that generational "revolt" will pull societies away from the frantic lifestyles, shallow materialism, and divisive competitiveness that are accompanying globalization. It should be kept in mind that youths in most cases are a positive force.

Rising to the Challenge

The Study Group found that youths in most parts of the world report being optimistic about their lives and that, despite the greater demands and longer ladders, the majority of young people are rising to the challenge. Rates of illiteracy among 15-year-olds have fallen from 37% to 20% since 1970, UNESCO statistics show. Rates of high school and college graduation across most nations continue to climb. And there is little question that many young women have more versatile skills for taking care of themselves and navigating public environments today than 50 years ago. In the United States, teenage rates of pregnancy and violence have fallen substantially across the last decade, indicating that fewer teens are getting off track.

The most convincing scientific evidence of the increasing abilities of youth comes from IQ test scores. New Zealand political scientist James Flynn gathered intelligence test scores of young people over the last 70 years. Because new norms for the

tests are established every few years, the publicly reported scores have shown little change. Once Flynn went back to the unadjusted scores, however, he found the IQs of young people rose dramatically over this period: The average IQ of a young adult today is 20 points higher than in 1940. There is no way to pinpoint what accounts for this increase, but it seems likely that youths' abilities have grown as they have responded to the increased complexity of modern life.

Web Resources on Youth Trends

- **Search Institute**, www.search-institute.org
  Social science organization focuses on youth development in multiple community and society settings.
- **2001 Monitoring the Future Study**,
  www.nida.nih.gov/Infofax/HSYouthtrends.html
  Study on the extent of drug abuse among eighth, tenth, and twelfth graders, conducted annually by the University of Michigan's Institute for Social Research and funded by the National Institute on Drug Abuse.
- **Ewing Marion Kauffman Foundation**,
  www.emkf.org
  Researches and identifies unfulfilled needs in society, then develops, implements, and/or funds solutions to help young people achieve success in school and life.
- **Youth Values 2000**, www.youthvalues.org
  International project, initiated by the International Sport and Culture Association, exploring young people's self-image, values, and beliefs about the world around them.
- **European Youth Forum**, www.youthforum.org
  Youth platform in Europe, composed of youth councils and nongovernmental youth organizations, that works to facilitate communication between young people and decision makers.

The general decrease in family size also contributes to youths' better preparedness for adulthood. Smaller families mean that parents can devote more attention and resources to each child. Parents in many parts of the world are adopting a more responsive and communicative parenting style, which research shows facilitates development of interpersonal skills and enhances mental health.

Other new supports and opportunities have also brightened the outlook for adolescents. Young people receive better health care than they did 50 years ago; consequently, youths around the world are much less likely to die from disease. The Internet provides an important new vehicle for some young people (though as yet a very small percentage of the world's youth) to access a wealth of information. Via the Net, adolescents can also run businesses, participate in social movements, and develop relationships; they are less handicapped by traditional barriers of age.

As a result of these opportunities and their own initiative, the current generation of youth is smarter, more mature, and more socially versatile than any generation in human history. They are better able to function in multiple worlds, collaborate in teams, and solve unstructured problems. We must not underestimate the ways in which adolescents in all parts of the world and of all social classes may draw on their youthful reservoirs of energy and optimism to forge fresh directions and develop new skills.

However, it would be a mistake to be too sanguine. Adolescence in the twenty-first century provides many opportunities for youths to make wrong turns or just become turned off, never to realize their true potential. In order to keep adolescents on the right track, society needs to provide more diverse kinds of ladders for people with different learning styles and socioeconomic backgrounds, regardless of sex or ethnicity. Many jobs involve skills that do not correspond to those tested in school, and we need to provide avenues for them to receive non-aca-demic opportunities to grow and shine—internships, job skills workshops, even art classes, to name a few.

There should also be way stations along the climb that allow young people to rest, gather themselves, and consider alternatives. The success of government, business, the arts, and private life in 2050 and beyond depends on how well we nurture and inspire the next generation to take over and give their best.

About the Author
Reed Larson leads the Study Group on Adolescence in the 21st Century, which was sponsored by the Society for Research on Adolescence and the International Society for Behavioral Development. He is a professor in the Department of Human and Community Development at the University of Illinois, 1105 West Nevada Street, Urbana, Illinois 61801. E-mail larsonR @uiuc.edu.

For more information on the Study Group, visit its Web site, www. s-r-a.org/studygroup.html.

Originally published in the November/December 2002 issue of *The Futurist.* Used with permission from the World Future Society, 7910 Woodmont Avenue, Suite 450, Bethesda, MD 20814. Telephone: 301/656-8274; Fax: 301/951-0394; http://www.wfs.org. © 2002.

Midlife Changes:
Utilizing a Social Work Perspective

ABSTRACT. The life stage that ranges from approximately age forty to sixty-five in human development is a time of major changes for both men and women, yet this time frame is often neglected or de-emphasized in the intervention context. This article reviews the philosophical, biological, cultural, psychological, and social areas of human development in mid-life. These factors are identified and practice suggestions are made as we enter the new millennium.

KEYWORDS. Human development, mid-life changes

Sophia F. Dziegielewski

Carolyn Heymann

Cheryl Green

Jannie E. Gichia

INTRODUCTION

The life stage that ranges in age from approximately forty to sixty-five is a time of major changes for both men and women. Yet this time frame is often neglected or de-emphasized in the treatment context. "It is a time of heartaches and heart attacks" (Clark, Shute, & Kelly, 2000). In the year 2000, 4.7 million people turned 40. This generation is different from those who came before them in that they are actively resisting growing up and old. Today's version of this period of life is the extreme sports of middle age (Clark et al., 2000). As people age at different rates (Shute, 1997), some forty year olds today resemble the 30 year olds of 10 years ago. They are having children later, cosmetic surgery sooner, and working harder in their jobs than their parents did at their age. This middle-aged population is busier, more stressed and more responsible than past generations. Women are spending far more time in the work place and men have more in-home responsibilities. In addition, these couples are more likely to have a newborn in their home and at the same time an elderly parent. Career changes occur more frequently and individuals remain in outside-the-home employment longer. With this extended period of productivity over one trillion dollars was spent in the past year. However, with all of this, this group which totals 15.4% of the population is five times more likely to be laid off or lose their jobs (Clark et al., 2000).

During these years, individuals begin to look at their lives and often begin to count the years left until death, instead of the years since birth. Changes that occur in this time period affect the biological, social and psychological areas of human development (Pillari, 1998). The purpose of this article is to review these changes while stressing how these factors interact with the culture and societal system.

THE PHILOSOPHY OF MIDLIFE

Traditionally, mid-life is noted as a time of questioning. The individual can be consumed with a flood of emotions and thoughts regarding personal issues, careers, family, and the future. Acceptance of the changes that occur at this stage of life have its origin in one's attitude. In terms of human development it seems the early years of life have an *external* focus. This makes the mid-life years crucial as they represent a time of change to an *internal focus* that provides wisdom for the later years. This in turn is commonly referred to as the "mid-life crisis," a theory first noted by Jaques (1965). More commonly, the fear of death and realization of mortality is placed into context of the person's view of their lifespan as the amount of time until death, hence creating an adaptation crisis (Shek, 1996).

Since the resolution of fear and anxiety often involve faith and knowledge the book of Ecclesiastes in the Bible and the writings of Carl Jung can help in understanding the struggles of individuals aged 40–55. Both offer valuable advice in successfully traversing the changes that occur in mid-life. The Philosopher in the book of Ecclesiastes: 1–12 expresses the feelings of many mid-life people with the message that through it all, people are not just killing time and life has purpose.

Jung believed in the importance of a successful transition from one phase of life to the next and that the first half of life serves as preparation for the second half, which embodies the pursuit of meaning (Brandes, 1986). This pursuit of meaning involves a coming to terms with mortality, a task that extends beyond the psychological into the spiritual. In fact many cultures, such as Judaism, literally restrict certain social roles and bodies of knowledge to the second half of life.

Therefore, according to Jung, mid-life is designed to usher in a new set of tasks. The main question individuals encounter at this stage is "What is the purpose of my existence from now on?" (p. 35). In puberty individuals experience a burst of hormones that can force sexual and aggressive instincts into an identity and a role. In mid-life, individuals can control these instincts and are able to evaluate goals and expectations formulated in these earlier developmental years. In midlife, a focus on current commitments is highlighted such as partner, family, and job. In reviewing these life partnerships it is important not to act on impulse. The secret to satisfaction is believed to be in the individual's integration of these factors and the shift from biological imperatives to introversion and imagination. Here the emphasis is on the expansion and cultivation of character. "Integration is an inward process of becoming open to other ways of being" (Brandes, 1986, p. 36). In midlife there is a decreased sense of competition and aggressiveness often found in youth yet at times the sense of emptiness and hunger for the old pleasures may build up and cause dissatisfaction with the current lifestyle.

Sometimes in midlife this results in a restlessness with an immediate reaction to make things work the way they used to. This action warrants caution as it can result in regression into past behaviors, which causes increased stress and anxiety. For some this may lead to the impulse to act out and experience feeling and emotions similar to those felt previously in puberty to reemerge. For others the primary goal is not the establishment of another concrete love relationship, but the development of openness to a partner. The problem is that our culture makes no provision and has no guidelines for this phase of development. Instead, we produce soap operas and movies about extramarital affairs. In midlife, the focus is inner not outer change. Wisdom as Jung describes it involves empathy, humor, and detachment—attitudes that ultimately enable one to begin to move into the last phase of life. This movement completes the circle of self, the capacity to be fully human. The moving out of oneself allows moving into others, which expands the personality and revitalizes the ego.

Western Culture: Men and Women

In examining the lives of many Westerners it is reported that an identity crisis can occur at age forty and beyond. Unfortunately, in terms of normal human growth and development, we accept the changes experienced by two-year olds and adolescents, but seem to interpret midlife as a downward turn. The negative attitude toward the age of forty, and the perception of older ages as being even worse, is almost exclusively a trait of Western cultures. America is infatuated with youth and this infatuation is perpetuating the idea of dysfunction with aging (Clark et al., 2000). In turn, this fosters the personal trauma we experience at mid-life, as noted previously the mid-life crisis (Kruger, 1996; Myers, 1998). Men have abandoned their jobs and left wives and children. Women spruce up and acquire lovers or change their previous life styles (Kruger, 1996; Myers, 1998; Clark et al., 2000). While these events may at first appear problematic, these experiences can serve to usher in a new life stage that requires the individual develop a more highly integrated personality structure with deeper insight.

Kruger (1994) reached a conclusion comparable to that of Margaret Mead when he questioned that there are cultural, rather than biological, reasons why the age of forty is perceived as transitional and is accorded such an unfavorable image. This finding on mid-life crisis was linked to the prosperity of white western cultures as the source for the belief that one should act out the associated behaviors of the crisis. Therefore, westerners increase their leisure time to allow for self-absorption (Kruger, 1994). In fact, Brandes reported that in one village in Mexico people do not even know their age (1986). Even the bourgeoisie of Barcelona did not focus on this age to the extent that Americans do. Myers (1998) further expounds with identifying the variance in recognition of mid-life between cultures with the idea of a social timetable theory in which people behave in a prescribed patterns (i.e., through education, career, marriage, and parenthood).

Middle aged women in central Europe, Turkey, Persia, North Africa, and Arabia who participated in an exhaustive study reported they heartily welcomed menopause, and did not want to mother infants. For these women, menopause and middle age brought more relief than anxiety and they dismissed the question of mid-life crisis. These women did not experience the social changes that women in Western societies reported (Jones, 1994).

BIOLOGICAL CHANGES IN MIDLIFE

It is clear from the latest information on mid life that what was old before is not now (Shute, 1997). In looking at the physiological consequences of older ages, there are some issues that are associated with aging that cannot be changed with mere attitude or restructuring of social norms. Physical activity actually starts to decrease in one's 20s and this change is absolutely normal; although, it is in the 40s that the realization of the loss of youth comes to fruition (Clark et al., 2000). Due to medical advancements heart disease and associated deaths are down since the 1970s by 50% and cancer is down by one third (Clark et al., 2000).

Biomedical Factors: Menopause and the Climacteric Response

To assist in clarification of terminology, the American Heritage Dictionary (1989) describes *climacteric* as: (1) a period or year of life when physiological changes, especially menopause occur; (2) a critical period. During this time frame *menopause* occurs and is described as: (1) the cessation of menstruation that occurs in women, usually between the ages of 45 and 50. However, recently climacteric has been used to include the general description of the mid-life crisis for men. Male Menopause or *Andropause* has been used adaptively in reference to male changes in hormone levels or functioning (LifeMD, 2000). The most prominent changes for both sexes are linked to hormone levels and age related physical functioning.

Men

Some people use the term *male menopause* or *Andropause* to describe changes that men undergo. Yet, such use of the term can be misleading. Men do not experience a sudden plunge in hormone levels. Instead, most men will show a long-term, and generally gradual decline in their testosterone level (over 10 to 15 years) between their seventh and ninth decades (LifeMD, 2000). The timing of hormone release also changes in men. In contrast to the morning surge of testosterone that was experienced in youth, most men will experience a leveling off of hormone production during the day when they approach mid-life similar to women (Skolnick, 1992).

This process consists of a reduction in cell production or intensity failure of the transmitter to reach the responder side. This decrease is also called hypogonadism. This results in decreased testosterone levels in the body. There are two kinds of testosterone produced in the body: free or bound. It is the free testosterone that aids in strength libido, sexual performance, sleep patterns, erectile function, mood, and sense of well being. However, there is a limited supply of free testosterone to begin with and over time the amount of bound testosterone increases. This couples with the increase in estrogen levels in the men over time. The effects of the increased estrogen levels are increased risk of heart attack and a negation of the effects of testosterone in the body. Obesity, zinc deficiency, and liver dysfunction as associated with alcohol use or side effects of prescription drugs can enhance estrogen increases. The end result is the men experience Andropausal symptoms such as depression, fatigue, irritability, anxiety, cognitive deficits, aches and pains, sweats, hot flashes, dysphoria, erectile dysfunction and dermatological issues (LifeMD, 2000; Perry, Lund, Arndt, Holman, Bever-Stille, Paulsen, & Demers, 2001; Tan, 2001).

Women

In women the pathologic consequences of the endocrine depletion state of menopause are evident but the degree of effect varies among individual woman. Generally, the specific hormones that are deficient are estradiol and progesterone. Testosterone is reduced to a greater degree after surgical menopause (Swartz, 1992). Attitudes toward menopause have changed in the past decade (Gunby, 1992). In "1981, the World Health Organization referred to menopause as an 'estrogen-deficiency disease' (which) conveys the message of post-menopausal *functionlessness* and decline" (Jones, 1994). However, Jacqueline Goodchilds, a social psychologist, suggests, "If the truth were known, we'd have to diagnose older women as having P.M.F.—Post-Menstrual Freedom" (Myers, 1998). While some women regret the inability to produce children, most relish the release from the burden of menstruation and pregnancy concerns (Berkun, 1986; McQuaide, 1998).

Most women actually experience a *climacteric*, or an overall time of change, which starts with the peri-menopause or pre-menopause. This time is marked by changes in the menstrual cycle, and ends with the full cessation of ovulation in the *menopause* stage. The most common symptoms of menopause are additional weight gain, vaginal dryness, and hot flashes. The "hot flash" affects approximately 75% of menopausal women. This symptom is caused by a malfunction to temperature control mechanisms in the hypothalamus, and can be experienced as a mild body flush, or severe perspiration, which soaks clothing and bedding, and interferes with sleep. This sleep disturbance contributes to the fatigue women experience in this stage (Myers, 1998; Sheehy, 1993). Not all these symptoms, however, are due to a cessation of estrogen production. Swartz (1992) cautions health care providers to initiate appropriate diagnostic procedures for all symptoms to avoid assuming symptoms in a menopausal female are due singularly to menopause. Also, many women have experienced the attitude from their physicians that postmenopausal women were simply neurotic. Neurosis and menopause troubles are not related. However, if a woman seeking help at mid-life is met with insinuations that she is neurotic, real distress could come from loss of self-confidence, thereby fulfilling the diagnosis. When this occurs, she will not receive the medical support she needs and if menopausal distress is hormonally caused it makes sense that the greatest success will come with a hormonal cure (Cutler & Garcia, 1992).

Differences Between Men and Women

In summary, the differences between male and female reproductive physiology are extensive. Similarly, evidence also supports there is a difference between the way that men and women perceive pain (Hoffman & Tarzian, 2001; Rubin, 2001). In general the term menopause describes the end of the egg-releasing menstrual years (Cutler & Garcia, 1992). For example, men produce a fresh supply of sperm each day, often into advanced age, while *women are born with all the eggs they will ever have.* While men do experience physiological changes in the middle adulthood life stage that can be major, they are not generally due to a severe, rapid decrease in several hormones. The change in hormones in women's bodies, however, can cause greater threats to health and quality of life, depending on the individual. Dr. Swartz and the sixteen scientists and recognized authorities in this field who produced *Hormone Replacement Therapy* (HRT) concluded from the data that HRT is generally beneficial to women who are not producing these hormones when adjusted individually for each patient. They indicate that though there remains some risk of cancer due to the HRT, the benefits far outweigh the risks. This data also indicate that while all are at risk, the diseases discussed above will not adversely affect most women. The FDA lists four contraindications for HRT, and these can be discussed with the physician (Cutler, 1993).

Treatment or Hormone Replacement

For men the treatment is similar to that of the women and what is lost needs to be replaced. This is not done to reverse the aging process but to alleviate symptoms of the decline. Although there is concern that testosterone supplementation may lead to prostate hypertrophy or cancer and increased risk of heart disease (Skolnick, 1992); research is limited because the practice of testosterone replacement is not commonly used. If implemented the treatment methods are simple given orally or with injection. Three common drugs are Testcypionate, Depotest, and Delatestryl. It is clear that further investigation into hormone therapy in men is needed to weigh side effects and potential risks to benefits known.

For women the use of hormones is similar in purpose with positive outcomes related to decreases in heart disease, vaginal dryness, vaginal atrophy, and osteoporosis (Branswell, 1998; McQuaide, 1998). Risks include primarily that of breast cancer. In this case family history is an indicator of risk that must be considered (Branswell, 1998; McQuaide, 1998). The last 15 years have seen a tremendous upsurge in information regarding female menopause, but data is still insufficient, particularly regarding the use of hormone replacement therapy. Until recently, most medical research was concentrated on men, primarily because men were easier to study (no monthly physical inconsistencies). Another problem surfaced with the realization that most women obtained hormone replacements from their personal obstetrician/gynecologist, who was not involved with the osteoporosis, cardiovascular, neurological, or psychosocial problems their patients were encountering. Similarly, a woman's cardiologist, or orthopedic surgeon was not communicating with her gynecologist (Swartz, 1992).

One recent change in medical data has been to decrease the fears associated with hormone replacement and cancer. Today physicians are looking for ways to minimize risk through the use and development of new drugs or designer estrogen such as Raloxifene to maximize hormonal therapies without the risk of cancer (Branswell, 1998). They are able to weigh the balance of risk and benefit in each patient.

Swartz (1992) recommended, and Branswell (1998) supports, noninvasive bone mass/density testing for all women entering menopause because the lifetime risk of suffering a hip fracture is approximately 15% and that risk equals the combined risk of breast, uterine, and ovarian cancer. This also appears to indicate that women have a 70% chance they will not experience any of the above. Swartz (1992) also stressed that estrogen therapy decreases the risk of coronary heart disease by approximately 50%. Combined regimens of estrogen and progestin lower LDL cholesterol and increase levels of HDL, an action that helps to prevent coronary heart disease. Hypertension, another health problem in this population is benefited by estrogen therapy (Branswell, 1998; McQuaide, 1998).

In addition to hormone replacement therapy (HRT), women are now utilizing herbal remedies such as the phytoestrogens in flaxseed and some soy products. However, it cannot be emphasized strongly enough that these herbs are not clinically proven or studied the way that the prescription drugs are (Dziegielewski & Leon, 2001). Extreme caution and medical consult should be obtained whenever an alternative remedy is sought. Until dietary evidence has been researched, women should restrict the soy products to one serving per day. Appropriate portions of soy intake have not been studied in American women and the model of protective effects is based on East Asian diets (Vincent & Fitzpatrick, 2000; Messina & Messina, 2000). Additionally, weight-bearing exercises such as running, jogging, weight training, aerobics, or stair climbing are a recommended prescription for bone health (Branswell, 1998; McQuaide, 1998). The overall physical benefits of exercise are so pervasive that all women should be encouraged to participate in exercise all of their lives. Other necessary health measures are decreasing alcohol consumption, monitoring nutrition, increasing calcium intake, and smoking cessation (Cutler & Garcia, 1992).

Other Physical Changes

The Journal of the American Medical Association states that there is no comparison of biological changes in men and women (Skolnick, 1992). However, there are some commonalties in aging. In addition to hormonal changes, there are several conditions that warrant examination. Both women and men have gained an average of 7.6 lbs in their median weight since the 1980s. With this increase in weight, there has been an overall decrease in physical functioning, and vitality (Fine et al., 1999). Another change shared is that of vision. With age, the lens in one's eyes becomes less flexible and hence creates farsightedness. The solution here is bifocals and even perhaps trifocals as one ends the period of middle age. In fact, 74% of all persons in their 40s and 94% of persons in their 50s use some reading aide such as glasses (Clark et al., 2000). In considering these effects, it is interesting to look by gender for commonalities.

Women may experience some hair loss, loss of firmness in labia and breasts, difficulty maintaining weight, body contour change, and loss of elasticity and strength in some muscles. Some itchiness, headaches, and insomnia may occur, and growth of hair on the upper lip and at the corners of the mouth. Estrogen replacement therapy and regular exercise can minimize these symptoms (Cutler & Garcia, 1992).

Other typical physical changes in men include decreased hair growth, voice depth, deterioration of the sex glands, wrinkles, slowing blood circulation, sluggish digestion, and the vulnerability of the prostate to problems, including prostate cancer. Shute (1997) notes that there are new Prostate Specific Antigen (PSA) screenings available, however, that may detect this form of cancer 10 years prior to manual detection.

Also men and women both may experience urinary problems; men as a result of prostate malfunctions, such as benign prostate hyperplasia or enlarged prostate. This condition causes urinary hesitancy and is linked to recurrent kidney malfunction and urinary tract infection (Prevention, 1999). Women have problems as a result of muscle weakness from childbirth, which manifests as stress incontinence. Women also experience increase in urinary tract infections due to changes in the bladder resulting from estrogen decrease. While men fear prostate cancer, women are concerned about the possibility of uterine cancer.

The principal physical change in both sexes, which may be categorized with mid-life crisis, is the decrease in sexual functioning. In men there is a decrease in sperm produced, and a delay in erection and ejaculation during sexual intercourse. For many men, however, the causes for difficulties with erections can be physical or psychological. Vascular impairment and some drugs can cause interference in sexual functioning (Koenaman, Mulhall, & Goldstein, 1997). Problems can also be psychogenic in origin, and for this psychotherapy is the recommended course of treatment (Cutler, 1993; Myers, 1998). For some men, the stimulation of a new, younger partner may assist with these problems, but not always as the younger partner may actually cause more frustration and realiza-

tion of the situation (Cutler, 1993). For women this dysfunction arises in vaginal dryness, painful intercourse, and decreased libido (Prevention, 1999). Overall, for both men and women, a partner of a similar age seems to make the situation and acceptance of each other's situations easier.

The heart is another organ in which both sexes manifest problems in midlife. There is an increase in heart disease found in women and men with age. It is the leading cause of death in women with 25,000 deaths a year (Branswell, 1998). Women now equal men in the prevalence of heart disease by age 65 (Alexander, 2000). Variations of heart disease include Coronary Artery Diseases (CAD), Angina, Myocardial Infarction (MI) and Hypertension (HTN) (Alexander, 2000). There are various theories as to why this is occurring and perhaps one of the most controversial has to do with increased levels of Estrogen, Estrogen to Androgen ratios, and life style (Stains, 1997). Risks for heart disease in mid life include smoking cigarettes, weight gain, sedentary life styles, alcohol use, and diet (Wannamathee, Shaper, Walker, & Ebraheim, 1998; Alexander, 2000).

Though the physical changes can be threatening, the most difficult aspects of mid-life for both men and women in this country are the psychosocial dimensions. The major difficulties with aging, in turn, are a reflection of the culture of the population. Men in the lower socioeconomic classes are severely affected because of the impact on their social role in this culture.

Social Changes That Occur in Midlife

Several areas are worthy of consideration in examining the effect age has on social development. Persons in midlife have more choices today and have to cope with more information, stress and responsibilities. The areas most widely affecting this group include family and socialization, work, education, and the effect of media/marketing.

To understand the depths of impact on the familial system, some basic facts are necessary. There is an increase in the range of midlife family definition. One in seven marriages end in divorce, which is double the numbers from 1975. This has led to a remarkable increase in remarriage and stepfamilies. One may have both a newborn and an elderly parent to care for. More people at midlife are raising grandchildren along side their own children while still others are coping with an empty nest (Clark et al., 2000; Wu & Penning, 1997).

Brandes (1985) indicates when many American parents are suffering through a mid-life crisis, they are also playing different roles. They are spouses, mothers and fathers, and caregivers or receivers. Parents may be burdened with mental and physical problems associated with midlife, while their children are weathering adolescence. The effect of illness has demonstrated a negative effect on family and work systems. Quality of life then becomes associated with an ability to meet financial stresses of satisfying medical needs or care giving roles. Despite the outcome, the roles held in the family or relationship will change (Walsh, 1997).

Walsh (1997) acknowledged that families are becoming increasingly unconventional and childbearing is now extending well into couples' forties and fifties. The forms are varied: adoption, single parenthood, in vitro fertilization, and sperm donors. In addition, middle-aged persons are increasingly tolerant of varied family forms such as cohabitation without marriage, step families, and families of mixed faith or race. With this change in definitions of family, there are some unforeseen realities such as attachment disordered internationally adopted children, custody issues of both spouses from former marriages, and increased work demands or conditions such as sudden lay off. Divorce is a primary area of concern for most persons in midlife.

Divorce rates are influenced by several factors. Wu and Penning (1997) found that increased length of time married before age forty increases the strength of the marriage after forty. Having young children in the home also aids the marital stability. Mutual interests and involvement are key to marital satisfaction during and after midlife. Persons who remarried during midlife are also more apt to experience marital stability. Increased education levels on the other hand negatively affect marital stability. This is especially true for women whose education level has far surpassed a spouse prior to mid life (Wu & Penning, 1997). Some adults experience empty nest syndrome, and some are caught in the sandwich generation. Parents who looked forward to freedom when the youngest child leaves home are sometimes depressed to find the oldest is back home. All of this equals a definitive rise in stress levels (Walsh, 1997). Minorities experience the greatest difficulties during the age due to the stress of discrimination and oppression on all members (Elman & O'Rand, 1998).

One such area of increased stress is care taking of elderly parents for both men and women, though men are not typically the caregivers. In the age of managed care, there has been an increase in the emphasis on family ties in the care taking process for elderly parents and ill spouses. The estimated reduction in cost to the system is approximately 7 to 10 thousand dollars per admission. The end result is that family members will either reside longer with their families with decreased professional assistance or the caregiver will expend their disposable income in addition to parental finances to maintain private services (Robinson, 1997). Women are unaffected by the actual multiplicity of roles, while for men there is evidence of both role buffering and strain from conflicting demands. However, in contrast to caring for their elderly parents, women find their well being is enhanced when assisting their adult children (Spitze et al., 1994).

Professionally, men and women both have substantial reason for age-related concerns. They are working longer hours. For example women in 1975 worked an average of 18 hours a week at age 40, and in 1995 that figure rose to an average of 28 hours a week (Clark, Shute, & Kelly, 2000). Age does seem to severely limit the opportunities for employment or career alternatives. Fortune (1999) noted the continuing trend to eliminate older workers as seniority is no longer valued. Despite this, there are some efforts when the structured approach to high tech fails to retreat to use of the older and wiser manager, to turn things around (Fortune, 1999). However, the reality remains that jobs of the midlife aged employee come under greater risk with each passing birthday (Clark, Shute, & Kelly, 2000). This situation can lead to malaise, depression, or other forms of self-destruction.

Research into this problem began as early as the 1920s, through Stanford University. It took until 1967 for Congress to pass the Age Discrimination Employment Act (ADEA). However, the Federal Regulation of Employment Service, 1981, p. 5, reported that the age of 40, not 70 as dictated by the Act, was the real upper limit for suspected discrimination of employees. Influxes of lawsuits based on age discrimination are continually filed, even in the academic fields. The situation, however, has not shown substantial improvement (Brandes, 1985; Shute, 1997; Hyuck, 1997; Fortune, 1997; Clark et al., 2000). In fact employers won 89% of all discrimination cases in the mid 1990s (Clark et al., 2000).

Insecurity leads some to invest in what Clark, Shute and Kelly (2000) called the "Grecian plan" (p. 73). One minimizes their job experience, leaves those date questions or details blank on resumes, dyes their hair, joins a gym, hires a personal shopper in their 20s, has a little cosmetic and dental surgery to gain increased hiring appeal. But is this really necessary? There are several proponents that note people do their best work in the first 10 to 20 years after beginning a career despite age when they start the career. In addition, figures show that the median age of employees in 2000 is 35 but by 2050 it will be in the 70s (Economist, 2000).

Despite these potential barriers, there is also evidence of occupational advantages of being over forty. For example, positions in administration are often reserved for more experienced employees. Requirements for political office also stipulate a minimum age, indicating the highest, most difficult posts are reserved for people forty years and older (Brandes, 1985). As women have entered the work force, they are finding they are now equal with men in the age-discrimination situation, but have not advanced to the level of the highest political offices. The solution it seems is to maintain one's training and to maintain flexibility as they approach the midlife barrier. The statistics show clearly that middle-aged persons are leaving career jobs earlier, changing tasks, benefits, and mobility, and thus, reexamining their lives. The outcome is that in retirement these people are experiencing a greater variety of experiences with varied rewards (Elman & O'Rand, 1998).

In addition to work experiences, one must also consider the educational trends in the middle-aged population. There has been a rapid reentry of persons in higher education and retraining in the past 5 years. Women in this age group are the most likely to retrain as well as whites and Hispanics. Change is encouraged in today's marketplace leading to increases in unemployment and the corresponding increased probability for the need to retrain. Factors affecting these trends appear to be those with stable employment and those with increased health issues (Elman & O'Rand, 1998). Brandes concludes his book, *Forty: The Age and the Symbol* with a discussion how the events of age 40 may later assume the significance that adolescence now holds.

Psychological Changes in Midlife

A review of psychological theories which include Erikson, Peck, Maslow, and Levinson, together with the moral theories of Piaget, Kohlberg and Gilligan aid in understanding people in mid-life transition (Myers, 1998; Chess & Nolin, 1991). Understanding the process of well being at this life stage, however, is sometimes easier if one is not living it. In addition, there is a contention that the primary psychological process, mid-life crisis resolution, is nothing more than the resolution of an adjustment disorder, complicated with the appropriate mood as it presents (Kruger, 1994). A look at this theory does hold some merit as the criteria for diagnosis does match the presenting symptoms of midlife transition (APA, 1996). However, a full examination of this theory and its implications are beyond the scope of the present work. For social work there are several current issues of concern and a look at five of these will assist in understanding for practice implementation. They are fear, anxiety, depression, creativity, and intelligence.

To understand the impact of psychological issues on functioning, a definition of well being in midlife is essential. Well being is the individual's perception of their emotional state. It is the ability to overcome the factors identified as problematic in midlife crisis that increases the ability to identify and maintain one's sense of well being. These factors include worries about the future, inability to enjoy leisure time, feelings of deteriorating health, and stress from care taking responsibilities to name a few (Sheck, 1996). As menopause is such a primary event in mid life, some have proposed that a decline in sense of well being can be linked to endocrinal changes. However, research has found the feelings of well being are directly linked to health status, psychosocial factors, and life style variables rather than changes in the endocrine system (Demerstein, Smith, & Morse, 1994). Furthermore, while there is an initial decline in feelings of well being at the onset of menopause, it is identified as improving two years post menopause. The intensity of these feelings is linked to levels of fear experienced (Demerstein & Berger, 1997).

Fear is a common phenomenon that both men and women experience at this stage of life. The fear is of aging, as related to potential loss of mental and physical abilities. One's sense of desirability and sexual prowess is particularly important. Women's fears center on the media's theme of the "sin of aging" and therefore "age discrimination, and abandonment by romantic partners or mates" (McQuaide, 1998, p. 532). Men are afraid women will reject them, or surpass them in sexual ability. Both are afraid of death and ending up alone. In business it is not uncommon to reward youth and flexibility over age and experience (Clark, Shute, & Kelly, 2000). Women join men in fear of losing their professional abilities, even employment security, as both have often closely related their identities with their work (Myers, 1998). Economic fears in men are more directly related to employment. However, in women, they are more related to life choices. If the woman has chosen a lesser career or has delayed career entry to raise children or support a partner's career, they are of greater disadvantage in mid life and face greater risks of economic peril (APA, 1997). All of these fears generally lead to feelings of anxiety.

The anxiety which women experience usually begins in the early stages of menopausal change. This anxiety seems to be largely due to fear of the unknown about coming changes in their bodies and psychosocial lives. Women consistently seek more knowledge about this life stage. Access to information successfully reduces the fear that accompanies the changes. The amount of anxiety is frequently relative to the degree to which a woman's identity and/or career is based on her appearance and physical abilities. The more value a woman has placed on her slim, youthful appearance, the more difficulty she is likely to experience in accepting this life stage (Jones, 1994; McQuaide, 1998). However, in time, these women are often able to refocus their life goals in new directions. Men, on the other hand, experience anxiety in the form of identity crisis where they have been socialized to believe that with age comes impotence and decreased power. The most threatening part of this stage of life for men is this depression. Men are often driven to thoughts of suicide over the impending decrease in sexual and success-centered abilities (Hyuck, 1996; Clarke, Shute, & Kelly, 2000). Men in mid life have high rates of success with their suicide attempts (two times that of women), which heightens the level of awareness for the practitioner (Maxmen & Ward, 1995).

Changes in life, such as children leaving home, becomes increasingly important due to hormonal fluctuations and life changes that naturally occur in mid life. In addition, there is an increase in health problems, loss of social group affiliation with retirement preparation, and a confrontation of one's mortality as parents age and friends and family members begin to pass on (Hyuck, 1996). If one's identity is surrounded by their original roles, these changes can spur depression. Creativity becomes a key factor when looking at dealing with anxiety and depression over role confusion or transition, and cited reasoning for exclusion of the middle aged in career aspects of the technology era (APA, 1997; Time, 2000). Midlife can highlight expertise, imaginative thinking skills, venturesome personality, and intrinsic motivation, and none of these factors are based on age. The bottom line is that Alzheimer's disease and severe cognitive dysfunction is very rare at this stage of life and memory difficulties are more likely related to depression, side effects of medication, and excess in alcohol use (Shute, 1997; Clark, Shute & Kelly, 2000). One researcher even reported that the heights of creative invention, and the ability to forge powerful intellectual syntheses, generally are not realized until mid-life (Brandes, 1992).

Forging synthesis of intelligence is discussed by Myers (1998) who reports that *crystallized intelligence*, the individual's accumulated knowledge, increases with age. *Fluid intelligence*, the individual's ability to reason abstractly, on the other hand, decreases with age. So, while the type of intelligence may change, the degree of intellectual ability does not. It is also noteworthy that there is an underlying constancy in most people's temperaments and personality traits, especially after age 30, and older ages do not signal a major change in personality (Myers, 1998; Shute, 1997).

PREPARATION: INTERVENTION SUGGESTIONS

This article has been clear to point out the philosophical thought as well as the many tasks of adjustment and development that will occur during this stage of the life cycle. Unfortunately, in terms of professional social work, this area is often neglected unless clients present with specific problems that need to be addressed. For all social workers, building individual client strengths and helping the client to achieve the steps required in this life transition phase remain important. Helping the client to accept these issues and to plan for them can only assist the client to adjust and accommodate as needed. With the noted increases to this age group's population size, this will only become more significant for the clinician. The baby boom generation is now in mid life and going strong. They have already collectively changed the rules with regards to family structure, retirement, and self-reinvention. There are several time-based factors to consider when working with this diverse group. First, take all the rules and theories based on the nuclear family of the '50s and '60s and throw them out the window. Secondly, understand that while the baby boomers strive to meet the expectations placed upon them by societal norms, they also yearn for more (Clark, Shute, & Kelly, 2000).

There are several basic rules for staying healthy in mid life such as get ample sleep, exercise body and mind, and take a healthy dose of realism (Clark, Shute, & Kelly, 2000). The APA recommends that talking to people you trust, avoid catastrophizing, make time for yourself, eat well, exercise, and seek psychological consultation if issues of depression, anxiety or identity become overwhelming. One potential tool for use in assisting persons in therapy for depression, anxiety and identity issues is the Myers Briggs Type Indicator due to its emphasis on "Who am I" questions (Myers, 1995).

Additionally, as we have noted midlife transition is clinically similar to that of an adjustment disorder, it is appropriate to utilize interventions shown effective in this condition. Although there is some debate on whether to treat these adjustment issues or to treat the clinical presentation of anxiety, depression, or identity, most therapists engage in a crisis intervention or brief time-limited cognitive approach (Maxmen & Ward, 1995; Tuner, 1996). This allows for a focus on the present maladaptive issues and a quick resolution to avoid unintended consequences of fostering dependence or over analysis. Regardless of the approach utilized areas that need to be discussed in the intervention process are: preparation for retirement, changing roles and relationships within families, careers, socialization with friends and family, and coping and problem solving skills related to potential health problems.

First, the social worker needs to help the client become aware of the need for planning early for a successful retirement life. This cannot only ensure financial security, it can also serve as a means of instilling positive thoughts about the later years in life. The concrete skills involved in financial planning are of obvious importance. A statement can be obtained from the Social Security Administration that provides the individual's projection of benefits. Tax-sheltered savings, individual retirement accounts (IRA), certificates of deposit are all-important considerations. This is the time to arrange for orderly transfer of accumulated resources and plan a will. It is important to recognize the need to plan for disposal of real estate, insurance benefits, and money upon one's death. This requires one to recognize the inevitable reality of one's mortality.

In addition, the importance of preparing for the adequacy of maintenance income and insurance coverage is critical. Generally, this is best accomplished by preparing for additional insurance needs in retirement years by investigating during the younger years. Unfortunately, with the fluctuating environment in terms of health care and finances this type of long-term preparation is not easily accomplished. To further complicate these attempts many people have been victimized by discrimination and oppression that has impaired their ability to prepare financially or ensure adequate insurance coverage for their retirement.

For those who are able, planning for appropriate living arrangements that will provide necessary services, social outlets, and other needs will make transition into retirement more successful. Planning for retirement cannot happen too early and all individuals need to be made aware of options that will be available to them in retirement, especially in regard to leisure activities.

Secondly, the social worker will assist the client in assessing their current relationships and roles in life. They will encourage creativity and development of alternative support networks to meet the change in life style of middle age. They will foster late bloomers through empowerment to reach for previously unattained goals. Social workers will work with couples and families to explore their interconnectedness and to strengthen potentially strained searches for identity. One cannot be too careful with this area in particular as study after study link decreased social inter-relatedness and familial discord to decrease in functioning and sense of well being.

Third, the social worker will examine health aspects and concerns from chronic or severe illnesses of the patient to care taking responsibilities as parents, grandparents, or children of elderly parents. Partializing, respite, and prioritizing are effective tools for handling these issues. For professionals, empathy is mandatory for true understanding of the client's needs in this area and when working with this age group the therapist needs to be educated as to the associated physiological and discrimination issues.

Lastly, it needs to be recognized that there can also be a sincere resistance to change. For individuals in mid-life the fear of change and avoidance for what they cannot predict can create a barrier to advance planning. At the current time they may have grown comfortable in their careers and achieved a sense of consistency with respect to job patterns. Gress (1994) suggests anticipating a change in relationships as clients lose contact with colleagues in the work place, and contact with friends and acquaintances is diminished due to geographic changes or deaths. It is suggested the client plan how to establish new relationships.

It is also projected that all individuals will someday be asking "Why am I here?" Continued formulation of a philosophy of life serves to offer a perspective on a direction of life for the later years. Finally, Gress (1994) emphasizes planning for good mental and physical health by anticipating the need for intellectual stimulation, social activity, proper nutrition, exercise, and medical care.

SUMMARY

The implications for social workers rest in understanding both the differences and similarities in this life stage for men and women. Social workers also need to be aware of the profound effects the biopsychosocial transition has on those who do not have access to proper care. The health effects are magnified by the physical changes in conjunction with the social and psychological needs associated with midlife evolution.

While there are similarities, there are also differences in biological changes between men and women; these changes can be substantial for both sexes and variance in

degree is expected (Henkel, 2000). These changes, though a somewhat greater threat to women physically, are effectively tolerable in both men and women who have access to proper physical and mental health care. The overall fears and anxieties are very similar for both sexes.

In the western culture the most difficult areas for both men and women are sexuality, economic security, and life direction and values. These areas have a direct impact on self-esteem, as it forces an evaluation of self-worth. The key to successful transition is in our attitudes toward aging, and in the values used when calculating one's worth as a person. The media continues to focus on youth to endorse products and demonstrate the positive aspects of life without consideration of the importance of wisdom and experience. Consequently, youth will continue to carry more power in the job markets. Research demonstrates that men and women make valuable contributions until a much later age. However, these contributions are often unrecognized in the nation's development and sustenance.

Western cultures seem to equate skill, talent, and intellectual ability with the competition and aggressiveness of youth. This is typical of Jung's description of the first half of life. The task now becomes making individuals aware of the value of the second half of life. By 2030, one in five people in North America will be over 65 years of age, and can expect to live until age 83 or beyond. The increased number of individuals at this age can provide encouragement for research, which compares intellectual productivity at the reproductive ages, and at the later mid-life years to support the presence or absence of correlation. Jung believed that all that is really needed to prosper is guidance into the transition stage of mid-life. Proper, holistic preparation for the later years will foster pleasant anticipation, and help to dispel the anxiety, fear and depression typical of the mid-life crisis.

REFERENCES

American Bible Society (1976). *Good News Bible*. New York: American Bible Society. Old Testament, 724–733.

Alexander, I. (2000). Check midlife women for vascular disease. *Contraceptive Technology Update, 21* (10), 125

APA (1996). How to achieve good mental health. *Psychology in daily life Fact Sheet* [Online] Available *http://www.apa.org/daily/index.html*

APA (1997). *Preparing for retirement means more than money in the bank.* [Online] Available *http://www.apa.org/daily/index.html*

Berkun, C. (1986). In behalf of women over 40: Understanding the importance of the menopause. *Social Work.* September–October. 378–384.

Brandes, S. (1986). *Forty: The age and the symbol.* Knoxville: The University of Tennessee Press. ix–126.

Branswell, B. (1998). The HRT conundrum. *Macleans, 111* (2), 54–55.

Clark, K., Shute, N., & Kelly, K. (2000, March). The new midlife. *US News and World Reports, 128* (100), 70–82.

Cutler, B. (1993). Marketing to menopausal men. *American Demographics.* 15:3. 49.

Cutler, W. & Garcia, C. (1992). *A guide for women and the men who love them.* New York: Norton & Company. 122–130.

Dziegielewski, S. F. & Leon, A. M. (2001). *Psychopharmacology and social work practice.* New York: Springer.

Economist (2000). When cultures collide. *The Economist, 8.*

Elman, C. & O'Rand, A. M. (1998, July). Midlife work pathways and educational reentry. *Research on Aging, 20* (4), 475–506.

Fine, J. et al. (1999). A prospective study of weight change and health-related quality of life in women. *JAMA, 282* (22), 2136.

Fortune (1999, February) Finished at forty. *Fortune, 139* (2), 50.

Gress, L. (1993). Make it happen! *Gerontological Nursing.* Editorial. September 3.

Gunby, P. (1992). "Climacteric gynecology" fellowships begin. *JAMA.* 268: 18. 2486.

Henkel, J. (2000). Keeping fit in those middle years. *FDA Consumer, 34* (6), 36.

Hoffman, D., & Tarzian, A. (2001). The girl who cried pain: A bias against women in the treatment of pain. *Journal of Law and Medicine & Ethics, 29,* 13–27.

Hyuck, M. (1993). Middle age. *Academic American Encyclopedia, 13,* 390–391.

Hyuck, C. (1996). The dynamic relationship between social support and health in older adults: Assessment implications. *Journal of Gerontological Social Work, 27* (1–2), 149–166.

Jones, J. (1994). Embodied meaning: Menopause and the change of life. *Women's health and social work: Feminist Perspectives.* 19:3/4. 43–65.

Koeneman, K. S., Mulhall, J. P., & Goldstein, I. (1997). Sexual health for the man at midlife: In-office workup. *Geriatrics, 52* (9), 76–82.

Kruger, A. (1994). The mid-life transition: Crisis or Chimers? *Psychological reports, 75,* 1299–1305.

McQuaide, S. (1998). Discontent at midlife: Issues and considerations in working toward women's well being. *Families in Society: The Journal of Contemporary Human Services, 79* (5), 532–543.

McQuaide, S. (1998). Women at Midlife. *Social Work, 43* (1), 21–32.

Messina, M. & Messina, V. (2000). Soyfoods, soybean isoflavones, and bone health: A brief overview. *Journal of Renal Nutrition, 10* (2), 63–68.

Myers, D. (1998). *Psychology, fifth edition. New York: Worth,* 107–121, 196–197.

Myers, S. (1995). Mid-life crisis. Psychiatry On-Line [Online] Available *http://www.pol-it.org/mbti2.htm*

Perry, P. J., Lund, B. C., Arndt, S., Holman, T., Bever-Stille, K. A., Paulsen, J., & Demers, L. M. (2001). Bioavailable testosterone as a correlate of cognition, psychological status, quality of life, and sexual function in aging males: Implications for testosterone replacement therapy. *Annals of Clinical Psychi-atry: Official Journal of the American Academy of Clinical Psychiatrists, 13* (2), 75–80.

Pillari, V. (1998). *Human behavior in the social environment* (second edition). Pacific Grove, CA: Brooks Cole.

Prevention (1999, Nov.) Sexuality during mid-life: A roundtable discussion. *Prevention, 51* (11), 1S1.

Robinson, K. M. (1997). Family caregiving: Who provides the care, and at what cost? *Nursing Economics, 15* (5), 243–248.

Rubin, R. (2001, October 9). Women react to pain differently than men. *USA Today,* 10D.

Sheehy, G. (1993). *Menopause: The silent passage.* New York: G. Merritt Corp. 57–81.

Shek, D. T. (1996). Mid-life crisis in Chinese men and women. *Journal of Psychology, 130,* 109–119.

Shute, N. (1997). A study for the ages: Generations of volunteers are helping scientists to comprehend time's toll. *US News & World Reports, 122* (22), 66–75.

Skolnick. A. (1992). Is "male menopause" real or just an excuse? *JAMA.* 268: 18. 2486.

Spitze, G. et al. (1994). Middle generation roles and the well being of men and women. *Journal of Gerontology.* 49:3. S107.

Stains, L. R. (1997). Escape middle-aged prostate woes. *Prevention, 49* (2), 96–104.

Swartz, D. (1992). *Hormone Replacement Therapy.* Baltimore: Williams & Wilkins. xiii–233.

Tan, R. S. (2001). Memory loss as a reported symptom of andropause. *Archives of Andrology, 47* (3), 185–189.

Vincent, A. & Fitzpatrick, L. A. (2000). Subspecialty clinics: Endocrinology, metabolism, and nutrition. Soy isoflavones: Are they useful in menopause?. *Mayo Clinic Proceedings, 75* (11), 1174–84.

Walsh, C. (1997). Many boomers rejoice in the freedom to form unconventional families. *America, 177* (11), 10.

Wannamathee, S. G., Shaper, G. A., Walker, M., & Ebrahim, S. (1998). Lifestyle and 15 year survival free of heart attack, stroke, and diabetes in middle aged British men. *Archives of Internal Medicine, 158* (22), 2433–2442.

Wu, Z. & Penning, M. J. (1997, Sept). Marital instability after midlife. *Journal of Family Issues, 18* (5), 459–479.

Sophia F. Dziegielewski, PhD, LCSW, is Professor, School of Social Work, University of Central Florida, Orlando, Florida.

Carolyn Heymann is Social Worker, Seattle, Washington.

Cheryl Green, PhD, is Assistant Professor, School of Social Work, University of Central Florida, Orlando, Florida.

Jannie E. Gichia, PhD, CNM, is Assistant Professor, School of Nursing, University of Central Florida.

Address correspondence to: Dr. Sophia F. Dziegielewski, School of Social Work, University of Central Florida, P.O. Box 163358, Orlando, FL, 32816-3358 (E-mail: sdziegie@mail.ucf.edu).

From *Journal of Human Behavior in the Social Environment,* Vol. 6, No. 4, pp. 65-86. Reprinted with permission of The Haworth Press, Inc.

Start the Conversation

The MODERN MATURITY guide to end-of-life care

The Body Speaks

Physically, dying means that "the body's various physiological systems, such as the circulatory, respiratory, and digestive systems, are no longer able to support the demands required to stay alive," says Barney Spivack, M.D., director of Geriatric Medicine for the Stamford (Connecticut) Health System. "When there is no meaningful chance for recovery, the physician should discuss realistic goals of care with the patient and family, which may include letting nature take its course. Lacking that direction," he says, "physicians differ in their perception of when enough is enough. We use our best judgment, taking into account the situation, the information available at the time, consultation with another doctor, or guidance from an ethics committee."

Without instructions from the patient or family, a doctor's obligation to a terminally ill person is to provide life-sustaining treatment. When a decision to "let nature take its course" has been made, the doctor will remove the treatment, based on the patient's needs. Early on, the patient or surrogate may choose to stop interventions such as antibiotics, dialysis, resuscitation, and defibrillation. Caregivers may want to offer food and fluids, but those can cause choking and the pooling of dangerous fluids in the lungs. A dying patient does not desire or need nourishment; without it he or she goes into a deep sleep and dies in days to weeks. A breathing machine would be the last support: It is uncomfortable for the patient, and may be disconnected when the patient or family finds that it is merely prolonging the dying process.

The Best Defense Against Pain

Pain-management activists are fervently trying to reeducate physicians about the importance and safety of making patients comfortable. "In medical school 30 years ago, we worried a lot about creating addicts," says Philadelphia internist Nicholas Scharff. "Now we know that addiction is not a problem: People who are in pain take pain medication as long as they need it, and then they stop." Spivack says, "We have new formulations and delivery systems, so a dying patient should never have unmet pain needs."

In Search of a Good Death

If we think about death at all, we say that we want to go quickly, in our sleep, or, perhaps, while fly-fishing. But in fact only 10 percent of us die suddenly. The more common process is a slow decline with episodes of organ or system failure. Most of us want to die at home; most of us won't. All of us hope to die without pain; many of us will be kept alive, in pain, beyond a time when we would choose to call a halt. Yet very few of us take steps ahead of time to spell out what kind of physical and emotional care we will want at the end.

The new movement to improve the end of life is pioneering ways to make available to each of us a good death—as we each define it. One goal of the movement is to bring death through the cultural process that childbirth has achieved; from an unconscious, solitary act in a cold hospital room to a situation in which one is buffered by pillows, pictures, music, loved ones, and the solaces of home. But as in the childbirth movement, the real goal is choice—here, to have the death you want. Much of death's sting can be averted by planning in advance, knowing the facts, and knowing what options we all have. Here, we have gathered new and relevant information to help us all make a difference for the people we are taking care of, and ultimately, for ourselves.

In 1999, the Joint Commission on Accreditation of Healthcare Organizations issued stern new guidelines about easing pain in both terminal and nonterminal patients. The movement intends to take pain seriously:

131

to measure and treat it as the fifth vital sign in hospitals, along with blood pressure, pulse, temperature, and respiration.

The best defense against pain, says Spivack, is a combination of education and assertiveness. "Don't be afraid to speak up," he says. "If your doctor isn't listening, talk to the nurses. They see more and usually have a good sense of what's happening." Hospice workers, too, are experts on physical comfort, and a good doctor will respond to a hospice worker's recommendations. "The best situation for pain management," says Scharff, "is at home with a family caregiver being guided by a hospice program."

The downsides to pain medication are, first, that narcotics given to a fragile body may have a double effect: The drug may ease the pain, but it may cause respiratory depression and possibly death. Second, pain medication may induce grogginess or unconsciousness when a patient wants to be alert. "Most people seem to be much more willing to tolerate pain than mental confusion," says senior research scientist M. Powell Lawton, Ph.D., of the Philadelphia Geriatric Center. Dying patients may choose to be alert one day for visitors, and asleep the next to cope with pain. Studies show that when patients control their own pain medication, they use less.

Final Symptoms

Depression This condition is not an inevitable part of dying but can and should be treated. In fact, untreated depression can prevent pain medications from working effectively, and antidepressant medication can help relieve pain. A dying patient should be kept in the best possible emotional state for the final stage of life. A combination of medications and psychotherapy works best to treat depression.

Anorexia In the last few days of life, anorexia—an unwillingness or inability to eat—often sets in. "It has a protective effect, releasing endorphins in the system and contributing to a greater feeling of well-being," says Spivack. "Force-feeding a dying patient could make him uncomfortable and cause choking."

Dehydration Most people want to drink little or nothing in their last days. Again, this is a protective mechanism, triggering a release of helpful endorphins.

Drowsiness and Unarousable Sleep In spite of a coma-like state, says Spivack, "presume that the patient hears everything that is being said in the room."

Agitation and Restlessness, Moaning and Groaning The features of "terminal delirium" occur when the patient's level of consciousness is markedly decreased; there is no significant likelihood that any pain sensation can reach consciousness. Family members and other caregivers may interpret what they see as "the patient is in pain" but as these signs arise at a point very close to death, terminal delirium should be suspected.

Hospice: The Comfort Team

Hospice is really a bundle of services. It organizes a team of people to help patients and their families, most often in the patient's home but also in hospice residences, nursing homes, and hospitals:

- Registered nurses who check medication and the patient's condition, communicate with the patient's doctor, and educate caregivers.
- Medical services by the patient's physician and a hospice's medical director, limited to pain medication and other comfort care.
- Medical supplies and equipment.
- Drugs for pain relief and symptom control.
- Home-care aides for personal care, homemakers for light housekeeping.
- Continuous care in the home as needed on a short-term basis.
- Trained volunteers for support services.
- Physical, occupational, and speech therapists to help patients adapt to new disabilities.
- Temporary hospitalization during a crisis.
- Counselors and social workers who provide emotional and spiritual support to the patient and family.
- Respite care—brief noncrisis hospitalization to provide relief for family caregivers for up to five days.
- Bereavement support for the family, including counseling, referral to support groups, and periodic check-ins during the first year after the death.

Hospice Residences Still rare, but a growing phenomenon. They provide all these services on-site. They're for patients without family caregivers; with frail, elderly spouses; and for families who cannot provide at-home care because of other commitments. At the moment, Medicare covers only hospice services; the patient must pay for room and board. In many states Medicaid also covers hospice services (see How Much Will It Cost?). Keep in mind that not all residences are certified, bonded, or licensed; and not all are covered by Medicare.

Getting In A physician can recommend hospice for a patient who is terminally ill and probably has less than six months to live. The aim of hospice is to help people cope with an illness, not to cure it. All patients entering hospice waive their rights to curative treatments, though only for conditions relating to their terminal illness. "If you break a leg, of course you'll be treated for that," says Karen Woods, executive director of the Hospice Association of America. No one is forced to accept a hospice referral, and patients may leave and opt for curative care at any time. Hospice programs are listed in the Yellow Pages. For more information, see Resources.

The Ultimate Emotional Challenge

Adying person is grieving the loss of control over life, of body image, of normal physical functions, mobility and strength, freedom and independence, security, and the illusion of immortality. He is also grieving the loss of an earthly future, and reorienting himself to an unknowable destiny.

At the same time, an emotionally healthy dying person will be trying to satisfy his survival drive by adapting to this new phase, making the most of life at the moment, calling in loved ones, examining and appreciating his own joys and accomplishments. Not all dying people are depressed; many embrace death easily.

Facing the Fact

Doctors are usually the ones to inform a patient that he or she is dying, and the end-of-life movement is training physicians to bring empathy to that conversation in place of medspeak and time estimates. The more sensitive doctor will first ask how the patient feels things are going. "The patient may say, 'Well, I don't think I'm getting better,' and I would say, 'I think you're right,' " says internist Nicholas Scharff.

At this point, a doctor might ask if the patient wants to hear more now or later, in broad strokes or in detail. Some people will need to first process the emotional blow with tears and anger before learning about the course of their disease in the future.

"Accept and understand whatever reaction the patient has," says Roni Lang, director of the Geriatric Assessment Program for the Stamford (Connecticut) Health System, and a social worker who is a longtime veteran of such conversations. "Don't be too quick with the tissue. That sends a message that it's not okay to be upset. It's okay for the patient to be however she is."

Getting to Acceptance

Some patients keep hoping that they will get better. Denial is one of the mind's miracles, a way to ward off painful realities until consciousness can deal with them. Denial may not be a problem for the dying person, but it can create difficulties for the family. The dying person could be leaving a lot of tough decisions, stress, and confusion behind. The classic stages of grief outlined by Elisabeth Kübler-Ross—denial, anger, bargaining, depression, and acceptance—are often used to describe post-death grieving, but were in fact delineated for the process of accepting impending loss. We now know that these states may not progress in order. "Most people oscillate between anger and sadness, embracing the prospect of death and unrealistic episodes of optimism," says Lang. Still, she says, "don't place demands on them

Survival Kit for Caregivers

A study published in the March 21, 2000, issue of **Annals of Internal Medicine** shows that caregivers of the dying are twice as likely to have depressive symptoms as the dying themselves.

No wonder. Caring for a dying parent, says social worker Roni Lang, "brings a fierce tangle of emotions. That part of us that is a child must grow up." Parallel struggles occur when caring for a spouse, a child, another relative, or a friend. Caregivers may also experience sibling rivalry, income loss, isolation, fatigue, burnout, and resentment.

To deal with these difficult stresses, Lang suggests that caregivers:

• Set limits in advance. How far am I willing to go? What level of care is needed? Who can I get to help? Resist the temptation to let the illness always take center stage, or to be drawn into guilt-inducing conversations with people who think you should be doing more.

• Join a caregiver support group, either disease-related like the Alzheimer's Association or Gilda's Club, or a more general support group like The Well Spouse Foundation. Ask the social services department at your hospital for advice. Telephone support and online chat rooms also exist (see Resources).

• Acknowledge anger and express it constructively by keeping a journal or talking to an understanding friend or family member. Anger is a normal reaction to powerlessness.

• When people offer to help, give them a specific assignment. And then, take time to do what energizes you and make a point of rewarding yourself.

• Remember that people who are critically ill are self-absorbed. If your empathy fails you and you lose patience, make amends and forgive yourself.

to accept their death. This is not a time to proselytize." It is enough for the family to accept the coming loss, and if necessary, introduce the idea of an advance directive and health-care proxy, approaching it as a "just in case" idea. When one member of the family cannot accept death, and insists that doctors do more, says Lang, "that's the worst nightmare. I would call a meeting, hear all views without interrupting, and get the conversation around to what the patient would want. You may need another person to come in, perhaps the doctor, to help 'hear' the voice of the patient."

What Are You Afraid Of?

The most important question for doctors and caregivers to ask a dying person is, What are you afraid of? "Fear aggravates pain," says Lang, "and pain aggravates fear." Fear of pain, says Spivack, is one of the most common problems, and can be dealt with rationally. Many people do not know, for example, that pain in dying is not inevitable. Other typical fears are of being separated from loved ones, from home, from work; fear of being a burden, losing control, being dependent, and leaving things undone. Voicing fear helps lessen it, and pinpointing fear helps a caregiver know how to respond.

How to Be With a Dying Person

Our usual instinct is to avoid everything about death, including the people moving most rapidly toward it. But, Spivack says, "In all my years of working with dying people, I've never heard one say 'I want to die alone.' " Dying people are greatly comforted by company; the benefit far outweighs the awkwardness of the visit. Lang offers these suggestions for visitors:

• Be close. Sit at eye level, and don't be afraid to touch. Let the dying person set the pace for the conversation. Allow for silence. Your presence alone is valuable.

• Don't contradict a patient who says he's going to die. Acceptance is okay. Allow for anger, guilt, and fear, without trying to "fix" it. Just listen and empathize.

• Give the patient as much decision-making power as possible, as long as possible. Allow for talk about unfinished business. Ask: "Who can I contact for you?"

• Encourage happy reminiscences. It's okay to laugh.

• Never pass up the chance to express love or say goodbye. But if you don't get the chance, remember that not everything is worked through. Do the best you can.

Taking Control Now

Sixty years ago, before the invention of dialysis, defibrillators, and ventilators, the failure of vital organs automatically meant death. There were few choices to be made to end suffering, and when there were—the fatal dose of morphine, for example—these decisions were made privately by family and doctors who knew each other well. Since the 1950s, medical technology has been capable of extending lives, but also of prolonging dying. In 1967, an organization called Choice in Dying (now the Partnership for Caring: America's Voices for the Dying; see Resources) designed the first advance directive—a document that allows you to designate under what conditions you would want life-sustaining treatment to be continued or terminated. But the idea did not gain popular understanding until 1976, when the parents of Karen Ann Quinlan won a long legal battle to disconnect her from respiratory support as she lay for months in a vegetative state. Some 75 percent of Americans are in favor of advance directives, although only 30–35 percent actually write them.

Designing the Care You Want

There are two kinds of advance directives, and you may use one or both. A Living Will details what kind of life-sustaining treatment you want or don't want, in the event of an illness when death is imminent. A durable power of attorney for health care appoints someone to be your decision-maker if you can't speak for yourself. This person is also called a surrogate, attorney-in-fact, or health-care proxy. An advance directive such as Five Wishes covers both.

Most experts agree that a Living Will alone is not sufficient. "You don't need to write specific instructions about different kinds of life support, as you don't yet know any of the facts of your situation, and they may change," says Charles Sabatino, assistant director of the American Bar Association's Commission on Legal Problems of the Elderly.

The proxy, Sabatino says, is far more important. "It means someone you trust will find out all the options and make a decision consistent with what you would want." In most states, you may write your own advance directive, though some states require a specific form, available at hospital admitting offices or at the state department of health.

When Should You Draw Up a Directive?

Without an advance directive, a hospital staff is legally bound to do everything to keep you alive as long as possible, until you or a family member decides otherwise. So advance directives are best written before emergency status or a terminal diagnosis. Some people write them at the same time they make a will. The process begins with discussions between you and your family and doctor. If anybody is reluctant to discuss the subject, Sabatino suggests starting the conversation with a story. "Remember what happened to Bob Jones and what his family went through? I want us to be different…." You can use existing tools—a booklet or questionnaire (see Resources)—to keep the conversation moving. Get your doctor's commitment to support your wishes. "If you're asking for something that is against your doctor's conscience" (such as prescribing a lethal dose of pain medication or removing life support at a time he considers premature), Sabatino says, "he may have an obligation to transfer you to another doctor." And make sure the person you name as surrogate agrees to act for you and understands your wishes.

Filing, Storing, Safekeeping…

An estimated 35 percent of advance directives cannot be found when needed.

• Give a copy to your surrogate, your doctor, your hospital, and other family members. Tell them where to find the original in the house—not in a safe deposit box where it might not be found until after death.

Five Wishes

Five Wishes is a questionnaire that guides people in making essential decisions about the care they want at the end of their life. About a million people have filled out the eight-page form in the past two years. This advance directive is legally valid in 34 states and the District of Columbia. (The other 16 require a specific state-mandated form.)

The document was designed by lawyer Jim Towey, founder of Aging With Dignity, a nonprofit organization that advocates for the needs of elders and their caregivers. Towey, who was legal counsel to Mother Teresa, visited her Home for the Dying in Calcutta in the 1980s. He was struck that in that haven in the Third World, "the dying people's hands were held, their pain was managed, and they weren't alone. In the First World, you see a lot of medical technology, but people die in pain, and alone." Towey talked to MODERN MATURITY about his directive and what it means.

What are the five wishes? Who do I want to make care decisions for me when I can't? What kind of medical treatment do I want toward the end? What would help me feel comfortable while I am dying? How do I want people to treat me? What do I want my loved ones to know about me and my feelings after I'm gone?

Why is it so vital to make advance decisions now? Medical technology has extended longevity, which is good, but it can prolong the dying process in ways that are almost cruel. Medical schools are still concentrating on curing, not caring for the dying. We can have a dignified season in our life, or die alone in pain with futile interventions. Most people only discover they have options when checking into the hospital, and often they no longer have the capacity to choose. This leaves the family members with a guessing game and, frequently, guilt.

What's the ideal way to use this document? First you do a little soul searching about what you want. Then discuss it with people you trust, in the livingroom instead of the waiting room—before a crisis. Just say, "I want a choice about how I spend my last days," talk about your choices, and pick someone to be your health-care surrogate.

What makes the Five Wishes directive unique? It's easy to use and understand, not written in the language of doctors or lawyers. It also allows people to discuss comfort dignity, and forgiveness, not just medical concerns. When my father filled it out, he said he wanted his favorite afghan blanket in his bed. It made a huge difference to me that, as he was dying, he had his wishes fulfilled.

For a copy of Five Wishes in English or Spanish, send a $5 check or money order to Aging With Dignity, PO Box 1661, Tallahassee, FL 32302. For more information, visit www.agingwithdignity.org.

• Some people carry a copy in their wallet or glove compartment of their car.

• Be aware that if you have more than one home and you split your time in several regions of the country, you should be registering your wishes with a hospital in each region, and consider naming more than one proxy.

• You may register your Living Will and health-care proxy online at uslivingwillregistry.com (or call 800-548-9455). The free, privately funded confidential service will instantly fax a copy to a hospital when the hospital requests one. It will also remind you to update it: You may want to choose a new surrogate, accommodate medical advances, or change your idea of when "enough is enough." M. Powell Lawton, who is doing a study on how people anticipate the terminal life stages, has discovered that "people adapt relatively well to states of poor health. The idea that life is still worth living continues to readjust itself."

Assisted Suicide: The Reality

While advance directives allow for the termination of life-sustaining treatment, assisted suicide means supplying the patient with a prescription for life-ending medication. A doctor writes the prescription for the medication; the patient takes the fatal dose him- or herself. Physician-assisted suicide is legal only in Oregon (and under consideration in Maine) but only with rigorous preconditions. Of the approximately 30,000 people who died in Oregon in 1999, only 33 received permission to have a lethal dose of medication and only 26 of those actually died of the medication. Surrogates may request an end to life support, but to assist in a suicide puts one at risk for charges of homicide.

Good Care: Can You Afford It?

The ordinary person is only one serious illness away from poverty," says Joanne Lynn, M.D., director of the Arlington, Virginia, Center to Improve Care of the Dying. An ethicist, hospice physician, and health-services researcher, she is one of the founding members of the end-of-life-care movement. "On the whole, hospitalization and the cost of suppressing symptoms is very easy to afford," says Lynn. Medicare and Medicaid will help cover that kind of acute medical care. But what is harder to afford is at-home medication, monitoring, daily help with eating and walking, and all the care that will go on for the rest of the patient's life.

"When people are dying," Lynn says, "an increasing proportion of their overall care does not need to be done by doctors. But when policymakers say the care is nonmedical, then it's second class, it's not important, and nobody will pay for it."

Bottom line, Medicare pays for about 57 percent of the cost of medical care for Medicare beneficiaries.

Another 11 percent is paid by Medicaid, 20 percent by the patient, 10 percent from private insurance, and the rest from other sources, such as charitable organizations.

Medi-what?

This public-plus-private network of funding sources for end-of-life care is complex, and who pays for how much of what is determined by diagnosis, age, site of care, and income. Besides the private health insurance that many of us have from our employers, other sources of funding may enter the picture when patients are terminally ill.

•**Medicare** A federal insurance program that covers health-care services for people 65 and over, some disabled people, and those with end-stage kidney disease. Medicare Part A covers inpatient care in hospitals, nursing homes, hospice, and some home health care. For most people, the Part A premium is free. Part B covers doctor fees, tests, and other outpatient medical services. Although Part B is optional, most people choose to enroll through their local Social Security office and pay the monthly premium ($45.50). Medicare beneficiaries share in the cost of care through deductibles and co-insurance. What Medicare does not cover at all is outpatient medication, long-term nonacute care, and support services.

•**Medicaid** A state and federally funded program that covers health-care services for people with income or assets below certain levels, which vary from state to state.

•**Medigap** Private insurance policies covering the gaps in Medicare, such as deductibles and co-payments, and in some cases additional health-care services, medical supplies, and outpatient prescription drugs.

Many of the services not paid for by Medicare can be covered by private long-term-care insurance. About 50 percent of us over the age of 65 will need long-term care at home or in a nursing home, and this insurance is an extra bit of protection for people with major assets to protect. It pays for skilled nursing care as well as non-health services, such as help with dressing, eating, and bathing. You select a dollar amount of coverage per day (for example, $100 in a nursing home, or $50 for at-home care), and a coverage period (for example, three years—the average nursing-home stay is 2.7 years). Depending on your age and the benefits you choose, the insurance can cost anywhere from around $500 to more than $8,000 a year. People with pre-existing conditions such as Alzheimer's or MS are usually not eligible.

How Much Will It Cost?

Where you get end-of-life care will affect the cost and who pays for it.

•**Hospital** Dying in a hospital costs about $1,000 a day. After a $766 deductible (per benefit period), Medicare reimburses the hospital a fixed rate per day, which varies by region and diagnosis. After the first 60 days in a hospital, a patient will pay a daily deductible ($194) that goes up (to $388) after 90 days. The patient is responsible

for all costs for each day beyond 150 days. Medicaid and some private insurance, either through an employer or a Medigap plan, often help cover these costs.

•**Nursing home** About $1,000 a week. Medicare covers up to 100 days of skilled nursing care after a three-day hospitalization, and most medication costs during that time. For days 21–100, your daily co-insurance of $97 is usually covered by private insurance—if you have it. For nursing-home care not covered by Medicare, you must use your private assets, or Medicaid if your assets run out, which happens to approximately one-third of nursing-home residents. Long-term-care insurance may also cover some of the costs.

•**Hospice care** About $100 a day for in-home care. Medicare covers hospice care to patients who have a life expectancy of less than six months. (See Hospice: The Comfort Team.) Such care may be provided at home, in a hospice facility, a hospital, or a nursing-home. Patients may be asked to pay up to $5 for each prescription and a 5 percent co-pay for in-patient respite care, which is a short hospital stay to relieve caregivers. Medicaid covers hospice care in all but six states, even for those without Medicare.

About 60 percent of full-time employees of medium and large firms also have coverage for hospice services, but the benefits vary widely.

•**Home care without hospice services** Medicare Part A pays the full cost of medical home health care for up to 100 visits following a hospital stay of at least three days. Medicare Part B covers home health-care visits beyond those 100 visits or without a hospital stay. To qualify, the patient must be homebound, require skilled nursing care or physical or speech therapy, be under a physician's care, and use services from a Medicare-participating home-health agency. Note that this coverage is for medical care only; hired help for personal nonmedical services, such as that often required by Alzheimer's patients, is not covered by Medicare. It is covered by Medicaid in some states.

A major financial disadvantage of dying at home without hospice is that Medicare does not cover out-patient prescription drugs, even those for pain. Medicaid does cover these drugs, but often with restrictions on their price and quantity. Private insurance can fill the gap to some extent. Long-term-care insurance may cover payments to family caregivers who have to stop work to care for a dying patient, but this type of coverage is very rare.

Resources

MEDICAL CARE

For information about pain relief and symptom management:
Supportive Care of the Dying (503-215-5053; careofdying.org).

For a comprehensive guide to living with the medical, emotional, and spiritual aspects of dying:
Handbook for Mortals by Joanne Lynn and Joan Harrold, Oxford University Press.

For a 24-hour hotline offering counseling, pain management, downloadable advance directives, and more:
The Partnership for Caring (800-989-9455; www.partnershipforcaring.org).

EMOTIONAL CARE

To find mental-health counselors with an emphasis on lifespan human development and spiritual discussion:
American Counseling Association (800-347-6647; counseling.org).

For disease-related support groups and general resources for caregivers:
Caregiver Survival Resources (caregiver911.com).

For AARP's online caregiver support chatroom, access **America Online** every Wednesday night, 8:30–9:30 EST (keyword: AARP).

Education and advocacy for family caregivers:
National Family Caregivers Association (800-896-3650; nfcacares.org).

For the booklet,
Understanding the Grief Process (D16832, EEO143C), e-mail order with title and numbers to member@aarp.org or send postcard to AARP Fulfillment, 601 E St NW, Washington DC 20049. Please allow two to four weeks for delivery.

To find a volunteer to help with supportive services to the frail and their caregivers:
National Federation of Interfaith Volunteer Caregivers (816-931-5442; nfivc.org).

For information on support to partners of the chronically ill and/or the disabled:
The Well Spouse Foundation (800-838-0879; www.wellspouse.org).

LEGAL HELP

AARP members are entitled to a free half-hour of legal advice with a lawyer from **AARP's Legal Services Network**. (800-424-3410; www.aarp.org/lsn).

For **Planning for Incapacity,** *a guide to advance directives in your state,* send $5 to Legal Counsel for the Elderly, Inc., PO Box 96474, Washington DC 20090-6474. Make out check to LCE Inc.

For a **Caring Conversations** *booklet on advance-directive discussion:*

Midwest Bioethics Center (816-221-1100; midbio.org).

For information on care at the end of life, online discussion groups, conferences:
Last Acts Campaign (800-844-7616; lastacts.org).

HOSPICE

To learn about end-of-life care options and grief issues through videotapes, books, newsletters, and brochures:
Hospice Foundation of America (800-854-3402; hospice-foundation.org).

For information on hospice programs, FAQs, and general facts about hospice:
National Hospice and Palliative Care Organization (800-658-8898; nhpco.org).

For **All About Hospice: A Consumer's Guide** (202-546-4759; www.hospice-america.org).

FINANCIAL HELP

For **Organizing Your Future,** *a simple guide to end-of-life financial decisions,* send $5 to Legal Counsel for the Elderly, Inc., PO Box 96474, Washington DC 20090-6474. Make out check to LCE Inc.

For **Medicare and You 2000** *and a* **2000 Guide to Health Insurance for People With Medicare** (800-MEDICARE [633-4227]; medicare.gov).

To find your State Agency on Aging: **Administration on Aging, U.S. Department of Health and Human Services** (800-677-1116; aoa.dhhs.gov).

GENERAL

For information on end-of-life planning and bereavement: (www.aarp.org/endoflife/).

For health professionals and others who want to start conversations on end-of-life issues in their community:

Discussion Guide: On Our Own Terms: Moyers on Dying, based on the PBS series, airing September 10–13. The guide provides essays, instructions, and contacts. From PBS, www.pbs.org/onourownterms Or send a postcard request to On Our Own Terms Discussion Guide, Thirteen/WNET New York, PO Box 245, Little Falls, NJ 07424-9766.

Funded with a grant from The Robert Wood Johnson Foundation, Princeton, N.J. *Editor* Amy Gross; *Writer* Louise Lague; *Designer* David Herbick

UNIT 8
Personality Processes

Unit Selections

29. **Psychoanalyst: Sigmund Freud**, Peter Gay
30. **Psychology Discovers Happiness. I'm OK, You're OK**, Gregg Easterbrook
31. **The Verdict on Media Violence: It's Ugly...and Getting Uglier**, Daphne Lavers

Key Points to Consider

- What is the study of personality; what is the definition of personality? What are some of the major tenets of personality theories? Do you know any personality theories? Can you differentiate one theory from another?

- Which do you think contributes most to our unique personalities, biology or environment? If you answered biology, what does this imply about the possibility of personality change? If you answered environment, do you think that biology plays any role in personality? Is personality stable or ever-changing across a lifetime? What are the advantages of a stable personality? What would be the advantages of an ever-changing personality?

- In a nutshell, what is Freud's theory of personality? What are some of the criticisms of his theory? Do you think his theory is sound? Based on logical thought? Based on science? What contributions did Freud make to psychology? What did Freud contribute to the average person?

- What is positive psychology? What is optimism? Why is it important to the human condition? What other aspects of personality play a role in the theories and research endeavors of positive psychologists? How does the notion of positive psychology compare to psychoanalysis? Where should psychology head in the future according to positive psychologists?

- What are learning theories of personality? What can be learned that shapes who we are? What role does the media play in influencing us in terms of our attitudes and behaviors? Why is media violence problematic? What would you recommend to reduce media violence?

- Out of all the personality theories that you studied, which do you think is best and why? Was your answer based on science, on anecdote, or something else?

 **Links: www.dushkin.com/online/**
These sites are annotated in the World Wide Web pages.

The Personality Project
http://personality-project.org/personality.html

Sabrina and Sadie are identical twins. When the girls were young children, their parents tried very hard to treat them equally. Whenever Sabrina received a present, Sadie received one. Both girls attended dance school and completed early classes in ballet and tap dance. In elementary school, the twins were both placed in the same class with the same teacher. The teacher also tried to treat them the same.

In junior high school, Sadie became a tomboy. She loved to play rough and tumble sports with the neighborhood boys. On the other hand, Sabrina remained indoors and practiced the piano. Sabrina was keenly interested in the domestic arts such as sewing, needlepoint, and crochet. Sadie was more interested in reading novels, especially science fiction, and in watching adventure programs on television.

As the twins matured, they decided it would be best to attend different colleges. Sabrina went to a small, quiet college in a rural setting, and Sadie matriculated at a large public university. Sabrina majored in English, with a specialty in poetry; Sadie switched majors several times and finally decided on a communications major.

Why, when these twins were exposed to the same early childhood environment, did their interests and paths diverge later? What makes people, even identical twins at times, so unique, so different from one another?

The study of individual differences is the domain of personality. The psychological study of personality has included two major thrusts. The first has focused on the search for the commonalties of human life and development. Its major question is: How are humans, especially their personalities, affected by specific events or activities? Personality theories are based on the assumption that a given event, if it is important, will affect almost all people in a similar way, or that the personality processes that affect people are common across events and people. Most psychological research into personality variables has made this assumption. Failures to replicate a research project are often the first clues that differences in individual responses require further investigation.

While some psychologists have focused on personality-related effects that are presumed to be universal among humans, others have devoted their efforts to discovering the bases on which individuals differ in their responses to environmental events. In the beginning, this specialty was called genetic psychology, because most people assumed that individual differences resulted from differences in genetic inheritance. By the 1950s the term genetic psychology had given way to the more current term: the psychology of individual differences.

Does this mean that genetic variables are no longer the key to understanding individual differences? Not at all. For a time, psychologists took up the philosophical debate over whether genetic or environmental factors were more important in determining behaviors. Even today, behavior geneticists compute the heritability coefficients for a number of personality and behavior traits, including intelligence. This is an expression of the degree

to which differences in a given trait can be attributed to differences in inherited capacity or ability. Most psychologists, however, accept the principle that both genetic and environmental determinants are important in any area of behavior. These researchers devote more of their efforts to discovering how the two sources of influence interact to produce the unique individual. Given the above, the focus of this unit is on personality characteristics and the differences and similarities among individuals.

What is personality? Most researchers in the area define personality as patterns of thoughts, feelings, and behaviors that persist over time and over situations, are characteristic or typical of the individual, and usually distinguish one person from another.

We will examine several different theories of personality in this unit. Sigmund Freud developed one of the first personality theories—psychoanalysis. In "Psychoanalyst: Sigmund Freud," Peter Gay reviews Freud's theory and his contributions to psychology. Gay further reminds us of the way Freud contributed to our vocabularies and how he influenced other psychologists.

We next look at a second idea or theme in personality: positive psychology. While Freud often focused on the negative aspects of human nature, the humanists focus on the positive aspects of humanity. Psychologists are becoming more and more interested in positive psychology that examines human contentment, optimism, and well-being.

The final selection in this unit pertains to learning theories. Social learning theory suggests that we learn by observation. Thus, watching television teaches us many new behaviors and attitudes. Some researchers loudly proclaim, therefore, that media violence teaches violent behavior to Americans. The final article critiques this notion with an eye to research on media violence.

PSYCHOANALYST
SIGMUND FREUD

He opened a window on the unconscious—where, he said, lust, rage and repression battle for supremacy—and changed the way we view ourselves

By PETER GAY

There are no neutrals in the Freud wars. Admiration, even downright adulation, on one side; skepticism, even downright disdain, on the other. This is not hyperbole. A psychoanalyst who is currently trying to enshrine Freud in the pantheon of cultural heroes must contend with a relentless critic who devotes his days to exposing Freud as a charlatan. But on one thing the contending parties agree: for good or ill, Sigmund Freud, more than any other explorer of the psyche, has shaped the mind of the 20th century. The very fierceness and persistence of his detractors are a wry tribute to the staying power of Freud's ideas.

BORN May 6, 1856, Freiberg, Moravia

1881 Earns medical degree

1885 Receives appointment as lecturer in neuropathology, University of Vienna

1886 Begins private neurology practice in Vienna; marries Martha Bernays

1900 Publishes *The Interpretation of Dreams*

1910 Establishes International Psychoanalytic Association

1938 Emigrates from Vienna to London

1939 Dies Sept. 23 in London

There is nothing new about such embittered confrontations; they have dogged Freud's footsteps since he developed the cluster of theories he would give the name of psychoanalysis. His fundamental idea—that all humans are endowed with an unconscious in which potent sexual and aggressive drives, and defenses against them, struggle for supremacy, as it were, behind a person's back—has struck many as a romantic, scientifically unprovable notion. His contention that the catalog of neurotic ailments to which humans are susceptible is nearly always the work of sexual maladjustments, and that erotic desire starts not in puberty but in infancy, seemed to the respectable nothing less than obscene. His dramatic evocation of a universal Oedipus complex, in which (to put a complicated issue too simply) the little boy loves his mother and hates his father, seems more like a literary conceit than a thesis worthy of a scientifically minded psychologist.

Freud first used the term psychoanalysis in 1896, when he was already 40. He had been driven by ambition from his earliest days and encouraged by his doting parents to think highly of himself. Born in 1856 to an impecunious Jewish family in the Moravian hamlet of Freiberg (now Pribor in the Czech Republic), he moved with the rest of a rapidly increasing brood to Vienna. He was his mother's firstborn, her "golden Siggie." In recognition of his brilliance, his parents privileged him over his siblings by giving him a room to himself, to study in peace. He did not disappoint them. After an impressive career in school, he matriculated in 1873 in the University of Vienna and drifted from one philosophical subject to another until he hit on medicine. His choice was less that of a dedicated healer than of an inquisitive explorer determined to solve some of nature's riddles.

As he pursued his medical researches, he came to the conclusion that the most intriguing mysteries lay concealed in the complex operations of the mind. By the early 1890s, he was specializing in "neurasthenics" (mainly severe hysterics); they taught him much, including the art of patient listening. At the same time he was beginning to write down his dreams, increasingly convinced that they might offer clues to the workings of the unconscious, a notion he borrowed from the Romantics. He saw himself as a scientist taking material both from his patients and from himself, through introspection. By the mid-1890s, he was launched on a full-blown self-analysis, an enterprise for which he had no guidelines and no predecessors.

TODAY WE ALL SPEAK FREUD

*His ideas—or ideas that can be traced, sometimes circuitously,
back to him—have permeated the language*

PENIS ENVY Freud's famous theory—not favored by feminists—that women wish they had what men are born with

FREUDIAN SLIP A seemingly meaningless slip of the tongue that is really e-mail direct from the unconscious

UNCONSCIOUS Repressed feelings, desires, ideas and memories that are hidden from the conscious mind

REPRESSION Involuntary blocking of an unsettling feeling or memory from conscious thought

OEDIPUS COMPLEX In classic Freudian theory, children in their phallic phase (ages three to six) form an erotic attachment to the parent of the opposite sex, and a concomitant hatred (occasionally murderous) of the parent of the same sex

CASTRATION ANXIETY A boy's unconscious fear of losing his penis, and his fantasy that girls have already lost theirs

SUBLIMATION Unconscious shifting of an unacceptable drive (lust for your sister, say) into culturally acceptable behavior (lust for your friend's sister)

TRANSFERENCE Unconscious shifting of feelings about one person (e.g., a parent) to another (e.g., your analyst)

ID The part of the mind from which primal needs and drives (e.g., lust, rage) emerge

SUPEREGO The part of the mind where your parents' and society's rules reside; the original guilt trip

EGO The mind's mechanism for keeping in touch with reality, it referees the wrestling match between id and superego

PHALLIC SYMBOLS Almost anything can look like a penis, but sometimes, as Freud is supposed to have remarked, "a cigar is just a cigar"

The book that made his reputation in the profession—although it sold poorly—was *The Interpretation of Dreams* (1900), an indefinable masterpiece—part dream analysis, part autobiography, part theory of the mind, part history of contemporary Vienna. The principle that underlay this work was that mental experiences and entities, like physical ones, are part of nature. This meant that Freud could admit no mere accidents in mental procedures. The most nonsensical notion, the most casual slip of the tongue, the most fantastic dream, must have a meaning and can be used to unriddle the often incomprehensible maneuvers we call thinking.

Although the second pillar of Freud's psychoanalytic structure, *Three Essays on the Theory of Sexuality* (1905), further alienated him from the mainstream of contemporary psychiatry, he soon found loyal recruits. They met weekly to hash out interesting case histories, converting themselves into the Vienna Psychoanalytic Society in 1908. Working on the frontiers of mental science, these often eccentric pioneers had their quarrels. The two best known "defectors" were Alfred Adler and Carl Jung. Adler, a Viennese physician and socialist, developed his own psychology, which stressed the aggression with which those people lacking in some quality they desire—say manliness—express their discontent by acting out. "Inferiority com-

plex," a much abused term, is Adlerian. Freud did not regret losing Adler, but Jung was something else. Freud was aware that most of his acolytes were Jews, and he did not want to turn psycho-analysis into a "Jewish science." Jung, a Swiss from a pious Protestant background, struck Freud as his logical successor, his "crown prince." The two men were close for several years, but Jung's ambition, and his growing commitment to religion and mysticism—most unwelcome to Freud, an aggressive atheist—finally drove them apart.

Freud was intent not merely on originating a sweeping theory of mental functioning and malfunctioning. He also wanted to develop the rules of psychoanalytic therapy and expand his picture of human nature to encompass not just the couch but the whole culture. As to the first, he created the largely silent listener who encourages the analysand to say whatever comes to mind, no matter how foolish, repetitive or outrageous, and who intervenes occasionally to interpret what the patient on the couch is struggling to say. While some adventurous early psychoanalysts thought they could quantify just what proportion of their analysands went away cured, improved or untouched by analytic therapy, such confident enumerations have more recently shown themselves untenable. The efficacy of analysis remains a matter of controversy, though the possibil-

ity of mixing psychoanalysis and drug therapy is gaining support.

"If often he was wrong and, at times, absurd, to us he is no more a person now but a whole climate of opinion."

W. H. AUDEN,
after Freud's death
in 1939

Freud's ventures into culture—history, anthropology, literature, art, sociology, the study of religion—have proved little less controversial, though they retain their fascination and plausibility and continue to enjoy a widespread reputation. As a loyal follower of 19th century positivists, Freud drew a sharp distinction between religious

POST-FREUDIAN ANALYSIS

Other psychologists continued the work that Freud began, though not always in ways that he would have approved

CARL JUNG A former disciple of Freud's, Jung shared his mentor's enthusiasm for dreams but not his obsession with the sex drive. Jung said humans are endowed with a "collective unconscious" from which myths, fairy tales and other archetypes spring.

ALFRED KINSEY A biologist who knew little about sex and less about statistics, Kinsey nonetheless led the first large-scale empirical study of sexual behavior. The Kinsey reports shocked readers by documenting high rates of masturbation and extramarital and homosexual sex.

BENJAMIN SPOCK One of the first pediatricians to get psychoanalytic training, Dr. Spock formed commonsense principles of child rearing that helped shape the baby-boom generation. Since 1946 his book on baby care has sold 50 million copies.

B. F. SKINNER A strict behaviorist who avoided all reference to internal mental states, Skinner believed that behavior can best be shaped through positive reinforcement. Contrary to popular misconception, he did not raise his daughter in the "Skinner box" used to train pigeons.

faith (which is not checkable or correctable) and scientific inquiry (which is both). For himself, this meant the denial of truth-value to any religion whatever, including Judaism. As for politics, he left little doubt and said so plainly in his late—and still best known—essay, *Civilization and Its Discontents* (1930), noting that the human animal, with its insatiable needs, must always remain an enemy to organized society, which exists largely to tamp down sexual and aggressive desires. At best, civilized living is a compromise between wishes and repression—not a comfortable doctrine. It ensures that Freud, taken straight, will never become truly popular, even if today we all speak Freud.

In mid-March 1938, when Freud was 81, the Nazis took over Austria, and after some reluctance, he immigrated to England with his wife and his favorite daughter and colleague Anna "to die in freedom." He got his wish, dying not long after the Nazis unleashed World War II by invading Poland. Listening to an idealistic broadcaster proclaiming this to be the last war, Freud, his stoical humor intact, commented wryly, "*My* last war."

Yale historian Peter Gay's 22 books include Freud: A Life for Our Times

Psychology discovers happiness.
I'm OK, You're OK

By Gregg Easterbrook

"Life is divided up into the horrible and the miserable," Woody Allen tells Diane Keaton in *Annie Hall*. "The horrible would be like terminal cases, blind people, cripples—I don't know how they get through life. It's amazing to me. And the miserable is everyone else. So, when you go through life, you should be thankful that you're miserable."

That's a fairly apt summary of the last century's consensus regarding the psyche. Psychiatry now recognizes some 14 "major" mental disorders, in addition to countless lesser maladies. Unipolar depression—unremitting blue feelings—has risen tenfold since World War II and now afflicts an estimated 18 million Americans. Increasingly, even children are prescribed psychotropic drugs, while frustrated drivers are described as not merely discourteous but enraged. In the past 100 years, academic journals have published 8,166 articles on "anger," compared with 416 on "forgiveness"; in its latest edition, the presumably encyclopedic *Encyclopedia of Human Emotions*, a reference for clinicians, lists page after page of detrimental mental states but has no entry for "gratitude." Sigmund Freud declared mental torment the normal human condition and suggested that most people's best possible outcome would be to rise from neurosis into "ordinary unhappiness." It's a wonder we don't all lose our minds.

And yet, somehow, most people turn out OK. Only a tiny fraction of the populace commit antisocial acts or lose their ability to function in society. Roughly 80 percent of Americans describe themselves as basically satisfied with their lives. Not only have we not all lost our minds, but, considering modern stress, most of our minds seem in surprisingly good condition.

This observation is leading to a revolutionary development in the theory of the psyche—positive psychology, which seeks to change the focus of inquiry from what causes psychosis to what causes sanity. Researchers "tend to study the things that can go wrong in people's minds but not the things that can go right," says Robert Emmons, a psychologist at the University of California at Davis. Yet what can go right is at least as important, not

just for individuals but for society. And, in contrast to much modern scholarship, positive psychology may produce knowledge that actually improves lives and makes the world a better place.

The initial ideas of positive psychology came to Martin Seligman 35 years ago when he and a colleague were giving electric shocks to dogs. Seligman, who has since become a professor of psychology at the University of Pennsylvania and is a past president of the American Psychological Association, found that by zapping dogs unless they jumped a barrier, he could reduce the animals to a state of cowering helplessness in which they would not attempt any other tasks. It may seem obvious that creatures exposed to regular pain would enter a state of wretchedness, but the psychology establishment of the time, dominated by behaviorists, rejected Seligman's result. Behaviorism claimed that dogs (or people) do that for which they are rewarded and avoid that for which they are punished: A dog shocked when performing one task should just move on to another. But the subjects of Seligman's experiment simply sat down and whimpered pitifully. Seligman took this as evidence that psychological states are in some sense *learned*, not merely involuntary reflexes to stimuli. And if negative mental states can be learned, he eventually realized, why not altruism or equanimity?

When Seligman proposed such rethinking to some older professors, it made them furious. After all, a fundamentally positive approach to psychology conflicted with the profession's modern history. Roughly since the Enlightenment, study of the mind had been flavored by the Cartesian notion that abstract thought is the brain's calling, while emotional states are handicaps. That view was briefly challenged by Charles Darwin, who, after publishing *The Origin of Species*, hypothesized that if physical traits had evolved, mental states must have, too. Darwin's final work, *The Expression of the Emotions in Man and Animals*, published in 1872, speculated that psychological qualities must be mainly beneficial or evolution would not have preserved them—loyalty, for instance, could have enhanced early humans' survival by causing them to care for one another.

But while Darwin's views on biology spread throughout the intellectual world, his views on the mind were quietly dismissed. Freud's much more negative interpretation—that the consciousness is steeped in self-delusion and emotions are repellent by-products of infantile sexual compulsions—fit the new century's zeitgeist of existential despair. When evidence for Freud's claims eventually turned out to be shaky, the equally uninviting model of behaviorism arose. Behaviorism held that we're all lab rats in a meaningless maze, and it viewed human feeling with open contempt. The dogma's low point came when the behaviorist guru John Watson pronounced that parents should "never hug and kiss" children, because this would only condition them to want affection.

At about the time behaviorism was reaching its zenith, the U.S. government established the National Institute of Mental Health and greatly expanded the Veterans Administration. The NIMH gave grants almost exclusively to researchers studying mental illness, while the VA (now the Department of Veterans Affairs) paid to train a generation of clinicians to treat World War II combat trauma. Between Freudianism, behaviorism, and a government that funded the study and treatment of the negative, psychology in the early postwar era became a truly dismal science.

Of course, this view had opponents. Humanistic psychology, founded by Abraham Maslow in the 1950s, argued both that life was well worth living and that people could find fulfillment by understanding that human needs come in a sequence, from physical to spiritual. (Seligman has been accused of borrowing ideas from humanistic psychology.) Around the same time, physicians accidentally discovered that some new tuberculosis drugs palliated depression. The discovery proved a hammer blow against Freudianism. As psychologists Fari Amini, Richard Lannon, and Thomas Lewis note in their book, *A General Theory of Love*, if a few molecules can alleviate psychological pain, "[h]ow does one square *that* with the supposed preeminence of repressed sexual urges as the cause of all matters emotional?"

The discovery that emotions have a biological component provided an opening for new views of the psyche. It meant mental states were not childhood curses (Freud) or involuntary twitches (behaviorism) but an integral element of the living world, evolving with life just as Darwin had guessed. Barbara Frederickson, a positive psychologist at the University of Michigan, has since expanded on Darwin's view, noting that while some negative emotions confer obvious survival advantages—fear causes you to run—natural selection may favor positive emotions in more subtle ways. A person who is joyful or outgoing, Frederickson supposes, is more likely to make friends; the friends would then come to the person's aid in times of crisis, increasing the odds that friendliness would be passed to offspring. Further, as Amini, Lannon, and Lewis put it, if emotional states have a biological basis, they must be "part of the physical universe" and therefore "lawful," subject to understanding.

By the early '90s, researchers had fashioned this cluster of insights into a new movement Seligman originally called "good life" studies—the effort to determine what psychological forces caused people such as Eleanor Roosevelt (one of his heroes) to live life admirably. But because "good life" can connote champagne and dancing girls, in the late '90s advocates renamed the framework "positive psychology." Since then, the concept has gained ground with researchers.

Positive psychology's first empirical focus was figuring out who exactly is happy. Edward Diener, a psychologist at the University of Illinois, has come to the following conclusions. First, poverty cáuses unhappiness but wealth does not cause happiness. Second, the old as a group have more "life satisfaction" than the young. (Diener notes, "The minds of the young are full of the things they want to achieve and have not, whereas most of the elderly have either achieved what they wanted or made their peace with the fact that they never will.") And, third, according to a well-being test designed by Diener, the norm is positive; most Americans' scores on his test indicate they are "slightly satisfied" with life.

Diener's discovery that the impoverished are unhappy is hardly surprising: In a classic confirm-the-obvious exercise, he went to Calcutta and produced irrefutable data that the poor there experience "a very low level of life satisfaction." Studies by Diener and others show that as a person's income rises toward the middle-class level, his or her sense of well-being rises as well. But once basic material needs are met, income decouples from happiness. Since the 1957 publication of John Kenneth Galbraith's *The Affluent Society*, real income for the average American has trebled. But during that same period the fraction of Americans who describe themselves as "very happy" in the University of Chicago's long-running National Opinion Research Center polls has not budged: It was one-third in 1957, and it is one-third today.

Researchers surmise that once people become middle-class, additional income ceases to correlate with happiness because people begin to perceive money primarily in relation to those around them. Most do not think, *Does my house meet my needs?* but rather, *How nice is my house compared with the neighbors'?* Upon reaching upper income brackets, people may grow obsessed with what they still don't have, activating some kind of "nature's revenge" law that denies extra contentment to the wealthy. When Diener gave his tests to a group of multimillionaires from the *Forbes 400*, he found that, on average, they were only a tiny bit happier than the typical suburbanite.

Through its studies of the relationship between income and happiness, positive psychology supports the philosophical-theological conclusion that longing for material things ultimately harms the person doing the longing. Materialism also causes people to spend rather than save, which embeds anxiety in daily life—a point championed by Harvard University economist Juliet Schor. Cross-cultural studies of happiness buttress these findings. Sociologist Ronald Inglehart has found that life satisfaction is highest in the Scandinavian countries (where income is fairly evenly distributed, mitigating neighbors'-house angst) and lowest in poor nations. Life satisfaction is also unusually high in Ireland, which boasts a "count your blessings" culture. Life satisfaction is distressingly low in affluent Japan—much lower than in Argentina or Hungary—perhaps because Japanese culture emphasizes money even more relentlessly than American culture.

Exactly how "happy" a person might be is ephemeral, of course. Psychologist Daniel Kahneman of Princeton University has been attempting for years to create a wholly objective measure of well-being, without much success. Kahneman found, for instance, that if he asked college students whether they were happy, most said yes. But if he first asked how many dates they had had in the last month and then asked if they were happy, most said no. Kahneman says he stopped asking subjects if they considered themselves unhappy because the question caused some to burst into tears.

Positive psychology further finds that happiness is hard. Laura King of Southern Methodist University, writing in the current issue of the *Journal of Humanistic Psychology*, shows that a positive attitude toward life requires considerable effort; people may slip into melancholy simply because it's the path of least resistance. Freud anticipated this when he noted that "unhappiness is much less difficult to experience" than elevated feelings. As a result, positive psychologists tend to view happiness as a condition that must be actively sought. Kahneman marvels at one study that found that quadriplegics have high emotional satisfaction relative to lottery winners. The lottery winners, we can guess, got swept up in and betrayed by materialism, while the quadriplegics worked hard to adjust to their condition and in so doing learned how to appreciate life better.

Finally, positive psychology suggests individual happiness is not self-indulgent but in the interest of society, since studies show happy people are more likely to do volunteer work, give to charity, and contribute to their communities in other ways. Robert Browning wrote, "[M]ake us happy and you make us good." A wonderful, quirky 1998 book by Dennis Prager, *Happiness Is a Serious Problem*, proposes that people actually have a civic duty to become happy because this will make them altruistic.

This isn't to say that positive psychology advocates an unrealistically rosy view of life. Psychologist Lisa Aspinwall of the University of Utah has found that one reason optimists generally have better "life outcomes" than pessimists is they pay more attention to safety and health warnings: Being optimistic doesn't make them blind to threats but rather makes them want to be around for the long haul.

Reversing the logic of dogs shocked into helplessness, Seligman advocates "learned optimism"—the idea that, by learning to expect tribulations and occasional unhappiness, people can avoid pessimism. Seligman thinks primary schools should teach children to expect difficulties, so that when problems start, as inevitably they will, children will not be traumatized but will view occasional setbacks as part of the natural course of events. An idealized anticipation of life, Seligman says, only creates disillusionment, whereas expecting to have some really bad days fosters a sustainable positive outlook. Managing one's expectations in this way, of course, requires self-control. And in fact Roy Baumeister, a researcher at Case Western Reserve University, has found that self-control is a better predictor of "life outcomes"—career and marriage success, overall happiness—than IQ.

Gratitude and forgiveness also turn out to promote happiness. Recent studies have shown that people who describe themselves as grateful—to others and to God or nature for the gift of life—tend to enjoy better health, more successful careers, and less depression than the population as a whole. These results hold even when researchers factor out age and income, equalizing for the fact that the affluent or good-looking might have more to be grateful for. And just as positive psychology doesn't recommend Pollyannaish optimism, it doesn't call for Panglossian gratitude. "To say we feel grateful is not to say that everything in our lives is necessarily great," says Emmons, the University of California psychologist. "It just means… if you only think about your disappointments and unsatisfied wants, you may be prone to unhappiness. If you're fully aware of your disappointments but at the same time thankful for the good that has happened and for your chance to live, you may show higher indices of well-being."

In this regard, the power of self-suggestion is considerable: Studies show that those who dwell on negative experiences become negative, while those who keep "gratitude journals," in which they write down what they're thankful for, experience improved well-being. Counting your blessings may sound corny, but if it helps you do better in life or simply have a good day, it's perfectly rational. Adam Smith anticipated this in his 1759 *Theory of Moral Sentiments*, one premise of which is that people who do not feel grateful cheat themselves out of their experience of life. Lack of gratitude leads to bitterness, Smith wrote, and bitterness only harms the person who feels it.

Likewise, positive psychology advises forgiveness because it benefits the person who forgives. If you bear a grudge or want retribution, your own well-being declines. Even in cases when someone has done you a severe wrong, such as a crime, forgiving the person is in your self-interest, because it prevents your own life from being subsumed in bitterness.

Depression is the malady of greatest concern to positive psychology, and here the figures are haunting. Incidence of bipolar depression—exaggerated mood swings—has not changed during the postwar era; the disorder is now believed to be primarily biological and is treated with medication. But the tenfold postwar increase in incidence of unipolar depression appears to have no biological explanation, and the rate holds in all developed nations. Steadily rising Western standards of living have been accompanied by a huge upswing in the percentage of the population that constantly feels bad. What's going on?

Seligman thinks most unipolar depression is a learned condition, and he offers four causes. First, too much individualism: "Unipolar depression is a disorder of the thwarting of the I, and we are increasingly taught to view all through the I." Past emphases on patriotism, family, and faith may sometimes have been suffocating but also let individuals view their private disappointments as minor within the larger context. Today, Seligman supposes, "rampant individualism causes us to think that our setbacks are of vast importance, and thus something to become depressed about."

Next, Seligman blames the self-esteem trend. "Self-esteem emphasis has made everybody think there's something fundamentally *wrong* if you don't feel good, as opposed to 'We just don't feel good right now but will later,'" he says. If something is fundamentally wrong with your life, that's pretty depressing. Self-esteem types maintain that people should feel good about themselves all the time, an idea positive psychology proponents deem totally unrealistic. The preaching of self-esteem in schools, Seligman thinks, has backfired by increasing melancholy.

Third, Seligman thinks depression is rising because of "the promiscuity of postwar teaching of victimology and helplessness." Intellectuals and the media have spent the last couple of decades discovering victims; surveys find that ever-higher percentages of incoming college freshmen describe themselves as having been victimized or possessing little control over their fates—though, objectively, personal freedom has never been higher. The "We're all victims" view discourages people from asserting control over their psyches.

Seligman finds particularly counterproductive the fad of adults claiming they were victimized by their parents. Only in extreme cases—such as sexual abuse—is there a clear link between parenting and adult personality: "You are entitled to blame your parents for the genes they gave you, but you are not entitled, by any research I know of, to blame them for the way they treated you," Seligman says. Depressed patients often attribute their condition to their parents, but once recovered they rarely say their parents were to blame for their disorder.

Fourth on Seligman's list of depression's causes is runaway consumerism. "Shopping, sports cars, expensive chocolates—these things are shortcuts to well-being," he says. While overall happiness has not increased as national income has trebled in the postwar period, surveys show that what Americans expect materially has grown in lockstep with the earnings curve. Like a street drug, materialism requires more and more to produce the same brief high. As David Myers, a social scientist at Hope College in Holland, Michigan, has noted of this predicament, "[T]he victor belongs to the spoils."

Whatever the causes of unipolar depression, there are two main treatments. One is Prozac and an expanding variety of related medications. The other is cognitive therapy, a psychological approach based on the premise that your mind can fix its own problems. Both pharmacology and cognitive therapy show similar effectiveness—about two-thirds of patients get better, and one-third do not respond. Proponents of positive psychology generally prefer the cognitive route.

The cognitive strategy against depression includes learning to recognize the "automatic" negative thoughts that flit through the mind as the blues are coming on and to counter such thoughts. To some extent this is simply common sense and echoes what is found in "power of positive thinking" books. But previous theories of the mind have distinctly lacked common sense and, therefore, have done little good. The University of Illinois's Diener says, "Freudian theory offered little of value to society, wanting to convince us we were all screwed up and there was nothing we could do beyond getting our misery under control. Positive psychology offers patients a realistic way to treat conditions and offers society as a whole a way to build virtues and human strengths."

Seligman is trying to convey this message on a broader scale with a pilot program in Philadelphia middle schools to teach students "learned optimism." Positive psychology is also integral to the "character education" movement blooming in schools and universities, which teaches both that virtue is a duty and that it improves individual lives. These efforts may soon gain a powerful new rationale, as growing research suggests that a positive psychological outlook not only improves "life outcomes" but enhances health directly. In her new book *The Balance Within*, Esther Sternberg, chief of neuroendocrine immunology and behavior at the National Institutes of Health, presents evidence that emotions play a role in regulating the immune system—the more positive your sense of well-being, the better your white blood cells function.

By focusing on improvement rather than dysfunction, the positive-psychology movement also hopes to destigmatize mental therapy. Today most insurers will not reimburse patients for therapy unless their diagnosis includes one of the standard codes for mental illness. The result is that many pay for treatment out of their own pockets to avoid having such an entry on medical records, while many others receive no care. Seligman and University of Michigan psychologist Christopher Peterson are trying to change this by working on a manual for classification of "the sanities," a handbook that would be the reverse of the *Diagnostic and Statistical Manual* that clinicians use to code mental illnesses. Such a volume, they believe, not only might solve the insurance records problem but could encourage the many who experience mild psychological pain to get help—just as physicians once thought patients should simply live with mild ailments, such as aching knees, but now believe people should seek every possible cure.

As positive psychology moves from the margins to the mainstream, millions may embrace the remarkable idea that it is not only in society's interest to be altruistic, optimistic, and forgiving but in your own. For roughly a century, academic theory has assumed that when people lose their minds, the awful truth about life is revealed. Now comes a theory that says the truth is revealed when people acquire happiness and virtue. Which model sounds better to you?

GREGG EASTERBROOK is a senior editor of TNR.

The Verdict On Media Violence: It's Ugly ... And Getting Uglier

Daphne Lavers

More than five decades after television's advent, its early promise "has been erased by the rapid degeneration of televised programming content," according to the Los Angeles-based Parents Television Council (PTC), which lobbies for more wholesome family TV fare.

The PTC recently quantified the general sense that television and film have increased the "raunch factor" in a study of the 2000-01 TV season titled The Sour Family Hour. The report showed "huge increases in coarse language," up 78 percent compared with the last study in 1998-99. (It equated coarse language with "verbal violence," seeing it as the starting point of the violence continuum.) TV violence was up a whopping 70 percent in the two years since the previous study. The sexual content fell into subcategories—including homosexuality, oral sex, pornography, masturbation and "kinky" practices such as phone sex, group sex and bondage—"covering topics which a generation ago would seldom have seen the light of day in 10 p.m. programming, let alone 8 p.m. fare."

Upset, the PTC wrote an open letter to the heads of the major TV networks asking for the reinstatement of the "family hour" between 8 p.m. and 9 p.m. The organization also launched a campaign to "publicly shame those advertisers who market and sponsor the violence, sexual raunch and vulgarity to our nation's children," says L. Brent Bozell, PTC president. "We will name names, and often. It saddens and frustrates me to no end that it has gotten to this point—publicly shaming adults for marketing trash to 10 million children every night."

But in many families, media have replaced teachers and parents as educators, role models and the primary sources of information about the world, according to the American Academy of Pediatrics (AAP). Children between 2 and 18 years of age spend six-and-a-half to eight hours a day with media, including television, videotapes, movies and video games—more time than on any other activity except sleeping, the AAP has found. By age 18, the average young person has seen 200,000 acts of violence on television alone.

The AAP also notes that, of 10,000 hours of broadcast programming reviewed by the National Television Violence Study, 61 percent portrayed interpersonal violence, much of it in an entertaining or glamorized manner. The highest proportion of violence was in children's programs: Of all animated films produced in the United States between 1937 and 1999, 100 percent portrayed violence.

Pushing such "trash" on children was the focus of a Federal Trade Commission (FTC) report in 2000 entitled Marketing Violent Entertainment to Children: A Review of Self-Regulation and Industry Practices in the Motion Picture, Music Recording and Electronic Game Industries. Prompted by the Columbine High School massacre, it found that the entertainment industries routinely and illegitimately target-marketed violent entertainment directly to adolescents and preadolescents and then denied doing so. In April 2001, the FTC reported some improvement in the movie and video-game industries, notably in limiting advertising to teens and in providing "rating information."

"Every year, the media use ever-greater quantities of violence to hook their audience," says Dave Grossman, a psychologist and media researcher. "Why did the alcohol and tobacco industries want so desperately to continue to sell their products to children? Because the addictive process is so much more powerful if they can start when they're children."

Grossman, a retired U.S. Army lieutenant colonel who studied and taught at West Point, researched how to overcome natural and instinctive barriers to killing, a task essential for the armed forces. He found that the psychological tools of repetition, desensitization and escalation, combined with the instinct for survival, all contribute to a soldier's—or a child's—capacity for violence.

Repetition is a psychological technique to reduce or eliminate phobias by increasing exposure, which increases tolerance levels—the same paradigm as addiction. The practice also is the foundation of the advertising industry: More "exposures" equal more familiarity and increased comfort levels. Repetition of violence does the same through the process of desensitization.

Over time, the phobic response against violence becomes less and less intense, according to Joanne Cantor, professor of communications at the University of Wisconsin. "Exposure to media violence, particularly that which entails bitter hostilities or the graphic display of injuries, initially induces an intense emotional reaction in viewers," Cantor told the American Psychological Association in an August 2000 speech. "Over time and with repeated exposure, however, many viewers exhibit decreasing emotional responses to the depiction of violence and injury."

That decreasing response necessitates an escalation of video violence—increasing the dose, as it were—to maintain a reaction. "People get jaded very quickly," says Neal Gabler, senior fellow at the Lear Center, a project of the University of

Southern California's Annenberg School of Communication. "I compare popular culture to a drug. In popular culture, there is always a ratcheting mechanism. Once you've had this experience, this sensation, you want more; once you've had that, you reach a plateau and you want more."

Once desensitization has begun, whether in viewers, addicts or soldiers, conditioning—both operant and classical—reinforces that learned behavior. "Operant conditioning teaches you to kill, but classical conditioning is a subtle but powerful mechanism that teaches you to like it," says Grossman.

Operant conditioning is the powerful, repetitive, stimulus-response training mechanism by which reactions are trained into automatic response, such as a police officer on a firing range or a pilot in a flight simulator. Video games, some based on movies and TV series, program exactly the same automatic, conditioned response and increasing skill level in children, often in marksmanship. In fact, law-enforcement agencies use the Firearms Training Simulator, more or less identical to the ultraviolent video game "Time Crisis", notes Toronto media activist Valerie Smith in her Media Violence 101 primer. The U.S. Army trains with the Multipurpose Arcade Combat Simulator, based on a modified Super Nintendo video game. Classical conditioning associates a stimulus with some pleasurable response, developed in the Pavlovian experiments with dogs in which food was associated with an audio cue. Television connects visual media-program content with advertising content.

"Our children watch vivid pictures of human suffering and death, and they learn to associate it with their favorite soft drink and candy bar or their girlfriend's perfume," says Grossman. "All the time in movie theaters when there is bloody violence, the young people laugh and cheer and keep right on eating popcorn and drinking soda. We have raised a generation of barbarians who have learned to associate violence with pleasure, like the Romans cheering and snacking as the Christians were slaughtered in the Coliseum."

The doubling of the murder rate following the introduction of television was discovered through an epidemiological study of murder by Brandon Centerwall, a professor of psychiatry and behavioral sciences at the University of Washington. "All Canadian and U.S. studies of the effect of prolonged childhood exposure to television (two years or more) demonstrate a positive relationship between earlier exposure and later physical aggressiveness," Centerwall wrote in the Journal of the American Medical Association. "The critical period of exposure to television is preadolescent childhood…. The aggression-enhancing effect of exposure to television is chronic, extending into later adolescence and adulthood."

The phenomenon of killers committing replica homicides learned through murderous teaching tools from movies and television has been linked to films such as Natural Born Killers, Reservoir Dogs, Child's Play 3 and The Basketball Diaries, as well as World Wrestling Federation TV broadcasts. The movie Scream, in which a slasher-murderer draped in black dons a mask inspired by Edvard Munch's painting The Scream continues to inspire replica murders both in North America and Europe. The same month that the AAP released its policy on media violence last year, a 24-year-old Belgian with no criminal record and no history of psychiatric problems dressed himself in-a long black tunic, donned a Scream mask and stabbed a 15-year-old schoolgirl 30 times. He told police the murder was premeditated and motivated by the Scream trilogy.

While most film and TV people deny any responsibility for the increase in crime and violence, one exception is veteran film director Robert Altman, who blamed Hollywood for recent terrorism attacks. Altman, director of M*A*S*H, told the BBC last October that violent action films with big explosions, usually targeted at young men, amount to training films. He observed that "nobody would have thought to commit an atrocity like that unless they'd seen it in a movie."

While young men are the target audience, young women are most often the victims, whether in TV series or serial-killer glorification movies. In her media-violence primer, activist Smith observed that "the most extreme form of film violence, the splatter or slasher genre, was launched in 1963." This form of entertainment features people, primarily teen-age girls and young women, being tortured, dismembered, disemboweled and beheaded with various construction tools: chain saws, tool guns, drills, jigsaws. The violence almost always takes place while the victims are naked or wearing skimpy lingerie.

Former FBI agent Robert Ressler and forensic psychiatrist Park Elliot Dietz, both experts on serial murder, believe these films have helped fuel the increase in serial killings because of the explicit linking of sex with torture and murder in films targeted at teen-age audiences. "If a mad scientist wanted to find a way to raise a generation of sexual sadists in America, he could hardly do better at our present state of knowledge than to try to expose a generation of teen-age boys to films showing women mutilated in the midst of a sexy scene," says Dietz.

Horror over television's content has prompted the creation of two technology fixes, the V-chip and CC+, both developed by Canadians for the North American market. The V-chip, widely available in new TV sets and some cable set-top boxes, combines hardware and software to block programming according to rating codes and content categories. Developed by Canadian engineering professor Tim Collings, the V-chip uses the controversial national ratings system for television and televised movie programs.

CC+ is a hardware and software technology that blocks swearwords. It was developed by Alberta forklift driver and mother of four Diane LaPierre, who was appalled when one of her sons began learning how to spell swearwords from the captions on PG-13 TV programs. CC+ works with the V-chip video technology, can be incorporated into new TV sets and also is available as a stand-alone black box.

Daphne Lavers is a Toronto-based free-lance journalist specializing in science, technology and broadcasting issues.

UNIT 9
Social Processes

Unit Selections

Key Points to Consider

- How do we perceive another person; that is, what processes do we depend on? When you assess another, how can you be sure that your judgment is accurate? What role does gaze play in our person perception? Why is it important to study eye gaze?

- What is friendship? Why are friends important? How do adulthood and childhood friendships differ? Why should adults salvage their friendships, especially today when life already seems so full?

- What types of events can be classified as terrorist attacks? How does terrorism affect the general population? How does it affect you? What can we do as a nation to better cope with terrorism? What can you do as an individual to better cope with terrorism? If the prospect of more terrorism causes the government to truncate certain individual rights, will you agree or disagree with the government? Why? Do you think it is fair to target "Arab looking" individuals as possible future terrorists?

- Why is human sexuality such a stigmatized topic? What are some of the social problems that relate to sexuality in America? How can we better address these types of problems?

 **Links: www.dushkin.com/online/**
These sites are annotated in the World Wide Web pages.

National Clearinghouse for Alcohol and Drug Information
http://www.health.org
Nonverbal Behavior and Nonverbal Communication
http://www3.usal.es/~nonverbal/

Everywhere we look there are groups of people. Your general psychology class is a group. It is what social psychologists would call a secondary group, a group that comes together for a particular, somewhat contractual reason and then disbands after its goals have been met. Other secondary groups include athletic teams, church associations, juries, committees, and so forth.

There are other types of groups, too. One other type is a primary group. A primary group has much face-to-face contact, and there is often a sense of "we-ness" in the group (cohesiveness as social psychologists would call it.) Examples of primary groups include families, suite mates, sororities, and teenage cliques.

Collectives or very large groups are loosely knit, massive groups of people. A bleacher full of football fans would be a collective. A long line of people waiting to get into a rock concert would also be a collective. A mob in a riot would be construed as a collective, too. As you might guess, collectives behave differently from primary and secondary groups.

Mainstream American society and any other large group that shares common rules and norms is also a group, albeit an extremely large group. While we might not always think about our society and how it shapes our behavior and our attitudes, society and culture nonetheless have a measureless influence on us. Psychologists, anthropologists, and sociologists alike are all interested in studying the effects of a culture on its members.

In this unit we will look at both positive and negative forms of social interaction. We will move from focused forms of social interaction to broader forms of social interaction. In other words, we will move from interpersonal to group to societal processes.

In the first few articles, we concentrate on interpersonal phenomena such as person perception and friendship. In the first essay about eye gaze, the authors explore the important role gaze plays in shaping interpersonal interactions and perceptions of others. Gazing at another person appears to do more than simply bring us visual information about another person.

Another important interpersonal issue is scrutinized in the next article. In "Got Time for Friends?" Andy Steiner considers why friendship remains so important to us. He asserts that friends are valuable for a number of psychological reasons. Steiner then concludes that adult friendships often fall by the wayside unlike childhood friendships. We need to renew adult friendships because they are just as valuable as our childhood ones.

Another timely social issue is terrorism and trauma or the fear of them. Erica Goode, writing for the *New York Times*, discusses recent terrorist events and how people usually respond to them in an irrational way. Events that are unfamiliar and threatening often produce terror.

One last issue of interest to society is human sexuality. The magazine *Psychology Today* takes a look at the topic of sex and why it is so discordant. Based on a report from David Satcher, former surgeon general, the article discusses what we need to do to overcome some of the social problems related to sexuality, for example, unwanted pregnancies and violent sexual encounters.

ARE YOU LOOKING AT ME?
Eye Gaze and Person Perception

Abstract—*Previous research has highlighted the pivotal role played by gaze detection and interpretation in the development of social cognition. Extending work of this kind, the present research investigated the effects of eye gaze on basic aspects of the person-perception process, namely, person construal and the extraction of category-related knowledge from semantic memory. It was anticipated that gaze direction would moderate the efficiency of the mental operations through which these social-cognitive products are generated. Specifically, eye gaze was expected to influence both the speed with which targets could be categorized as men and women and the rate at which associated stereotypic material could be accessed from semantic memory. The results of two experiments supported these predictions: Targets with nondeviated (i.e., direct) eye gaze elicited facilitated categorical responses. The implications of these findings for recent treatments of person perception are considered.*

C. Neil Macrae, Bruce M. Hood, Alan B. Milne, Angela C. Rowe, and Malia F. Mason

Humans and many other species tend to look at things in their environment that are of immediate interest to them. You might be the recipient of another's gaze, for instance, because you are a potential meal, a mate or simply because you are someone with whom they would like to interact. (Langton, Watt, & Bruce, 2000, pp. 51–52)

Direction of eye gaze is a crucial medium through which humans and other animals can transmit socially relevant information. In some contexts, the mere establishment of eye contact can be interpreted as a sign of hostility or anger (Argyle & Cook, 1976). Indeed, in many primate societies, staring is deemed to be an unambiguously threatening gesture (Hinde & Rowell, 1962). Yet mutual eye contact can also convey positive messages. For example, staring can be taken to be a sign of friendliness, romantic attraction, or general interest (Argyle & Cook, 1976; Kellerman, Lewis, & Laird, 1989; Kleinke, 1986). As von Grünau and Anston (1995) have noted, "whether maintained stare is a sign of dislike or like, it is certainly an indication for a potential social interaction" (p. 1297).

Given the acknowledged informational value of eye gaze, it makes sound evolutionary sense that people should be sensitized to eye gaze in others. As gaze direction signals the appearance and relative importance of objects in the environment (e.g., friends, predators, food), considerable adaptive advantages can be gained from an information processing system that is finely tuned to gaze detection and interpretation (see Baron-Cohen, 1994, 1995; Perrett & Emery, 1994). Luckily for the

smooth running of everyday life, the available evidence confirms that people are indeed highly sensitive to gaze direction, an ability that emerges in the very early stages of childhood. Young infants prefer to look at the eyes more than at other regions of the face (Morton & Johnson, 1991) and by the age of 4 months can discriminate staring from averted eyes (Vecera & Johnson, 1995). This fascination with gaze continues into adulthood, particularly with respect to mutual eye contact (Baron-Cohen, 1994, 1995). Although this sensitivity to eye gaze undoubtedly serves a variety of useful functions (e.g., reflexive visual orienting; see Driver et al., 1999; Friesen & Kingstone, 1998; Hood, Willen, & Driver, 1998), one function in particular is of considerable social importance. Understanding the nonverbal language of the eyes facilitates the development of social cognition, notably the cognitive and affective construal processes that guide people's daily interactions with others (see Baron-Cohen, 1994, 1995; Perrett & Emery, 1994).

EYE GAZE AND SOCIAL COGNITION

An intriguing account of the role that eye gaze may play in social cognition has been offered by Baron-Cohen (1995) in his writings on mind reading (i.e., theory of mind). According to Baron-Cohen (1994, 1995), the mind contains a series of specialized modules that have evolved to enable humans to attribute mental states to others (see also Brothers, 1990). One of these modules, the *eye-direction detector* (EDD), deals explicitly with gaze detection and interpretation and plays a critical role in the development of social cognition. In summary, the EDD has three basic functions: It (a) detects the presence of eyes or eyelike stimuli in the environment, (b) computes the direction of gaze (e.g., direct or averted), and (c) attributes the mental state of "seeing" to the gazer. As Baron-Cohen (1995) put it, the "EDD is a mindreading mechanism specific to the visual system; it computes whether there are eyes out there and, if so, whether those eyes are looking at me or looking at not-me" (p. 43). Such a system is believed to occupy a pivotal role in everyday social interaction. Indeed, without the ability to read the language of the eyes, perceivers would find it difficult to adopt the "intentional stance" (Dennett, 1987) when interpreting the actions of others (Baron-Cohen, 1994, 1995).

Whether or not one endorses the view that the mind contains an EDD or some functionally equivalent module (e.g., *direction of attention detector,* DAD; see Perrett & Emery, 1994), it is apparent that a specialized processing system deals with the problem of gaze detection and interpretation. Electrophysiological research has suggested that such a system may be localized in the superior temporal sulcus (STS; see Allison, Puce, & McCarthy, 2000; Haxby, Hoffman, & Gobbini, 2000; Hoffman & Haxby, 2000). A number of early studies identified cells in areas of temporal cortex that were highly receptive to facial stimuli (Bruce, Desimone, & Gross, 1981; Perrett, Rolls, & Cann, 1982). In subsequent research, Perrett and his colleagues located specific cells in the STS that responded selectively to the direction of gaze (Perrett et al., 1985). In particular, whereas some cells were tuned to eye contact, others were tuned to detect averted gaze. As it turns out, however, these cells appear to be only part of a broader system that is dedicated to the detection of social attention (Perrett & Emery, 1994). In recent research, individual cells in the STS region of the macaque brain have been shown to be responsive to particular conjunctions of eye, head, and body position (Perrett & Emery, 1994), suggesting that the direction of social attention can be signaled by a variety of stimulus cues.

Given, then, the fundamental role that gaze detection and interpretation plays in the development of social cognition (Baron-Cohen, 1994, 1995; Perrett & Emery, 1994), it is surprising that no empirical studies have yet investigated the effects of eye gaze on basic aspects of social-cognitive functioning, such as the pivotal process of person construal (i.e., person categorization). This oversight is puzzling as the categorical inferences that people draw about others are widely acknowledged to be the building blocks of social cognition (Allport, 1954; Brewer, 1988; Bodenhausen & Macrae, 1998; Fiske & Neuberg, 1990; Macrae & Bodenhausen, 2000). Rather than construing people in terms of their unique collections of attributes and proclivities, perceivers typically characterize them instead on the basis of the social groups to which they belong (Allport, 1954; Bargh, 1999). They do so for good reason, however. Not only does categorical thinking simplify the complexities of person perception, but also the products of this process shape the direction and nature of people's social interactions. Specifically, once targets have been categorized in a particular way, associated knowledge structures (e.g., stereotypes) guide people's impressions, evaluations, and recollections of others (Bodenhausen & Macrae, 1998; Brewer, 1988; Fiske & Neuberg, 1990; Macrae & Bodenhausen, 2000). Given this state of affairs, one might expect the efficiency of the person-construal process to be moderated by factors that have obvious biological significance to perceivers, such as the eye gaze of others (Baron-Cohen, 1994, 1995; Perrett & Emery, 1994). That is, in making sense of the persons who populate their social worlds, perceivers may use eye gaze as a cue for computing the relative importance or relevance of the individuals they encounter (e.g., looking at me vs. not looking at me). In turn, this cuing process may moderate the efficiency of the mental operations that furnish perceivers with category-related knowledge about others (Macrae & Bodenhausen, 2000).

EYE GAZE AND PERSON CONSTRUAL

There is good reason to suspect that the efficiency of the person-construal process may be influenced by a target's direction of gaze. Given that eye gaze can signal the potential intentions of friend and foe alike, it is useful to have an information processing system that can deal with this perceptual input in a rapid and effective manner (Baron-Cohen, 1994, 1995; Perrett & Emery, 1994). As Baron-Cohen (1995) has argued, "it makes...sense that we should be hypersensitive to when another organism is watching us, since this is about the best early warning system that another organism may be about to attack us, or may be interested in us for some other reason" (p. 98). Of course, in such a situation it is not simply enough to detect the presence of eyes or eyelike stimuli in the environment. To discern the potential intentions or motives of another organism (e.g., friend, enemy, predator, potential mate), it is also necessary to establish the identity of the organism in question and then to access any relevant information that may be stored in memory. After all, it is only after this knowledge has been accessed that appropriate action plans can be generated and implemented. For this reason, we suspect that the efficiency of the person-construal process may be moderated by the direction of eye gaze. As the most relevant stimulus targets are usually those with whom mutual eye contact has been established, we hypothesized that individuals would be categorized most rapidly when they display nondeviated (i.e., direct) eye gaze. Moreover, as a result of this categorization advantage, we expected that generic category-related knowledge (i.e., stereotypic information) would be highly accessible for these persons. We investigated these predictions in the following two experiments.

EXPERIMENT 1: EYE GAZE AND PERSON CATEGORIZATION

Method

Participants and design

Thirty-two undergraduates (14 men, 18 women) participated in the experiment for course credit. The experiment had a single-factor (eye gaze: full face, direct vs. 3/4 face, direct vs. averted vs. closed) repeated measures design.

Table 1. *Gender categorization times and knowledge accessibility as a function of eye gaze*

Measure	Eye Gaze			
	3/4 face, direct	Full face, direct	Laterally averted	Closed
Gender categorization (ms)	Experiment 1			
	534	525	630	611
Knowledge accessibility (ms)	Experiment 2			
Stereotypic items	—	587	626	621
Counterstereotypic items	—	647	645	650
Nonwords	—	692	690	684

Procedure and stimulus materials

Upon arrival in the laboratory, each participant was greeted by a female experimenter and seated facing the monitor of an Apple Macintosh iMac microcomputer. The experimenter explained that the study involved a classification task in which participants had to judge the gender of persons depicted in a series of photographs. Each photograph appeared in the center of the screen, and the participant responded by pressing, as quickly and accurately as possible, one of two appropriately labeled keys ("male" or "female"). Throughout the experiment, the participant was instructed to fixate on a small black cross that was located in the center of the screen. It was explained that the photographs would always be located on the fixation cross. On each trial, the fixation cross was blanked out 30 ms before the onset of the stimulus. Each photograph remained on the screen until the participant made a response, and the intertrial interval was 2,000 ms.

In total, 48 black-and-white photographs were presented (i.e., 24 men and 24 women). Across the stimulus set, 12 targets (6 men and 6 women) displayed full-face, direct gaze; 12 targets (6 men and 6 women) displayed 3/4-face, direct gaze; 12 targets (6 men and 6 women) displayed laterally averted gaze (i.e., 6 laterally averted to the right and 6 laterally averted to the left); and 12 targets (6 men and 6 women) had their eyes closed. The 3/4-face, direct condition was included to confirm that any effects observed were not driven by low-level properties of the images (e.g., symmetry, which holds only for direct gaze in full-face views; see George, Driver, & Dolan, 2001). The eyes-closed targets were included as an additional control condition because it is possible that laterally averted gaze may cue covert shifts in visual attention, which in turn may impair categorization performance (Driver et al., 1999; Hood et al., 1998). Presentation of the stimuli was randomized for each participant by computer software. On completion of the task, participants were debriefed, thanked for their participation, and dismissed.

Results and Discussion

The dependent measure of interest in this experiment was the mean time taken by participants to categorize the photo-graphs by gender. Given the presence of outlying responses in the data set, categorization times that were slower than 3 SDs from the mean were excluded from the analysis, as were trials in which participants categorized the targets incorrectly. This resulted in 3.2% of the data being excluded from the statistical analysis. Prior to the statistical analysis, a log transformation was performed on the data. For ease of interpretation, however, the nontransformed treatment means are reported in Table 1. Participants' mean gender-categorization times were submitted to a single-factor (eye gaze: full face, direct vs. 3/4 face, direct vs. averted vs. closed) repeated measures analysis of variance (ANOVA). This revealed an effect of eye gaze on categorization times, $F(3, 93) = 11.47, p < .0001$ (see Table 1 for treatment means). Post hoc Tukey tests confirmed that gender-categorization times were faster for targets with direct gaze (both 3/4 face and full face) than for either targets with laterally averted gaze or targets with their eyes closed (all ps < .01). No other differences were significant.

As expected, therefore, basic aspects of the person-construal process were moderated by the direction of eye gaze of to-be-categorized targets. Confirming the importance and informational value of mutual eye contact (Baron-Cohen, 1994, 1995; Perrett & Emery, 1994), gender-categorization times were fastest when targets were looking straight ahead. This effect was independent of the orientation of the face (i.e., 3/4 face or full face), thereby confirming that gaze direction was driving the observed effect (see also George et al., 2001).

Of course, identifying social objects is only one aspect of the person-construal process. Equally important is the task of accessing information about the social objects of interest (e.g., what do I know about the person?). After all, once this material has been generated, social interaction can be guided in an appropriate (e.g., purposive) manner (Bargh, 1999; Bodenhausen & Macrae, 1998; Macrae & Bodenhausen, 2000). The results of Experiment 1 suggest a possible route through which perceivers may gain enhanced access to category-related material in memory. Specifically, given the observed differences in gender-categorization times, it is possible that categorical knowledge may also be moderated by a person's direction of gaze. That is, just as category identification is facilitated for targets displaying direct eye gaze, so too associated categorical knowledge may be highly accessible for such targets. If this is indeed the case, then it should be possible to detect such an effect in a semantic priming task (Blair & Banaji, 1996; Macrae, Bodenhausen, & Milne, 1995; Macrae, Bodenhausen, Milne, Thorn, & Castelli, 1997). That is, priming effects should be most pronounced when category-related items follow the presentation of targets who are displaying nondeviated (i.e., direct) eye gaze. We investigated this prediction in our second experiment.

EXPERIMENT 2: EYE GAZE AND KNOWLEDGE ACCESSIBILITY

Method

Participants and design

Eighteen undergraduates (9 men, 9 women) participated in the experiment. The experiment had a 3 (eye gaze: direct vs. averted vs. closed) × 2 (item type: stereotypic vs. counterstereotypic) repeated measures design.

Procedure and stimulus materials

Participants arrived at the laboratory individually, were greeted by a female experimenter, and were seated facing the monitor of an Apple Macintosh G3 microcomputer. Written instructions explained that the experiment involved an investigation of the speed with which people could categorize letter strings as words. Participants were informed that, on the computer screen, they would see a series of letter strings (e.g., *jeep, dlab*). Their task was simply to decide, as quickly and accurately as possible, whether each letter string was a word or a nonword. Responses were made by pressing one of two appropriately labeled keys ("word" or "nonword"). In total, 72 letter strings (36 words and 36 nonwords) were used in the experiment. The target words were selected from those normed by Blair and Banaji (1996) and comprised 18 masculine (e.g., *jeep, cigars, rebellious*) and 18 feminine (e.g., *flowers, lingerie, passive*) items. The nonwords were rearranged (but pronounceable) versions of the target items. Participants were told that, prior to the presentation of each letter string, they would briefly see another item appear on the screen. It was emphasized, however, that these items were irrelevant to the task and should be ignored (in reality, of course, these items were the critical priming photographs).

Thirty-six photographs were used as priming stimuli in the experiment: 18 male faces and 18 female faces. Of these priming stimuli, 12 depicted targets (6 men and 6 women) displaying full-face, direct gaze; 12 depicted targets (6 men and 6 women) displaying laterally averted gaze (6 laterally averted to the left and 6 laterally averted to the right); and 12 depicted targets (6 men and 6 women) with their eyes closed. As the two direct-gaze conditions produced comparable effects in Experiment 1, only the full-face, direct targets were used in the second experiment. Each priming stimulus was followed by a stereotypic item, a counterstereotypic item, and a nonword, giving a total of 108 experimental trials. For all trials, the priming stimulus appeared for 150 ms, a blank screen was presented for 100 ms, and then the letter string appeared and remained on the screen until participants made a response (i.e., stimulus onset asynchrony = 250 ms). The intertrial interval was 2,000 ms. The computer recorded the accuracy and latency of each response. On completion of the task, participants were debriefed, thanked for their participation, and dismissed.

Results and Discussion

The dependent measure of interest in this experiment was the mean time taken by participants to classify the category-related letter strings as words. These data were trimmed and normalized using the procedures outlined in Experiment 1. In total, 2.6% of the trials were excluded from the statistical analysis. Prior to the statistical analysis, a log transformation was performed on the data. For ease of interpretation, however, the nontransformed treatment means are reported in Table 1.

Participants' mean lexical decision times were submitted to a 3 (eye gaze: direct vs. averted vs. closed) × 2 (item type: stereotypic vs. counterstereotypic) repeated measures ANOVA. This analysis revealed main effects of eye gaze, $F(2, 34) = 3.26$, $p < .05$, and item type, $F(1, 17) = 7.33$, $p < .02$, on participants' responses. As expected, however, these effects were qualified by an Eye Gaze × Item Type interaction, $F(2, 34) = 3.50$, $p < .04$ (see Table 1 for treatment means). Simple effects analysis confirmed an effect of eye gaze on participants' responses to the stereotypic items, $F(2, 34) = 4.90$, $p < .02$. Lexical decisions were faster when stereotypic items were preceded by targets with direct gaze than when they were preceded by either targets with laterally averted gaze or targets with their eyes closed (both $ps < .05$). In addition, responses were faster to stereotypic than counterstereotypic items when the priming stimuli were targets with direct gaze, $F(1, 17) = 11.40$, $p < .004$. Interestingly, this priming effect (i.e., faster responses to stereotypic than counterstereotypic items) was only marginally significant for targets with laterally averted gaze or targets with their eyes closed.

The time taken by participants to classify letter strings as nonwords was not affected by gaze direction, $F(2, 34) < 1$, n.s. (see Table 1), thereby confirming that direct eye gaze does not prompt a general enhancement in task performance. Instead, the effects of gaze direction were confined to the accessibility of categorical knowledge. This study extends the results of Experiment 1, showing that stereotypic knowledge as most accessible when targets were looking directly ahead. This finding is important as it demonstrates that the task of understanding other persons (i.e., accessing relevant material in semantic memory) is facilitated when mutual eye contact is established between the perceiver and target of interest.

GENERAL DISCUSSION

According to recent writings, the detection and interpretation of eye gaze plays a prominent role in both the development of social cognition and the smooth running of everyday social interaction (Baron-Cohen, 1994, 1995; Perrett & Emery, 1994). Understanding the language of eyes enables perceivers to attribute mental states to others, and hence describe their behavior using a rich variety of mentalistic terms (e.g., intentions, desires, hopes, plans; see Baron-Cohen 1995; Dennett, 1978). This turns out to be an important ability. As Dennett (1987) has argued, "we use folk psychology all the time, to explain and predict each other's behavior; we attribute beliefs and desires to each other with confidence—and quite unselfconsciously—and spend a substantial portion of our waking lives formulating the world—not excluding ourselves—in these terms" (p. 48). We suspected that people's sensitivity to eye gaze would also prompt the emergence of some important social-cognitive effects pertaining to the efficiency of the person-construal process. Our results corroborated this prediction. The speed with which targets were categorized according to their gender and the rate at which associated knowledge was extracted from semantic memory were shown to be contingent upon the target's direction of gaze. Specifically, person construal was facilitated when targets displayed direct eye gaze. This finding not only is of theoretical significance (Baron-Cohen, 1994, 1995; Perrett & Emery, 1994), but also has important practical implications for the dynamics of everyday social interaction. It is obviously beneficial if perceivers can respond to significant (i.e., relevant, salient) others as quickly and effectively as possible. Through enhancements in the efficiency of the person-construal process when mutual eye contact has been established between perceiver and target, this objective can clearly be attained.

Interestingly, recent neuroimaging research has investigated the neural mechanisms that underlie the detection of eye gaze (Kawashima et al., 1999). It has long been known that the amygdala plays an important role in the processing of emotional stimuli (Adolphs, Tranel, Damasio, & Damasio, 1994). For example, studies have demonstrated activation within the amygdala in response to overt (Adolphs et al., 1994) or masked (Morris, Öhman, & Dolan, 1998) emotionally expressive (i.e., angry) faces and in response to threatening or fear-provoking stimuli (LaBar, Gatenby, Gore, LeDoux, & Phelps, 1998). Similar effects have also been obtained when eye gaze is directed toward a person (Kawashima et al., 1999), suggesting that mutual eye contact induces a strong emotional response. This is perhaps to be expected if shared gaze signals the relevance or importance of another person in the environment (Baron-Cohen, 1995). It is possible, therefore, that the social-cognitive effects demonstrated in the present study may be mediated by differential amygdala activation as perceivers strive to understand the people who populate their social worlds. One task for future research will be to investigate this intriguing possibility.

By emphasizing the functional nature of categorical thinking, researchers have unraveled some of the more perplexing mysteries of the person-perception process (Macrae & Bodenhausen, 2000). As economizing mental devices (Macrae, Milne, & Bodenhausen, 1994), categorical knowledge structures confer order, meaning, and predictability to an otherwise chaotic social world. Notwithstanding the acknowledged benefits that accrue from a category-based conception of others, however, some unresolved issues remain. Notable among these is the question of when exactly perceivers activate categorical knowledge structures in their dealings with others. Is categorical thinking an inevitable aspect of the person-perception process, or is its occurrence regulated by a variety of cognitive and mo-tivational factors (see Bargh, 1999; Macrae & Bodenhausen, 2000)? Rather than attempting to resolve this thorny debate, we considered a closely related issue in the present study: Are there factors that moderate the relative efficiency of person construal, such that targets are processed more rapidly (and effectively) under some circumstances than others? Our results confirmed that this is indeed the case, with eye gaze moderating the efficiency of the construal processes that furnish perceivers with categorical knowledge about others. This finding is theoretically noteworthy as it provides an initial demonstration of the important role that biological factors play in the regulation of social cognition. To gain a complete understanding of the dynamics of person construal, it may therefore be useful to consider the wider evolutionary context in which this process emerged.

Acknowledgments— The authors would like to thank Giff Weary, Bill von Hippel, Norman Freeman, Dave Turk, and an anonymous reviewer for their helpful comments on this work.

REFERENCES

Adolphs, R., Tranel, D., Damasio, H., & Damasio, A. (1994). Impaired recognition of emotion in facial expressions following bilateral damage to the human amygdala. *Nature, 372,* 669–672.

Allison, T., Puce, A., & McCarthy, G. (2000). Social perception from visual cues: Role of the STS region. *Trends in Cognitive Sciences, 4,* 267–278.

Allport, G. W. (1954). *The nature of prejudice.* Reading, MA: Addison-Wesley.

Argyle, M., & Cook, M. (1976). *Gaze and mutual gaze.* Cambridge, England: Cambridge University Press.

Bargh, J. A. (1999). The cognitive monster: The case against the controllability of automatic stereotype effects. In S. Chaiken & Y. Trope (Eds.), *Dual process theories in social psychology* (pp. 361–382). New York: Guilford.

Baron-Cohen, S. (1994). How to build a baby that reads minds: Cognitive mechanisms in mindreading. *Cahiers de Psychologie Cognitive, 13,* 513–552.

Baron-Cohen, S. (1995). *Mindblindness: An essay on autism and theory of mind.* Cambridge, MA: MIT Press.

Blair, I. V., & Banaji, M. R. (1996). Automatic and controlled processes in stereotype priming. *Journal of Personality and Social Psychology, 70,* 1142–1163.

Bodenhausen, G. V., & Macrae, C. N. (1998). Stereotype activation and inhibition. In R. S. Wyer, Jr. (Ed.), *Stereotype activation and inhibition: Advances in social cognition* (Vol. 11, pp. 1–52). Hillsdale, NJ: Erlbaum.

Brewer, M. B. (1988). A dual process model of impression formation. In R. S. Wyer, Jr., & T. K. Srull (Eds.), *Advances in social cognition* (Vol. 1, pp. 1–36). Hillsdale, NJ: Erlbaum.

Brothers, L. (1990). The social brain: A project for integrating primate behavior and neurophysiology in a new domain. *Concepts in Neuroscience, 1,* 27–51.

Bruce, C., Desimone, R., & Gross, C. (1981). Visual properties of neurones in a polysensory area in superior temporal sulcus of the macaque. *Journal of Neurophysiology, 46,* 369–384.

Dennett, D. (1978). *Brainstorms: Philosophical essays on mind and psychology.* London: Harvester.

Dennett, D. (1987). *The intentional stance.* Cambridge, MA: MIT Press.

Driver, J., Davis, G., Ricciardelli, P., Kidd, P., Maxwell, E., & Baron-Cohen, S. (1999). Gaze perception triggers visuospatial orienting. *Visual Cognition, 6,* 509–540.

Fiske, S. T., & Neuberg, S. L. (1990). A continuum model of impression formation from category based to individuating processes: Influences of information and motivation on attention and interpretation. In M. P. Zanna (Ed.), *Advances in experimental social psychology* (Vol. 3, pp. 1–74). San Diego, CA: Academic Press.

Friesen, C. K., & Kingstone, A. (1998). The eyes have it!: Reflexive orienting is triggered by nonpredictive gaze. *Psychonomic Bulletin & Review, 5*, 490–495.

George, N., Driver, J., & Dolan, R. J. (2001). Seen gaze-direction modulates fusiform activity and its coupling with other brain areas during face processing. *NeuroImage, 13*, 1102–1112.

Haxby, J. V., Hoffman, E. A., & Gobbini, M. I. (2000). The distributed human neural system for face perception. *Trends in Cognitive Sciences, 4*, 223–233.

Hinde, R. A., & Rowell, T. E. (1962). Communication by posture and facial expression in the rhesus monkey. *Proceedings of the Zoological Society of London, 138*, 1–21.

Hoffman, E. A., & Haxby, J. V. (2000). Distinct representations of eye gaze and identity in the distributed human neural system for face processing. *Nature Neuroscience, 3*, 80–84.

Hood, B. M., Willen, J. D., & Driver, J. (1998). Gaze perception triggers corresponding shifts of visual attention in young infants. *Psychological Science, 9*, 131–134.

Kawashima, R., Sugiura, M., Kato, T., Nakamura, A., Hatano, K., Ito, K., Fukuda, H., Kojima, S., & Nakamura, K. (1999). The human amygdala plays an important role in gaze monitoring: A PET study. *Brain, 122*, 779–783.

Kellerman, J., Lewis, J., & Laird, J. D. (1989). Looking and loving: The effects of mutual gaze on feelings of romantic love. *Journal of Research in Personality, 23*, 145–161.

Kleinke, C. L. (1986). Gaze and eye contact: A research review. *Psychological Review, 100*, 78–100.

LaBar, K. S., Gatenby, J. C., Gore, J. C., LeDoux, J. E., & Phelps, E. A. (1998). Human amygdala activation during conditioned fear acquisition and extinction: A mixed-trial fMRI study. *Neuron, 20*, 937–945.

Langton, S. R. H., Watt, R. J., & Bruce, V. (2000). Do the eyes have it? Cues to the direction of social attention. *Trends in Cognitive Sciences, 4*, 50–59.

Macrae, C. N., & Bodenhausen, G. V. (2000). Social cognition: Thinking categorically about others. *Annual Review of Psychology, 51*, 93–120.

Macrae, C. N., Bodenhausen, G. V., & Milne, A. B. (1995). The dissection of selection in person perception: Inhibitory processes in social stereotyping. *Journal of Personality and Social Psychology, 69*. 397–407.

Macrae, C. N., Bodenhausen, G. V., Milne, A. B., Thorn, T. M. J., & Castelli, L. (1997). On the activation of social stereotypes: The moderating role of processing objectives. *Journal of Experimental Social Psychology, 33*, 471–489.

Macrae, C. N., Milne, A. B., & Bodenhausen, G. V. (1994). Stereotypes as energy-saving devices: A peek inside the cognitive toolbox. *Journal of Personality and Social Psychology, 66*, 37–47.

Morris, J. S., Öhman, A., & Dolan, R. J. (1998). Conscious and unconscious emotional learning in the human amygdala. *Nature, 393*, 417–418.

Morton, J., & Johnson, M. (1991). CONSPEC and CONLEARN: A two-process theory of infant face recognition. *Psychological Review, 98*, 164–181.

Perrett, D., & Emery, N. J. (1994). Understanding the intentions of others from visual signals: Neuropsychological evidence. *Cahiers de Psychologie Cognitive, 13*, 683–694.

Perrett, D., Rolls, E., & Cann, W. (1982). Visual neurones responsive to faces in the monkey temporal cortex. *Experimental Brain Research, 47*, 329–342.

Perrett, D., Smith, P., Potter, D., Mistlin, A., Head, A., Milner, A., & Jeeves, M. (1985). Visual cells in the temporal cortex sensitive to face view and gaze direction. *Proceedings of the Royal Society of London B, 223*, 293–317.

Vecera, S., & Johnson, M. (1995). Gaze detection and the cortical processing of faces: Evidence from infants and adults. *Visual Cognition, 2*, 59–87.

von Grünau, M., & Anston, C. (1995). The detection of gaze direction: A stare-in-the-crowd effect. *Perception, 24*, 1297–1313.

(RECEIVED 5/23/01; REVISION ACCEPTED 12/01)

C. Neil Macrae, *Dartmouth College*

Bruce M. Hood, *University of Bristol, Bristol, England*

Alan B. Milne, *University of Aberdeen, Aberdeen, Scotland*

Angela C. Rowe, *University of Bristol, Bristol, England*

Malia F. Mason, *Dartmouth College*

Address correspondence to Neil Macrae, Department of Psychological and Brain Sciences, Dartmouth College, Moore Hall, Hanover, NH 03755; e-mail: c.n.macrae@dartmouth.edu.

From *Psychological Science*, September 2002, pp. 460–464. © 2002 by Blackwell Publishing Ltd., Oxford, UK. Reprinted by permission.

Got time for Friends?

Sure, you're busy. But are you paying attention to what's really important?
Why finding—and keeping—friends is the key to a happy life.

BY ANDY STEINER

It's not the last time my daughter will make me look foolish, but it was one of the first. Maybe it was silly to take a toddler to an art opening, but there we were, the effervescent Astrid and her uptight mama. As I hovered near her, hoping to intercept toppling *objets d'art*, Astrid spotted Claire across the room.

Maybe their attraction was predestined, since Claire and Astrid, 18 and 16 months respectively, were the only under-three-footers in what to them must have looked like a sea of kneecaps. Still, Astrid's eyes lit up when she saw young Claire, and she turned on the charm, hopping and squealing and running in some strange kiddie ritual. Claire squealed back, Astrid flashed her tummy, and that was it: They were fast friends.

The culture-at-large tells us that once school is over or we hit 30, friendship ought to take a backseat to more pressing concerns.

It wasn't so easy for Claire's mother and me. When our kids started making nice, we smiled politely, and as the junior friendship heated up, we attempted shy (on my part at least) and distracted attempts at conversation. "How old is she?" I asked. "What's her name?" she countered. I'd like to say that today Claire's mommy is a good friend, but that's not the case. We continued to exchange pleasantries while our daughters pranced around together, but when our partners appeared, we picked up our squirmy squirts and said good-bye. We haven't seen each other since. Too bad, because I could have used a new friend. Who couldn't?

In college, and for several years after, I was immersed in a warm circle of friends, the kind of exciting and exotic people I'd spent my small-town youth dreaming about. These friends came to my college from around the world, and after graduation, many of them stayed. We had a great time. We went to movies—and for a bit created our own monthly film group. We gathered at each other's apartments to cook big dinners and stay up late, sharing our opinions on music, sex, and dreams. We even took a few trips together—to a friend's wedding in the mountains of Colorado and to a cabin on the edge of a loon-covered lake. But time passes, and as these friends moved on, got married, or found great jobs, my gang of compatriots began to dwindle.

"We cannot tell the precise moment when friendship is formed. As in filling a vessel drop by drop, there is at last a drop which makes it run over; so in a series of kindnesses there is at last one which makes the heart run over."

Samuel Johnson

Now many of them have moved to other states—other countries, even. Though a precious core group still lives within shouting distance, I worry that grown-up life will soon scatter them all and I'll be left, lonely and missing them.

So it goes for many of us as we leave our youth behind and face "real" life. While generations of young adults have probably felt the same way, the yearning for close friends takes on a greater sense of urgency now as modern life makes our lives busier and more fragmented. "It's not that it's so hard to make friends when you're older," says sociologist Jan Yager, author of *Friendshifts*, "but making friends—and finding time to maintain and nurture old friendships as well as new ones—is just one of the many concerns that occupy your time."

Astrid's encounter with Claire (and my parallel one with her mother) cast a spotlight on one reality: Kids see potential friends everywhere. Adults, on the other hand, have a harder time of it, especially as we (and our potential friends) enter the realm of romantic commitments, full-time jobs, motherhood and fatherhood. While we may wish to add to our collection of friends, we feel too busy, too consumed by other obligations, too caught up in everyday bustle to make time to help a friendship blossom and grow.

"Be a friend to thyself, and others will befriend thee."

English proverb

And we may be following subtle clues from the culture-at-large telling us that, once school is over or we near 30, friendship ought to take a back seat to more pressing concerns. Despite the central role that idealized gangs of pals play on sitcoms, our primary sources of information—self-help books, magazines, and personal interest TV shows—rarely talk about how to get—or keep—friends. Instead they barrage us with detailed advice on how to attract a lover, get ahead in a career, rekindle a marriage, or keep peace in the family. Friendships, unlike these other kinds of relationships, are supposed to just happen, with little effort on your part. But what if they don't?

"Friends can get relegated to secondary status," says Aurora Sherman, assistant professor of psychology at Brandeis University. "Even if you don't have children or a partner or aging parents, the pressures of adult responsibility can force people to place friendship in the background."

"All I can do is to urge you to put friendship ahead of all other human concerns, for there is nothing so suited to man's nature, nothing that can mean so much to him, whether in good times or in bad... I am inclined to think that with the exception of wisdom, the gods have given nothing finer to men than this."

Marcus Tullius Cicero

Children's full-scale focus on friendship may have to do with more than just their carefree attitude about life. Sherman cites the research theorizing that kids' interest in making friends serves a larger developmental purpose.

"A young person's primary motivation for social interaction is to get information and to learn about the world," Sherman explains. "When you're a kid, practically everybody that you meet has the potential to help you learn about something that you didn't know." Grown-ups already know most things (or at least they think they do), so as you get older, you may feel less of a drive to make new friends.

So, if you're someone who embraces the goal of lifelong learning, it's important not to write off friendship as a thing of the past. Meeting new people is a lot less work than going back to college for another degree, and more fun, too. Want to learn yoga or steep yourself in South American culture? How about sharpening your skills as an entrepreneur or activist? Think outside the classroom by finding someone eager to show what they know. An added benefit is that you, too, can share your passion about knitting or bocce ball or radical history. If the people you currently hang out with don't know much about the things you want to know, maybe it's time to break into some new circles.

"The proper office of a friend is to side with you when you are in the wrong. Nearly anybody will side with you when you are in the right."

Mark Twain

The tangible rewards of friendship go far beyond exchanges of information. In 1970 Lenny Dee left New York and moved across the country to Portland, Oregon, where he knew barely a soul. "The first week I was there I met probably half the people who became my lifelong friends," says Dee. "It was like I walked through this magic door and a whole world opened up for me." Within a day of his arrival, he had moved into a house that was an epicenter of the city's alternative culture. He could barely step out of the house without running into one of his new friends.

"At one point in my life all of the people I knew were footloose and fancy free," Dee says, "but over the years that changed. A certain segment of my friends in Portland became more settled while I remained less settled. People got families and jobs, and they started disappearing. Now you have to make an appointment to get together."

Still, Dee has been vigilant in nurturing old friendships; people all across the country can count on a birthday phone call from Portland. "I have always thought you could invest your energies in making money or making friends," Dee says, "and they achieve much the same ends—security, new experiences, personal options, travel, and so forth. I have always found it more fulfilling to make friends."

And Dee's life has been shaped in many ways by the enduring connections he's maintained, including a key position at the start-up of a now successful educational software company and a recent vacation in Corsica at the summer home of an old Portland friend who now lives in Paris.

A slew of recent research supports Dee's example that friends make life complete.

"As hard as it is with everyone so busy and consumed with the day-to-day workings of their lives, it's important to understand that making and maintaining friendships is really pivotal to social, emotional, and physical well-being," says Yager. She ticks off research that touts the value of building strong nonfamilial bonds, including: an in-depth study of thousands of Northern California residents that revealed that having ties to at least one close friend extends a person's life, and another study of 257 human resource managers that discovered adults who have friends at work report not only higher productivity but also higher workplace satisfaction.

When you know who his friend is, you know who he is.
Senegal proverb

For New York psychotherapist Kathlyn Conway, a three-time cancer survivor and author of the memoir *An Ordinary Life*, friends provided an anchor during times when she felt her life was drifting off course.

"I had friends I could talk to at any time," Conway says of her 1993 battle with breast cancer. "If I was upset, it was easy for me to call someone and expect them to listen—no matter what."

And when the busy mother of two needed physical help, friends came to her aid. "One friend went to the hospital after my mastectomy and helped me wash my hair," Conway recalled in an article she wrote for the women's cancer magazine *Mamm*. "Another, who herself had had breast cancer, visited and stealthily, humorously, kindly opened her blouse to show me her implanted breast in order to reassure me. Yet another left her very busy job in the middle of the week to go shopping with me for a wig."

One time when adults tend to make new friends is during major life changes, like a move, a new job, or the birth of a child. Ellen Goodman and Patricia O'Brien, authors of *I Know Just What You Mean*, a book chronicling their quarter-century friendship, met in 1973 when both were completing Neiman fellowships at Harvard. At the time, Goodman, now a nationally syndicated newspaper columnist, and O'Brien, a novelist and former editorial writer for the *Chicago Sun-Times*, were both newly divorced mothers in their 30s.

"We were both broke and busy and we were not at all alike—at least on the surface," Goodman recalls, "but we bonded, maybe out of some sense of great urgency, and during that year we spent an enormous amount of time in Harvard Square, drinking coffee and talking. We missed a lot of classes, but those times together were some of the best seminars either of us ever attended."

"Life shifts—like a divorce or an illness or another unexpected change—can occur at any time, and when that happens, there's always this powerful draw to another person who's going through the same thing," O'Brien says. "For Ellen and me there was this wonderful opportunity to talk to another woman who was hitting the same bumps in the road as we were. We could talk for hours and always understand what the other person was saying." After the short spell at Harvard, they never again lived in the same place but kept the friendship going with letters, phone calls, and frequent visits.

Three is the magic number

When it comes to making friends, there's much we can learn from kids about flashing a wide grin and harboring a playful spirit. But Stanford University psychology professor Laura Carstensen emphasizes that an important lesson also comes from the over-65 set. In studying senior citizens' social networks, she has found that "it is the *quality* of their relationships that matters—not the *quantity*. In our work we find that three is the critical friend number. If you have three people in your life that you can really count on, then you are doing as well as someone who has 10 friends. Or 20, for that matter. If you have fewer than three friends, then you could be a little precarious."

So sit down, get out a piece of paper, and start listing your friends. Got three folks you're always excited about seeing and feel certain you can trust? Then put down the pencil. Who says you can't put a number on success?

—*Andy Steiner*

A while back—inspired by my daughter's happy, open face and ready giggle—I resolved that making new friends might be just the cure for the post-baby blahs I was experiencing.

So I set my sights on one particular woman. Even though I have wonderful old friends, people I wouldn't trade for a billion dollars, this particular woman caught my eye. She seemed smart and funny. We were both writers. I'd heard that she lived in my neighborhood. Then, the kicker: Someone we both knew suggested that we would hit it off. So I called her—out of the blue—and invited her to coffee. Sure, she said. So we met.

Just the other day, this woman told me that at the time she wondered about my motivation, this strange, nervously enthusiastic young woman who peppered her with questions about writing and reading and her impressions of the university we'd both attended, she as an undergraduate, I as a master's student. Still, a few weeks later she took me up on my invitation to go for a walk, and our conversation soon became natural and fun. Suddenly, she became my new friend.

Astrid, riding in her stroller, witnessed it all. Besides babbling and napping, she was watching closely as my new friend and I laughed and told the stories of our lives. Taking a risk and extending yourself is one way to form a bond with someone. We weren't squealing or flashing our tummies, but it was close.

Andy Steiner, mother of gregarious Astrid, is a senior editor of Utne Reader.

Rational and Irrational Fears Combine in Terrorism's Wake

By ERICA GOODE

The familiar became strange, the ordinary perilous.

On Sept. 11, Americans entered a new and frightening geography, where the continents of safety and danger seemed forever shifted.

Is it safe to fly? Will terrorists wage germ warfare? Where is the line between reasonable precaution and panic?

Jittery, uncertain and assuming the worst, many people have answered these questions by forswearing air travel, purchasing gas masks and radiation detectors, placing frantic calls to pediatricians demanding vaccinations against exotic diseases or rushing out to fill prescriptions for Cipro, an antibiotic most experts consider an unnecessary defense against anthrax.

Psychologists who study how people perceive potential hazards say such responses are not surprising, given the intense emotions inspired by the terrorist attacks.

"People are particularly vulnerable to this sort of thing when they're in a state of high anxiety, fear for their own well-being and have a great deal of uncertainty about the future," said Dr. Daniel Gilbert, a professor of psychology at Harvard.

"We don't like that feeling," Dr. Gilbert said. "We want to do something about it. And, at the moment, there isn't anything particular we can do, so we buy a gas mask and put an American decal on our car and take trains instead of airplanes."

But, he added, "I'll be very surprised if five years from now even one life was saved by these efforts."

Still, many psychologists said avoiding flying might be perfectly reasonable if someone is going to spend the entire flight in white-knuckled terror. And though experts say gas masks will offer dubious protection in a chemical attack, if buying them helps calm people down, it can do no harm.

"The feelings may be irrational, but once you have the feelings, the behavior is perfectly rational," said Dr. George Lowenstein, a professor of economics and psychology at Carnegie Mellon University. "It doesn't make sense to take a risk just because it's rational if it's going to make you miserable. The rational thing is to do what makes you comfortable."

The public's fears may be heightened, he and other experts said, by the sense that the government failed to predict or prevent the Sept. 11 attacks, making people less trusting of the reassurances offered by the authorities, who have said that biological attacks are unlikely and, with vastly heightened security, air travel is safe.

The vivid, the involuntary and the unfamiliar seem to be more threatening.

Checkpoints on highways, closed parking structures at airports, flyovers by military aircraft and other security measures, they added, while reassuring many people, may for others increase anxiety by providing a constant reminder of danger.

In fact, the threats now uppermost in many people's minds, Dr. Lowenstein and other psychologists said, are examples of the kinds of risks that people find most frightening.

"All the buttons are being pushed here," said Dr. Paul Slovic, a professor of psychology at the University of Oregon and the author of "The Perception of Risk." Threats posed by terrorism, he said, "are horrific to contemplate, seem relatively uncontrollable and are catastrophic."

He and other researchers have found that risks that evoke vivid images, that are seen as involuntary, that are unfamiliar or that kill many people at once are often perceived as more threatening than risks that are voluntary, familiar and less extreme in their effects. For example, in studies, people rank threats like plane crashes and nuclear accidents higher than dangers like smoking or car accidents, which actually cause many more deaths each year.

This fact is a source of endless frustration to some scientists, who cannot understand why people panic over almost undetectable quantities of pesticides on vegetables but happily devour charcoal-broiled hamburgers and steaks, which contain known carcinogens formed in grilling. And, when asked to rank the relative dangers of a variety of potential hazards, scientific experts routinely give lower ratings to things like nuclear power and pesticides than do laypeople, researchers have found.

"Everything in some sense is dangerous, in some concentration and some place, and usually not in others," said Dr. James Collman, a chemistry professor at Stanford and the author of "Naturally Dangerous: Surprising Facts About Food, Health and the Environment."

He said his daughter called him after the terrorist attacks to ask if she should buy a gas mask.

"I told her not to panic," he said. "I thought it was sort of statistically a silly thing to do, and were there ever any toxic gases out there, whatever mask she had might or might not be effective anyway."

Yet psychologists say the average person's responses make sense if one realizes that human beings are not the cool, rational evaluators that economists and other social scientists once assumed them to be.

Rather, the human brain reacts to danger through the activation of two systems, one an instant, emotional response, the other a higher level, more deliberate reaction.

The emotional response to risk, Dr. Lowenstein said, is deeply rooted in evolution and shared with most other animals. But rationality—including the ability to base decisions about risk on statistical likelihood—is unique to humans.

Yet the two responses, he said, often come into conflict, "just as the experts clash with the laypeople."

"People often even within themselves don't believe that a risk is objectively that great, and yet they have feelings that contradict their cognitive evaluations," Dr. Lowenstein said.

For example, he said, "The objective risk of driving for four or five hours at high speeds still has got to be way higher than the risk of flying."

What You Don't Know . . .

Whether people fear something depends not only on how dangerous it actually is, but also on how much they know about it and how much control they believe they have over their exposure to it. Researchers use diagrams like this to chart perceptions of risk.

VERTICAL AXIS
At bottom, risks that subjects view as known and observable; at top, those whose effects are hardest to observe.

UNKNOWN RISKS

Less risky, less frightening
- Marijuana
- Aspirin
- Sunbathing

Most frightening
- Terrorism
- Nuclear weapons
- Nuclear power
- Nerve gas

CONTROLLABLE RISKS   UNCONTROLLABLE RISKS

HORIZONTAL AXIS ▶
At left, things described as controllable. At right, things that seem beyond one's control.

Least frightening
- Surfing
- Motorcycles
- Alcoholic beverages
- Hunting

KNOWN RISKS

More risky, more frightening
- Smoking
- Heroin
- Crime
- Open-heart surgery

Items are shown in no special order.

Source: "The Perception of Risk," by Paul Slovic

The New York Times

Yet Dr. Lowenstein added that a group of his colleagues, all academic experts on risk assessment, chose to drive rather than fly to a conference after the terrorist attacks.

"If you ask them which is objectively more dangerous, they would probably say that driving is," Dr. Lowenstein said. And though his colleagues cited potential airport delays, he said he suspected fear might also have played into their decision.

President Bush and other policy makers in Washington, Dr. Lowenstein said, must contend with a similar struggle between reason and emotion in shaping their response to the attacks.

"A lot of what's going on is this battle where the emotions are pushing us to respond in a way that would give us quick release but would have all sorts of long-term consequences," Dr. Lowenstein said.

In fact, studies show that once awakened, fear and other emotions heighten people's reactions to other potential hazards. In one study, for example, students shown sad films perceived a variety of risks as more threatening than students who saw emotionally neutral films.

Fear can also spread from person to person, resulting in wild rumors and panic.

One example often cited by sociologists who study collective behavior is the so-called Seattle windshield pitting epidemic, which occurred in 1954, a time when cold war fears ran high and the United States was testing the hydrogen bomb.

That year, tiny holes in car windshields were noticed in Bellingham, Wash., north of Seattle. A week later, similar pitting was seen by residents of towns south of Bellingham. Soon, people in Seattle and all over the state were reporting mysterious damage to their windshields. Many speculated that fallout from the H-bomb tests was the cause. Others blamed cosmic rays from the sun. At the height of the panic, the mayor of Seattle even called President Dwight D. Eisenhower for help.

But eventually, a more mundane explanation revealed itself: In the usual course of events, people did not examine their windshields that closely. The holes, pits and dings turned out to be a result of normal wear and tear, which few had noticed until it was drawn to their attention.

The antidote to such fears, psychologists say, is straightforward information from trustworthy sources.

"Trustworthiness has two elements," said Dr. Baruch Fischhoff, a psychologist in Carnegie Mellon's department of social and decision sciences. "One is honesty and the other is competence."

Attempts by the authorities to use persuasion often fall flat, Dr. Fischhoff said, because "if people feel they have to peel away the agenda of the communicator in order to understand the content of the message, that's debilitating."

"Give me the facts in a comprehensible way, and leave it to me to decide what's right for me," he said.

Yet what psychologists can say with some certainty is that, if no further attacks occur in the near future, people's fears are likely to fade quickly—even faster than the fearful themselves would predict.

Studies suggest, Dr. Gilbert said, that "people underestimate their resilience and adaptiveness."

We have remarkable both psychological and physiological mechanisms to adapt to change," he said. "I guarantee you that in six months whatever New Yorkers are feeling will seem pretty normal to them, even if it is not exactly what they were feeling before."

SEX IN AMERICA

LAST SUMMER THE OUTGOING SURGEON GENERAL DAVID SATCHER ISSUED HIS REPORT ON THE STATE OF THIS COUNTRY'S SEXUAL HEALTH. *PT* PUTS A FACE ON THE HARD FACTS.

By Michael W. Ross, Ph.D., and PT Staff

PUBLIC POLICY ON SEXUAL HEALTH HAS A TROUBLED history. Competing agendas, dismissed administrators and shrill representatives often obscure the facts rather than inform the public.

Surgeon General David Satcher, M.D., Ph.D., sought to change this contentious tone by bringing together health professionals representing diverse disciplines and points of view. These meetings produced the surgeon general's report on sex in America, *Call to Action to Promote Sexual Health and Responsible Sexual Behavior*.

Without scientific debate, says Satcher, discussion would continue to be fueled by special interests, salacious media and schoolyard mythology. *Call to Action* emphasizes that our first task is to encourage honest discussion about sexuality. We then need to find realistic responses to increased rates of sexually transmitted diseases (STD) and HIV, sexual violence, unintended pregnancies and abortions.

Satcher recognizes that different communities may have different values and approaches as well as different answers. Thus, *Call to Action* is a starting point, not an end point, from which to develop solutions.

Psychology Today takes a closer look at the statistics and talks to some of the people they represent.

Unintended pregnancies

Nearly half of all pregnancies in the U.S. are unintended. While women of all ages, incomes and ethnic backgrounds

MANDY OLIVARES

It hasn't been an easy life for Mandy and John Olivares. When the young couple found out she was pregnant last year, they were worried. They hadn't intended to have children so soon. Mandy, however, doesn't believe in abortion. So at age 20, she is the mother of a three-month-old infant and a three-year-old boy. She was 16 when she had her first child. Receiving an eviction notice—their apartment building was converted into a cooperative—added to the couple's stress.

To cover their expenses, Mandy returned to work as a sales clerk. John who already holds down a day job as a clerical worker, plans to take on a night job to help make ends meet. Still, the couple has never relied on welfare. "I got myself into this situation," says Mandy. "I'd rather do it on my own and work with my husband than depend on others." She even has ambitions to return to college and major in interior design and business. "I had two jabs before I got pregnant with my second child, I can do that again." She says she's not worried' "I have faith."

have unintended pregnancies, numbers are highest among adolescents, low-income women and women of African-American descent. Unintended pregnancies are also medically costly. They can, for example, increase risk for low birth weight and infant mortality. Aside from higher medical expenses, the cost to society is palpable. Intended pregnancies affect education rates, welfare dependency and even subsequent child abuse and neglect.

STDs

An estimated 45 million people in the U.S. are infected with genital herpes, and 1 million new cases occur every year. Sexually transmitted disease (STD) rates in the U.S. are the highest in the developed world. Chlamydia and gonorrhea are approaching epidemic proportions among some adolescent populations, and one in five sexually active adults may be infected with genital herpes. Education is critical, as is breaking the chains of transmission through abstinence, condom use or screening and treatment. Silence is unacceptable.

LAURA ZIMMER

Barely 18 years old and a freshman in college, Laura Zimmer was just beginning to explore her sexuality when she contracted genital herpes. "I was a naive little Catholic girl," Zimmer admits. When she confronted her boyfriend, he denied knowing he carried the disease. But rather than face possible rejection by other, noninfected men, she stayed with and eventually married him.

Ten years later, Zimmer realized that she and her husband weren't compatible and they divorced. Soon she found herself facing the same challenge she had avoided as a teenager. "I'd date someone until I had to reveal that I had herpes," she says. "Then I'd sabotage it-let my very worst traits come out—so if he rejected me it wasn't because I had shared something personal." But Zimmer couldn't continue living with her fear of rejection. She wanted people to know her story; so she wrote it and then e-mailed it to nearly everyone she knew. "It's the best thing I ever did," says Zimmer, who's now in a healthy, honest relationship. "Everyone responded with such love and respect. This is part of me that won't change, and I'm not going to reject myself."

Homosexuality

Some 80 percent of gay men and women have experienced verbal or physical harassment, 45 percent have been threatened with violence and 17 percent have been physically attacked. Strengthening families—whatever their structure—and encouraging stable, enduring adult relationships is important to sexual health. The stigma of this sexual orientation can lead to harassment, depression and suicide.

AIDS

The AIDS epidemic is shifting toward women. While women accounted for 28 percent of HIV cases reported between 1981 and 1999, they accounted for 32 percent of reported cases between June 1999 and July 2000. We need to observe that the enemy is the virus—not those infected. We need to team up with those infected to stem the spread of HIV. With their help, we can increase awareness of the need for responsible sexual behavior.

HARA ESTROFF MARANO

"I have had two abortions," says Hara Estroff Marano. At the time of her first, in the early 1960s, abortion was illegal. Marano ended up on a dining-room table with a coat hanger and a little Italian woman standing over her. The then 21-year-old college student "was oddly confident." Yet two nights later she was bleeding to death, so a friend whisked her to a Boston hospital for an emergency D and C. She woke up at three in the morning inside an oxygen tank, scared and without the emotional support of her family. "I felt I had screwed up and I wasn't going to get any sympathy from my family."

Year's later, in her midthirties, Marano faced an impending divorce and another unwanted pregnancy. Already the mother of two young children, she chose to have an abortion. This time, the procedure was professional and not in the least traumatic. "Being a mother is the most important job we have. To be a parent we need resources—emotional, financial and social," says Marano, *PT*'s editor at large and editor of the magazine's *Blues Buster* newsletter.

BILL AND DWAYNE

When Bill told his mother he was gay, she was less than understanding. "She made comments that I would go to hell," he recalls. That winter his mother didn't invite Bill's partner Dwayne to celebrate Christmas with the family. Consequently, Bill didn't see her either. Her reaction has made it hard for Bill to disclose his life to others: "I'm very guarded. I don't feel like explaining myself." At his former place of employment, one coworker compared gay people with child molesters. Although Bill, a 31-year-old cardiac sonographer, wanted to tell his co-worker to relax, he didn't: "I prefer not to have the confrontation."

Bill lives with Dwayne, a 33-year-old hotel worker, and their three dogs and two cats in Long Island, New York. They bought an abandoned house in a culturally diverse community and renovated it to the delight of their neighbors. But they realize that living in New York is much different than living in the South. "People here have more experience with gays who are out," says Bill. While the couple feels comfortable in their neighborhood, Bill and Dwayne still keep a low profile. "We don't walk around holding hands—not that we don't want to," says Dwayne.

Abortion

An estimated 1.37 million women underwent abortions in the U.S. in 1996. Of that figure, nearly 45 percent had already received at least one abortion. Teenage pregnancy has become a focus, but abortion rates are, in fact, higher for women in their early twenties. There is general agreement that rates should be lower. One way to achieve this is by providing information on, access to and use of contraception.

The Opposition

Surgeon General David Satcher isn't exactly a popular public figure in many circles. The Family Research Council, for one, has demanded his resignation. So it is no surprise that Satcher's *Call* has met with a chorus of controversy. The Bush administration and numerous other groups, including the American Family Association, Focus on the Family and the Family Research Council have denounced the report.

These various organizations disagree with several points in the report. For example, the surgeon general advises schools to teach abstinence, while also recommending that students be educated about birth control. This approach, known as "abstinence plus," has drawn the most fire. "The safe-sex campaign has been a disaster," says Ed Vitagliano, of the American Family Association.

The report also concludes that there is no valid scientific evidence that sexual orientation can be changed—another point of contention. "The conclusion was basically down the line with that promoted by homosexuality advocacy groups," says Vitagliano, who objects to the view that "sexual orientation is determined at an early age and that there is no valid evidence that orientation can be changed."

—PT Staff

MICHELLE LOPEZ

Michelle Lopez turned tricks on the streets of New York in the mid-1980s, soon after she arrived from her native Trinidad. But when she became infected with HIV in 1988, it was through sexual intercourse with her husband. Their daughter, Raven, was born HIV-positive two years later and was diagnosed in 1992. Everything changed. Lopez kicked drugs and compulsively researched the disease: "I saw what the gay white male population did. I saw what worked for the ones who wanted to live: learning about research and drug side effects and developing relationships with drug companies." Lopez has had full-blown AIDS since 1996. She takes a cocktail of five drugs a day as well as Zoloft for depression.

Today, Lopez is an AIDS educator at the health clinic where she first sought treatment nine years ago. Some 75 percent of the patients are women and, like Lopez, many emigrated from the Caribbean. Raven is now 12 and speaks publicly about being HIV-positive. Lopez feels that she herself has come full circle: "I want to help people live. A lot of people did that for me. When Raven and I were diagnosed, I was on a mission to live. Now I'm on a mission to save my child's life."

Michael W. Ross, Ph.D., is professor of public health at the University of Texas and a scientific editor of the surgeon general's Call to Action *For information see: www.surgeongeneral.gov/library/sexualhealth/*

UNIT 10
Psychological Disorders

Unit Selections

Key Points to Consider

- Do you believe everyone has the potential for developing a mental disorder? Just how widespread is mental disorder in the United States? What circumstances lead an individual to emotional problems? In general, what can be done to reduce the number of cases of mental disorder or to promote better mental health in the United States?

- What is depression? How widespread are depressive episodes? What causes depression? How are ordinary episodes of depression different from clinical depression? Why are the elderly of interest to specialists in the field of depression? What biological causes are implicated in depression? Are there psychological causes for depression? What are some promising treatments for this disorder?

- What are anxiety disorders? What are specific anxiety disorders and their symptoms? What causes anxiety disorders? What role does the nervous system play in anxiety and anxiety disorders?

- Why did some individuals recover from the trauma of September 11, 2001 while others remain adversely affected? What is post-traumatic stress disorder? How does it differ from everyday stress? What can we do to assist people suffering from post-traumatic stress disorder? What can you do for yourself should another major terrorist event occur?

- What is schizophrenia? What are its symptoms? Can a person with schizophrenia appear "normal" at times? What are the suspected causes of schizophrenia? What are the currently available treatments for schizophrenia?

- Do you know anyone with a mental illness? If yes, can you describe the symptoms experienced by the individual? Do the symptoms appear to be consistent with several diagnostic categories or of one particular disorder? What type of dilemmas do multiple symptoms pose for psychologists and psychiatrists? How, then, can such professionals make an accurate diagnosis?

 **Links: www.dushkin.com/online/**
These sites are annotated in the World Wide Web pages.

American Association of Suicidology
http://www.suicidology.org

Anxiety Disorders
http://www.adaa.org/mediaroom/index.cfm

Ask NOAH About: Mental Health
http://www.noah-health.org/english//illness/mentalhealth/mental.html

Mental Health Net Disorders and Treatments
http://www.mentalhelp.net/

Mental Health Net: Eating Disorder Resources
http://www.mentalhelp.net/poc/center_index.php/id/46

National Women's Health Resource Center (NWHRC)
http://www.healthywomen.org

Jay and Harry were two brothers who owned a service station. They were the middle children of four. The other two children were sisters, the oldest of whom had married and moved out of the family home. Their father who retired and turned it over to his sons once owned the service station.

Harry and Jay had a good working relationship. Harry was the "up-front" man. Taking customer orders, accepting payments, and working with parts distributors, Harry was the individual who dealt most directly with the public, delivery personnel, and other people accessing the station. Jay worked behind the scenes. While Harry made the mechanical diagnoses, Jay was the one who did the corrective work. Some of his friends thought Jay was a mechanical genius.

Preferring to spend time by himself, Jay had always been a little odd and a bit of a loner. Jay's friends thought his emotions had been more inappropriate and intense than other people's emotional states, but they passed it off as part of his eccentric genius. On the other hand, Harry was the stalwart in the family. He was the acknowledged leader and decision maker when it came to family finances.

One day Jay did not show up for work on time. When he did, he was dressed in the most garish outfit and was laughing hysterically and talking to himself. Harry at first suspected that his brother had taken some illegal drugs. However, Jay's condition persisted and, in fact, worsened. Out of concern, his family took him to their physician who immediately sent Jay and his family to a psychiatrist. After several visits, the diagnosis was schizophrenia. Jay's maternal uncle had also been schizophrenic. The family grimly left the psychiatrist's office and traveled to the local pharmacy to fill a prescription for antipsychotic medications. They knew they would make many such trips to retrieve the medicine that Jay would probably take the rest of his life.

What caused Jay's drastic and rather sudden change in mental health? Was Jay destined to be schizophrenic because of his family tree? Did competitiveness with his brother and the feeling that he was less revered than Harry cause Jay's descent into mental disorder? How can psychiatrists and clinical psychologists make accurate diagnoses? Once a diagnosis of mental disorder is made, can the individual ever completely recover?

These and other questions are the emphasis in this unit. Mental disorder has fascinated and, on the other hand, haunted us for centuries. At various times in our history those who suffered from these disorders were persecuted as witches, tortured to drive out demons, punished as sinners, jailed as a danger to society, confined to insane asylums, or at best hospitalized for simply being too ill to care for themselves.

Today, psychologists propose that the view of mental disorders as "illnesses" has outlived its usefulness. We should think of mental disorders as either biochemical disturbances or disorders of learning in which the person develops a maladaptive pattern of behavior that is then maintained by the environment. At the same time, we need to recognize that these reactions to stressors in the environment or to the inappropriate learning situations may be genetically preordained; some people may be

more susceptible to disorders than others. Serious disorders are serious problems and not just for the individual who is the patient or client. The impact of mental disorder on the family (just as for Jay's family) and friends deserves our full attention, too. Diagnosis, symptoms, and the implications of the disorders are covered in some of the articles in this section. The following unit, 11, will explore further the concept of treatment of mental disorders.

The first article in this unit offers a general introduction to the concept of mental disorder. In it, David Satcher reveals his agenda for better mental health care in the United States. Mental disorder, he concludes, is more widespread than previously thought. Only an active policy of assisting those who need help can change the status of those with mental disorders in this country.

We turn next to some specific disorders. Depression is one of the most common forms of mental disorder. Depression in its severe form can sometimes lead to suicide. In "The Lowdown on Depression," the author looks at the causes, symptoms, and treatments for clinical depression. Both pharmaceutical and psychological treatments are addressed.

Another common mental affliction is anxiety and fear. Anxiety disorders take several forms—such as panic attacks—that are addressed in the next article. The role of the nervous system in anxiety disorders is also revealed.

An increasingly common disorder is post-traumatic stress disorder. Some individuals were able to recover from the events of September 11, 2001; others were not. An article in the *Harvard Health Letter* explains why this is the case. It also helps the reader identify post-traumatic stress disorder from reactions to normal stress. The article would be incomplete if it did not also include advice about how to cope with either type of stress—everyday or traumatic.

The final disorder covered in this unit is the one from which Jay suffered—schizophrenia. Sharon Begley in her article "The Schizophrenic Mind" examines the causes, symptoms, and treatments for this baffling and debilitating disorder.

MENTAL HEALTH GETS NOTICED

The First-Ever Surgeon General's Report on Mental Health

BY DAVID SATCHER, M.D., PH.D., UNITED STATES SURGEON GENERAL

I am pleased to issue the first-ever Surgeon General's Report on Mental Health. In doing so, I am alerting the American people that mental illness is a critical public health problem that must be addressed immediately. As a society, we assign a high priority to disease prevention and health promotion; so, too, must we ensure that mental health and the prevention of mental disorders share that priority.

Mental illness is the second leading cause of disability in major market economies such as the United States, with mental disorders collectively accounting for more than 15% of all disabilities. Mental disorders—depression, schizophrenia, eating disorders, depressive (bipolar) illness, anxiety disorders, attention deficit hyperactivity disorder and Alzheimer's disease, to name a few—are as disabling and serious as cancer and heart disease in terms of premature death and lost productivity.

Few Americans are untouched by mental illness, whether it occurs within one's family or among neighbors, coworkers or members of the community. In fact, in any one year, one in five Americans—including children, adolescents, adults and the elderly—experience a mental disorder. Unfortunately, over half of those with severe mental illness do not seek treatment. This is mostly due to some very real barriers to access, foremost among them the stigma that people attach to mental illness and the lack of parity between insurance coverage for mental health services and other health care services.

Over the past 25 years, there has been a scientific revolution in the fields of mental health and mental illness that has helped remove the stigma. The brain has emerged as the central focus for studies of mental health and mental illness, with emphasis on the activities that underlie our abilities to feel, learn, remember and, when brain activity goes awry, experience mental health problems or a mental illness. We now know that not only do the workings of the brain affect behavior, emotions and memory, but that experience, emotion and behavior also affect the workings of the brain

As information about the brain accumulates, the challenge then becomes to apply this new knowledge to clinical practice.

Today, mental disorders can be correctly diagnosed and, for the most part, treated with medications or short-term

GREG GIANNINI

I'd describe myself as a regular person.... Most of the time I like taking walks around my house. Before I was living in a group home out in the country and there weren't that many stores or streets to walk on. I like walking to 7-Eleven and Mr. D's fast food.

ROSE CLARK

Sometimes I wake up so sick, but then I go to work and feel better. Being with animals makes me feel 100% better. Does that sound funny?

I love my boss. He's crazy. When he does surgery he dances, does the jitterbug. Sometimes I go into surgery with him to make sure all the animals are lying down straight and not awake. Mostly my responsibilities are taking care of the cages and general cleaning.

I've been with this program for four years. Since then I've gone back to school and gotten a job. I live in my own apartment, got two cats, and have a checking and savings account.

psychotherapy, or with a combination of approaches. The single most explicit recommendation I make in my report is to seek help if you have a mental health problem or think you have symptoms of a mental disorder. It is my firm conviction that mental health is indispensable to personal well-being and balanced living. Overall quality of life is tremendously improved when a mental disorder is diagnosed early and treated appropriately.

My report presents an in-depth look at mental health services in the U.S. and at the scientific research that supports treatment interventions for people with mental disorders. Summarized briefly below, it attempts to describe trends in the mental health field; explore mental health across the human life span; examine the organization and financing of mental health services; and recommend courses of action to further improve the quality and availability of mental health services for all Americans. The report's conclusions are based on a review of more than 3,000 research articles and other materials, including first person accounts from people who have experienced mental disorders.

A Vision for the Future

I cannot emphasize enough the principal recommendation of my report: Seek help if you think you have a mental health problem or symptoms of a mental disorder. But because stigma and substantial gaps in the accessibility to state-of-the-art mental health services keep many from seeking help, I offer the nation the following additional recommendations, which are intended to overcome some of these barriers:

- **Continue to Build the Science Base:** As scientific progress propels us into the next century, there should be a special effort to address pronounced gaps in current knowledge, including the urgent need for research relating to mental health promotion and illness prevention.
- **Overcome Stigma:** An emerging consumer and family movement has, through vigorous advocacy, sought to overcome stigma and prevent discrimination against people with mental illness. Powerful and pervasive, stigma prevents people from acknowledging their mental health problems and disclosing them to others. To improve access

to care, stigma must no longer be tolerated. Research and more effective treatments will help move this country toward care and support of the ill—and away from blame and stigma.

- **Improve Public Awareness of Effective Treatments:** Mental health treatments have improved by leaps and bounds over the past 25 years, but those treatments do no good unless people are aware they exist and seek them out. There are effective treatments for virtually every mental disorder. For more information on how to take advantage of them, call (877) MHEALTH.
- **Ensure the Supply of Mental Health Services and Providers:** Currently, there is a shortage of mental health professionals serving children and adolescents, elderly people with serious mental disorders and those who suffer from mental illness-related substance abuse. There is also a shortage of specialists with expertise in cognitive behavioral therapy and interpersonal therapy—two forms of psychotherapy that have proven effective for many types of mental health problems.
- **Ensure Delivery of State-of-the-Art Treatments:** A wide variety of effective, community-based services—carefully refined through years of research—exist for even the most severe mental illnesses, but they are not yet widely available in community settings. We need to ensure that mental health services are as universally accessible as other health services in the continuously changing health care delivery system. We must speed the transfer of new information from the research setting into the service delivery setting.
- **Tailor Treatment to Individuals, Acknowledging Age, Gender, Race and Culture:** To be optimally effective, diagnosis and treatment of mental illness must be attentive to these factors. Patients often prefer to be treated by mental health professionals who are of the same racial and ethnic background, a fact that underscores the need to train more minorities in the mental health professions.
- **Facilitate Entry into Treatment:** Access to mental health services

can be improved immediately if we enhance the abilities of primary care providers, public schools, the child welfare system and others to help people with mental health problems seek treatment. In addition, ensuring ready access to appropriate services for people with severe mental disorders promises to significantly reduce the need for involuntary care, which is sometimes required in order to prevent behavior that could be harmful to oneself or others.

- **Reduce Financial Barriers to Treatment:** Equality or parity between mental health coverage and other health coverage is an affordable and effective way to decrease the number of ill people who are not receiving proper treatment.

TONY RIVERA

When I first came to the Pastimes Cafe & Antiques I told them that it reminds me of the coffee shops in Baltimore and Maryland. They laughed and we've been friends for two years. They know my name when I walk in. I used to know all their names now and I can't remember. They make me feel comfortable, like I'm not bothering anybody.

KATHY MOLYNEAUX

I didn't know I was depressed until after college. I just thought everyone felt the same way I did. I had problems sleeping, feeling down, overwhelmed, worried and not happy. My graduation from DePaul University in 1983 was a good day. After college, I worked successfully as a nurse for 13 years. I felt like I could relate to the patients because I had been there myself.

The U.S. system is extremely complex; it is a hybrid system that serves many people well, but often seems fragmented and inaccessible to those with the most extensive problems and fewest financial resources. Critical gaps exist between those who need services and those who receive them; only about 40% of those with severe disorders use any services at all.

Although research shows little direct evidence of problems with quality in mental health service programs, there are signs that programs could be better implemented, especially ones that serve children and people with serious impairment. While an array of quality monitoring and improvement methods have been developed, incentives to improve conditions lag behind incentives to reduce costs.

These inequities in insurance coverage for mental and physical health care have prompted 27 states to adopt legislation requiring parity, and compelled President Clinton to order the Federal Employees Health Benefits Program to provide parity for federal employees by the year 2001. Some localized attempts at creating parity so far have resulted in better mental health service access at negligible cost increases for managed care organizations.

Issues relating to mental health and mental illness have been overlooked or ignored in this country too often and for too long. While we cannot change the past, I am convinced that we can shape a better future.

SHERYL CAUDLE

My family at first didn't understand why I was so depressed. My dad kept asking me why couldn't I be happy?... I never thought I'd be able to work again because of my illness. I've had to quit other jobs in the past, but I don't want to quit cleaning the Roxy [a local movie theater]; I want to have an apartment someday and a job in the community. Both of these things would be special to me because it would mean I've come a long way.

PATTI REID

I used to live in a house with my family, but I have a rare disorder that makes me think about the past. In 1992, I got this disorder and I couldn't drive my car anymore. I miss driving the most. My two big battles are smiling and taking my medications. Both of these are very hard.

David Satcher, M.D., Ph.D., is the 16th surgeon general of the United States. He is also Assistant Secretary for Health, advising the Secretary on public health matters and directing the Office of Public Health and Science.

The Lowdown on Depression

Thirty-three-year-old Saritza Velilla of Frisco, Tex., was just 7 years old when she first started feeling worthless. As the years went by, these feelings intensified and she became more withdrawn from social activities. But it wasn't until 1996 that Velilla was diagnosed with clinical depression, and only recently that she found relief from her ongoing symptoms.

By Carol Lewis

"I always felt outside the mainstream," she remembers. "I could feel alone in a roomful of people." Velilla grew up for the most part with a great void in what she calls "that important emotional need" for parental care, affection, or attention. "Without those bonds in place," she says, "I did not develop emotionally and had trouble relating to others."

Velilla is not alone in grappling with the consequences of mental illness. An estimated 22 percent of Americans 18 and older—about 1 in 5 adults—have a diagnosable mental disorder in any given year, according to the National Institute of Mental Health (NIMH). To complicate matters, many people struggle with more than one mental disorder at a time. The pain and suffering that goes along with these illnesses is felt not only by those who have a disorder, but also by the people who care about them.

Family members often watch their loved ones cycle in and out of treatment, on and off medications, and, in some cases, in and out of jail. Pete Earley of Fairfax, Va., says that if medical experts had responded to his son's mental condition as quickly as law enforcement reacted to his criminal behavior, his son would be receiving therapy instead of facing a possible prison term.

Earley's son has bipolar disorder—also called manic-depressive illness—a form of mental illness different from Velilla's that can cause extreme shifts in mood, energy and functioning. Earley says his son is frequently de-

lusional, paranoid, and psychotic. If he discontinues his medications, he exhibits bizarre, irrational behavior.

According to the NIMH, most people with a depressive illness do not get the help they need, although the great majority—even those whose depression is severe—can be helped. Without treatment, the symptoms of depression can last for weeks, months, or even years. With treatment, many people can find relief from their symptoms and lead a normal, healthy life.

More Than a Mood Swing

Clinical depression, one of the more common categories of mental illnesses, is a serious brain disorder that affects the way nearly 19 million American adults feel, think, and interact. In contrast to the normal emotional experiences of sadness, loss, or passing mood states, clinical depression is extreme and persistent and can interfere significantly with a person's ability to function. People with depression cannot merely "pull themselves together" and get better. Depression cannot be willed or wished away.

There are three main types of clinical depression: major depressive disorder; dysthymic disorder; and bipolar depression, the depressed phase of bipolar disorder. Within these types are variations in the number of associated mental symptoms, and their severity and persistence.

A person experiencing major depressive disorder suffers from, among other symptoms, a depressed mood or loss of interest in normal activities that lasts most of the day, nearly every day, for at least two weeks. Such episodes may occur only once, but more commonly occur several times in a lifetime.

Unlike major depressive disorder, dysthymic disorder—a chronic but less severe type—doesn't strike in episodes, but is instead characterized by milder, persistent symptoms that may last for years. Although it usually doesn't interfere with everyday tasks, people with this milder form of depression rarely feel like they are functioning at their full capacities.

Bipolar disorder cycles between episodes of major depression, similar to those seen in major depressive disorder, and highs known as mania. In a manic phase, a person might act on delusional grand schemes that could range from unwise business decisions to romantic sprees. Mania left untreated may deteriorate into a psychotic state.

For Earley, one of his son's recent psychotic episodes played out in a burglary charge. The pair was headed home from a local hospital where doctors had refused to treat him involuntarily. Earley's son suddenly leapt from their moving car, ran away, and broke into a stranger's house. After throwing a potted plant through a glass door and smashing some furniture, he then ran upstairs and drew himself a bubble bath. Earley says his son has never been in trouble with the law before and that he did not take anything from the house.

It's Not 'All In The Head'

Because the symptoms, course of illness, and response to treatment vary so much among people with depression, doctors believe that depression may have a number of complex and interacting causes.

Some factors include another medical illness, losing a loved one, stressful life events, and drug or alcohol abuse. Any of these factors also may contribute to recurrent major depressive episodes.

Modern brain imaging technologies are revealing that neural circuits responsible for the regulation of moods, thinking, sleep, appetite, and behavior fail to function properly in people with depression. Imaging studies also indicate that critical neurotransmitters—chemicals used by nerve cells to communicate—are out of balance.

Moreover, genetics research suggests that vulnerability to depression results from the influence of multiple genes acting together with environmental factors. The hormonal system that regulates the body's response to stress also is overactive in many depressed people.

Research conducted in the fields of psychiatry, behavioral science, neuroscience, biology, and genetics, including studies of twins, lead scientists to believe that the risk of developing mental illness increases if another family member is similarly affected, suggesting a hereditary component.

This was the case for 34-year-old Susan Poage of Thornton, Colo. She recently was diagnosed with clinical depression, like her mother before her. Poage recalls a dismal childhood.

"There was a lot of silent crying, promiscuity, alcohol and drugs," she says, "and I don't remember having any good times." With the help of her doctor and a five-year struggle with drug therapy, Poage today is managing her symptoms of depression, including thoughts of suicide.

Despite strong evidence for genetic susceptibility, scientists still don't know the number of genes that might be involved in making someone more likely to develop a mental disorder. Identification of these genes has proved to be extremely difficult.

Similarly, the role of environmental effects in the development of mental illness remains largely unknown.

Diagnosing Depression

Medical professionals generally base a diagnosis of mental illness on the presence of certain symptoms listed in the 4th edition of the American Psychiatric Association's *Diagnostic and Statistical Manual of Mental Disorders* (DSM-IV). The symptoms listed for a major depressive episode include:

- sadness
- loss of interest or pleasure in activities once enjoyed
- change in appetite or weight
- difficulty sleeping or oversleeping
- physical slowing or agitation
- energy loss
- feelings of worthlessness or inappropriate guilt
- difficulty thinking or concentrating
- recurrent thoughts of death or suicide.

A person is clinically depressed if he or she has five or more of these symptoms and has not been functioning normally for most days during the same two-week period.

Dysthymic disorder is diagnosed when depressed mood persists for at least two years (one year in children) and is accompanied by at least two other symptoms of depression.

The episodes of depression that occur in people with bipolar disorder alternate with mania, which is characterized by abnormally and persistently elevated mood or irritability. Symptoms of mania include overly inflated self-esteem, decreased need for sleep, increased talkativeness, racing thoughts, distractibility, physical agitation, and excessive risk-taking. Because bipolar disorder requires different treatment than major depression or dysthymia, obtaining an accurate diagnosis is extremely important.

Treating Depression

Finding the right treatment for depression can be as difficult as convincing someone that they need help. However, according to the NIMH, clinical depression is one of the most treatable of all medical illnesses.

Classification of Antidepressant Drugs

Function	Antidepressant
Monoamine oxidase inhibitor	Marplan (isocarboxazid) Nardil (phenelzine) Parnate (tranylcypromine)
Norepinephrine transport blocker	Asendin (amoxapine) Norpramin Pertofrane (desipramine) Adapin Sinequan (doxepin) Ludiomil (maprotiline) Aventyl Pamelor (nortriptyline) Vivactil (protriptyline)
Serotonin transport blocker (selective serotonin reuptake inhibitor)	Elavil (amitriptyline) Celexa (citalopram) Anafranil (clomipramine)* Prozac (fluoxetine) Luvox (fluvoxamine) Tofranil (imipramine) Paxil (paroxetine) Zoloft (sertraline) Surmontil (trimipramine) Effexor (venlafaxine)
Dopamine transport blocker	Wellbutrin (bupropion)
Serotonin 5-HT-2A receptor blocker	Remeron (mirtazapine) Serzone (nefazodone) Desyrel (trazodone)

*Approved for use in the U.S. only for the treatment of obsessive-compulsive disorder

Source: Mayo Clinic

Currently, a broad range of antidepressant drugs is available. Although their actions are not well understood, they all work to influence the levels of certain neurotransmitters in the brain. The type of action and drug names are listed in the above chart.

Because it is currently against the law in Virginia, where the Earleys live, to force someone into medical treatment, Earley must rely on his son's willingness to take his medicines. Typically, bipolar patients periodically stop taking their medications.

"Part of my son's illness," Earley explains, "is believing he is perfectly fine when he goes off his medicines.

"Even though it was obvious that my son was clearly out of his mind, the law still insisted that he was capable of deciding whether or not he needed treatment," says Earley. "In these cases, you are asking an irrational person to make a rational decision. It's like expecting a person with a broken leg to run a marathon."

Today, most people with depression can be treated successfully with antidepressant medications, "talk" therapy (psychotherapy), or a combination of the two.

(See "Classification of Antidepressants.") Experts agree that successful treatment also hinges on early intervention. And early treatment increases the likelihood of preventing serious recurrences.

Drug Treatment

Existing antidepressant drugs are known to influence the functioning primarily of either or both of two neurotransmitters in the brain—serotonin and norepinephrine. Older medications—tricyclic antidepressants (TCAs) and monoamine oxidase inhibitors (MAOIs)—affect the activity of both of these neurotransmitters simultaneously. Their disadvantage is that they can be difficult to tolerate due to significant side effects, or, in the case of MAOIs, dietary and medication restrictions.

Newer medications, such as the selective serotonin re-uptake inhibitors (SSRIs), have fewer side effects than the older drugs, making it easier for people, including older adults, to adhere to treatment. Both generations of medications are effective in relieving depression, although some people will respond to one type of drug, but not another.

"Clinicians tell us that different drugs seem to work for different people," says Thomas Laughren, M.D., team leader for the review of psychiatric drugs in the Food and Drug Administration's Division of Neuropharmacological Drug Products. "And it's difficult to predict which people will respond to which drug or who will experience what side effects." So, Laughren says, it may take more than one try to find the appropriate medication. "Now that we've made a distinction between different depression subtypes, this seems to have stimulated additional drug research. Drug companies are also conducting more longer-term studies in depression, and this is important since depression tends to be a chronic illness."

Although some improvement may be seen in the first few weeks, antidepressants usually must be taken regularly for three to four weeks (and sometimes longer) before full therapeutic benefits occur. "If we had a better understanding of the biological basis for depression, it would help in the discovery of newer antidepressants that hopefully would work faster and better," says Laughren. "Unfortunately we do not really understand the mechanism for the antidepressant drugs."

The medication most often used to treat bipolar disorder is lithium (Eskalith, Lithane, Lithobid, Cibalith-S). Lithium evens out mood swings in both directions—from mania to depression, and depression to mania. It is used not just for manic attacks or flare-ups of the illness, but also as an ongoing maintenance treatment for bipolar disorder.

Non-Drug Treatments

In psychotherapy, also called "talk therapy," a person discusses with a mental health professional the feelings, thoughts and behaviors that seem to cause difficulty. The goal of psychotherapy is to help people understand and manage their problems so that they can function better.

"Finding a therapist who believes in recovery is the first step," says Velilla. "Someone who can teach you to think differently and learn new behaviors." She believes that her feelings of neglect, coupled with the eventual divorce of her parents, ultimately triggered many of her bouts with depression. Her own divorce some years later, she says, only heightened her feelings of worthlessness. "My therapist finally put a name to what I'd been feeling since I was 7 years old."

Psychotherapy can help people with bipolar disorder, and their families, identify early warning signs and manage emotional stress, which may help prevent a bipolar episode.

Richard O'Connor, Ph.D., a psychotherapist in Canaan, Conn., and the author of several books on depression, believes that people need to help themselves "break the bad habits in their lives that set them up for depression." Waking up and going to sleep at the same time each day, for example, might help those people prone to bouts of insomnia due to irregular sleep patterns.

A depression sufferer himself, O'Connor came to this belief after many of the people he was treating "thought it was too late for them to help themselves, and they wanted us to pick up the pieces," he says. "People are responsible for their own recovery. They must learn to take care of themselves and structure their lives so that they're less likely to trigger an episode."

When people are unresponsive to psychotherapy and medications, or the combination of the two works too slowly to relieve severe symptoms, such as psychosis or recurring thoughts of suicide, electroconvulsive therapy (ECT) may be considered. Electrodes are placed at precise locations on the head to deliver electrical impulses. The stimulation causes a 30-second seizure within the brain; however, the person does not consciously feel the stimulus. Three sessions per week typically are given for full therapeutic benefit. Like antidepressants, ECT is believed to affect the chemical balance of the brain's neurotransmitters.

Interest is rapidly growing as well in the use of herbs for treating depression. But, according to a study published in the April 10, 2002, issue of the *Journal of the American Medical Association*, an extract of the popular herb St. John's wort was no more effective for treating major depression of moderate severity than an inactive pill (placebo). The multi-site trial, involving 340 people, also compared the FDA-approved antidepressant drug Zoloft (sertraline) to a placebo as a way to measure how sensitive the trial was to detecting antidepressant effects. Since Zoloft was also found to be no different than the placebo in that study, Laughren says it can best be thought of as a "failed study" that isn't informative about the antidepressant effectiveness of St. John's wort.

The NIMH cautions people who think they may be depressed not to use dietary supplements without first being evaluated by a psychiatrist or examined by a physician. The risks, according to the institute, can outweigh any potential benefits.

Following Prescribed Treatment

Antidepressant drugs are not considered to be candidates for abuse. However, as is the case with any type of medication, use of antidepressants must be carefully monitored to make sure the correct dosage is being given. Care also is needed when antidepressants are discontinued.

As is often seen with antibiotics, people may be tempted to stop antidepressants too soon. They may feel better and think they no longer need the medication, or they may believe the medication isn't working. But quickly stopping certain antidepressants is linked to side effects ranging from flu-like symptoms to sensory disturbances. As a result, new labeling, as specified by the FDA, recommends that patients taper off these medications slowly. If a person encounters problems going off a drug, he or she is advised to consult a physician rather than reduce dosage without supervision.

After spending 11 days in the hospital following the burglary, Earley's son was released to his parents. He is currently awaiting trial on two counts of felony breaking and entering and destruction of property. He is attending a 15-week treatment program that includes routine medications, and he now has a job and hopes to return to college to finish his education.

"He doesn't want to be delusional," says Earley. "He's embarrassed and ashamed about what happened. But now he's got no choice but to admit that he is sick and always will be. The question is, will that be enough to keep him taking his medications?"

When a patient and the health-care provider think that medication can be discontinued or scaled back, they will discuss how best to ease off the medication gradually.

The NIMH says it is important to keep taking prescribed medication until it has had a chance to work, even though side effects may appear before antidepressant activity does.

As for Velilla, "I'm still not taking any medication," she says, "but I think I may not need it after all. I continue to read books that will inspire and give me tools to deal with life. I feel like I am making progress in counseling and in all areas of my life and that makes me feel pretty good and optimistic about recovering."

Where to Get More Information:

National Institute of Mental Health (NIMH)
Public Inquiries
6001 Executive Blvd., Rm. 8184,
MSC 9663 Bethesda, MD 20892-9663
301-443-4513
www.nimh.nih.gov

National Foundation for Depressive Illness, Inc.
PO Box 2257 New York, NY 10116
1-800-239-1265
www.depression.org

National Mental Health Association (NMHA)
2001 N. Beauregard St., 12th Floor
Alexandria, VA 22311
1-800-969-NMHA (1-800-969-6642) TTY: 1-800-443-5959
www.nmha.org

From *FDA Consumer*, January/February 2003, pp. 29-33. © 2003 by FDA Consumer, the magazine of the U.S. Food and Drug Administration.

THE SCIENCE OF ANXIETY

WHY DO WE WORRY OURSELVES SICK? BECAUSE THE BRAIN IS HARDWIRED FOR FEAR, AND SOMETIMES IT SHORT-CIRCUITS

By CHRISTINE GORMAN

IT'S 4 A.M., AND YOU'RE WIDE AWAKE—PALMS SWEATY, HEART racing. You're worried about your kids. Your aging parents. Your 401(k). Your health. Your sex life. Breathing evenly beside you, your spouse is oblivious. Doesn't he—or she—see the dangers that lurk in every shadow? He must not. Otherwise, how could he, with all that's going on in the world, have talked so calmly at dinner last night about flying to Florida for a vacation?

How is it that two people facing the same circumstances can react so differently? Why are some folks buffeted by the vicissitudes of life while others glide through them with grace and calm? Are some of us just born more nervous than others? And if you're one of them, is there anything you can do about it?

The key to these questions is the emotional response we call anxiety. Unlike hunger or thirst, which build and dissipate in the immediate present, anxiety is the sort of feeling that sneaks up on you from the day after tomorrow. It's supposed to keep you from feeling too safe. Without it, few of us would survive.

All animals, especially the small, scurrying kind, appear to feel anxiety. Humans have felt it since the days they shared the planet with saber-toothed tigers. (Notice which species is still around to tell the tale.) But we live in a particularly anxious age. The initial shock of Sept. 11 has worn off, and the fear has lifted, but millions of Americans continue to share a kind of generalized mass anxiety. A recent TIME/CNN poll found that eight months after the event, nearly two-thirds of Americans think about the terror attacks at least several times a week. And it doesn't take much for all the old fears to come rushing back. What was surprising about the recent drumbeat of terror warnings was how quickly it triggered the anxiety so many of us thought we had put behind us.

This is one of the mysteries of anxiety. While it is a normal response to physical danger—and can be a useful tool for focusing the mind when there's a deadline looming—anxiety becomes a problem when it persists too long beyond the immediate threat. Sometimes there's an obvious cause, as with the shell-shocked soldiers of World War I or the terror-scarred civilians of the World Trade Center collapse. Other times, we don't know why we can't stop worrying.

GLOSSARY

STRESS Any external stimulus, from threatening words to the sound of a gunshot, that the brain interprets as dangerous

FEAR The short-term physiological response produced by both the brain and the body in response to stress

ANXIETY A sense of apprehension that shares many of the same symptoms as fear but builds more slowly and lingers longer

DEPRESSION Prolonged sadness that results in a blunting of emotions and a sense of futility; often more serious when accompanied by anxiety disorder

There is certainly a lot of anxiety going around. Anxiety disorder—which is what health experts call any anxiety that persists to the point that it interferes with one's life—is the most common mental illness in the U.S. In its various forms, ranging from very specific phobias to generalized anxiety disorder, it afflicts 19 million Americans (see "Are You Too Anxious?").

And yet, according to a survey published last January by researchers from UCLA, less than 25% of Americans with anxiety disorders receive any kind of treatment for their condition. "If mental health is the stepchild of the health-care system," says Jerilyn Ross, president of the Anxiety Disorders Association of America, "then anxiety is the stepchild of the stepchild."

Sigmund Freud was fascinated with anxiety and recognized early on that there is more than one kind. He identified two major forms of anxiety: one more biological in nature and the other more dependent on psychological factors. Unfortunately, his followers were so obsessed with his ideas about sex drives and unresolved conflicts that studies of the physical basis of anxiety languished.

In recent years, however, researchers have made significant progress in nailing down the underlying science of anxiety. In just the past decade, they have come to appreciate that whatever the factors that trigger anxiety, it grows out of a response that is hardwired in our brains. They have learned, among other things:

ARE YOU TOO ANXIOUS?

Everybody feels a bit of anxiety from time to time, but a clinical anxiety disorder is a different matter. If you suspect you may be suffering from one, you should consult a professional for a diagnosis. The psychological diagnostic manual lists 12 anxiety conditions. Here are the signs of five of the most common ones:

PANIC DISORDER

WHAT IT IS: Recurrent, unexpected attacks of acute anxiety, peaking within 10 minutes. Such panic may occur in a familiar situation, such as a crowded elevator
WHAT IT ISN'T: Occasional episodes of extreme anxiety in response to a real threat
WHAT TO LOOK FOR: Palpitations; chest pains, sweating, chills or hot flushes; trembling; shortness of breath or choking; nausea; light-headedness or feeling of unreality; fear of losing control or dying
BOTTOM LINE: Four or more of these symptoms in at least two discrete episodes could spell trouble

SPECIFIC PHOBIA

WHAT IT IS: Consuming fear of a specific object or situation, often accompanied by extreme anxiety symptoms
WHAT IT ISN'T: Powerful aversion to certain places or things
WHAT TO LOOK FOR:
- Do you come up with elaborate ways to avoid the object or situation?
- Do you dread the next possible encounter?
- Are you aware that the fear is excessive but you are unable to control it?
- Does merely thinking about the thing you fear make you anxious?

BOTTOM LINE: Don't worry if you just plain hate, say, snakes or crowds or heights. The key is how powerful your feelings are— and how you handle them

OBSESSIVE-COMPULSIVE DISORDER

WHAT IT IS: A preoccupation with specific thoughts, images or impulses, accompanied by elaborate and sometimes bizarre rituals
WHAT IT ISN'T: Fastidious—even idiosyncratic—behavior that does not significantly interfere with your quality of life
WHAT TO LOOK FOR: Are the obsessive thoughts persistent and intrusive?
- Do you expend a lot of energy suppressing the thoughts, usually unsuccessfully?
- Are you generally aware that the thoughts are irrational?

- Is the anxiety temporarily eased by a repetitive ritual such as hand washing or a thought ritual such as praying?
- Are the rituals time consuming?

BOTTOM LINE: Some researchers question whether OCD is a genuine anxiety disorder. Whatever it is, it does respond to treatment—provided you seek help

POST-TRAUMATIC STRESS DISORDER

WHAT IT IS: Repeated, anxious reliving of a horrifying event over an extended period of time
WHAT IT ISN'T: Anxiety following a trauma that fades steadily over the course of a month or so
WHAT TO LOOK FOR: After witnessing, experiencing or hearing about an event that caused or threatened to cause serious injury, do you:
- Have recurrent recollections or dreams about the experience?
- Feel emotionally or physically as if the event were still occurring?
- Experience intense anxiety when something reminds you of the event?
- Try to avoid thoughts, feelings, activities or places associated with the event?
- Have difficulty recalling details of the event?
- Experience anxiety symptoms such as irritability, jumpiness, difficulty sleeping, feelings of detachment from others, diminished interest in things, feelings that your future is in some way limited?

BOTTOM LINE: Sometimes, PTSD will not appear until six months after the event. Seek help whenever symptoms occur

GENERALIZED ANXIETY DISORDER

WHAT IT IS: Excessive anxiety or worry, occurring more days than not for six months
WHAT IT ISN'T: Occasional serious worry that doesn't markedly diminish quality of life
WHAT TO LOOK FOR: Restlessness; difficulty concentrating or sleeping; irritability; fatigue; muscle tension
BOTTOM LINE: If you have three or more symptoms for the required six months, the diagnosis may fit

—*By Jeffrey Kluger*

- There is a genetic component to anxiety; some people seem to be born worriers.
- Brain scans can reveal differences in the way patients who suffer from anxiety disorders respond to danger signals.
- Due to a shortcut in our brain's information-processing system, we can respond to threats before we become aware of them.
- The root of an anxiety disorder may not be the threat that triggers it but a breakdown in the mechanism that keeps the anxiety response from careening out of control.

Before we delve into the latest research, let's define a few terms. Though we all have our own intuitive sense of what the words stress and fear mean, scientists use these words in very specific ways. For them, stress is an external stimulus that signals danger, often by causing pain. Fear is the short-term response such stresses produce in men, women or lab rats. Anxiety has a lot of the same symptoms as fear, but it's a feeling that lingers long after the stress has lifted and the threat has passed.

In general, science has a hard time pinning down emotions because they are by nature so slippery and subjective. You can't

THE ANATOMY OF ANXIETY

WHAT TRIGGERS IT...

When the senses pick up a threat—a loud noise, a scary sight, a creepy feeling—the information takes two different routes through the brain

.... AND HOW THE BODY RESPONDS

By putting the brain on alert, the amygdala triggers a series of changes in brain chemicals and hormones that puts the entire body in anxiety mode

A THE SHORTCUT

When startled, the brain automatically engages an emergecy hot line to its fear center, the amygdala. Once activated, the amygdala sends the equivalent of an all-points bulletin that alerts other brain structures. The result is the classic fear response: sweaty palms, rapid heartbeat, increased blood pressure and a burst of adrenaline. All this happens before the mind is conscious of having smelled or touched anything. Before you know why you're afraid, you are

B THE HIGH ROAD

Only after the fear response is activated does the conscious mind kick into gear. Some sensory information, rather than traveling directly to the amygdala, takes a more circuitous route, stopping first at the thalamus— the processing hub for sensory cues—and then the cortex—the outer layer of brain cells. The cortex analyzes the raw data streaming in through the senses and decides whether they require a fear response. If they do, the cortex signals the amygdala, and the body stays on alert

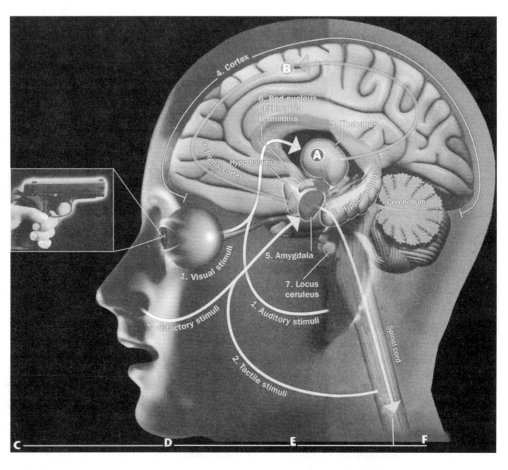

C Stress-Hormone Boost

Responding to signals from the hypothalamus and pituitary gland, the adrenal glands pump out high levels of the stress hormone cortisol. Too much cortisol shortcircuits the cells in the hippocampus, making it difficult to organize the memory of a trauma or stressful experience. Memories lose their context and become fragmented

D Racing Heartbeat

The body's sympathetic nervous system, responsible for heart rate and breathing, shifts into overdrive. The heart beats faster, blood pressure rises and the lungs hyperventilate. sweat increases, and even the nerve endings on the skin tingle into action, creating goose bumps

E Fight, Flight or Fright

The senses become hyperalert, drinking in every detail of the surroundings and looking for potential new threats. Adrenaline shoots to the muscles, preparing the body to fight or flee

F Digestion shutdown

The brain stops thinking about things that bring pleasure, shifting its focus instead to identifying potential dangers. To ensure that no energy is wasted on digestion, the body will sometimes respond by emptying the digestive tract through involuntary vomiting, urination or defecation

(Continued on following page)

Source: Dennis S. Charney, M.D., National Institute of Mental Health.   TIME Diagram by Joe Lertola.   Text by Alice Park

THE ANATOMY OF ANXIETY

continued

1. Auditory and visual stimuli

Sights and sounds are processed first by the thalamus, which filters the incoming cues and shunts them either directly to the amygdala or to the appropriate parts of the cortex

2. Olfactory and tactile stimuli

Smells and touch sensations bypass the thalamus altogether, taking a shortcut directly to the amygdala. Smells, therefore, often evoke stronger memories or feelings than do sights or sounds

3. Thalamus

The hub for sights and sounds, the thalamus breaks down incoming visual cues by size, shape and color, and auditory cues by volume and dissonance, and then signals the appropriate parts of the cortex

4. Cortex

It gives raw sights and sounds meaning, enabling the brain to become conscious of what it is seeing or hearing. One region, the prefrontal cortex, may be vital to turning off the anxiety response once a threat has passed

5. Amygdala

The emotional core of the brain, the amygdala has the primary role of triggering the fear response. Information that passes through the amygdala is tagged with emotional significance

6. Bed nucleus of the stria terminalis

Unlike the amygdala, which sets off an immediate burst of fear, the BNST perpetuates the fear response, causing the longer-term unease typical of anxiety

7. Locus ceruleus

It receives signals from the amygdala and is responsible for initiating many of the classic anxiety responses: rapid heartbeat, increased blood pressure, sweating and pupil dilation

8. Hippocampus

This is the memory center, vital to storing the raw information coming in from the senses, along with the emotional baggage attached to the data during their trip through the amygdala

ask a rat if it's anxious or depressed. Even most people are as clueless about why they have certain feelings as they are about how their lungs work. But fear is the one aspect of anxiety that's easy to recognize. Rats freeze in place. Humans break out in a

cold sweat. Heartbeats race, and blood pressure rises. That gives scientists something they can control and measure. "You can bring on a sensory stimulus that makes an animal—or human—fearful and study its effects," says Dr. Wayne Drevets of the National Institute of Mental Health (NIMH). "Then you can take the stimulus away and see how the animal calms down."

Indeed, a lot of what researchers have learned about the biology of anxiety comes from scaring rats and then cutting them open. Just as the Russian physiologist Ivan Pavlov showed 100 years ago that you could condition a dog to salivate at the sound of a bell, scientists today have taught rats to fear all kinds of things—from buzzers to lights—by giving them electrical shocks when they hear the buzzer or see the light. The animals quickly learn to fear the stimulus even in the absence of a shock. Then researchers destroy small portions of the rats' brains to see what effect that has on their reactions (an experiment that would be impossible to conduct in humans). By painstakingly matching the damaged areas with changes in behavior, scientists have, bit by bit, created a road map of fear as it travels through the rat's brain.

The journey begins when a rat (we'll get to humans later) feels the stress, in this case an electric shock. The rat's senses immediately send a message to the central portion of its brain, where the stimulus activates two neural pathways. One of these pathways is a relatively long, circuitous route through the cortex, where the brain does its most elaborate and accurate processing of information. The other route is a kind of emergency shortcut that quickly reaches an almond-shaped cluster of cells called the amygdala.

What's special about the amygdala is that it can quickly activate just about every system in the body to fight like the devil or run like crazy. It's not designed to be accurate, just fast. If you have ever gone hiking and been startled by a snake that turned out to be a stick, you can thank your amygdala. Joseph LeDoux, a neuroscientist at New York University, calls it "the hub in a wheel of fear."

But while the amygdala is busy telling the body what to do, it also fires up a nearby curved cluster of neurons called the hippocampus. (A 16th century anatomist named it after the Greek word for seahorse.) The job of the hippocampus is to help the brain learn and form new memories. And not just any memories. The hippocampus allows a rat to remember where it was when it got shocked and what was going on around it at the time. Such contextual learning helps the poor rodent avoid dangerous places in the future. It probably also helps it recognize what situations are likely to be relatively safe.

By this point, the other half of the stress signal has reached the cortex, which confirms that there's a danger present and figures out that it's causing pain. Once the shock has warn off, a part of the brain called the prefrontal cortex sends out an all-clear message and lets the amygdala know that it's O.K. to stand down. At least it's supposed to. It seems that it's harder to turn off a stress response than to turn it on. This makes sense, in terms of survival. After all, it's better to panic unnecessarily than to be too relaxed in the face of life-threatening danger.

Discovering this basic neural circuitry turned out to be a key breakthrough in understanding anxiety. It showed that the anx-

WHAT CAN YOU DO

There are as many ways to relieve anxiety as there are things that make us anxious. The key is to find the way that works for you—and use it

BEHAVIORAL THERAPY

When the brain sets anxiety alarms ringing, our first inclination is to find the off switch. Behavioral scientists take the opposite approach. They want you to get so accustomed to the noise that you don't hear it anymore. The standard behavioral treatment for such anxiety conditions as phobias, obsessive-compulsive disorder (OCD) and panic disorder is to expose patients to a tiny bit of the very thing that causes them anxiety, ratcheting up the exposure over a number of sessions until the brain habituates to the fear. A patient suffering from a blood phobia, for example, might first be shown a picture of a scalpel or syringe, then a real syringe, then a vial of blood and so on up the anxiety ladder until there are no more rungs to climb. There is a risk that if treatment is cut short (before the patient has become inured to the anxiety triggers), the anxious feelings could be exacerbated. But done right, behavioral therapy can bring relief from specific phobias in as little as two or three sessions. Social anxiety takes somewhat longer, and OCD may take a good deal longer still.

COGNITIVE THERAPY

Rather than expect patients to embrace anxiety, cognitive therapists encourage them to use the power of the mind to reason through it. First popularized in the 1980s, cognitive therapy teaches people who are anxious or depressed to reconfigure their view of the world and develop a more realistic perspective on the risks or obstacles they face. Patients suffering from social-anxiety disorder, for example, might see a group of people whispering at a party and assume the gossip is about them. A cognitive therapist would teach them to rethink that assumption. Some behavioral therapists question cognitive techniques, arguing—not without some justification—that a brain that was so receptive to reason wouldn't be all that anxious in the first place. Cognitive therapists dispute that idea, though some have begun incorporating behavior-modification techniques into their treatment.

ANTIDEPRESSANTS

When talk therapy doesn't work—or needs a boost—drugs can help, especially the class of antidepressants called selective serotonin reuptake inhibitors. Prozac is the best known of these drugs, which work by preventing the brain from reabsorbing too much of the neurotransmitter serotonin, leaving more in nerve synapses and thus helping to improve mood. Another SSRI, Paxil, was recently approved by the Food and Drug Administration specifically for the treatment of social-anxiety disorder, though the others seem to work as well. A third, Zoloft, has been approved for OCD and panic disorder. Each formulation of SSRI is subtly different—targeting specific subclasses of serotonin. And side effects—which can include dry mouth, fatigue and sexual dysfunction—will vary from person to person. A new group of antidepressants, known as serotonin-norepinephrine reuptake inhibitors, may be even more effective in treating anxiety disorders than the SSRIs are. As the name implies, SNRIs target a second neurotransmitter called norepinephrine, which is secreted by the adrenal fight-or-flight response—thus actually increasing anxiety symptoms in many situations. However, norepinephrine also helps control emotion and stabilize mood, and, properly manipulated along with serotonin, may be able to do just that for the anxious person.

MINOR TRANQUILIZERS

If the antidepressants have a flaw, it's that they sometimes don't start working for weeks—a lifetime for the acutely anxious. For this reason, many doctors recommend judicious doses of fast-acting relaxants such as the benzodiazepines Xanax, Valium or Klonopin to serve as a temporary bridge until the SSRIs have a chance to kick in. The downside of such drugs is that they can be highly addictive and may merely mask symptoms. For this reason, doctors will prescribe them very carefully and strictly limit refills.

EXERCISE

Before turning to drugs or talk therapy, many people prefer to try to bring their anxiety under control on their own. Unlike most emotional or physical conditions, anxiety disorders respond well to such self-medication—provided you know how to administer the treatment. One of the most effective techniques is simple exercise. It's no secret that a good workout or a brisk walk can take the edge off even the most acute anxiety. Scientists once believed the effect to be due to the release of natural opiates known as endorphins, but new research has called this into question. Regardless, working out regularly—most days of the week, if possible for at least 30 minutes or so—may well help recalibrate the anxious brain.

ALTERNATIVE TREATMENTS

One of the most popular self-treatments is yoga, which is both a form of exercise and a way to quiet the mind by focusing attention on breathing. Indeed, even without yoga, breathing exercises can help quell an anxiety episode, if only by slowing a racing heart and lengthening the short, shallow breaths of a panic attack. Many anxiety sufferers have relief through meditation or massage—even just a 10-min. foot treatment. For those willing to travel a little farther from the mainstream there's aromatherapy (enthusiasts recommend rose and lavender scents), guided imager (a form of directed meditation used with some success by people recovering from cancer and open-heart surgery) and acupuncture.

LIFESTYLE CHANGES

If all else fails, go back to basics and try cleaning up your lifestyle. For starters, you can cut back or eliminate the use of sugar, caffeine, nicotine, alcohol and any recreational drugs you may be taking. Are you eating right and getting enough sleep and leisure time? Finally, if your job or the place you live is making you anxious, you might consider moving to a less stressful environment or finding a different line of work.

—By Jeffrey Kluger. With reporting by Sora Song/New York

iety response isn't necessarily caused by an external threat; rather, it may be traced to a breakdown in the mechanism that signals the brain to stop responding. Just as a car can go out of control due to either a stuck accelerator or failed brakes, it's not always clear which part of the brain is at fault. It may turn out that some anxiety disorders are caused by an overactive amygdala (the accelerator) while others are caused by an underactive prefrontal cortex (call it the brake).

It may also be that an entirely different part of the brain holds the key to understanding anxiety. Michael Davis, a behavioral neuroscientist at Emory University in Atlanta, has spent six years studying a pea-size knot of neurons located near the amygdala with an impossible name: the bed nucleus of the stria terminalis, or BNST. Rats whose BNST has been injected with stress hormones are much jumpier than those that have got a shot in their amygdala. Could the BNST be at the root of all anxiety disorders? The clues are intriguing, but as scientists are so fond of saying, more research is needed.

Of course, what you would really like to know is whether any of the work done in rats applies to humans. Clearly researchers can't go around performing brain surgery on the amygdalas of living patients to see if it affects their anxiety levels. But the fascinating case of a woman known only by her research number, SM046, suggests that when it comes to fear, rodents and hominids really aren't so different.

Owing to an unusual brain disorder, SM046 has a defective amygdala. As a result, her behavior is abnormal in a very particular way. When scientists at the University of Iowa show SM046 pictures of a series of faces, she has no trouble picking out those that are happy, sad or angry. But if the face is displaying fear, she cannot recognize the feeling. She identifies it as a face expressing some intense emotion, but that is all. Her unusual condition strongly suggests that even in *Homo sapiens*, fear takes hold in the amygdala.

But studying brain-damaged patients can teach scientists only so much. They would also like to know how anxiety works in normal, intact brains. For this, brain scans have proved invaluable.

For years, doctors have used CAT scans and MRIs to help them diagnose strokes, brain tumors and other neurological conditions. But as the technology has become more sophisticated, researchers have started to employ it to tease out some of the subtle changes associated with mental illness. "We're not yet able to use these scans in a diagnostic way," says Dr. David Silbersweig of the Weill Cornell Medical College in New York City. "But we're getting pretty specific about the areas of the brain that are implicated in a number of psychiatric disorders."

One type of brain scan helps identify structures that are the wrong size or shape. Two years ago, researchers at the University of Pittsburgh showed that the amygdalas of a group of overanxious young children were, on average, much larger than those of their unaffected peers. Perhaps they just had more fear circuits to contend with? Neuroscientists are tempted to say yes, but they admit the conclusion is pretty speculative. Another group of researchers found that patients with post-traumatic stress disorder had a smaller hippocampus than normal. Perhaps their stressful experiences had somehow interfered with the hippocampus' ability to make new memories and, just as important, forget the old ones? Again, no one knows for sure.

Another type of brain scan tells scientists which brain cells are using the most oxygen or soaking up the most nutrients. The idea, explains Dr. Scott Rauch of Massachusetts General Hospital, is that any area that seems more active than usual while someone is anxious may play an important role in making the person that way. Rauch's team has spent the past eight years scanning groups of combat veterans, some with post-traumatic stress disorder and some without, to see which areas of the brain light up when they hear tapes recounting their most troubling memories. So far, the signals in the amygdala appear to be more active in those with PTSD than in those without. In addition, signals to the prefrontal cortex of PTSD subjects seem to be weaker than in those without the disorder. Perhaps this explains why the patients still feel threatened even when they are perfectly safe.

The next step, Rauch says, is to scan groups of people who are likely to be thrust into dangerous situations—fire fighters, say, or police officers. Then it may be possible to determine if any changes in their brains are the result of traumatic situations or if the changes predate them. Either is plausible. The stress of surviving a building collapse, for example, could turn a normal amygdala into an overactive one. Or an already overactive amygdala may overwhelm the brain in the wake of a disaster.

Eventually, researchers would like to learn what role our genes, as opposed to our environment, play in the development of anxiety. "It has been known for some time that these disorders run in families," says Kenneth Kendler, a psychiatric geneticist at Virginia Commonwealth University in Richmond, Va. "So the next logical question is the nature-nurture issue." In other words, are anxious people born that way, or do they become anxious as a result of their life experiences?

Kendler and his colleagues approached the question by studying groups of identical twins, who share virtually all their genes, and fraternal twins, who, like any other siblings, share only some of them. What Kendler's group found was that both identical twins were somewhat more likely than both fraternal twins to suffer from generalized anxiety disorder, phobias or panic attacks. (The researchers have not yet studied twins with post-traumatic stress disorder or obsessive-compulsive disorder.)

The correlation isn't 100%, however. "Most of the heritability is in the range of 30% to 40%," Kendler says. That's a fairly moderate genetic impact, he notes, akin to the chances that you will have the same cholesterol count as your parents. "Your genes set your general vulnerability," he concludes. "You can be a low-vulnerable, intermediate-vulnerable or a high-vulnerable person." But your upbringing and your experiences still have a major role to play. Someone with a low genetic vulnerability, for example, could easily develop a fear of flying after surviving a horrific plane crash.

There is plenty to learn about how anxiety and fear shape the brain. One of the biggest mysteries is the relationship between anxiety and depression. Researchers know that adults who suffer from depression were often very anxious as children. (It's also true that many kids outgrow their anxiety disorders to become perfectly well-adjusted adults.) Is that just a coincidence, as many believe, or does anxiety somehow prime the brain to become depressed later in life? Brain scans show that the amygdala is very active in depressed patients, even when they are sleeping. Studies of twins suggest that many of the same genes could be involved. "There's a lot of overlap," says Dr. Dennis Charney, chief of the research program for mood and anxiety disorders at the NIMH. "Anxiety and depression have a similar underlying biology, and the genetics may be such that anxiety surfaces early in life and depression later on." Still, no one can say for sure.

Certainly antidepressants, like the serotonin reuptake inhibitors (Prozac and others) have proved very helpful in treating anxiety; some doctors think they are even more effective against anxiety than they are against depression. Although no one knows exactly why these antidepressants work, one important clue is that their effects don't show up until after a few weeks of treatment. The pathways for toning down anxiety are apparently much more resistant than those for ratcheting it up.

It's a mistake, however, to think that pills alone can soothe your neurochemistry. Remember the cortex? That's where you would expect psychotherapy to work, increasing the repertoire of calming messages that can be passed along to the amygdala. Certain desensitization techniques can also help the brain learn, through the hippocampus, to be less reactive. Of course, you have to do it right. Reliving a trauma too soon after it happened could also make the memory harder to erase.

There are no guidebooks to tell you when it's safe to venture out again. In many ways, the whole country last September was made part of an unwitting experiment in mass anxiety. Our brains are even now in the process of rewiring themselves. How successfully we navigate this delicate transition will depend a lot on our genes, our environment and any future attacks.

—Reported by Alice Park/Bethesda, Leslie Whitaker/Chicago and Dan Cray/Los Angeles

9/11/01

Post-Traumatic Stress Disorder

September 11th affected all of us, and even at this short interval it seems to mark a new, frightening turn in history. But obviously, anyone who lost a loved one or who was in direct danger that day had an emotional experience that was altogether different than the general reaction. The thousands of rescue workers who dug through the ruins afterward also shouldered special emotional burdens.

Grief, shock, and their elements of disbelief, apathy, and sometimes anger are normal—and healthy—responses to terrible events and sudden loss. Remarkably, many people recover—daunted and with a darker world view perhaps, but ready to continue on with their lives. Studies have shown this to be true of Holocaust survivors, combat veterans, and rape victims. The human psyche is resilient.

Some will have psychiatric problems

But if past experience is any indication, a significant fraction of September 11th survivors and the families of the deceased will have psychiatric problems. The symptoms vary but can include an intense irritability, jumpiness, emotional numbness, flashbacks, and nightmares. Sufferers may struggle with sleep problems. Marriages and personal relationships may fray under the strain.

All of this falls under the heading of *post-traumatic stress disorder* (PTSD), a diagnosis many Americans associate with Vietnam War veterans. Many people diagnosed with PTSD are afflicted with overlapping mental health problems, including depression. *Acute stress disorder* shares some of the same symptoms as PTSD, but is a diagnosis reserved for the first month after a traumatic experience.

It is hard to say how many will suffer from full-fledged PTSD. For Americans, the attacks two months ago have no real parallel either in kind or degree. The closest precedent is the 1995 bombing of the federal office building in Oklahoma City that killed 167 people. A study of survivors of that terrorist attack was published in the Aug. 25, 1999, *Journal of the American Medical Association*. The researchers interviewed approximately 200 people six months after the explosion. A person was eligible for the study if they were within a couple of hundred yards from the blast. Forty-five percent met the criteria for having some kind of psychiatric disorder and 34% had PTSD.

What qualifies as exposure?

By definition, PTSD is a consequence of exposure to a traumatic experience, with trauma being some kind of serious harm. In 1994, the American Psychiatry Association broadened the definition of exposure considerably. In addition to facing a threat of death or serious injury directly, it now includes "witnessing or learning about the unexpected or violent death, serious harm, or threat of death or injury experienced by a family member or close associate."

Who is vulnerable?

It stands to reason that the more direct and severe the traumatic experience, the more likely PTSD will develop. But there isn't a predictable dose-response relationship. Some people with a fairly remote connection to an event will have a strong psychiatric reaction, whereas others will go through a horrifying experience and bounce back.

Researchers have found some patterns. Studies have shown consistently, for example, that women are more susceptible to developing PTSD than men. In the Oklahoma City survivor study, women had twice the PTSD rate as men (45% vs. 23%). A traumatic experience is more likely to trigger PTSD in someone who has had a prior experience. A study done several years ago of women recovering from rape found that those who had been raped before were three times more likely to develop PTSD. Most vulnerable of all are people with prior psychiatric problems such as depression, anxiety, or a personality disorder.

Well shy of mental illness, certain personality traits seem to make PTSD more likely. *Neuroticism* is a tendency to react with strong emotion to adverse events. People with this kind of personality are more sensitive to stress: their response is faster, stronger, and slower to level off than normal. Research has connected high-test scores for neuroticism to PTSD. There may also be a link between PTSD and *impulsivity*, because it leads to recklessness that puts people in harm's way.

Researchers have looked at brain anatomy for clues. Several studies have found that an unusually small *hippocampus*, the part of the brain believed to control the narrative structure of memories, is associated with PTSD. It isn't settled, however, whether that is a cause or an effect.

Acute stress

During the traumatic event itself, some people often enter a *dissociative state*, perhaps as a defense mechanism. They imagine they are elsewhere. In their mind's eye, they see it happening to someone else. People with this kind response are more likely to develop PTSD. If they get stuck in this detached phase, it can turn into total amnesia or various identity disorders. Yet particularly during disasters, many survivors stay amazingly levelheaded and focus on saving themselves—and often others. As horrible as the collapse of the World Trade Center Towers was, it would have been much worse if so many hadn't stayed calm and gotten out of the buildings.

More on PTSD symptoms

PTSD symptoms don't stick to a decipherable time line. They can happen right away or emerge months or years later. After disasters, however, they usually begin within three months, perhaps because there isn't much stigma and people feel freer to express their emotions. In the case of the Oklahoma City bombing, 76% of the survivors said their PTSD started the same day.

The first set of PTSD symptoms includes insomnia, edginess, and irritability. People are easily startled. They have a hard time concentrating. Then, sometimes, an emotional flatness sets in as if the mind is struggling to bury or get rid of the whole experience. People feel listless. They may withdraw socially. They may start to have stomachaches, headaches, dizzy spells, and feel profoundly tired. At odds with this numbness is another set of classic PTSD symptoms that include nightmares, flashbacks, and what psychiatrists aptly term *intrusive thoughts*. The slightest reminder of the traumatic experience can set people off and cause emotional suffering.

How are family members and close friends affected?

The sudden death of a significant other can create a special kind of grief that includes *separation* and *traumatic distress*. People can't stop thinking about the deceased person. They may feel as though part of them has died. Life seems to have no purpose. Some have *facsimile illness symptoms*, which involve reliving the symptoms or pain of the person who died. Relatives of homicide victims may relive the crime, putting themselves in the place of their loved ones. Some psychiatrists believe *traumatic bereavement* should be added as a diagnosis, related to but separate from PTSD. Certainly, normal grief has some of these qualities. The difference is that normal grief tends to taper off. People adjust and find they can lead meaningful lives again.

Are rescue workers vulnerable?

Technically, the PTSD diagnosis won't apply to rescue workers who are not themselves in serious danger. Several studies have shown, however, that up to 40% of people responsible for body handling and recovery after a disaster show signs of distress and are at risk of developing PTSD.

How can it be treated?

No consensus exists about how to best treat PTSD. A wide range of antidepressants are used. Antiseizure medications like carbamazepine and valproate are sometimes prescribed on the theory that a traumatic experience may lower the arousal threshold of the brain's *limbic system*, which is where seizures originate but it also controls emotions. Beta-blockers, traditionally prescribed to lower blood pressure, may quiet the nervous system and thereby reduce anxiety and restlessness.

Several varieties of psychotherapy have been tried, too, most with some but not complete success. *Cognitive therapy* focuses on memories and breaking negative thought patterns. *Behavioral therapy* aims to cut off a conditioned response that has become automatic.

Many therapists advocate using a technique called *debriefing* right after a traumatic event. It involves getting people to talk, usually in a group, about their experiences and vent their emotions. Some experts believe this is the best way to head off PTSD. Others see it as possibly stirring up thoughts and emotions that people might not otherwise have had.

Are we all suffering from PTSD?

Edgy? The possibility of future attacks has jangled many people's nerves. Waves of bad economic news have added to the background anxiety. Numb? Many Americans say September 11th changed the way in which they look at the world. They no longer feel safe. They are looking for meaning. They pray more. Intrusive thoughts and flashbacks? We don't need to think them up ourselves. Television and other news media bring up plenty of frightening pictures.

No, we don't have PTSD. To say we do trivializes the suffering of others. Still, we're allowed a pang of self-recognition in the broad outlines and descriptions of the condition. These are, after all, disordered times we're living in.

From *Harvard Health Letter*, November 2001, pp. 4-5. © 2001 by President and Fellows of Harvard College. Reprinted by permission.

The Schizophrenic Mind

A popular movie and a murder trial bring this tragic disease to light. How can the voices sound so real?

BY SHARON BEGLEY

THE FIRST TIME CHRIS COLES HEARD THE VOICE, IT SPOKE TO him after midnight. In a gentle tone, it instructed him to meet his friend at a beach cove, right then, and apologize: Chris, the voice told him, had been planning to date the friend's girlfriend. Although Coles was planning no such thing, he did as instructed, arriving at the cove at 2 a.m. It was deserted. He dismissed the incident; imagination, after all, can play tricks in the twilight between waking and dreaming. But the voices kept intruding. Coles saw visions, too. At the beach near his California home, he often saw a profusion of whales and dolphins swimming onto the beach, and a golden Buddha glowing from the bushes by the dunes. "I also had delusions of grandeur," says Coles, now 47. "I felt that I had power over things in nature, influence over the whales and dolphins and waves. I thought I could make things happen magically in the water."

Yates has the **public face** of schizophrenia, gripped by evil forces; Nash has the **hidden one**

Donna Willey's visions came out of a darker world. She saw "bloody images, cut-up people, dismembered people," she says. Voices, too, began haunting her and, despite medication, still won't stop. "They say terrible things," says Willey, 43. "That what I'm doing is not important. They cuss and yell, trying to get me down, saying I shouldn't have done something that way. They're in my head, and they keep yelling." Even as she talks to a reporter in her office at the National Alliance for the Mentally Ill (NAMI) of Greater Chicago, the demons screech "You shouldn't say that," or "Don't say it that way." "The noise, the chaos in my head—it's hard to keep everything separate," she says.

The disease that came to be termed schizophrenia was first described by German psychiatrist Emil Kraepelin in the 1890s, but it remains one of the most tragic and mysterious of mental illnesses. Whether it brings the voices of heaven or of hell, it causes what must surely be the worst affliction a sentient, conscious being can suffer: the inability to tell what is real from what is imaginary. To the person with schizophrenia the voices and visions sound and look as authentic as the announcer on the radio and the furniture in the room. Some 2.5 million Americans have the disease, which transcends economic status, education, geography and even the loving kindness of family. Neither doctors nor scientists can accurately predict who will become schizophrenic. The cause is largely unknown. Although the disease almost surely arises from neurons that take a wrong turn during fetal development, it strikes people just on the cusp of adulthood. Whatever the cause, it seems not to change in frequency: the incidence of schizophrenia has remained at about 1 percent of the population for all the decades doctors have surveyed it. There is surely a genetic predisposition, but not an omnipotent one: when one identical twin has schizophrenia, his or her twin has the disease in fewer than half the cases. Treatment is improving, but a cure is not even on the horizon.

Williamson would eat only **canned food**, so **paranoid** was he that he was being poisoned

Diagnosing schizophrenia can take years. Soon after Andrea Yates confessed that she had drowned her five children, one by one, in a bathtub last year, the prison psychiatrist diagnosed her as having postpartum depression "with psychotic features." So had the psychiatrist who treated Yates after her 1999 suicide attempt. Since psychosis—the inability to distinguish reality from imagination—lies at the core of schizophrenia, both psychiatrists recommended that Yates be tested for that disease. Dr. Phillip Resnick of Case Western Reserve University did so. Last week, taking the witness stand for the defense at Yates's murder trial, he testified that she had a combination of schizophrenia and depression when she killed her children. In 1994, after her first child was born, she said she heard Satan's voice telling her to "get a knife" and hurt baby Noah.

If Yates's is the public face of schizophrenia—bedeviled by voices, gripped by evil forces—then John Nash's is the hidden one. As shown in the Academy Award-nominated picture "A Beautiful Mind," the disease, at least in its early stages, can inspire Olympian leaps of creativity and insight. "That's the wonderful paradox of schizophrenia," says Dr. Nancy Andreasen, professor of psychiatry at the University of Iowa. "People see things others don't, most of which aren't there. But because they perceive the world in a different way, they sometimes also notice things—real things—that normal people don't."

Schizophrenia is marked by the persistent presence of at least two of these symptoms: delusions, hallucinations, frequently derailed or incoherent speech, hugely disorganized or catatonic behavior, or the absence of feeling or volition. If the delusions are especially bizarre, or the hallucinations consist of either a running commentary on what the person is doing or thinking, or multiple voices carrying on a conversation, then that alone qualifies the person as schizophrenic. In one subtype, catatonic schizophrenia, the patient often seems to be in a stupor, resisting all entreaties and instructions, or engages in purposeless movements, bizarre postures, exaggerated mannerisms or grimacing. Yates would sit and stare into space for two hours; she would scratch her head bald and pat her foot obsessively. Before the drownings she rarely spoke, testified family members. Police officers responding to the crime described her as emotionless.

In paranoid schizophrenia, the patient becomes convinced of beliefs at odds with reality, hears voices that aren't there or sees images that exist nowhere but in his mind. Eric Williamson has had paranoid schizophrenia for 15 of his 31 years. As a teen he was terrified that someone would enter his room at night, and so would barricade the door and dangle hangers from the window to alert him to intruders. He would eat only canned food, so paranoid was he that someone was trying to poison him. Once, when his mother walked past the kitchen table as he ate, he cried out, "Why did you put that poison in my soup!?" He soon lost his grip on reality altogether, telling her, "Look how my eyelashes are growing. That's because [my brother] is messing with me."

Despite medication, Willey's voices still **burst** through, especially during **times of stress**

Andrea Yates may have had paranoid as well as catatonic schizophrenia. At the trial, Andrea's mother-in-law, Dora Yates, recalled the time Andrea stood transfixed in front of the television, neither moving nor speaking, for more than half an hour, as her children watched cartoons. Later, Yates told a prison psychiatrist that the cartoon characters were speaking to her, calling her a bad mother and scolding her for allowing her children to consume too much sugar. Yet even after her two suicide attempts, and even after she became nearly mute, her husband, Rusty, testified, he never suspected how severely ill she was.

Neuroscientists have now traced such hallucinations to malfunctions of the brain. In a 1995 study, researchers led by Drs. David Silbersweig and Emily Stern of Cornell Medical School teamed with colleagues in London to scan the brains of schizophrenics in the throes of hallucinations. As soon as an imagined voice spoke, or a vision appeared, a patient pressed a button. That told the scientists when to scrutinize the scans for abnormal activity. They found plenty. When one patient reported seeing dripping colors and severed heads, for instance, the parts of the sensory cortex that process movement, color and objects became active. Still, the complex visions depicted in "Beautiful Mind" are not typical. "The visual hallucinations are usually fragmentary," says Dr. Richard Wyatt, chief of neuropsychiatry at the National Institute of Mental Health, "not the elaborate things in the movie. They're an outline, or a figure without features."

When patients heard voices, the auditory cortex as well as the language-processing areas became active. "These regions process complex auditory, linguistic information, not just beeps or buzzes," says Silbersweig. The voices the patients heard were therefore as real to them as the conversations in the hallways they passed through en route to the lab.

The Chemistry of Mental Chaos

High-tech brain scans and new treatments are beginning to solve the mysteries of this debilitating disease, which affects 1% of the population. But much remains unknown.

Neurological Roots

Schizophrenia is associated with over-activity in the part of the brain normally involved in arousal and motivation, known as the mesolimbic pathway. This can produce hallucinations and delusions.

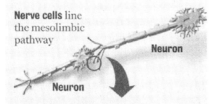

Nerve cells line the mesolimbic pathway

Neuron

Neuron

Dopamine receptors

The disease has been linked to an excess of the brain chemical dopamine, which helps signals pass between nerve cells.

Normal dopamine system In healthy people, the flow of dopamine between brain cells is carefully regulated.

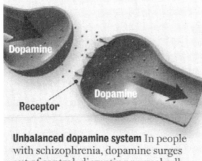

Dopamine

Dopamine

Receptor

Unbalanced dopamine system In people with schizophrenia, dopamine surges out of control, disrupting normal cell communications.

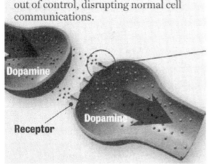

Dopamine

Dopamine

Receptor

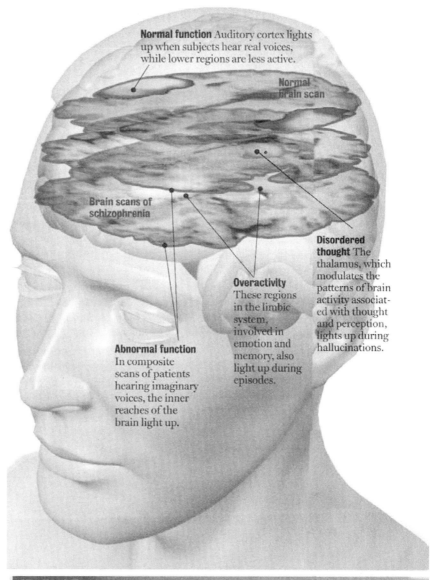

Normal function Auditory cortex lights up when subjects hear real voices, while lower regions are less active.

Normal brain scan

Brain scans of schizophrenia

Disordered thought The thalamus, which modulates the patterns of brain activity associated with thought and perception, lights up during hallucinations.

Overactivity These regions in the limbic system, involved in emotion and memory, also light up during episodes.

Abnormal function In composite scans of patients hearing imaginary voices, the inner reaches of the brain light up.

Medical Treatments

Traditional antipsychotics blocked dopamine in the mesolimbic pathway, but they also blocked it in other parts of the brain, creating troublesome side effects.

Old drugs

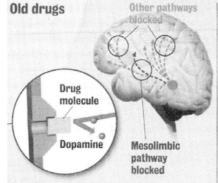

Other pathways blocked

Drug molecule

Dopamine

Mesolimbic pathway blocked

Older drugs reduced dopamine by completely blocking receptors on mesolimbic cells. In other pathways, this blocking led to impaired movement and cognition.

New drugs

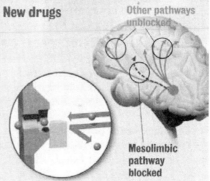

Other pathways unblocked

Mesolimbic pathway blocked

New drugs bind less strongly to receptors. They block enough dopamine to ease symptoms in the mesolimbic pathway, without causing shortages elsewhere.

Sources for this and following page: David Silbersweig, M. D., and Emily Stern, M. D., Cornell University Medical School. Sources: Jeffery Lieberman, M.D. University of North Carolina Medical School. Images courtesy of David Silbersweig M. D. and Emily Stern M. D.; Text and research by Josh Ulick, Graphic by Kevin Hand—Newsweek.

Taking Pictures

By scanning the brains of people with schizophrenia in the midst of auditory and visual hallucinations, scientists can pinpoint the overactive regions that cause these symptoms.

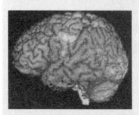

In this image of a hallucinating brain, taken from PET scans, the parts of the outer shell (known as the cerebral cortex) involved in vision and hearing light up.

Statistical Snapshot

Schizophrenia afflicts an estimated 2.5 million Americans, and cuts across all segments of society. Direct treatment costs run about $20 billion a year.

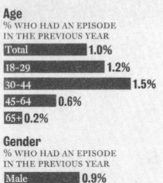

Age
% WHO HAD AN EPISODE IN THE PREVIOUS YEAR

Total	1.0%
18-29	1.2%
30-44	1.5%
45-64	0.6%
65+	0.2%

Gender
% WHO HAD AN EPISODE IN THE PREVIOUS YEAR

Male	0.9%
Female	1.1%

Ethnic group
% WHO HAD AN EPISODE IN THE PREVIOUS YEAR

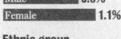

White/other	0.9%
Black	1.6%
Hisp.	0.4%

Employment status
% OF LIFETIME SCHIZOPHRENIA SUFFERERS

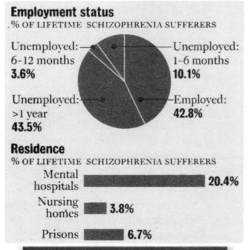

Unemployed: 6-12 months **3.6%**
Unemployed: 1-6 months **10.1%**
Unemployed: >1 year **43.5%**
Employed: **42.8%**

Residence
% OF LIFETIME SCHIZOPHRENIA SUFFERERS

Mental hospitals	20.4%
Nursing homes	3.8%
Prisons	6.7%

How to Get Help

National Schizophrenia Foundation
Provides information about the disease and support groups. Call 800-482-9534 or log on to sanonymous.org.

National Mental Health Association
Lobbies federal and state governments on mental-health issues. Call 800-969-6642 or check out www.nmha.org.

National Alliance for the Mentally Ill
Supports a help line. Call 800-950-6264 or go to www.nami.org.

American Psychiatric Association
Provides referrals to psychiatrists around the country. Call 888-357-7924 or log on to www.psych.org.

Deep within the brain during hallucinations, structures involved in memory (the little sea-horse-shaped hippocampus), in emotions (the amygdala) and in consciousness (the thalamus) all flick on like streetlights at dusk. That suggests why hallucinations are packed with rare emotional power—the power to make Chris Coles ashamed enough to venture to a deserted beach at night, the power to make Eric Williamson so terrified he ate only canned food. Sensory signals are conveyed deep into the brain, where they link up with memories and emotions. The neuronal traffic might go the other way, too, with activity in the emotional and memory regions triggering voices and visions.schizophrenia.

Why one person sees whales and another sees severed heads remains poorly understood. But the content of hallucinations probably reflects personal experience: in one patient the neuronal pathways activated during a hallucination run through the memories of seashore visits, while in another they intersect memories of pain and terror. Yates, who has a deeply religious background, had satanic hallucinations. Soon after a relative tried to rape her at the age of 11, Joanne Verbanic became convinced that strangers were trying to break into her house. Fourteen years later ominous voices started telling her that her brother would be killed. "I thought I was being followed and my phone was being tapped," she says. "There was a hole in the ceiling of my closet, and I thought there was a wire up there. I thought they had installed microphones in my eyeglasses and a dental filling." Other voices told her to kill herself; at 25 she tried to throw herself from a moving car, but her husband yanked her back.

"What's so cruel about voices is that they come from your very own brain," says Carol North, now a respected psychiatrist and researcher at Washington University, who first heard voices when she was 16. "They know all your innermost secrets and the things that bother you most." North's voices tormented her about failing a neurophysiology exam. "That was a horrible thing for me. The voices said, 'Carol North got an F.' They'd say things like, 'She can't do it [get into medical school],' 'She's just not smart enough'."

Another key brain area involved in schizophrenia is nearly silent. The Cornell/London brain-imaging study showed that schizophrenia is marked by abnormally low activity in the frontal lobes (just behind the forehead). These regions rein in the emotional system, provide insight and evaluate sensory information. They provide, in other words, a reality check. "You may need a double hit to suffer the psychotic symptoms of schizophrenia," says Silbersweig. "You need the aberrant sensory and emotional functioning, but you also need aberrant frontal-lobe function, which leaves you with no inhibition of these hallucinations and no reality check. That makes the hallucinations so believable."

The absence of a reality check makes "willing" yourself out of schizophrenia just about impossible. "It is very unlikely for somebody to will themselves to get better,"

Famous Figures, Troubled Minds

Throughout history, many well-known people, diagnosed or not, have exhibited some of the bizarre behaviors that are now associated with schizophrenia.

David Helfgott: His doctor says the famed pianist with the strange speech and other odd behaviors has schizoaffective disorder, not schizophrenia.

Vaslav Nijinsky: After six weeks of nearly nonstop diary writing, the Russian ballet dancer was diagnosed with schizophrenia by Eugen Bleuler, who coined the term.

Mary Todd Lincoln: The president's wife said she was haunted, wandered hotel hallways in her nightgown and sewed large sums of money in her clothes to foil imaginary thieves.

Zelda Fitzgerald: Hospitalized with nervous exhaustion at 27 and diagnosed with schizophrenia by Karl Jung, she received an early form of shock therapy.

Vincent van Gogh: Besides famously slicing off his ear, the erratic genius suffered hallucinations and memory lapses and once swallowed paint.

---

says NIMH's Wyatt. Toward the end of the film, when Nash recognizes that he has a mental illness, he says, "I just choose not to acknowledge" the figures he hallucinates. The reality is grimmer. Even among people who have had their illness for decades, and who have periods of clarity (thanks to medication), only some learn to discriminate between the voices everyone hears and the voices only they can hear. Verbanic, who founded Schizophrenics Anonymous in 1985, had been hospitalized often enough to recognize her symptoms. While working on bankruptcies for Ford Motor Credit, "I thought the attorneys weren't really attorneys and the files were phony," she says. She asked a supervisor to take her to the hospital.

Some **2.5 million** Americans have the disease, which eludes even the **loving kindness** of family.

Identifying what happens in the brain during schizophrenic hallucinations is one step short of understanding why they happen. The old theory that cold, rejecting mothers make their children schizophrenic has long been discredited. Although the actual cause remains elusive, scientists know a few things. The age of the father mat-

ters. A 25-year-old has a 1-in-198 chance of fathering a child who will develop schizophrenia by 21, finds Dr. Dolores Malaspina of Columbia University. That risk nearly doubles when the father is 40, and triples when he passes 50. Viruses or stresses that interfere with a fetus's brain development also raise the risk; mothers who suffer rubella or malnutrition while pregnant have a greater chance of bearing children who develop the disease. And if there is schizophrenia in your family, you run a higher-than-average risk of developing it. Last year researchers led by NIMH's Dr. Daniel Weinberger linked a gene on chromosome 22 to a near-doubled risk of schizophrenia. When the gene, called COMT, is abnormal, it effectively depletes the frontal lobes of the neurochemical dopamine. That can both unleash hallucinations and impair the brain's reality check.

The seeming authenticity of the voices means that people with schizophrenia can be barraged by commands that, they are convinced, come from God or Satan. That inference is not illogical: who else can speak to you, unseen, from inside your head? Some patients have heard commands to shoplift, some to commit suicide. Believing she was possessed by Satan, Yates thought that her children "were not righteous." If she killed them while they were young, she told a psychiatrist, then "God would take them up" to heaven. Legally, "insanity" means the inability to tell right from wrong. There is no evidence that people with schizophrenia have impaired moral judgment. Then why do some obey commands to break the law, or worse? Perhaps one need look no further than Genesis 22. When Abraham heard God's command to sacrifice his only son, Isaac, he did not hesitate to take the boy up the mountain to the place of sacrifice and raise the knife.

Another misconception about schizophrenia involves creativity. In real life, bipolar disorder, with its alternating mania and depression, is more closely associated with creativity than schizophrenia is. "Most of John Nash's inventiveness came before his illness," says NIMH's Wyatt. "With schizophrenia, you can have brilliant thoughts, but they're hard to translate into something others understand." Untreated schizophrenia is so crippling that patients can barely buy groceries or pay bills, let alone pen a novel or compose a concerto. It may, however, inspire feats of genius in math and physics. "Creativity in these fields doesn't require sustained discipline," notes Iowa's Andreasen. "Many insights come as intuitions rather than brute proof by empirical evidence." Sadly, though, many of the creative breakthroughs that people with schizophrenia claim are not: thanks to delusions of grandeur, a crazy doodle can seem a Nobel Prize-winning insight. "I thought there were 10,000 universal truths that I needed to understand, that there were messages in the pattern of paint on the wall and in the pattern of concrete," recalls Carol North.

There is, as yet, no cure for schizophrenia, for drugs cannot unscramble tangled neuronal circuits. But drugs can quiet them. Those that give rise to the delusions and

'Is There Trouble With Jim?'

When someone you love hears voices through walls

BY DIRK JOHNSON

THREE YEARS AGO, MINDY GREILING SAT IN A PSYCHOLogist's office and listened to her son, Jim, talk about wanting to kill her. "I want to shoot you in the face," he said, "because you look so evil." As a boy growing up in suburban Minneapolis, Jim Greiling was a Cub Scout, a Little Leaguer, a math whiz. Now 24, he suffers from schizophrenia, a disease that tortures families as it haunts the ill. Like millions of American families with a sufferer at home—or one who is off wandering somewhere in the world—Mindy and Roger Greiling are on intimate terms with this disease. They know the helplessness of trying to force treatment on an adult who refuses. They know the grief of letting go of dreams. "When he is young, you think about what the future might be for him," his father said. "It wasn't this."

Schizophrenia rains down guilt on some families— old notions held that poor parenting was to blame, with a finger usually pointed at the mother. Today it is believed to have a strong genetic component, leaving some relatives feeling as though they handed down a curse. The disease still brings shame, and it can ruin a family's finances. The Greilings were in a better position than most. They are well-educated and prosperous—and enlightened enough to know that schizophrenia is nobody's fault. But they also know the feeling of standing in the living room of their split-level home amid the wreckage of their son's hallucinations: smashed flowerpots, holes punched in the wall, kitty litter kicked across the floor. Their son's bouts have meant calling the police, with his terrified mother pleading: "He's 6-foot-4, and I'm afraid of him."

For Jim's sister, Angela Greiling Keane, a journalist in Washington, it means feelings of helplessness, a thousand miles from crisis. Unexpected telephone calls trigger anxiety. "When it's 7 a.m., and the caller ID says it's my parents, I automatically worry: is there trouble with Jim?"

Theirs are ghastly struggles. After one of Jim's rampages at home his parents called the police and asked them to take him to the hospital. But the police refused, since the mentally ill cannot be committed until they pose a threat. "You reach the point," said Mindy, "where you're actually hoping for something to happen, so he'll be forced to go to a hospital."

There had been worries for years—during high school Jim smoked marijuana, and the family wanted to believe drugs were behind his erratic behavior. But while he was a student at the University of Montana he called home and said something that gave his mother chills. "He said he could hear the voices of women through the walls of the next apartment," said Mindy. "He said they were talking about him."

Mindy Greiling, a state representative, was busy at a late-night legislative session last year when another call came from Montana. Jim had been arrested. "After the session adjourned, she drove through the night to the jail. She felt "heart-broken," she says, as she saw her son behind the glass wearing an orange prisoner's suit, looking gaunt and whiskered. Jim had broken a window in a neighboring apartment, then climbed inside, lay down on a sofa and fell asleep. The judge in Montana released Jim, who entered a state mental hospital where he underwent treatment for three months. Now he lives in a house in St. Paul with four other patients. Everybody is assigned a job; Jim drives a van on the late shift. He is taking his medicine and seems to have gotten accustomed to his routine.

But for his family, the worries have scarcely stopped. Just the other day, the old voices came back. Jim was sitting on the sofa with his father, when he turned and asked: "Did you just say that you didn't like me?" The father said no. Jim smiled, reassured. For his parents, it is frightening to know that Jim still hears those voices. They can only hope that he ignores them.

hallucinations of schizophrenia are awash in the neurochemical dopamine. Thorazine, an early antipsychotic, blocked dopamine receptors, with the result that dopamine had no effect on neurons. But since dopamine is also involved in movement, Thorazine leaves patients slow and stiff, "doing the Thorazine shuffle," says Suzanne Andriukaitis of NAMI. Dopamine also courses through circuits responsible for attention and pleasure, so Thorazine puts patients in a mental fog and deadens feelings. "The old drugs are a nuclear weapon against dopamine," says Dr. Peter Weiden of Downstate Medical Center in Brooklyn, N.Y. "They eliminate your sense of pleasure and reward. Patients lose their joy."

People with schizophrenia can be **barraged** by commands that, they are convinced, come from **God**

The new antipsychotics, called "atypicals," are more like smart bombs. Drugs including Clozaril, Risperdal,

Zyprexa, Geodon and Seroquel target mainly the dopamine-flooded regions, so patients no longer feel as if the voices of 40 radio stations, as different as NPR and the local hip-hop station, are blaring in their ears. "The volume is softer, the speed is slower, it's making more sense," says Donna Willey. Although the voices and visions don't always disappear, the new drugs can allow people with schizophrenia to hold jobs and have families. Still, they increase appetite, and may alter metabolism, resulting in what NIMH's Wyatt calls "the enormous problem" of huge weight gain. Willey gains 20 pounds a year on Zyprexa, and has ballooned from 120 pounds to her current 280. That makes some reluctant to take the drugs. Another side effect is foggy thinking, the feeling that brain signals are trying to push through caramel. Patients may also lose their libido. For all the power of the new drugs, they are treatment and not cure.

Sometimes Chris Coles misses the angelic voices. "They said complimentary things," he remembers. "They were sweet voices, telling me about the sunrise or sunset." But Zyprexa and Seroquel have stilled the angels. Willey wishes her voices would fall silent. Although Zyprexa has hushed them, they still burst through perhaps once a day, especially during times of stress. And she still, 20 years after she first heard the voices, isn't always completely, totally sure that they're not real.

With ANNE UNDERWOOD *in New York*, KAREN SPRINGEN *in Chicago and* ANNE BELLI GESALMAN *in Houston*

UNIT 11
Psychological Treatments

Unit Selections

Key Points to Consider

- Do you know what varieties of psychotherapy are commonly available? Does psychotherapy work? Why are Americans in love with psychotherapy? Or are they? Do you think that supportive lay persons can be as effective as psychotherapists? Is professional assistance for psychological problems always necessary? Can people successfully change themselves without benefit of therapy?

- Can therapists easily differentiate their brand of therapy from another? What makes therapy successful? Whom do you think is more important to the therapeutic alliance, the client or the therapist? What characteristics of each person make therapy effective? Do you think one type of therapy would work better for you than another?

- Why would doing research on psychotherapy as a process be difficult? Besides the process itself and how it works (for example, empathy), what other measures would be important to research?

- Why are more and more people turning to cybertherapy or the Internet for help with mental disorders? How can we research whether this form of therapy is effective? Why is this an important research topic?

- Are Americans "nuts"? Why do you agree or disagree? What varieties of psychotherapy are commonly available to your knowledge? Does psychotherapy work? Why are Americans "in love with psychotherapy"? Do you think that supportive lay persons can be as effective as psychotherapists? Is professional assistance for psychological problems always necessary? How and why is psychotherapy replacing spirituality, according to Mary McNamara?

- Can people successfully change themselves? Why do people turn to self-help groups rather than to professionals? What disorders are amenable to intervention by support groups? What does research show about the efficacy of support groups? Can support groups be dangerous? How can we be sure that we are receiving good advice from self-help groups? Do you think support groups should include a trained professional or trained facilitator? Why or why not?

 **Links: www.dushkin.com/online/**
These sites are annotated in the World Wide Web pages.

The C.G. Jung Page
http://www.cgjungpage.org
Knowledge Exchange Network (KEN)
http://www.mentalhealth.org
NetPsychology
http://netpsych.com/index.htm
Sigmund Freud and the Freud Archives
http://plaza.interport.net/nypsan/freudarc.html

Have you ever had the nightmare that you are trapped in a dark, dismal place? No one will let you out. Your pleas for freedom go unanswered and, in fact, are suppressed or ignored by domineering authority figures around you. You keep begging for mercy but to no avail. What a nightmare! You are fortunate to awake to your normal bedroom and to the realities of your daily life. For the mentally ill, the nightmare of institutionalization, where individuals can be held against their will in what are sometimes terribly dreary, restrictive surroundings, is a reality. Have you ever wondered what would happen if we took perfectly normal individuals and institutionalized them in such a place? In one well-known and remarkable study, that is exactly what happened.

In 1973, eight people, including a pediatrician, a psychiatrist, and some psychologists, presented themselves to psychiatric hospitals. Each claimed that he or she was hearing voices. The voices, they reported, seemed unclear but appeared to be saying "empty" or "thud." Each of these individuals was admitted to a mental hospital, and most were diagnosed as being schizophrenic. Upon admission, the "pseudopatients," or fake patients, gave truthful information and thereafter acted like their usual, normal selves.

Their hospital stays lasted anywhere from 7 to 52 days. The nurses, doctors, psychologists, and other staff members treated them as if they were schizophrenic and never saw through their trickery. Some of the real patients in the hospital, however, did recognize that the pseudopatients were perfectly normal. Upon discharge almost all of the pseudopatients received the diagnosis of "schizophrenic in remission," meaning that they were still clearly defined as schizophrenic; they just weren't exhibiting any of the symptoms at the time of release.

What does this study demonstrate about mental illness? Is true mental illness readily detectable? If we can't always pinpoint mental disorders (the more professionally accepted term for mental illness), how can we treat them? What treatments are available, and which treatments work better for various diagnoses? The treatment of mental disorders is a challenge. The array of available treatments is ever-increasing and can be downright bewildering—and not just to the patient or client! In order to demystify and simplify your understanding of various treatments, we will look at them in this unit.

We commence with a general article on psychotherapy. There are as many forms of therapy as there are theories. Can all of the various practitioners differentiate one form of psychotherapy from another? Is there any such thing as a pure form of psychotherapy as practiced today? The answers will surprise you.

In the second article in this unit, research receives great emphasis, as well it should. What aspects of therapy seem most important? That is, what characteristics of therapy does research reveal as making therapy effective? These and other questions are answered in this incisive summary of research.

People more and more are turning to the Internet for help with mental disorders. Researchers are just now researching whether this trend bodes well for the future. As you will read in the next article of this unit, much more research is needed.

In the next article, Mary McNamara asks, "Are We Nuts?" If one examines the popularity of psychotherapy today, then one might indeed conclude that, yes, Americans appear to be crazy because so many of us are in therapy. Some therapy clients consider psychotherapy to be fashionable. Why are we in love with psychotherapy? Is therapy truly helpful? Both questions are explored in McNamara's article.

Ina a companion article, support groups are put under the scientific microscope. Such groups are becoming more and more popular. Do such groups work? Do they result in positive change? The answers are not easy. Support groups may or may not be beneficial, according to recent research.

In the final article, the editors review the recent trends in the use of outpatient psychotherapy in the United States.

Psychotherapies: Can we tell the difference?

If, as a patient or a therapist, you have tried one kind of psychotherapy, you may have tried more than one. Despite labels, different kinds of psychotherapy are often almost indistinguishable in practice. At least that's the conclusion some Harvard and Berkeley researchers have arrived at after examining the records of the National Institute of Mental Health (NIMH) Treatment of Depression Collaborative Research Program.

That clinical trial, one of the most carefully conducted ever, compared antidepressant medication, interpersonal psychotherapy, and cognitive behavioral therapy in the treatment of depressed patients. Cognitive behavioral therapy concentrates on changing maladaptive habits, irrational beliefs, and self-defeating attitudes. Interpersonal therapy, in principle, is concerned mainly with life changes and personal relationships, especially grief and loss. Detailed manuals lay out procedures for both forms of therapy.

The researchers asked experts to compare their own understanding of interpersonal and cognitive behavioral therapy with a process rating list—100 statements describing some typical features of psychotherapy sessions. The experts rated each item on the list from 1 to 100, depending on how accurately it described the proceedings during an ideal session of interpersonal or cognitive behavioral therapy. Then, without being told which kind of therapy they were observing, independent judges read transcripts of sessions from the NIMH trial and sorted items on the process rating list to match what they were reading.

Cognitive behavioral therapists rated five items as best representing their practice:

1. discussing specific activities and tasks for the patient to attempt outside of psychotherapy sessions;
2. discussing the patient's ideas or belief systems;
3. discussing the patient's treatment goals;
4. encouraging the patient to test new ways of behaving with others;
5. controlling the interaction between therapist and patient by introducing new topics.

For interpersonal therapists, the top five items were:

1. emphasizing the patient's personal relationships;
2. emphasizing the patient's feelings to help him or her experience them more deeply;
3. encouraging the patient to talk of feelings about being close to or needing someone;
4. discussing love or romantic relationships;
5. explaining the reasons for their approach to treatment.

The transcripts of 35 interpersonal and 29 cognitive behavioral therapy sessions did not show the expected contrast. No matter what the label, process ratings resembled the cognitive behavioral model more than the interpersonal model (although the interpersonal therapy sessions matched more features of the interpersonal ideal than cognitive behavioral therapy sessions did). Use of cognitive behavioral procedures was generally associated with a better outcome, but the interpersonal therapists, despite the label, were also using those procedures most of the time, and they were just as successful as the cognitive behavioral therapists.

According to the authors, other studies—including some of their own—show that in practice psychodynamic therapists often use cognitive behavioral methods as well. And in this study, even the ideal forms of cognitive behavioral therapy and interpersonal therapy as described by experts were not as different as they may seem. Six of the first 20 items on the process rating list were common to both. Successful therapists of all persuasions, the authors believe, adopt an authoritative and benevolent manner, offer advice and reassurance, and coach patients in ways to change their behavior.

The patient's contribution was also important. Readers of the transcripts found that if they judged by the patient's statements alone, the two forms of psychotherapy were almost indistinguishable. In an earlier study, what patients did and said during therapy sessions proved to be more important in determining the outcome than what therapists did and said.

The authors believe that most comparative tests of psychotherapy are based on the wrong assumptions. The standard description of a form of psychotherapy may be unrelated to what actually goes on in the encounters between a therapist and a patient. Better understanding of how change occurs during those encounters, they say, is the key to improving psychotherapeutic practice.

Reference

Ablon, J. et al. "Validity of Controlled Clinical Trials of Psychotherapy: Findings from the NIMH Treatment of Depression Collaborative Research Program," American Journal of Psychiatry (May 2002): Vol. 159, No. 5, pp. 775–83.

Characteristics of Empirically Supported Treatments

This study presents a survey of general characteristics of empirically supported treatments (ESTs) identified by the American Psychological Association Division 12 Task Force on the Promotion and Dissemination of Psychological Procedures. Results indicate that the ESTs share the following characteristics: they involve skill building, have a specific problem focus, incorporate continuous assessment of client progress, and involve brief treatment contact, requiring 20 or fewer sessions. Traditional assessment methods, such as intelligence testing, projectives, and objective personality tests such as the MMPI-2, are rarely used in these treatments. Although it is recognized that these findings are in part an artifact of sociological factors present in contemporary psychotherapy development and research, the findings may also serve as a heuristic aid in the development of therapies. (The Journal of Psychotherapy Practice and Research 2000; 9:69–74)

William O'Donohue, Ph.D.
Jeffrey A. Buchanan, M.A.
Jane E. Fisher, Ph.D.

In 1995 the American Psychological Association Division 12 Task Force on the Promotion and Dissemination of Psychological Procedures was formed and charged with identifying psychotherapies with proven efficacy. The rationale was partly to educate those who might become involved (e.g., potential clients, third-party payors, and treatment providers) about the benefits that could be derived from psychotherapy. The task force included members with a variety of theoretical preferences in an attempt to minimize the intrusion of antecedent theoretical commitments. The committee agreed on standards for the adequacy of research evidence to warrant the positive judgment that the treatment was "empirically validated" or "empirically supported." The 1995 task force identified 18 well-established empirically supported treatments (ESTs) and 7 probably efficacious treatments.[1] The 1998 task force updated this list and found 16 well-established treatments and 56 probably efficacious treatments.[2]

Although at each step the task force has attracted a great deal of controversy, its findings serve an important purpose because it is the first time in the history of psychotherapy that some consensus has emerged across psychologists with differing theoretical orientations regarding what psychotherapies have evidential support. This list of ESTs is an interesting data set in itself. It can be examined in an attempt to identify trends or commonalities among these

TABLE 1 Empirically supported treatments for which data were requested (data were not received from those in bold)

Well-established treatments

Behavior modification for developmentally disabled individuals (1995)
Behavior therapy for erectile dysfunction (1995)
Token economy programs (1995)
Cognitive-behavioral therapy (CBT) for panic disorder with and without agoraphobia
CBT for generalized anxiety disorder
Exposure treatment for agoraphobia
Exposure/guided mastery for specific phobia
Exposure and response prevention for obsessive-compulsive disorder (OCD)
Stress inoculation training for coping with stressors
Behavior therapy for depression
Cognitive therapy for depression
Interpersonal therapy for depression
Behavior therapy for headache
CBT for bulimia
Multicomponent CBT for pain associated with rheumatic disease
Multicomponent CBT with relapse prevention for smoking cessation
Behavior modification for enuresis
Parent training programs for children with oppositional behavior
Behavioral marital therapy

Probably efficacious treatments

Lewinsohn's psychoeducational treatment for depression (1995)
Applied relaxation for panic disorder
Applied relaxation for generalized anxiety disorder
CBT for social phobia
Cognitive therapy for OCD
Couples communication training adjunctive to exposure with agoraphobia
Eye movement desensitization and reprocessing for civilian posttraumatic stress disorder (PTSD)
Exposure treatment for PTSD
Exposure treatment for social phobia
Stress inoculation training for PTSD
Relapse prevention program for OCD
Systematic desensitization for animal phobia
Systematic desensitization for public speaking anxiety
Systematic desensitization for social anxiety
Behavior therapy for cocaine dependence
Brief dynamic therapy for opiate dependence
Cognitive-behavioral relapse prevention therapy for cocaine dependence

Cognitive therapy for opiate dependence
CBT for benzodiazepine withdrawl in panic disorder patients
Community Reinforcement Approach for alchohol dependence
Cue exposure adjunctive treatment for alcohol dependence
Project CALM for mixed alcohol abuse and dependence
Social skills training adjunctive to inpatient treatment for alcohol dependence
Brief dynamic therapy for depression
Cognitive therapy for geriatric patients with depression
Reminiscence therapy for geriatric patients with depression
Self-control therapy for depression
Social problem-solving therapy for depression
Behavior therapy for childhood obesity
CBT for binge eating disorder
CBT adjunctive to physical therapy for chronic pain
CBT for chronic low back pain
Electromyographic biofeedback for chronic pain
Hypnosis as an adjunct to CBT for obesity
Interpersonal therapy for binge eating disorder
Interpersonal therapy for bulimia
Multicomponent cognitive therapy for irritable bowel syndrome
Multicomponent CBT for pain of sickle cell disease
Multicomponent operant behavior therapy for chronic pain
Scheduled, reduced smoking adjunctive to multicomponent behavior therapy for smoking cessation
Thermal biofeedback for Raynaud's syndrome
Thermal biofeedback plus autogenic relaxation training for migraine
Emotionally focused couples therapy for moderately distressed couples
Insight-oriented marital therapy
Behavior modification of encopresis
CBT for anxious children (overanxious,, separation anxiety, and aviodant disorders)
Exposure for simple phobia
Family anxiety management training for anxiety disorders
Hurlbert's combined treatment approach for female hypoactive sexual desire
Masters and Johnson's sex therapy for female orgasmic dysfunction
Zimmer's combined sex and marital therapy for female hypoactive sexual desire
Behavior modification for sex offenders
Dialectical behavior therapy for borderline personality disorder
Family intervention for schizophrenia
Habit-reversal and control techniques
Social skills training for improving social adjustment of schizophrenic patients
Supported employment for severely mentally ill clients

treatments. Modern psychotherapies range widely in their assumptions on issues such as the importance of the psychotherapeutic relationship in the change process, the exact role of assessment and psychodiagnostics, the length of therapy, and the roles of skill building versus personality restructuring, among other issues. Trends in these relatively successful therapies might be useful in evaluating assumptions about the nature of effective therapy as well as a heuristic aid in the discovery of other effective therapies.

Table 2. Questionnaire items and responses

Item	Response n(%)		
	Yes	No	Other
1. Please estimate how many 1-hour sessions, on average, this therapy takes before completion (this can be a rough estimate).[a]			
2. Is a DSM-IV diagnosis essential for making treatment decisions?	23 (38)	37 (61)	1 (2)
3. Is homework (i.e., structured tasks for the client to complete outside of therapy sessions) an essential component of this therapy?	52 (85)	8 (13)	1 (2)
4. Are traditional assessment devices (e.g., MMPI, Rorschach) used for the purpose of treatment entry or planning?	4 (7)	56 (92)	1 (2)
5. Please estimate how many hours per week a client must devote to treatment (both in and out of session) for optimal outcome.[b]			
6. Is the formation of the therapeutic relationship a key process variable (i.e., one of the important mechanisms of change necessary for successful outcome) in this therapy?	33 (54)	19 (31)	9 (15)
7. Is the primary in-session activity discussion of client problems leading to insight or catharsis, and the history of those problems (as opposed to teaching of skills)?	7 (11)	52 (85)	2 (4)
8. Estimate the frequency with which assessment (i.e., some sort of measurement beyond the unstructured clinical interview) is conducted.[c]			
9. Does assessment (as defined above) occur continuously throughout therapy?	47 (77)	8 (13)	6 (10)
10. Would you say that therapy is problem-focused (i.e., building skills) as opposed to focused on restructuring the client's personality?	55 (90)	2 (3)	4 (7)
11. Is knowledge of the client's history (i.e., origins of the presenting problem) essential for treatment planning or necessary for successful outcome?	19 (31)	33 (54)	7 (11)

⇒ [a]See Figure 1. [b] See Figure 2. [c] See Table 3.

METHODS

Participants

Participants in this study were authors of studies cited as supporting the inclusion of the treatment as a "well-established" empirically supported treatment or a "probable" EST in the APA Division 12 Task Force reports on empirically supported treatments.[1,2] For each EST, the Task Force cited either one or two articles that were used to support the conclusion regarding efficacy of the treatment. In cases where one study was cited, attempts were made to locate both the first and the second author. If this could not be done, additional authors (third, fourth, etc.) were contacted. In cases where two studies were cited, attempts were made to locate the first author of each study. If these individuals could not be located, additional authors were contacted, with the goal of contacting one author from each study. As can be seen in Table 1, a total of 76 distinct well-established and probably efficacious ESTs were identified, 4 from the 1995 Task Force report and 72 from the 1998 report. Overall, we distributed in this way 120 of the questionnaires described above.

Procedures

An 11-item questionnaire designed to assess various characteristics of ESTs was mailed to each participant. Specific questions can be found in Table 2. The response format for eight questions was "yes-no-other." However, three questions (#1, #5, and #8) required respondents to give a specific quantified response. The questionnaire included a

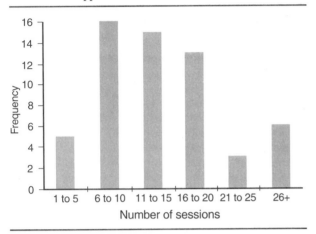

FIGURE 1. Total number of sessions required for empirically supported treatments (N=58).

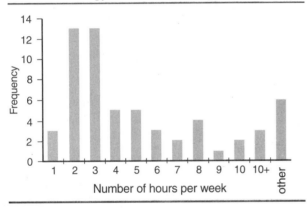

FIGURE 2. Number of total hours clients must devote to therapy in and out of session per week (N=60).

percentage agreement [agreements/(agreements + disagreements)]. Interrater reliability for this data set was 76%.

When examining the reliability data further, we found that a greater number of disagreements occurred for questions #6, #8, and #11 (each of these having nearly equal numbers of agreements and disagreements). Question #6 concerned the importance of the therapeutic relationship, question #8 concerned the frequency of assessment, and question #11 concerned the importance of knowing a client's history for treatment planning. It is impossible to know exactly why more disagreements occurred for these questions, but it could be due to the ambiguity of the question, different interpretations of the question, or simple disagreements among professionals.

Table 3. Responses to question #8 (frequency of assessment)

Response	Frequency
Weekly	14
Every session	12
Daily	7
Ongoing	3
None	1
1–2 times	2
3–4 times	12
5–6 times	1
7–8 times	1
9+ times	2
Other	4

cover letter explaining the purpose of the study, instructions concerning how to complete the questionnaire, and the name of the EST. After approximately 6 weeks, if at least one response had not been received concerning a particular EST, another questionnaire was sent to the author(s).

Our goal was to obtain one completed questionnaire for each full and probable EST, although often two authors for a particular EST were sent questionnaires in order to increase the likelihood of obtaining a completed questionnaire. If two completed questionnaires were received for an EST, one questionnaire was randomly chosen and that one was used to gather data; this occurred 11 times. Questions #1, #5, and #8 required respondents to provide quantitative answers. When these answers included a range of numbers, the median of these two numbers was the datum used in the results.

Reliability

Fortuitously, two sets of data were collected for a total of 11 ESTs, and interrater reliability was calculated by using

RESULTS AND DISCUSSION

Overall, the response rate was 80% (61 of 76 ESTs). Responses for questions with a "yes-no-other" format are presented in Table 2. Specific trends derived from these data indicate that ESTs, in general, share certain characteristics. For instance, responses to question #3 indicate that homework is a component of most ESTs (85%). In addition, responses to question #4 show that traditional assessment devices (e.g., the Minnesota Multiphasic Personality Inventory [MMPI] or the Rorschach test) are generally not used because they do not aid in treatment planning; 92% reported not using these devices.

Other clear trends that emerged from the data show that ESTs generally 1) focus on skill building, not insight or catharsis (#7; 85%); 2) involve continuous assessment to monitor a client's progress (#9; 77%); and 3) are problem-focused (#10; 90%).

Trends were less clear concerning three questions. First, the necessity of knowing the history of a client's presenting problem for treatment planning showed no clear trend

(#11). More specifically, 54% of respondents reported that knowing a client's history was not essential for treatment planning, whereas the other 46% either indicated that knowledge of the history was important or provided an "other" response. The necessity of making a DSM-IV diagnosis for treatment planning (question #2) is also somewhat less clear because responses were more evenly divided between "yes" and "no" responses. The majority of responses obtained (61%) indicated that diagnosis was not essential for making treatment decisions, but it appears that for at least a substantial minority of ESTs (38%), a DSM-IV diagnosis is an important aspect of treatment planning. Finally, 54% of respondents indicated that the formation of the therapeutic relationship was an important mechanism of change (#6), whereas 46% responded either "no" or "other."

Table 4. Data for well-established versus probably efficacious empirically supported treatments

Ques-tion #	Percentage					
	Well-Established (n=18)			Probably Efficacious (n=43)		
	Yes	No	Other	Yes	No	Other
2	33	67	0	40	58	2
3	89	5.5	5.5	84	16	0
4	6	94	0	7	91	2
6	50	33	17	56	30	14
7	11	83	6	12	86	2
9	78	11	11	78	14	9
10	100	0	0	86	5	9
11	39	56	6	28	54	19

Responses for question #1, concerning the total number of sessions required for the treatment, are presented in Figure 1. The vast majority of ESTs (80%) require 20 or fewer sessions. Responses of "other" to this question indicated that certain ESTs require very large amounts of time so a specific number could not be given (e.g., behavior modification for developmentally disabled individuals).

Figure 2 shows data regarding the number of hours a client must devote to treatment both in and outside of the session per week. It was found that all ESTs require some out-of-session work, with a large percentage requiring between 2 and 5 hours per week (59%). "Other" responses to this question usually indicated that it would be difficult to calculate the actual number of hours because of large between-subject variability (as in token economy programs or interpersonal therapy for bulimia).

Responses to question #8, concerning the frequency of assessment during treatment, are summarized in Table 3. A variety of responses were given to this question. In general,

though, it is evident that most ESTs involve periodic assessment throughout the treatment process. This finding contradicts the common notion among the general public that assessment is a process that occurs prior to treatment and then stops. It cannot be concluded, however, that continuous assessment is essential for positive treatment outcomes; it may be the case that continuous assessment is part of the research protocol used to evaluate many ESTs.

The response rate to the questionnaire was 80%, which leaves 20% of ESTs unaccounted for. As is always the case, it could be argued that had data been collected for these particular ESTs, the results of this study might have been somewhat different. Table 1 lists in boldface the ESTs for which no data were collected. These ESTs do not appear to differ in any important way from those for which responses were obtained. For instance, the majority of these therapies are behavioral or cognitive-behavioral, and they address a number of different problems (e.g., opiate dependence, obesity, sexual dysfunction). Therefore, we conclude that the data reported here are representative of ESTs in general.

Trends could, in theory, be different for the well-established ESTs versus the probably efficacious ESTs. To test this hypothesis, data for well-established and probably efficacious ESTs were compared for each of the "yes-no-other" questions. As can be seen in Table 4, the trends discussed above for the entire data set seem to apply equally well to the well-established ESTs and the probably efficacious ESTs. Furthermore, when data for particular questions are compared among the two sets of data, no appreciable differences emerge. Overall, the two sets of data show similar trends.

The trends found thus far in these relatively effective therapies tend to vindicate assumptions that an effective therapy is one in which the treatment is short-term; the emphasis is present-and problem-focused; skill building is stressed; the therapeutic relationship is considered to be important; homework is assigned; assessment is periodic; and traditional psychological tests such as intelligence testing, the MMPI-2, and the Rorschach are superfluous. However, there was some variation to this general pattern.

Philosophers of science have suggested that there is no logic of discovery; that is, in the context of discovery, "anything goes."[3] We do not disagree with this. However, we believe that the pattern of similarities that we have identified across therapies for a wide variety of problems (e.g., enuresis, depression, coping with stressors, bulimia, oppositional children, headache, and marital problems) is important to acknowledge because it can serve as a guide in the numerous choice points the researcher faces in therapy development.

We also want to offer one caveat. This trend may be partly an artifact of certain sociological factors that pertain to contemporary psychotherapy development and research. That is, the individuals who are meeting the research burden indicated by the Task Force are largely cognitive and behavioral researchers who generally adhere to the trends we have identified. Moreover, contemporary evaluative methods fit better with some types of therapies than others (e.g., short-term therapies). Still, this is an interesting sociological sketch regarding this discipline at this point in time. The future will show whether those with other, radically different positions regarding the nature of effective psychotherapy can vindicate those positions in reasonably designed outcome research.

References

1. Chambless DL: Training and dissemination of empirically validated psychological treatments: report and recommendations. The Clinical Psychologist 1995; 48:3–23

2. Chambless DL, Baker MJ, Baucom DH, et al: Update on empirically validated therapies, II. The Clinical Psychologist 1998; 51:3–16

3. Feyerabend PK: Against Method. New York, Verso, 1993

Received August 25, 1999; revised October 29, 1999; accepted November 22, 1999. From the Department of Psychology, University of Nevada, Reno. Address correspondence to Dr. O'Donohue, Department of Psychology/MS 298, University of Nevada, Reno, NV 89557; e-mail: wto@unr.edu

Computer- and Internet-Based Psychotherapy Interventions

Abstract

Computers and Internet-based programs have great potential to make psychological assessment and treatment more cost-effective. Computer-assisted therapy appears to be as effective as face-to-face treatment for treating anxiety disorders and depression. Internet support groups also may be effective and have advantages over face-to-face therapy. However, research on this approach remains meager.

Keywords

computer applications; Internet applications; psychotherapy and technology

C. Barr Taylor[1] and Kristine H. Luce
Department of Psychiatry, Stanford University Medical Center, Stanford, California

In recent years, the increasing number of users of computer and Internet technology has greatly expanded the potential of computer- and Internet-based therapy programs. Computer- and Internet-assisted assessment methods and therapy programs have the potential to increase the cost-effectiveness of standardized psychotherapeutic treatments by reducing contact time with the therapist, increasing clients' participation in therapeutic activities outside the standard clinical hour, and streamlining input and processing of clients' data related to their participation in therapeutic activities. Unfortunately, the scientific study of these programs has seriously lagged behind their purported potential, and these interventions pose important ethical and professional questions.

COMPUTER-BASED PROGRAMS

Information

A number of studies have demonstrated that computers can provide information effectively and economically. An analysis of a large number of studies of computer-assisted instruction (CAI) found that CAI is consistently effective in improving knowledge (Fletcher-Flinn & Gravatt, 1995). Surprisingly, few studies evaluating the use of CAI for providing information related to mental health or psychotherapy have been conducted.

Assessment

Traditional paper-based self-report instruments are easily adapted to the computer format and offer a number of advantages that include ensuring data completeness and standardization. Research has found that computer-administered assessment instruments work as well as other kinds of self-report instruments and as well as therapist-administered ones. Clients may feel less embarrassed about reporting sensitive or potentially stigmatizing information (e.g., about sexual behavior or illegal drug use) during a computer-assisted assessment than during a face-to-face assessment, allowing for more accurate estimates of mental health behaviors. Studies show that more symptoms, including suicidal thoughts, are reported during computer-assisted interviews than face-to-face interviews. Overall, the evidence suggests that computers can make assessments more efficient, more accurate, and less expensive. Yet computer-based assessment interviews do not allow for clinical intuition and nuance, assessment of behavior, and nonverbal emotional expression, nor do they foster a therapeutic alliance between client and therapist as information is collected.

Recently, handheld computers or personal digital assistants (PDAs) have been used to collect real-time, naturalistic data on a variety of variables. For example, clients can record their thoughts, behaviors, mood, and other variables at the same time and when directed to do so by an alarm or through instructions from the program. The assessment of events as they occur avoids retrospective recall biases. PDAs can be programmed to beep to cue a response and also to check data to determine, for instance, if responses are in the right range. The data are easily downloaded into computer databases for further analysis. PDAs with interactive transmission capabilities further expand the potential for real-time data collection. Although PDAs have been demonstrated to be useful for research, they have not been incorporated into clinical practice.

Computer-Assisted Psychotherapy

Much research on computer-based programs has focused on anxiety disorders (Newman, Consoli, & Taylor, 1997). Researchers have developed computer programs that direct participants through exercises in relaxation and restfulness; changes in breathing frequency, regularity, and pattern; gradual and progressive exposure to aspects of the situation, sensation, or objects they are afraid of; and changes in thinking patterns. Although the majority of studies report symptom reduction, most are uncontrolled trials or case studies and have additional methodological weaknesses (e.g., small sample sizes, no follow-up to assess whether treatment gains are maintained, focus on individuals who do not have clinical diagnoses).

Computer programs have been developed to reduce symptoms of simple phobias, panic disorder, obsessive-compulsive disorder (OCD), generalized anxiety disorder, and social phobia. In a multi-center, international treatment trial (Kenardy et al., 2002), study participants who received a primary diagnosis of panic disorder were randomly assigned to one of four groups: (a) a group that received 12 sessions of therapist-delivered cognitive behavior therapy (CBT), (b) a group that received 6 sessions of therapist-delivered CBT augmented by use of a handheld computer, (c) a group that received 6 sessions of therapist-delivered CBT augmented with a manual, or (d) a control group that was assigned to a wait list. Assessments at the end of treatment and 6 months later showed that the 12-session CBT and the 6-session CBT with the computer were equally effective. The results suggested that use of a handheld computer can reduce therapist contact time without compromising outcomes and may speed the rate of improvement.

An interactive computer program was developed to help clients with OCD, which is considered one type of anxiety disorder. The computer provided three weekly 45-min sessions of therapy involving vicarious exposure to their obsessive thoughts and response prevention (a technique by which clients with OCD are taught and encouraged not to engage in their customary rituals when they have an urge to do so). Compared with a control group, the clients who received the intervention had significantly greater improvement in symptoms. In a follow-up study with clients diagnosed with OCD, computer guided telephone behavior therapy was effective; however, clinician-guided behavior therapy was even more effective. Thus, computer-guided behavior therapy can be a helpful first step in treating patients with OCD, particularly when clinician-guided behavior therapy is unavailable. Computers have also been used to help treat individuals with other anxiety disorders, including social

phobia and generalized anxiety disorder, a condition characterized by excessive worry and constant anxiety without specific fears or avoidances.

CBT also has been adapted for the computer-delivered treatment of depressive disorders. Selmi, Klein, Greist, Sorrell, and Erdman (1990) conducted the only randomized, controlled treatment trial comparing computer- and therapist-administered CBT for depression. Participants who met the study's criteria for major, minor, or intermittent depressive disorder were randomly assigned to computer-administered CBT, therapist-administered CBT, or a wait-list control. Compared with the control group, both treatment groups reported significant improvements on depression indices. The treatment groups did not differ from each other, and treatment gains were maintained at a 2-month follow-up.

Little information exists on the use of computer-assisted therapy for treating patients with complicated anxiety disorders or other mental health problems. Thus, further study is needed.

THE INTERNET

Internet-based programs have several advantages over stand-alone computer-delivered programs. The Internet makes health care information and programs accessible to individuals who may have economic, transportation, or other restrictions that limit access to face-to-face services. The Internet is constantly available and accessible from a variety of locations. Because text and other information on the Internet can be presented in a variety of formats, languages, and styles, and at various educational levels, it is possible to tailor messages to the learning preferences and strengths of the user. The Internet can facilitate the collection, coordination, dissemination, and interpretation of data. These features allow for interactivity among the various individuals (e.g., physicians, clients, family members, caregivers) who may participate in a comprehensive treatment plan. As guidelines, information, and other aspects of programs change, it is possible to rapidly update information on Web pages. The medium also allows for personalization of information. Users may select features and information most relevant to them, and, conversely, programs can automatically determine a user's needs and strengths and display content accordingly.

Information

Patients widely search the Internet for mental health information. For example, the National Institute of Mental Health (NIMH) public information Web site receives more than 7 million "hits" each month. However, the mental health information on commercial Web sites is often inaccurate, misleading, or related to commercial interests. Sites sponsored by nonprofit organizations provide better and more balanced information, but search engines often list for-profit sites before they generate nonprofit sites. Furthermore, education Web sites rarely follow solid pedagogical principles.

Screening and Assessment

Many mental health Web sites have implemented screening programs that assess individuals for signs or symptoms of various psychiatric disorders. These programs generally recommend that participants who score above a predetermined cutoff contact a mental health provider for further assessment. The NIMH and many other professional organizations provide high-quality, easily accessible information combined with screening instruments. Houston and colleagues (2001) evaluated the use of a Web site that offered a computerized version of the Center for Epidemiological Studies' depression scale (CES-D; Ogles, France, Lunnen, Bell, & Goldfarb, 1998). The scale was completed 24,479 times during the 8-month study period. Fifty-eight percent of participants screened positive for depression, and fewer than half of those had previously been treated for depression. The Internet can incorporate interactive screening, which already has been extensively developed for desktop computers. Screening can then be linked to strategies that are designed to increase the likelihood that a participant will accept a referral and initiate further assessment or treatment.

On-Line Support Groups

Because Internet-delivered group interventions can be accessed constantly from any location that has Internet access, they offer distinct advantages over their face-to-face counterparts. Face-to-face support groups often are difficult to schedule, meet at limited times and locations, and must accommodate inconsistent attendance patterns because of variations in participants' health status and schedules. On-line groups have the potential to help rural residents and individuals who are chronically ill or physically or psychiatrically disabled increase their access to psychological interventions.

A wide array of social support groups is available to consumers in synchronous (i.e., participants on-line at the same time) or asynchronous formats. The Pew Internet and American Life Project (www.pewinternet.org) estimated that 28% of Internet users have attended an on-line support group for a medical condition or personal problem on at least one occasion. After a morning television show featured Edward M. Kennedy, Jr., promoting free on-line support groups sponsored by the Wellness Community (www.wellness-community.org), the organization received more than 440,000 inquiries during the following week! The majority of published studies on Internet-based support groups suggest that the groups are beneficial; however, scientific understanding of how and when is limited. Studies that examine the patterns of discourse that occur in these groups indicate that members' communication is similar to that found in face-to-face support groups (e.g., high levels of mutual support, acceptance, positive feelings).

Only a few controlled studies have examined the effects of Internet-based support programs. One such study investigated the effects of a program named Bosom Buddies on reducing psychosocial distress in women with breast cancer (Winzelberg et al., in press). Compared with a wait-list control group, the intervention group reported significantly reduced depression, cancer-related trauma, and perceived stress.

On-Line Consultation

On-line consultation with "experts" is readily available on the Internet. There are organizations for on-line therapists (e.g., the International Society for Mental Health Online, www.ismho.org) and sites that verify the credentials of on-line providers. However, little is known about the efficacy, reach, utility, or other aspects of on-line consultation.

Advocacy

The Internet has become an important medium for advocacy and political issues. Many organizations use the Internet to facilitate communication among members and to encourage members to support public policy (e.g., the National Alliance for the Mentally Ill, www.nami.org).

Internet-Based Psychotherapy

The Internet facilitates the creation of treatment programs that combine a variety of interactive components. The basic components that can be combined include psychoeducation; social support; chat groups; monitoring of symptoms, progress, and use of the program; feedback; and interactions with providers. Although many psychotherapy programs developed for desktop computers and manuals are readily translatable to the Internet format, surprisingly few have been adapted in this way, and almost none have been evaluated. Studies show that Internet-based treatments are effective for reducing symptoms of panic disorder. Compared with patients in a wait-list control group, those who participated in an Internet-based posttraumatic stress group reported significantly greater improvements on trauma-related symptoms. During the initial 6-month period of operation, an Australian CBT program for depression, MoodGYM, had more than 800,000 hits (Christensen, Griffiths, & Korten, 2002). In an uncontrolled study of a small subsample of participants who registered on this site, program use was associated with significant decreases in anxiety and depression. Internet-based programs also have been shown to reduce symptoms of eating disorders and associated behaviors. Users consistently report high satisfaction with these programs.

Treatment programs for depression, mood swings, and other mental health disorders are being designed to blend computer-assisted psychotherapy and psychoeducation with case management (in which a therapist helps to manage a client's problems by following treatment and therapy guidelines) and telephone-based care. These programs might also include limited face-to-face interventions, medication, and support groups. The effectiveness of these programs remains to be demonstrated.

Eventually, the most important use of the Internet might be to deliver integrated, home-based, case-managed, psychoeducational programs that are combined with some face-to-face contact and support groups. Unfortunately, although a number of such programs are "under development," none have been evaluated in controlled trials.

ETHICAL AND PROFESSIONAL ISSUES

Web-based interventions present a number of ethical and professional issues (Hsiung, 2001). Privacy is perhaps the most significant concern. The Internet creates an environment where information about patients can be easily accessed and disseminated. Patients may purposely or inadvertently disclose private information about themselves and, in on-line support groups, about their peers. Although programs can be password-protected, and electronic records must follow federal privacy guidelines, participants must be clearly informed that confidentiality of records cannot be guaranteed.

Internet interventions create the potential that services will be provided to patients who have not been seen by a professional or who live in other states or countries where the professionals providing the services are not licensed to provide therapy. Professional organizations are struggling to develop guidelines to address these concerns (e.g., Hsiung, 2001; Kane & Sands, 1998).

Because of its accessibility and relative anonymity, patients may use the Internet during crises and report suicidal and homicidal thoughts. Although providers who use Internet support groups develop statements to clearly inform patients that the medium is not to be used for psychiatric emergencies, patients may ignore these instructions. Thus, providers need to identify ancillary procedures to reduce and manage potential crises.

Given the continuing advances in technology and the demonstrated effectiveness and advantages of computer- and Internet-based interventions, one might expect that providers would readily integrate these programs into their standard care practice. Yet few do, in part because programs that are easy to install and use are not available, there is no professional or market demand for the use of computer-assisted therapy, and practitioners may have ethical and professional concerns about applying this technology in their clinical practice. Thus, in the near future this technology may primarily be used for situations in which the cost-effectiveness advantages are particularly great.

CONCLUSION

Computers have the potential to make psychological assessments more efficient, more accurate, and less expensive. Computer-assisted therapy appears to be as effective as face-to-face therapy for treating anxiety disorders and depression and can be delivered at lower cost. However, applications of this technology are in the early stages.

A high priority is to clearly demonstrate the efficacy of this approach, particularly compared with standard face-to-face, "manualized" treatments that have been shown to be effective for common mental health disorders. Studies that compare two potentially efficacious treatments require large samples for us to safely conclude that the therapies are comparable if no statistically significant differences are found. Kenardy et al. (2002) demonstrated that multi-site, international studies sampling large populations could be conducted relatively inexpensively, in part because the intervention they examined was standardized. If a treatment's efficacy is demonstrated, the next step would be to determine if the therapy, provided by a range of mental health professionals, is useful in large, diverse populations. Examination of combinations of therapies (e.g., CBT plus medication) and treatment modalities (Taylor, Cameron, Newman, & Junge, 2002) should follow. As the empirical study of this technology advances, research might examine the utility and cost-effectiveness of adapting these approaches to treating everyone in a community who wants therapy.

Continued use of the Internet to provide psychosocial support and group therapy is another promising avenue. As in the case of individual therapy, research is needed to compare the advantages and disadvantages between Internet and face-to-face groups, determine which patients benefit from which modality, compare the effectiveness of professionally moderated groups and self- or peer-directed groups, and compare the effectiveness of synchronous and asynchronous groups.

As research progresses, new and exciting applications can be explored. Because on-line text is stored, word content can be examined. This information may teach us more about the therapeutic process or may automatically alert providers to patients who are depressed, dangerous, or deteriorating.

Although research in many aspects of computer-assisted therapy is needed, and the professional and ethical concerns are substantial, computers and the Internet are likely to play a progressively important role in providing mental health assessment and interventions to clients. Thus, mental health professionals will need to decide how they will incorporate such programs into their practices.

RECOMMENDED READING

Taylor, C. B., Winzelberg, A. J., & Celio, A. A. (2001). The use of interactive media to prevent eating disorders. In R. H. Striegal-Moore & L. Smolak (Eds., *Eating disorders: Innovative directions in research and practice* (pp. 255–269). Washington, DC: American Psychological Association.

Yellowlees, P. (2001). *Your guide to e-health: Third millennium medicine on the Internet.* Brisbane, Australia: University of Queensland Press.

REFERENCES

Christensen, H., Griffiths, K. M., & Korten, A. (2002). Web-based cognitive behavior therapy: Analysis of site usage and changes in depression and anxiety scores. *Journal of Medical Internet Research, 4*(1), Article e3. Retrieved July 16, 2002, from http://www.jmir.org/2002/1/e3

Fletcher-Flinn, C. M., & Gravatt, B. (1995). The efficacy of computer assisted instruction (CAI): A meta-analysis. *Journal of Educational Computing Research, 3,* 219–241.

Houston, T. K., Cooper, L. A., Vu, H. T., Kahn, J., Toser, J., & Ford, D. E. (2001). Screening the public for depression through the Internet. *Psychiatric Services, 52,* 362–367.

Hsiung, R. C. (2001). Suggested principles of professional ethics for the online provision of mental health services. *Medinfo, 10,* 296–300.

Kane, B., & Sands, D. Z. (1998). Guidelines for the clinical use of electronic mail with patients: The AMIA Internet Working Group, Task Force on Guidelines for the Use of Clinic-Patient Electronic Mail. *Journal of the American Medical Informatics Association, 5,* 104–111.

Kenardy, J. A., Dow, M. G. T., Johnston, D. W., Newman, M. G., Thompson, A., & Taylor, C. B. (2002). *A comparison of delivery methods of cognitive behavioural therapy for panic disorder: An international multicentre trial.* Manuscript submitted for publication.

Newman, M. G., Consoli, A., & Taylor, C. B. (1997). Computers in assessment and cognitive behavioral treatment of clinical disorders: Anxiety as a case in point. *Behavior Therapy, 28,* 211–235.

Ogles, B. M., France, C. R., Lunnen, K. M., Bell, M. T., & Goldfarb, M. (1998). Computerized depression screening and awareness. *Community Mental Health Journal, 34* (1), 27–38.

Selmi, P. M., Klein, M. H., Greist, J. H., Sorrell, S. P., & Erdman, H. P. (1990). Computer-administered cognitive-behavioral therapy for depression. *American Journal of Psychiatry, 147,* 51–56.

Taylor, C. B., Cameron, R., Newman, M., & Junge, J. (2002). Issues related to combining risk factor reduction and clinical treatment for eating disorders in defined populations. *The Journal of Behavioral Health Services and Research, 29,* 81–90.

Winzelberg, A. J., Classen, C., Alpers, G., Roberts, H., Koopman, C., Adams, R., Ernst, H., Dev, P., & Taylor, C. B. (in press). An evaluation of an Internet support group for women with primary breast cancer. *Cancer.*

NOTE

1. Address correspondence to C. Barr Taylor, Department of Psychiatry, Stanford University Medical Center, Stanford, CA 94305-5722; e-mail: btaylor@stanford.edu.

From *Current Directions in Psychological Science,* February 2003, pp. 18-22. © 2003 by Blackwell Publishing Ltd., Oxford, UK. Reprinted by permission.

ARE WE Nuts?

By Mary McNamara Los Angeles Times

Americans have long been in love with the idea of psychotherapy. When Sigmund Freud made his first and only visit to the United States in 1909, American intelligentsia flocked to his lectures. Since then, psychotherapy has spread like kudzu, morphing from the medical treatment of specific, diagnosable mental illnesses into a sort of societal support system offered by psychiatrists, psychologists, counselors, therapists, self-help gurus and TV talk-show hosts.

"Seek professional help" is our standard answer to everything from episodes of psychotic rage to dating problems, and "self-help" has become its own industry. We use terms like "manic depressive," "obsessive compulsive" and "neurotic" to describe the most benign, everyday sort of behaviors.

And should true tragedy occur, the psychologists and counselors are there on the front lines, elbowing out the friends and clergy if not the paramedics. No other area of science or medicine so informs our national discussions or perceptions of who we are and who we should be.

But is it working? Are we getting any better? Is our mental health improving? And is our increased self-awareness benefiting society?

"It's difficult to gauge, compared to other parts of medicine," says Rochester, N.Y., psychiatrist John McIntyre. "There's no question that treatment of specific mental disorders is very effective—the efficacy rate is often higher than in other medical procedures. But when you broaden it to other issues, it gets fuzzy. It's had the overall beneficial effect of increasing knowledge of human nature, but are people better? How do you measure that?"

'Hysterical misery'

There is no arguing the fact that psychotherapy and psychiatry have improved the lives of millions suffering from often devastating chemical and mental imbalances. And, certainly, Freud had no personal illusions about transforming the human condition. He was content, he once said, to turn people's "hysterical misery into ordinary human unhappiness."

But here in America, we want to teach the world to sing, in perfect harmony. And so we look to psychology to provide us with answers and solutions to everything from a president's mendacity (there was that abusive stepfather) to relations between the sexes (which planet am I from?) to a baseball player's overt racism and homophobia (don't fire him, send him to a therapist).

According to Surgeon General David Satcher, the next decades will put the effectiveness of psychotherapy and psychiatry to the test. One out of five baby boomers can expect to suffer a mental disorder, from substance abuse to late-onset schizophrenia, while almost 21 percent of children ages 9 to 17 suffer from diagnosable mental disorders.

But measuring a nation's mental health is a difficult thing to undertake. One traditional method is to look at a society's tendency toward "social deviance"—its rates of crime, divorce, suicide, drug use and out-of-wedlock births. Most of these have decreased in recent years, although the divorce rate is significantly higher than it was even half a century ago.

But how valid are these numbers as indicators of mental health?

"Crime is not a good measure because there are a lot of social and economic reasons for crime," says Wendy Kaminer, pop psychology critic and author of "I'm Dysfunctional, You're Dysfunctional" and more recently "Sleeping With Extraterrestrials." "And to use divorce, well, if you have a sick norm [of troubled marriages], what is mentally healthy? To conform or rebel?"

Even using drug use as an indicator of mental instability is dangerous, she says, because there are many possible reasons for drug abuse; many in the scientific community believe the propensity for abuse is genetic.

Political movements have a complex relationship with the psychoanalytical movement. At one level, political movements by definition reject the psychological paradigm, their premise being that discontent stems not from our selves but from the System. On the other hand, Freud's identification of the id and the unconscious had a profound effect, particularly on the youth movements of the '60s and '70s.

Age of the id

"The id really came out in the '60s," says Peter Wolson, a Beverly Hills, Calif., psychoanalyst. "Suddenly, the thing is to be happy, not to lead a good life. Have fun, have orgasms, and this leads into the '70s and '80s, which is about getting ahead, still about 'me,' and then you have a backlash, mainly from fundamentalists. But even the backlash is very self-centered, very much of the id."

The United States has a long, complicated relationship with the culture of self—with self-government, self-actualization, self-discovery, self-aggrandizement. We celebrate nonconformity in a way that absolutely defines conformity and claim to treasure individualism while mass-producing more products than any other country in the world. "I gotta be me," we say, and if that "me" doesn't work out, well, we'll just try on a new one.

Psychology seems to provide both the means and the motive for the culture of self, and therein lies its greatest strength and its greatest failings.

"In a way, psychology has replaced religion," says David Blankenhorn of

the Institute for American Values, based in New York. "It is who we are, the air we breathe. And it can truly help people who suffer and can yield important insights. But the assumptions of the paradigm are so relentlessly centered on self, all other structures of meaning and authority evaporate. 'What do I want?' becomes the governing question."

Much of Blankenhorn's work centers on marriage and fatherhood, two areas greatly affected by the mass marketing of psychological theories in very different ways.

"For men, there are clearly advantages," he says. "They are more able to express emotions. Most fathers today hug their children and say, 'I love you.' For our fathers and grandfathers, such emotional intimacy was not there, and there is a whole generation of men walking around wounded from that."

But while fatherhood has benefited, he says, marriage has not.

"If talking about marriage and relationships was the basis of good marriage and relationships, we'd have the best in the history of the world," he says. "But they are now more fragile than they have ever been. Men and women seem unhappier with each other than ever."

Self-invention

Freud argued that it is pointless to try to make people happy because that's not what they want. Yet happiness seems to be the carrot at the end of psychology's stick—if you know yourself, you can change yourself and you can be happy. All the time. The creation of such expectations may be one of the psych-culture's greatest drawbacks.

"It's a mixed blessing," says University of Washington sociologist

Pepper Schwartz. "We've hugely increased our sensitivity to each other. We understand, for example, how much damage words can do. More people take responsibility for their actions, and if they don't, someone makes them. But we've also created whole new categories of what people should worry about, hundreds of new ways in which we can fail or people can fail us."

Our expectations from relationships have become much higher.

"Just look at the area of sex therapy," she says. "We have a hundred new ways to create inadequacies."

On the other hand, we have become more informed consumers, of theories as well as products.

"It used to be if Dr. So-and-So said something in the newspaper, readers would assume it was true," Schwartz says. "Not anymore. An easy example is how we have examined and rejected corporal punishment."

Like Blankenhorn, Schwartz believes the successes of the psychological movement are most evident in our attitudes toward parenting.

"If nothing else, I know we've made better fathers, although the numbers of fathers who leave is an area where we have possibly slid. But the ones who stay are much more participatory. No one's shocked to see a man in the grocery store alone with his kids. When I was a young woman, you would have assumed the mother was dead."

But again, are such changes the result of psychologically increased self-awareness, or the women's movement?

"The only real answer to 'Are we better yet?'" says Kaminer, "is, 'We don't know yet.'"

Cancer

Support Groups: Study Casts Some Doubt

In the past decade or so, many people have come to believe that healing can be a question of mind over matter. The notion that medical fate can be determined not only by the power of positive thinking but also through focused mental efforts of friends, relatives, and even strangers was once confined to "alternative" medicine. But scores of scientific studies have documented that support groups, social connectedness, and even prayer are not just effective in improving life but extending it. Mainstream medicine hasn't embraced all of these studies by any means, nor should it. But, at a minimum, most doctors acknowledge that psychosocial support has real consequences for health beyond just making people feel better.

The first study

If this phenomenon can be traced to a single source, it is a study in the Oct. 14, 1989, *Lancet* led by Stanford psychiatrist David Spiegel. He randomly assigned women with advanced breast cancer to either a support group and standard care, or standard care alone. Before the study, Spiegel and his team thought that participating in the support group would improve the quality of life, but they doubted it would affect survival. To their surprise, women in the support group lived, on average, 18 months longer than the women who received just standard care.

Other researchers have attempted to duplicate Spiegel's findings. The results are split down the middle. Half of the 10 investigations on record suggest that participating in a support group could, in fact, increase survival time. The others found no such effect. But the positive results seem to have gotten more attention. Support groups have sprung up everywhere. The promise of living longer isn't the only reason people join, but it has been dangling out there as a possible benefit.

No survival benefit

Now the largest study to date seems to have dashed the notion that support groups make patients live longer. In a multicenter investigation in Canada, 255 women with metastatic breast cancer were randomly assigned to two groups—158 attended support groups, 77 didn't. All the women received similar medical care. The women who went to a support group reported less pain and greater improvement in depression and other psychological symptoms. And those who were in the greatest distress

when they entered the study got the most benefit. But a key finding was that the support groups didn't add extra months to the lives of participants. With or without support group participation, the women lived for about a year and a half.

In an editorial in the Dec. 13, 2001, *New England Journal of Medicine* in which the Canadian study appeared, Spiegel said that the disparity between these results and his findings a dozen years ago might say as much about the state of breast-cancer treatment as it does about the value of support groups. He pointed to the substantial strides in breast-cancer detection and therapy. Indeed, the breast-cancer death rate finally started to drop in the 1990s.

Attitudes have changed

Maybe more importantly, attitudes about breast cancer have changed. No longer is it a condition that invokes an embarrassed silence. It's discussed in every conceivable forum, motivates powerful advocacy groups, and garners millions of research dollars each year. When women faced breast cancer virtually alone, joining a support group may have been one of the few ways to escape demoralizing—and unhealthy—isolation. Now breast cancer is out of the closet. With friends and family more likely to be understanding, the support group may be less of a lifeline. While participating in one might have been enough to tip the balance in the 1980s, it is now just one of several factors that can improve a patient's well-being.

Still helpful

Although a support group may not guarantee a longer life, it may mean a happier one. At the very least, support groups—whether for breast cancer, heart disease, emphysema, or myriad other conditions—offer an opportunity to vent about your condition without the fear of burdening or boring friends and family. They can spawn new friendships, offer coping strategies, and alleviate stress.

For people who prefer to keep their problems to themselves, a support group may just be a source of practical advice that is hard to find elsewhere. What better place to learn where to get a decent wig or a dentist with experience in treating people who are undergoing chemotherapy than a room of cancer survivors? Who is more likely to know which supermarket in your community has the best supply of sugar-free foods than a group of people with diabetes? It usually doesn't take long to tell if a support group is for you. If it isn't, you can drop out.

If you have a common condition like breast or prostate cancer, obesity, diabetes, emphysema, arthritis, diabetes, or heart disease, or are caring for someone with Alzheimer's disease, a support group is likely to be as close as the nearest hospital. You may need to travel farther, but an increasing number of groups exist for people with rare conditions. A host of other organizations, including health plans, foundations, advocacy groups, wellness centers, and adult education programs run them, partly because it's in their self-interest to do so. Support groups bring in potential customers or patients. Regardless of the sponsor, it's best to find a group run by a health professional. They can keep the discussion on track and ensure that the medical information exchanged is accurate.

Support online

If you want to communicate with others who have your condition, but don't want to do it in person, you may want to look into an Internet chat room or bulletin board. They are usually "hosted" by a Web site of some kind. You don't have to wait until the next scheduled meeting to voice a new concern or to pick up the thread of an ongoing discussion. Online interaction is also attractive to the many people who prefer to share their thoughts in writing.

But the Internet is also a free-for-all, especially when it comes to health information. Also, remember that while you may enjoy Internet anonymity, there's the danger that others will abuse it to peddle half-baked ideas or lie about who they are. For that reason, it's safest to start with the chat rooms or discussion groups on the Web sites of reputable non-profit organizations like the American Heart Association or the American Cancer Society. Such groups have experts who monitor the discussion boards to check that the information posted is sound.

Not do or die

Some people just aren't joiners. Perhaps they get the support they need from friends, family, or a particularly strong inner life. But if you believed the research findings that support groups extended life, not to join a support group seemed almost reckless. This latest study should send the message that support groups are a matter of choice, not a do-or-die-sooner situation. At the same time, both science and common sense say people in almost any dire circumstances can help each other out in innumerable ways. What's more, the more comfortable you are in a group, whether in person or through a computer hookup, the more you'll get out of it.

National Trends in the Use of Outpatient Psychotherapy

Objective: This article reports recent trends in the use of outpatient psychotherapy in the United States.

Method: Data from the household sections of the 1987 National Medical Expenditure Survey and the 1997 Medical Expenditure Panel Survey were analyzed. Trends in the rate of psychotherapy use from these nationally representative samples are presented by age, sex, race/ethnicity, marital status, education, employment status, and income. Psychotherapy users are compared over time by provider specialty, concomitant psychotropic medication use, number of annual visits, and costs. In addition, trends in payment source and primary diagnosis are assessed for psychotherapy visits.

Results: Between 1987 and 1997, there was no statistically significant change in the overall rate of psychotherapy use (3.2 per 100 persons in 1987 and 3.6 per 100 in 1997). However, significant increases were observed in psychotherapy use by adults aged 55–64 years and by unemployed adults. Among psychotherapy patients, there was a marked increase in the use of antidepressant medications (14.4% to 48.6%), mood stabilizers (5.3% to 14.5%), stimulants (1.9% to 6.4%), and psychotherapy provided by physicians (48.1% to 64.7%). A smaller proportion of patients made more than 20 psychotherapy visits in 1997 (10.3%) than in 1987 (15.7%). Over this period, psychotherapy visits for mood disorders became more common. In 1997, 9.7 million Americans spent $5.7 billion on outpatient psychotherapy.

Conclusions: From 1987 to 1997, access to psychotherapy in the United States remained constant overall but was characterized by increased use by some socioeconomically disadvantaged groups. However, the number of visits per user markedly decreased during this period. Psychotherapy was increasingly administered by physicians and provided in conjunction with psychotropic medications. These changes occurred during a period of expansion in the number of available psychotropic medications and growth in managed behavioral health care.

Mark Olfson, M.D., M.P.H.

Steven C. Marcus, Ph.D.

Benjamin Druss, M.D.

Harold Alan Pincus, M.D.

The provision and financing of outpatient psychotherapy has long been a matter of contention and controversy. Pointed disagreements have occurred among health policy analysts, mental health professionals, third-party payers, and patients over who should receive psychotherapy, how much they should receive, and who should pay for it. However, policies governing the provision and financing of outpatient psychotherapy have developed with little access to basic information about current patterns of psychotherapy utilization (1, 2). One reason that so little is known about patterns of psychotherapy use is that most large community mental health surveys do not distinguish psychotherapy from other outpatient mental health services. For example, neither the Epidemiologic Catchment Area study (3) nor the National Comorbidity Survey (4) identified whether psychotherapy was provided during outpatient psychiatric visits, nor did they provide an opportunity to assess changes in psychotherapy use over time.

The most recently published national estimates of psychotherapy use are based on data collected in 1987 (5, 6). Since that time, there have been profound changes in the organization and financing of mental health care in the United States. In addition,

new generations of antidepressant medications and other psychotropic medications that might complement or replace psychotherapy have become available. How these and other changes in the health care environment have altered patterns in use of psychotherapy remain unknown.

In this report, we examine recent national trends in the utilization and financing of outpatient psychotherapy using two large nationally representative surveys. We consider changes in who provided, received, and paid for outpatient psychotherapy in the United States during the period from 1987 to 1997. We also present national estimates of trends in access to outpatient psychotherapy and examine patterns of costs, reasons for use of psychotherapy, professional specialties of psychotherapists, and concurrent treatment with psychotropic medication for psychotherapy users.

Method

Data were drawn from the household component of the 1987 National Medical Expenditure Survey (7) and the 1997 Medical

Expenditure Panel Survey (8). Both surveys were sponsored by the Agency for Healthcare Research and Quality to provide national estimates of the use of, expenditures for, and financing of health care services. The National Medical Expenditure Survey and the Medical Expenditure Panel Survey were conducted with national probability samples of the U.S. civilian, noninstitutionalized population and were designed to provide nationally representative estimates to be compared over time.

Study Samples

The 1987 National Medical Expenditure Survey used a sampling design in which 15,590 households were selected from within 165 geographic regions across the United States. A sample of 34,459 individuals was included in the study, representing a response rate of 80.1%. Respondents for the 1997 Medical Expenditure Panel Survey household component were drawn from a nationally representative subsample of the 1995 National Health Interview Survey sample, which was selected by using a sampling design similar to that of the 1987 National Medical Expenditure Survey. A total of 32,636 participants from 14,147 households were interviewed, representing a 74.1% response rate. For both surveys, a designated informant was queried about all related persons who lived in the household.

The Agency for Healthcare Research and Quality devised weights to adjust for the complex survey design and yield unbiased national estimates. The sampling weights also adjusted for nonresponse and poststratification to population totals based on U.S. census data. More complete discussions of the design, sampling, and adjustment methods are presented elsewhere (9, 10).

Survey Structure

Households selected for the National Medical Expenditure Survey were interviewed four times to obtain health care utilization information for the 1987 calendar year. The Medical Expenditure Panel Survey included a series of three in-person interviews for 1997. In both surveys, respondents were asked to record medical events as they occurred in a calendar/diary that was reviewed during each in-person interview. Selected survey participants provided written permission to contact medical providers mentioned during the interview to verify service use, charges, and sources and amounts of payment.

Psychotherapy

The National Medical Expenditure Survey and the Medical Expenditure Panel Survey used a flash card with various response categories to ask respondents the type of care provided during each outpatient visit. Visits that included psychotherapy or mental health counseling were considered "psychotherapy" visits.

Psychotropic Medications

The National Medical Expenditure Survey and Medical Expenditure Panel Survey asked for a description of each prescribed medicine bought or otherwise obtained by survey participants during the survey year. We focused on prescribed psychotropic medications used by persons who had one or more psychotherapy visits during the survey year. Psychotropic medications were grouped by using the following American Hospital Formulary System therapeutic classes: antidepressants, antipsychotics, benzodiazepines, other anxiolytics, stimulants, and mood stabilizers (11).

Providers

The Medical Expenditure Panel Survey and National Medical Expenditure Survey solicited information on the type of health care professionals who provided treatment at each visit. We classified providers of psychotherapy into the following groups: physicians of all specialties (a breakdown by physician specialty was not available for 1997), social workers, psychologists, and a residual group of other providers that included nurses, nurse practitioners, physician assistants, chiropractors, and other health care providers. A psychotherapy user was considered to have been treated by a provider group if the user reported making one or more visits to that group during the survey year. Some respondents used psychotherapy from more than one provider group.

Diagnosis

The surveys collected information from the respondents on the primary reason for each ambulatory care visit. This information was grouped to permit classification according to ICD-9 categories by professional coders. The interviewers each underwent 80 hours of training, and coders all had degrees in nursing or medical record administration. A total of 5% of records were rechecked for errors; error rates in these rechecks were less than 2.5%. A staff psychiatric nurse determined mental disorder diagnoses in cases of diagnostic ambiguity or uncertainty.

The ICD-9 diagnoses associated with the psychotherapy visits were grouped into ten categories: schizophrenia and related disorders (ICD-9 codes 295, 297–299), mood disorders (296, 311), anxiety disorders (300), childhood disorders/mental retardation (312–319), adjustment disorders (308, 309), substance use disorders (291, 292, 303–305), personality disorders (301), other mental disorders (290, 293, 294, 302, 306, 307, 310), psychosocial circumstances (V40, V60–V62), and general medical conditions (all other codes). A separate category was constructed for visits in which the diagnosis was not specified. Patients who received one or more psychotherapy visits for the treatment of schizophrenia, affective psychoses, paranoid states, or other nonorganic psychoses (ICD-9 codes 295–299) were considered to have received treatment for a severe mental disorder (12).

Source of Payment

The survey interviewers asked respondents their sources of payment for each outpatient psychotherapy visit. From these data, summary variables of the following six potentially overlapping groups were constructed: self-payment, private insurance, Medicaid, Medicare, other Federal programs, and a residual group of other sources.

TABLE 1. Outpatient Psychotherapy Use in 1987 and 1997 National Probability Samples of the United States Civilian, Noninstitutionalized Population, by Sociodemographic Characteristics[a]

Characteristic	Rate of Psychotherapy Use per 100 Persons		Analysis	
	1987 (N=34,459)	1997 (N=32,636)	χ^2 (df=1)	p
Total	3.24	3.59	3.00	0.08
Age (years)				
<13	1.85	1.97	0.16	0.69
13–17	4.32	4.01	0.21	0.65
18–24	2.51	2.42	0.05	0.82
25–34	4.56	4.95	0.42	0.52
35–44	5.52	5.34	0.10	0.75
45–54	4.05	5.02	2.46	0.12
55–64	2.02	3.92	8.22	0.004
≥65	1.12	1.32	0.58	0.45
Sex				
Female	3.77	4.16	2.06	0.15
Male	2.67	2.96	1.46	0.23
Race/ethinicity				
White	3.69	4.26	4.91	0.03
Black	1.63	1.97	1.35	0.25
Hispanic	1.95	1.94	0.00	0.97
Other	1.75	0.93	2.34	0.13
Marital status[b]				
Married	2.92	3.31	1.90	0.17
Divorced/separated	7.04	6.55	0.31	0.58
Widowed	1.81	2.14	0.53	0.47
Not married	3.99	4.62	1.76	0.18
Education (years)[b]				
<12	2.38	3.08	5.90	0.02
12	3.18	3.49	0.70	0.40
13–16	4.29	4.79	1.28	0.26
≥17	6.65	5.66	0.93	0.34
Employment[b]				
Employed	3.20	3.24	0.03	0.88
Unemployed	3.33	4.62	10.67	0.001
Income status				
Poor	3.50	4.60	4.13	0.04
Near poor	2.41	3.73	3.55	0.06
Low income	3.32	2.91	0.72	0.40
Middle income	2.69	3.09	1.71	0.19
High income	3.79	3.89	0.06	0.80

[a]Data from the 1987 National Medial Expenditure Survey (7) and the 1997 Medical Expenditure Panel Survey (8).

[b]Analysis limited to persons at least 18 years of age.

Analysis Plan

Rates of psychotherapy use per 100 persons for each survey year were computed overall and stratified by key sociodemographic characteristics. Psychotherapy use was compared over time by provider specialty, concomitant psychotropic medication use, number of annual visits, and costs. In addition, trends in payment source and primary diagnosis for the psychotherapy visit were examined.

To adjust for changes in patient characteristics over time, we used a logistic regression model to evaluate the strength of the association between survey year and use of psychotherapy while controlling for the effects of background sociodemographic characteristics.

All statistical analyses were performed with the SUDAAN software package (13) to accommodate the complex sample design and the weighting of observations. Z tests were used to evaluate the statistical significance of changes in proportional cost distributions. The Wald chi-square test was used for all other comparisons. All tests were two-tailed, and alpha was set conservatively at 0.01 to compensate for multiple comparisons.

Results

Rate of Psychotherapy Use

The overall rate of outpatient psychotherapy use did not significantly change between 1987 (3.2 per 100 population) and 1997 (3.6 per 100 population). However, a significant increase in the rate of psychotherapy use was observed among adults age 55–64 years and among unemployed persons (Table 1). After controlling for patient sociodemographic characteristics, individuals were 1.14 (99% confidence interval=1.01–1.29) times more likely to receive at least one psychotherapy visit in 1997 than in 1987.

In 1987, there were approximately 7.75 million users of outpatient psychotherapy who made a total of approximately 83.68 million visits. In 1997, there were approximately 9.69 million psychotherapy users who made approximately 86.19 million visits.

Clinical Characteristics of Psychotherapy Users

During the survey period, there were significant increases in the proportion of psychotherapy users who made one or more psychotherapy visits to a physician or a social worker and a decline in the proportion of psychotherapy visits to other health care professionals who were not psychologists. Little change occurred in the proportion of psychotherapy users who received psychotherapy from psychologists (Table 2). In 1997, nearly two-thirds (64.7%) of outpatient psychotherapy users had at least one psychotherapy visit with a physician, compared with roughly one-half (48.1%) in 1987.

During the study period, psychotherapy patients sharply increased their use of psychotropic medications. Whereas approximately one-third (31.5%) of psychotherapy users received a psychotropic medication in 1987, almost two-thirds (61.5%) received a psychotropic medication in 1997 (Table 2). This increase was largely attributable to a rise in the proportion of psychotherapy users who received antidepressant medications, from 14.4% in 1987 to 48.6% in 1997. The proportion of psychotherapy users who reported using stimulants or mood stabilizers also increased significantly, although those medications were used substantially less often than antidepressants.

TABLE 2. Characteristics of Psychotherapy Received in 1987 and 1997 National Probability Samples of the United States Civilian, Noninstitutionalized Population[a]

Characteristic	Percentage of Respondents Reporting Use of Psychotherapy		Analysis	
	1987 (N=993)	1997 (N=1,139)	χ^2 (df=1)	p
Provider specialty				
Physician	48.09	64.73	31.15	<0.0001
Psychologist	31.81	35.18	1.47	0.23
Social worker	6.84	12.54	10.06	0.002
Other	22.78	14.67	12.46	0.0004
Psychotropic medication				
Any	31.52	61.52	126.42	<0.0001
Antidepressants	14.38	48.63	175.87	<0.0001
Antipsychotics	8.83	10.69	1.48	0.23
Benzodiazepines	16.26	14.75	0.68	0.41
Other anxiolytics	0.54	4.83	28.48	<0.0001
Stimulants	1.86	6.41	22.77	<0.0001
Mood stabilizers	5.28	14.51	33.49	<0.0001
Number of visits				
1 or 2	33.54	35.27	0.39	0.53
3–10	37.10	39.80	0.96	0.33
11–20	13.67	14.67	0.29	0.59
>20	15.69	10.26	8.38	0.004
Cost distribution by number of visits[b]			z	p
1 or 2	3.82	6.07	2.24	0.03
3–10	19.87	24.99	1.40	0.16
11–20	15.16	25.83	2.71	0.006
>20	61.15	43.11	3.09	0.002

[a]Data from the 1987 National Medical Expenditure Survey (7) and the 1997 Medical Expenditure Panel Survey (8).

[b]Data represent percentages of total annual expenditures for outpatient psychotherapy.

The proportion of psychotherapy patients who made more than 20 visits (long-term psychotherapy) during the survey year significantly declined over the study period. In addition, there was a substantial decline in the proportion of total psychotherapy costs attributed to patients who made more than 20 visits during the survey year (Table 2).

The proportion of patients in long-term psychotherapy (>20 visits) who were treated for a severe mental disorder diagnosis increased from 7.4% in 1987 to 20.9% in 1997 (χ^2=6.0, df=1, p=0.01). However, there was also an increase in the percentage of shorter-term (≤20 visits) psychotherapy users who received treatment for a severe mental disorder diagnosis (4.4% to 9.6%) (χ^2=13.2, df=1, p=0.0003).

In both survey years, a substantial proportion of psychotherapy users made only one or two psychotherapy visits (33.5% in 1987; 35.3% in 1997). In 1997, roughly one-third (35.7%) of psychotherapy users treated by physicians, one-quarter (27.9%) treated by psychologists, and one-tenth (10.3%) treated by social workers had episodes of treatment that were one or two visits in length.

Characteristics of Psychotherapy Visits

There were several significant changes in the distribution of primary diagnoses for outpatient psychotherapy visits. Specifically, a large increase occurred in the proportion of psychotherapy visits that were primarily for the treatment of mood disorders. The proportion of visits in which no condition was specified significantly declined. The proportion of psychotherapy visits for substance use disorders and general medical conditions declined, although the change was not significant (Table 3).

Between 1987 and 1997, Medicare tended to become more common as a primary source of payment for psychotherapy visits, and self-payment tended to become less common (Table 3). However, these changes did not reach the level of statistical significance. In 1997, the cost of outpatient psychotherapy was approximately 5.74 billion dollars.

Discussion

During the decade between 1987 and 1997, the nature of psychotherapy in the United States underwent several important changes. There was an increase in use of psychotherapy by socioeconomically disadvantaged individuals, a rise in psychotherapy for mood disorders, a decline in psychotherapy for nonspecific conditions, greater use of psychotropic medications and involvement of physicians, and a decline in longer-term psychotherapy. We briefly consider each of these trends.

A significant increase was evident in the rate of psychotherapy for unemployed adults, and there were nonsignificant gains among the poor and those with little formal education. These groups are at especially high risk for untreated mental health problems. Poor and less well-educated people have higher rates of mental disorders than their more affluent counterparts (14, 15) and are also less likely to seek mental health treatment (16). Increasing access to outpatient psychotherapy for these vulnerable populations is a welcomed development.

The use of psychotherapy for the treatment of mood disorders increased. Advances in clinical assessment and psychopharmacological treatment may have contributed to this trend. During the decade, a new generation of rapid screening and diagnostic instruments became available for clinical use (17–19). In addition, the availability of selective serotonin reuptake inhibitors and other newer antidepressants may have increased the demand for treatment of depression and secondarily increased the use of psychotherapy for patients receiving these medications (20). Increased public awareness of depression and its relative destigmatization may have further increased help seeking for mood disorders (21). Once patients were in treatment, incomplete or unsatisfactory response to pharmacological treatments, preferences of patients or clinicians, or treatment history considerations may have led to initiation of psychotherapy.

The use of mood stabilizers among psychotherapy patients also increased. In recent years, several anticonvulsants have

TABLE 3. Primary Diagnoses and Sources of Payment for Psychotherapy Visits in 1987 and 1997 National Probability Samples of the United States Civilian, Noninstitutionalized Population[a]

Primary Payment Source and Diagnosis	Visits in 1987 (N=10,113)	Visits in 1997 (N=10,078)	Analysis	
			z	p
Primary payment source				
Self-payment	44.29	37.44	1.53	0.12
Private insurance	25.71	33.39	1.31	0.19
Medicaid	16.01	15.61	0.07	0.93
Medicare	2.65	4.05	2.02	0.04
Other federal	6.84	2.70	1.35	0.17
Other	4.47	6.80	0.88	0.38
			χ^2 (df=1)	p
Primary diagnosis and ICD-9 category codes				
Schizophrenia (295, 297–299)	4.36	5.58	0.22	0.64
Mood disorders (296, 311)	19.51	39.09	22.50	<0.0001
Anxiety disorders (300)	10.45	12.56	0.54	0.47
Disorders of childhood/mental retardation (312–319)	3.34	4.02	0.30	0.58
Adjustment disorders (308, 309)	8.28	9.00	0.10	0.76
Substance use disorders (291, 292, 303–305)	4.09	1.47	4.68	0.031
Personality disorders (301)	1.11	0.05	2.04	0.15
Other mental disorders (290, 293, 294, 302, 306, 307, 310)	0.49	0.89	0.45	0.50
Psychosocial circumstances (V40, V60–V62)	7.01	4.64	1.58	0.21
General medical condition (all other ICD-9 codes)	16.25	10.31	4.46	0.035
No condition specified	25.11	12.38	14.92	0.0001

[a]Data from the 1987 National Medical Expenditure Survey (7) and the 1997 Medical Expenditure Panel Survey (8).

been discovered to have mood-stabilizing properties (22, 23). Mood stabilizers have become accepted pharmacological options for a widening array of bipolar spectrum disorders (24), schizoaffective disorder (25), posttraumatic stress disorder (26), and borderline personality disorder (27). Growth in the number of mood stabilizers and their emerging clinical applications may have contributed to their increased use by psychotherapy patients.

Stimulants have also become more commonly used by psychotherapy patients. Recent growth in the use of stimulants has been reported from analyses of bulk methylphenidate production (28), pharmacy-based audits (29), surveys of physicians (30, 31), school-based surveys (32, 33), and Medicaid claims (34, 35). The development of grassroots advocacy groups for attention deficit hyperactivity disorder (ADHD), including Children With Attention Deficit Disorder and the Attention Deficit Disorder Association, as well as federal reform affecting eligibility for special education services, is believed to have promoted recognition of ADHD and use of stimulants (36).

Psychotherapy for unspecified conditions has become less frequent. The dramatic expansion of managed behavioral health care during the decade may have played a role in the decline of psychotherapy for poorly defined conditions. Under managed behavioral health care, approval of psychotherapy is often linked to "medical necessity" or other precertification utilization review criteria (37). Such cost containment measures may encourage greater clinical efforts to focus psychotherapy on well-defined psychiatric conditions.

It is widely believed that managed care has shifted the provision of psychotherapy from psychologists, psychiatrists, and other physicians to other lower cost professionals (38, 39). The current findings belie this belief. We found that physicians were increasingly involved in the provision of psychotherapy. Unfortunately, it is not possible to distinguish psychotherapy visits in the 1997 survey that were provided by psychiatrists from those provided by other physicians. According to the 1987 survey, however, psychiatrists provided more than five times as many psychotherapy visits as nonpsychiatrist physicians (5).

The surveys also do not permit an assessment of whether patients treated with psychotherapy and psychotropic medications received integrated care (i.e., both pharmacotherapy and psychotherapy provided by a psychiatrist or other physician) or split treatment (i.e., pharmacotherapy provided by a physician and psychotherapy provided by another health professional). Some evidence suggests a recent growth in split treatment, although the effectiveness of such treatment and the cost implications of this development remain unclear (40, 41).

Long-term psychotherapy became less common during the survey period. This change in the nature of psychotherapy may be related to growth in the number of private health plans that limit outpatient mental visits (42, 43). It may also be a consequence of the resurgence of interest in cognitive behavior treatments (44, 45) and of other evidence supporting time-limited psychotherapies (46).

Approximately one-third of psychotherapy patients received only one or two sessions. Across a variety of patient populations and types of psychotherapy, there tends to be a dose-response relationship between the number of psychotherapy sessions and the amount of patient benefit (47, 48). These findings suggest that much of the psychotherapy in the United States is shallow and of limited benefit. At the same time, it should be acknowledged that a group of experimental studies has supported the efficacy of single-session cognitive behavior therapies for a variety of specific phobias (49–52).

The surveys had several limitations. The National Medical Expenditure Survey and the Medical Expenditure Panel Survey collected data from household informants who may not have been fully aware of all of the services utilized by household members. Recall errors, stigma, and problems distinguishing psychotherapy from other health counseling pose threats to the survey data. A broad definition of psychotherapy also makes it impossible to distinguish simple nonspecific support and generic counseling from established formal psychotherapies. It would be useful if future national surveys characterized psychotherapies in a manner that differentiates various well-defined clinical techniques. Without an independent measure of symptoms, assessment of the validity of the reported diagnostic codes associated with the psychotherapy visits is not possible. Finally, while the National Medical Expenditure Survey and the Medical Expenditure Panel Survey collected information on services provided by the full range of health care professionals, several of these groups typically receive little or no formal training in the provision of psychotherapy.

In summary, the pattern of psychotherapy utilization in the United States underwent several important changes during the decade under study. The use of long-term psychotherapy declined overall, and the use of psychotropic medications increased. At the same time, some socioeconomically disadvantaged groups increased their use of psychotherapy, and individuals with severe mental disorders accounted for an increasing share of long-term patients. These changes occurred in the context of advances in psychopharmacological treatments, development of tools for rapid diagnosis, changing public attitudes toward mental health care treatment, and major revisions in the organization and financing of mental health services.

There is broad consumer satisfaction with psychotherapy (53), even very brief forms of psychotherapy (54). However, the effects of commonly available psychotherapies on patient outcomes remain poorly studied. Key challenges ahead include defining technical dimensions of psychotherapy in community practice and determining the clinical effectiveness of psychotherapy for the large number of individuals who receive this intervention.

Received Oct. 9, 2001; revision received March 20, 2002; accepted June 25, 2002. From the New York State Psychiatric Institute and the Department of Psychiatry, College of Physicians and Surgeons of Columbia University; the School of Social Work, University of Pennsylvania, Philadelphia; the Department of Psychiatry, Yale University School of Medicine, New Haven, Conn.; the Department of Psychiatry, University of Pittsburgh; and the RAND Corporation, Pittsburgh. Address reprint requests to Dr. Olfson, New York State Psychiatric Institute, Department of Psychiatry, College of Physicians and Surgeons of Columbia University, 1051 Riverside Dr., New York, NY; olfsonm@child.cpmc.columbia.edu (e-mail).

Supported by a grant from the Robert Wood Johnson Foundation.

References

1. Hennessy KD, Green-Hennessy S: An economic and clinical rationale for changing utilization review practices for outpatient psychotherapy. J Ment Health Admin 1997; 24:340–349
2. Moran PW: The adaptive practice of psychotherapy in the managed care era. Psychiatr Clin North Am 2000; 23:383–402
3. Robins LN, Regier DA (eds): Psychiatric Disorders in America: The Epidemiological Catchment Area Study. New York, Free Press, 1991
4. Kessler RC, McGonagle KA, Zhao S, Nelson CB, Hughes M, Eshleman S, Wittchen H-U, Kendler KS: Lifetime and 12-month prevalence of DSM-III-R psychiatric disorders in the United States: results from the National Comorbidity Survey. Arch Gen Psychiatry 1994; 51:8–19
5. Olfson M, Pincus HA: Outpatient psychotherapy in the United States, I: volume, costs, and user characteristics. Am J Psychiatry 1994; 151:1281–1288
6. Olfson M, Pincus HA: Outpatient psychotherapy in the United States, II: patterns of utilization. Am J Psychiatry 1994; 151:1289–1294
7. Edwards WS, Berlin M: National Medical Expenditure Survey: Questionnaires and Data Collection Methods for the Household Survey and Survey of American Indians and Alaska Natives: DHHS Publication PHS 89–3450. Washington, DC, US Department of Health and Human Services, 1989
8. Cohen SB: Sample Design of the 1997 Medical Expenditure Panel Survey Household Component: MEPS Methodology Report 11: AHRQ Publication 01–0001. Rockville, Md, Agency for Healthcare Research and Quality, 2000
9. Cohen S, DiGaetano R, Waksberg J: Sample Design of the 1987 Household Survey: National Medical Expenditure Survey Methods 3: AHCPR Publication 91–0037. Rockville, Md, Agency for Health Care Policy and Research, 1991
10. Cohen SB: Sample Design of the 1997 Medical Expenditure Panel Survey Household Component: MEPS Methodology Report 11, AHRQ Publication 01–0001. Rockville, Md, Agency for Healthcare Research and Quality, 2000
11. McEvoy GK (ed): American Hospital Formulary Service Drug Information 97. Bethesda, Md, American Society of Health-System Pharmacists, 1997
12. Thompson JW, Burns BJ, Taube CA: The severely mentally ill in general hospital psychiatric units. Gen Hosp Psychiatry 1988; 10:1–9
13. Shah BV, Barnwell BG, Dieler GS: SUDAAN User's Manual, Release 7.5. Research Triangle Park, NC, Research Triangle Institute, 1997
14. Dohrenwend BP, Itzhak L, Shrout P, Schwartz S, Naveh G, Link B, Skodol A, Steve A: Socioeconomic status and psychiatric disorders: the causation-selection issue. Science 1992; 255:946–952
15. Regier DA, Farmer ME, Rae DS, Myers JK, Kramer M, Robins LN, George LK, Karno M, Locke BZ: One-month prevalence of mental disorders in the United States and sociodemographic characteristics: the Epidemiologic Catchment Area study. Acta Psychiatr Scand 1993; 88:35–47
16. Howard KI, Corniolle TA, Lyons JS, Vessey JT, Lueger RJ, Saunders SM: Patterns of mental health service utilization. Arch Gen Psychiatry 1996; 53:696–703

17. Spitzer RL, Williams JB, Kroenke K, Linzer M, deGruy FV III, Hahn SR, Brody D, Johnson JG: Utility of a new procedure for diagnosing mental disorders in primary care: the PRIME-MD 1000 study. JAMA 1994; 272:1749–1756

18. Leon AC, Olfson M, Weissman MM, Portera L, Fireman BH, Blacklow RS, Hoven C, Broadhead WE: Brief screens for mental disorders in primary care. J Gen Intern Med 1996; 11:426–430

19. Zimmerman M, Lish JD, Farber NJ, Hartung J, Lush D, Kuzma MA, Plescia G: Screening for depression in medical patients: is the focus too narrow? Gen Hosp Psychiatry 1994; 16:388–396

20. Olfson M, Marcus SC, Druss B, Elinson L, Tanielian T, Pincus HA: National trends in the outpatient treatment of depression. JAMA 2002; 287:203–209

21. Pincus HA, Tanielian TL, Marcus SC, Olfson M, Zarin DA, Thompson J, Zito JM: Prescribing trends in psychotropic medications: primary care, psychiatry, and other medical specialties. JAMA 1998; 279:529–531

22. American Psychiatric Association: Practice Guideline for the Treatment of Patients With Bipolar Disorder. Am J Psychiatry 1994; 151(Dec suppl)

23. Expert Consensus Panel for Bipolar Disorder: Treatment of bipolar disorder. J Clin Psychiatry 1996; 57(suppl 12A):3–88

24. Akiskal HS, Pinto O: The evolving bipolar spectrum: prototypes I, II, III, and IV. Psychiatr Clin North Am 1999; 22:517–534

25. Keck PE, McElroy SL, Strakowski SM: New developments in the pharmacologic treatment of schizoaffective disorder. J Clin Psychiatry 1996; 57(suppl 9):41–48

26. Davidson JR: Biological therapies for posttraumatic stress disorder: an overview. J Clin Psychiatry 1997; 58(suppl 9):29–32

27. Hollander E: Managing aggressive behavior in patients with obsessive-compulsive disorder and borderline personality disorder. J Clin Psychiatry 1999; 60(suppl 15):38–44

28. Morrow RC, Morrow AL, Haislip G: Methylphenidate in the United States, 1990 through 1995 (letter). Am J Public Health 1998; 88:1121

29. Batoosingh KA: Ritalin prescriptions triple over last 4 years. Clin Psychiatr News 1995; 23:1–2

30. Hoagwood K, Kelleher KJ, Feil M, Comer DM: Treatment services for children with ADHD: a national perspective. J Am Acad Child Adolesc Psychiatry 2000; 39:198–206

31. Zito JM, Safer DJ, dosReis S, Magder LS, Gardner JF, Zarin DA: Psychotherapeutic medication patterns for youths with attention-deficit/hyperactivity disorder. Arch Pediatr Adolesc Med 1999; 153:1257–1263

32. Safer DJ, Magder LS: Stimulant treatment in Maryland public schools. Pediatrics 2000; 106:533–539

33. Safer DJ, Krager JM: The increased rate of stimulant treatment for hyperactive/inattentive students in secondary schools. Pediatrics 1994; 94:462–464

34. Zito JM, Riddle MA, Safer DJ, Johnson R, Fox M, Speedie S, Scerbo M: Pharmacoepidemiology of youth with treatments for mental disorders (abstract). Psychopharmacol Bull 1995; 31:540

35. Rushton JL, Whitmire JT: Pediatric stimulant and selective serotonin reuptake inhibitor prescription trends: 1992 to 1998. Arch Pediatr Adolesc Med 2001; 155:560–565

36. Swanson JM, McBurnett K, Christian DL, Wigal T: Stimulant medications and the treatment of children with ADHD, in Advances in Clinical Child Psychology, vol 17. Edited by Ollendick TH, Prinz RJ. New York, Plenum, 1995, pp 265–307

37. Bennett MJ: Is psychotherapy ever medically necessary? Psychiatr Serv 1996; 47:966–970

38. Humphreys K: Clinical psychologists as psychotherapists: history, future, and alternatives. Am Psychol 1996; 51:190–197

39. Detre T, McDonald MC: Managed care and the future of psychiatry. Arch Gen Psychiatry 1997; 54:201–204

40. Goldman W, McCulloch J, Cuffel B, Zarin DA, Suarez A, Burns BJ: Outpatient utilization patterns of integrated and split psychotherapy and pharmacotherapy for depression. Psychiatr Serv 1998; 49:477–482

41. Dewan M: Are psychiatrists cost-effective? an analysis of integrated versus split treatment. Am J Psychiatry 1999; 156:324–326

42. Health Care Plan Design and Cost Trends—1988 through 1997. Washington, Hay Group, May 1998

43. Buck JA, Teich JL, Stein M: Behavioral health benefits in employer-sponsored health plans, 1997. Health Affairs 1999; 18(2):67–78

44. Thompson LW, Coon DW, Gallagher-Thompson D, Sommer BR, Koin D: Comparison of desipramine and cognitive/behavioral therapy in the treatment of elderly outpatients with mild-to-moderate depression. Am J Geriatr Psychiatry 2001; 9:225–240

45. Clarke GN, Rohde P, Lewinsohn PM, Hops H, Seeley JR: Cognitive-behavioral treatment of adolescent depression: efficacy of acute group treatment and booster sessions. J Am Acad Child Adolesc Psychiatry 1999; 38:272–279

46. Markowitz JC: Developments in interpersonal psychotherapy. Can J Psychiatry 1999; 44:556–561

47. Lutz W, Lowry J, Kopta SM, Eisensten DA, Howard KI: Prediction of dose-response relations based on patient characteristics. J Clin Psychol 2001; 57:889–900

48. Howard KI, Kopta SM, Krause MS, Orlinsky DE: The dose-effect relationship in psychotherapy. Am Psychol 1986; 41:159–164

49. Ost LG, Alm T, Brandberg M, Breitholtz E: One vs five sessions of exposure and five sessions of cognitive therapy in the treatment of claustrophobia. Behav Res Ther 2001; 39:167–183

50. Ost LG, Brandberg M, Alm T: One versus five sessions of exposure in the treatment of flying phobia. Behav Res Ther 1997; 35:987–996

51. Ost LG, Ferebee I, Furmark T: One session group therapy of spider phobias. Behav Res Ther 1997; 35:721–732

52. Ost LG, Salkovskis PM, Hellstrom K: One-session therapist directed exposure versus self-exposure in the treatment of spider phobias. Behav Res Ther 1991; 22:407–422

53. Seligman ME: The effectiveness of psychotherapy: the *Consumer Reports* study. Am Psychol 1995; 50:965–974

54. Sherman WH, Beech RP: Length of intervention and client assessed outcome. J Clin Psychol 1984; 40:475–480

Index

Index

Test Your Knowledge Form

We encourage you to photocopy and use this page as a tool to assess how the articles in *Annual Editions* expand on the information in your textbook. By reflecting on the articles you will gain enhanced text information. You can also access this useful form on a product's book support Web site at *http://www.dushkin.com/online/*.

NAME: _____ DATE: _____

TITLE AND NUMBER OF ARTICLE: _____

BRIEFLY STATE THE MAIN IDEA OF THIS ARTICLE: _____

LIST THREE IMPORTANT FACTS THAT THE AUTHOR USES TO SUPPORT THE MAIN IDEA:

WHAT INFORMATION OR IDEAS DISCUSSED IN THIS ARTICLE ARE ALSO DISCUSSED IN YOUR TEXTBOOK OR OTHER READINGS THAT YOU HAVE DONE? LIST THE TEXTBOOK CHAPTERS AND PAGE NUMBERS:

LIST ANY EXAMPLES OF BIAS OR FAULTY REASONING THAT YOU FOUND IN THE ARTICLE:

LIST ANY NEW TERMS/CONCEPTS THAT WERE DISCUSSED IN THE ARTICLE, AND WRITE A SHORT DEFINITION:

We Want Your Advice

ANNUAL EDITIONS revisions depend on two major opinion sources: one is our Advisory Board, listed in the front of this volume, which works with us in scanning the thousands of articles published in the public press each year; the other is you—the person actually using the book. Please help us and the users of the next edition by completing the prepaid article rating form on this page and returning it to us. Thank you for your help!

ANNUAL EDITIONS: Psychology 04/05

ARTICLE RATING FORM

Here is an opportunity for you to have direct input into the next revision of this volume.
We would like you to rate each of the articles listed below, using the following scale:

1. **Excellent: should definitely be retained**
2. **Above average: should probably be retained**
3. **Below average: should probably be deleted**
4. **Poor: should definitely be deleted**

Your ratings will play a vital part in the next revision.
Please mail this prepaid form to us as soon as possible.
Thanks for your help!

RATING	ARTICLE	RATING	ARTICLE
	1. Mind Games: Psychological Warfare Between Therapists and Scientists		32. Are You Looking at Me? Eye Gaze and Person Perception
	2. Teaching Skepticism via the CRITIC Acronym and the Skeptical Inquirer		33. Got Time for Friends?
	3. Causes and Correlations		34. Rational and Irrational Fears Combine in Terrorism's Wake
	4. What Makes You Who You Are		35. Sex in America
	5. The Blank Slate		36. Mental Health Gets Noticed
	6. Neuroscience: Breaking Down Scientific Barriers to the Study of Brain and Mind		37. The Lowdown on Depression
	7. Sight Unseen		38. The Science of Anxiety
	8. Different Shades of Perception		39. Post-Traumatic Stress Disorder
	9. It's a Noisy, Noisy World Out There!		40. The Schizophrenic Mind
	10. Pain and Its Mysteries		41. Psychotherapies: Can We Tell the Difference?
	11. Brains in Dreamland		42. Characteristics of Empirically Supported Treatments
	12. Implicit Learning		43. Computer- and Internet-Based Psychotherapy Interventions
	13. New Evidence for the Benefits of Never Spanking		44. Are We Nuts?
	14. The Seven Sins of Memory: How the Mind Forgets and Remembers		45. Support Groups: Study Casts Some Doubts
	15. Memory's Mind Games		46. National Trends in the Use of Outpatient Psychotherapy
	16. Mind in a Mirror		
	17. Intelligent Intelligence Testing		
	18. The Inner Savant		
	19. Fundamental Feelings		
	20. Medical Detection of False Witness		
	21. Emotions and the Brain: Laughter		
	22. How to Multitask		
	23. The Biology of Aging		
	24. Inside the Womb		
	25. Parenting: The Lost Art		
	26. The Future of Adolescence: Lengthening Ladders to Adulthood		
	27. Midlife Changes: Utilizing a Social Work Perspective		
	28. Start the Conversation		
	29. Psychoanalyst: Sigmund Freud		
	30. Psychology Discovers Happiness. I'm OK, You're OK		
	31. The Verdict on Media Violence: It's Ugly...and Getting Uglier		

(Continued on next page)

NO POSTAGE
NECESSARY
IF MAILED
IN THE
UNITED STATES

BUSINESS REPLY MAIL
FIRST-CLASS MAIL PERMIT NO. 84 GUILFORD CT

POSTAGE WILL BE PAID BY ADDRESSEE

McGraw-Hill/Dushkin
530 Old Whitfield Street
Guilford, Ct 06437-9989

ABOUT YOU

Name   Date
_____   _____

Are you a teacher? ☐   A student? ☐
Your school's name
_____

Department
_____

Address   City   State   Zip
_____

School telephone #
_____

YOUR COMMENTS ARE IMPORTANT TO US!

Please fill in the following information:
For which course did you use this book?
_____

Did you use a text with this ANNUAL EDITION?   ☐   yes ☐   no
What was the title of the text?
_____

What are your general reactions to the *Annual Editions* concept?
_____

Have you read any pertinent articles recently that you think should be included in the next edition? Explain.
_____

Are there any articles that you feel should be replaced in the next edition? Why?
_____

Are there any World Wide Web sites that you feel should be included in the next edition? Please annotate.
_____

May we contact you for editorial input?   ☐   yes ☐   no
May we quote your comments? ☐   yes ☐   no